PENGUIN BOOKS

MERCHANTS OF GRAIN

Dan Morgan was born in 1937 and grew up on farms in Maryland and upstate New York. He was graduated from Harvard College in 1958. As a *Washington Post* foreign correspondent from 1967 to 1973 he covered Europe from bases in Bonn and Belgrade, and his assignments included coverage of the Soviet occupation of Czechoslovakia. Since returning home, he has reported for the *Post* on agriculture and international resources at home and abroad. A three-time winner of the Front Page award of the Washington-Baltimore Newspaper Guild, he has also written for *Saturday Review* and other magazines.

Dan Morgan

Merchants of Grain

PENGUIN BOOKS

Penguin Books Ltd, Harmondsworth,
Middlesex, England
Penguin Books, 625 Madison Avenue,
New York, New York 10022, U.S.A.
Penguin Books Australia Ltd, Ringwood,
Victoria, Australia
Penguin Books Canada Limited, 2801 John Street,
Markham, Ontario, Canada L3R IB4
Penguin Books (N.Z.) Ltd, 182–190 Wairau Road,
Auckland 10, New Zealand

First published in the United States of America by
The Viking Press 1979
Published in Penguin Books 1980
Reprinted 1980

LIBRARY OF CONGRESS CATALOGING IN PUBLICATION DATA
Morgan, Dan, 1937–
Merchants of grain.
Bibliography: p. 485.
Includes Index.
1. Grain trade. 2. Food supply. 3. Grain trade—United States. I. Title.
[HD9030.6.M68   1980]   382'.4131   80-11849
ISBN 0 14 00.5502 9

Printed in the United States of America by
Offset Paperback Mfrs., Inc., Dallas, Pennsylvania
Set in CRT Caledonia

Maps and charts by Paul J. Pugliese, GCI

To Thomas and Andrea

Contents

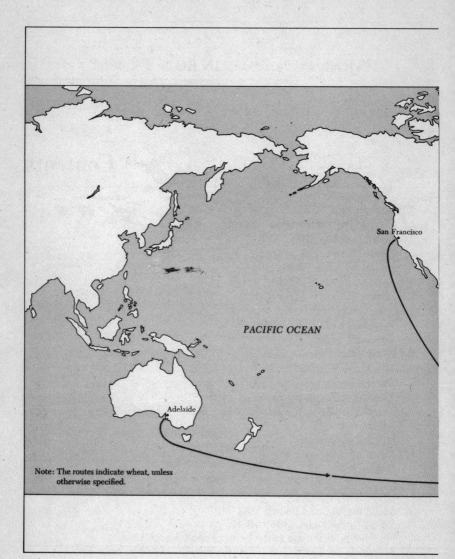

San Francisco

PACIFIC OCEAN

Adelaide

Note: The routes indicate wheat, unless
otherwise specified.

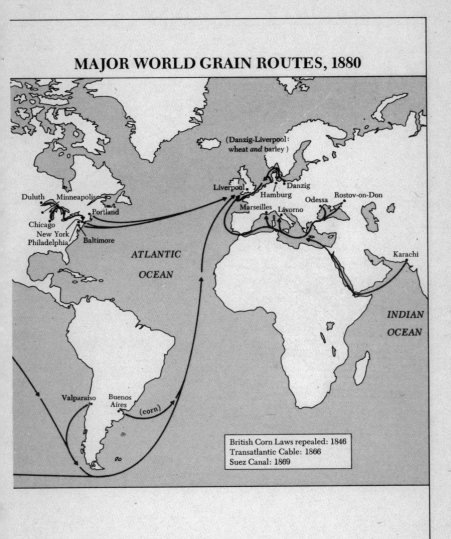

MAJOR WORLD GRAIN ROUTES, 1880

(Danzig-Liverpool: wheat *and* barley)

Liverpool
Danzig
Hamburg
Marseilles
Odessa
Rostov-on-Don
Livorno

Duluth
Minneapolis
Portland
Chicago
New York
Philadelphia
Baltimore

Karachi

ATLANTIC

OCEAN

INDIAN

OCEAN

Valparaiso
Buenos Aires
(corn)

British Corn Laws repealed: 1846
Transatlantic Cable: 1866
Suez Canal: 1869

MAJOR WORLD GRAIN ROUTES, 1978

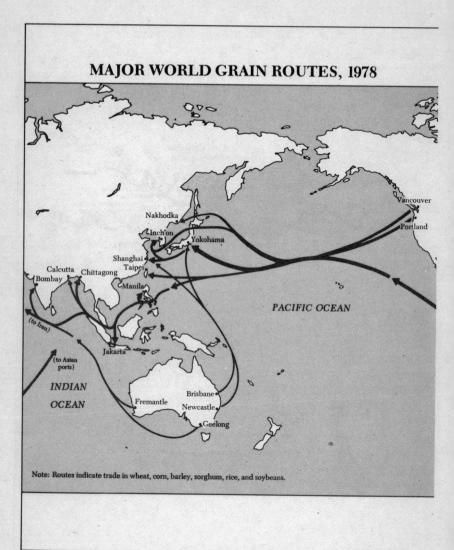

Note: Routes indicate trade in wheat, corn, barley, sorghum, rice, and soybeans.

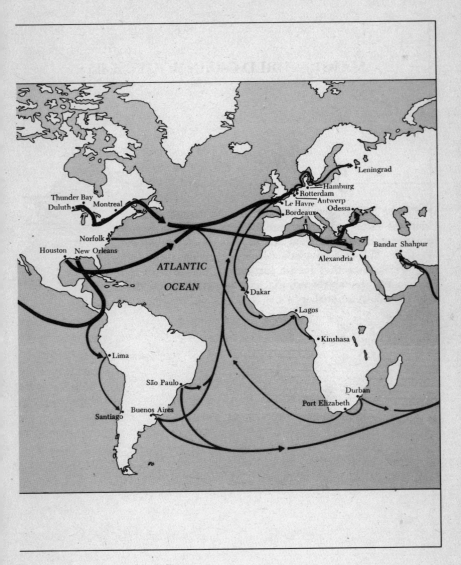

Thunder Bay
Duluth• •Montreal
Norfolk•
Houston• •New Orleans

ATLANTIC

OCEAN

•Lima

São Paulo•

Santiago• •Buenos Aires

•Dakar

•Lagos

•Kinshasa

Port Elizabeth• •Durban

Leningrad•
•Hamburg
•Rotterdam
Le Havre• Antwerp
•Bordeaux Odessa•

Alexandria•

Bandar Shahpur•

It was the Wheat, the Wheat! It was on the move again. From the farms of Illinois and Iowa, from the ranches of Kansas and Nebraska, from all the reaches of the Middle West, the Wheat, like a tidal wave, was rising, rising. Almighty, blood-brother to the earthquake, coeval with the volcano and the whirlwind, that gigantic world force, that colossal billow, Nourisher of the Nations, was swelling and advancing.

—FRANK NORRIS, *The Pit*

Introduction

It is difficult to understand how the international grain companies could have slipped through history as inconspicuously as they have. Grain is the only resource in the world that is even more central to modern civilization than oil. It goes without saying that grain is essential to human lives and health. But as much as oil, grain has its politics, its history, its effect on foreign affairs. After World War II, dozens of countries that had once fed themselves began to depend on a distant source—the United States—for a substantial part of their food supply. As America became the center of the planetary food system, trade routes were transformed, new economic relationships took shape, and grain became one of the foundations of the postwar American Empire. Food prices, diets, the dollar, politics, and diplomacy all were affected.

At the center of these changes are the five companies that are the subject of this book: Cargill, Continental, Louis Dreyfus, Bunge, and André. The stories of their growth and of America's emergence as a grain power are interwoven. Yet the companies remain shadowy and unknown, and it has taken the transformation of the global economy in the 1970s to make them of public interest. The grain companies were involved in the well-publicized and controversial sales of American grain to the Soviet Union in 1972. But it was really only a year later, with the quadrupling of oil prices, that public awareness of the critical importance of basic resources deepened.

This book is intended to contribute to a better understanding of the world that was so suddenly and painfully revealed to us in 1972 and 1973—a world in which nations all depend on each other for basic needs, and a few giant international companies and banks allocate and distribute the essential raw materials and the capital required to produce them. As much as possible, I have tried to illuminate the basic economics with anecdote and with descriptions of the personalities involved. And indeed, from the oligopoly of seven families that control the grain companies to the traders hawking grain futures in the Chicago "pit," the grain business is rich in mystery, color, and folklore. But it is no more possible to write about the people of Cargill, say, apart from the political and economic context in which the company operates, than it would be to write about Exxon without mentioning OPEC and U.S. policy in the Middle East.

My own introduction to the grain companies came in the summer of 1972 when I suddenly experienced every reporter's nightmare: I found myself in the middle of a big story, and I had no source. *The Washington Post* had assigned me to a brief stint in Moscow, and I arrived in the Soviet capital at about the time when rumors began circulating in the United States that some companies had sold the Russians $1 billion worth of grain. How to confirm the story? What were these companies? Where were they? We had no idea. As usual, the Russians were not talking. And the American government was not much help either. The U.S. Embassy seemed as ignorant as the foreign correspondents. Political and economic journalists back home were as bewildered as we were in Moscow. Only one thing was clear: The grain companies were no mere paper-shuffling middlemen, jotting down orders with stubby pencils. The Russian government, second most powerful in the world, was negotiating with them, and the most powerful government apparently did not know what they were up to. The companies had authority, aura, mystery. It was weeks before a full account of what came to be known as "the great grain robbery" was available.

This was my first experience with the traditional and well-protected secrecy of the grain companies. Later, when I let my curiosity lead me into the research for this book, I had no illusions that obtaining information would be easy. As it was, the task was much more complicated than I had anticipated.

In the first place, I had assumed that a considerable amount of my background work would already have been done for me by trained historians. I guessed that I would find, on library shelves, many scholarly works tracing the political and economic history of grain, charting the trade routes, and, perhaps, sketching the profiles of the great traders. The business had, after all, been around for centuries. Instead, I soon found myself fashioning my own historical narrative out of the bits and pieces that were available. This was an interesting lesson in its own right. Multinational scholarship of the kind required for inquiry into a subject like the grain trade is still in its infancy. The focus of historical research still seems to be on individual countries and their rulers, rather than on the world and its resources.

It is not that scholars have necessarily been derelict in their pursuits. Rather, the world and the way we look at it has changed faster than the scholarship. That is why unlicensed "historians" such as myself—free as we are from academic conventions—have made the perilous crossing into the historians' territory for better or for worse.

The subject of grain has not been ignored by academic researchers. I found many useful books, pamphlets, articles, and reports covering pieces of the history—even rather large pieces. The Odessa wheat port; the early grain trade in the Mediterranean; the Irish "potato famine"; the repeal of the English Corn Laws; the settlement of the Argentine Pampas and the Great Plains; the California wheat trade; and the grain races from Australia—all of this has been chronicled, often in fascinating and compelling detail. What I could not find was any work that brought together and gave significance to all these strands of grain's history when European civilization was industrializing and expanding in the nineteenth century (although the French historian Fernand Braudel does so for a period preceding the modern grain trade). As it is, the literature on oil, rubber, timber, or railroads provides more accessible information on the origins of these basic industries than anything I was able to find on grain.

Others, with more resources at their disposal than I, have had comparable difficulties. When in 1975 the staff of the Senate Subcommittee on Multinational Corporations began investigating the companies' role in foreign policy, it routinely asked libraries around the country to send material about the firms. One library after another informed the subcommittee that no such material existed. Senator Frank Church was to say of the grain multinationals, "No one knows how they operate, what their profits are, what they pay in taxes and what effect they have on our foreign policy—or much of anything else about them."

The hearings he conducted did expand our knowledge of the grain business, but they also clearly demonstrated the difficulties of probing deeply. For the questioning of grain-company officials was called off after only one bruising day. Cargill simply blitzed the subcommittee. Rows of experts from the Minneapolis headquarters showed up, ready to refute every hostile reference to the firm. These "wall-to-wall" witnesses were lined up like a Napoleonic musket regiment going into battle; and they were not content passively to defend themselves but turned the attack back on the subcommittee and accused it of attempting to smear the grain business. Further scheduled hearings were postponed—indefinitely—and there never was any questioning of Continental, Bunge, and the other big companies.

Later on, as I pursued my investigations, I began to see how the companies had been able to remain out of the public eye so long. Continental, a legacy of the Fribourg family (which has been in the grain business since the start of the nineteenth century), has never published a company brochure. The French magazine *L'Expansion,* introducing an article in 1976 about the Paris-based firm of Louis Dreyfus, called this company "a commercial empire of which one knows nothing, but which covers five continents." Discretion, I learned, may be the most valuable commodity of all in the grain business. "Economy is desirable, but secrecy is essential," wrote the Boston representative of the British merchant house of Baring Brothers to his New Orleans agent in 1844. (He was instructing the agent to buy American corn for the relief of the Irish famine. The precautions were effective: The corn had been safely in Cork harbor aboard a vessel for two weeks before its presence on that side of the Atlantic became known.)

Secrecy is not unusual in the corporate world, of course. Huge corporations do not live by the standards of openness that apply in American political life. Company officials do not have the same protection from reprisal by their superiors as government civil servants do. But most large American companies today take the view that they have some responsibility to account to the public, to disclose and explain their actions. This is not the prevailing view among the five major grain companies. The code of secrecy that applied in 1844 has been not only perpetuated but fortified as the control of the major companies became centralized in the hands of a few people. The result is often suspicion, reticence—and arrogance. The grain companies don't presume that the public has a right to know anything about what they are doing—and this despite the fact that they have received billions of dollars in U.S. government subsidies over the years. My impression that grain companies are secretive even by corporate standards was confirmed by—of all people—an oil executive. The petroleum giants have not been known to be loose with their own information, but as this high officer of a petroleum company said to me, "Those Cargill boys are *really* secretive!"

Some old-timers in the grain business who had been retired from active service for a decade or more refused to have anything to do with me. A French grain trader hurried me out of his office in Geneva, telling me that I would find no Watergate sources tucked away in the Swiss mountains. Even the grain trade's in-house historian, Bunge's vice-president Harry Fornari, declined to see me. I had read his book *Bread Upon the Waters*, and to dispel any concerns he might have, I suggested we limit our discussion to historical events occurring before 1945. But this history was still too recent for Fornari to agree to talk about it.

I still vividly remember an encounter with a grain trader in Paris in which the fears generated by outside inquiries were evident. I had telephoned a Lebanese grain broker who was said to have arranged many transactions with Czechoslovakia. Would he agree to see me about the book I was writing? The Lebanese replied in rather poor English that he would. At his office the next day, I thought I finally had encountered the original gnome of Zurich. A pale, moon-faced man peered at me across his desk and asked what commodity I was selling. More than a little surprised, I explained that I was a prospective author, not a merchant. He blinked at me. There had been a serious misunderstanding, he said. It was his poor English, he explained. Now, he had remembered an urgent appointment and must leave at once. And tomorrow, I asked? Engaged also, he replied. And the following day? "In your case I will *always* be engaged," he said impatiently as he swooped out the door. I caught up with him on the stairs, where he seemed to calm down. "I really do have an appointment," he told me. "At the bank. With some Russians." With that, he hurried off down the street.

On another occasion I had been visiting a grain merchant in his office in downtown New York. Talk turned to the question whether his company would be selling grain to China this year. It seemed unlikely, he replied. The Chinese had expressed little or no interest. He acted as if this were a very tedious subject, but as he accompanied me to the elevator we passed a large glass-enclosed conference room where I could see several American businessmen engrossed in conversation with several Oriental men clad in unmistakable "Mao suits."

Of course, leaks of information to competitors or to the public can be exceedingly costly to a company in the grain-trading business. But I had difficulties that went beyond the expected secrecy. The structure of the companies seemed most responsible for the unusual wariness. The grain merchant houses are private, centralized oligopolies that do not publish financial statements. There are no public stockholders, which greatly limits the obligation to disclose information. Ownership of the companies is vested in the hands of seven of the world's richest and most uncommunicative families, and the same families also have operating control of the companies. Information and decision-making are tightly controlled at the top by a very few people.

With several exceptions, the companies provided minimal assistance, or none at all, in the preparation of this book. I was granted a one-hour interview with the most prominent grain merchant in the world, Michel Fribourg, president of Continental. This was a signal honor, for Fribourg is a man who virtually embodies the retiring traditions of grain men, who shuns publicity and guards his privacy. The setting for our meeting was his office atop a Park Avenue skyscraper, but the ambience was European. Freshly cut flowers were on the table between us and off to the side was the beautiful Louis XV desk on which he signs the papers that send grain ships around the world. I was greeted by a trim, elegant man with graying hair and delicate features. He could have been some country's foreign minister, or the curator of a European museum—except for one thing: Michel Fribourg, a man whose family's wealth has been estimated to be in the vicinity of half a billion dollars and whose company stretches around the world, was clearly more ill at ease than I was. He was pleasant and articulate, but the quick, practiced smile suggested discomfort. Several months later, a letter came from Continental saying, "It has been decided that we choose not to participate in further interviews with you." Michel Fribourg had decided, and that was that.

I did not get near the Hirsches or the Borns, the ruling families of the Bunge Company. President Walter Klein of Bunge's North American division saw me for an hour and then had his public-relations agent inform me that he had "neither the time nor the inclination for further discussions."

Pierre Louis-Dreyfus, the current patriarch of the Paris company with that name,* invited me to lunch in his private dining room. M. Louis-Dreyfus, a short, mustachioed man who speaks flawless English, told many fascinating stories about his early interest in shipping and his wartime exploits flying bombing missions for the Free French. The fish with cream sauce was superb, as was the wine. But I left with a strong impression that I could not and would not unearth many secrets from M. Louis-Dreyfus. Back in the United States, repeated efforts to arrange a meeting with his son Gerard (who had succeeded him as president) were futile.

Georges André, patriarch of the family that controls the Swiss company of that name, kindly received me in his chalet, gave me hours of his time, provided some historical data, and invited me to an excellent lunch of brook trout in a village restaurant.

But only Cargill, the Minneapolis-based concern that is the world's largest grain company, was helpful on matters of substance. Perhaps this is because of all the houses, it is Cargill that is most secure, most successful, most thoroughly convinced of the rightness of its corporate cause. Cargill itself decides which executives outsiders have access to, and in my case these did not include either the chairman of the board, Whitney MacMillan, or President M. D. (Pete) McVay. Permission for me to see two of the merchants in Cargill's important Geneva office was also denied. But Cargill, through its vice-president for public affairs,

---

* The family hyphenates the name; the company does not.

William Pearce (an unusual grain executive, as we shall see), does accept questions and answers specific inquiries—although the answer may be "no comment." Cargill certainly does not volunteer anything. And Cargill has not, to anybody's knowledge, ever admitted it was wrong. But in mid-1978 it did take the unusual step of starting to publish a newsletter. (The second number described the ground-breaking for Cargill's $70-million *steel* plant—so the newsletter does shed light on the company's wealth and diversity.) But it raised eyebrows among company traditionalists. "Some of us don't feel very comfortable with this sort of thing," a Cargill man allowed.

In the absence of company cooperation or published material, I employed the tried-and-true techniques of investigative reporting. I developed what sources I could inside the companies, talked to former officials, and wore out shoe leather. My travels took me to the prairies of Manitoba, the towering grain terminals along the lower Mississippi River, the hubbub of commodity exchanges in Chicago, Kansas City, and Minneapolis, and the quiet offices of grain and shipping brokers in New York City. I crossed over the sandhills of western Kansas into the irrigated, pancake-flat wheat country and spent a Saturday night "on the town" with the local wheat farmers and cowboys. I also made three trips to Europe and spent weeks in the more sedate settings of London, Paris, and Geneva, talking with traders who run the "offshore" operations of the European and U.S.-based companies.

And through all this there were the glimpses of the world of the grain merchants—a sort of art deco room in the garish house of commerce.

These were all worthwhile journeys. For grain is a subject that takes its student down a thousand paths—back into history, forward into the future of an already overcrowded planet, and always across borders, borders of ideology, nationality, and geography. Through wheat, for example, I saw the close connection between two enormous events, the settling of the North

American prairies and the Industrial Revolution, with its insatiable need for bread. Instantly the nineteenth century seemed less remote and more in focus. Study grain long enough and the world shrinks. The wheat rising here and the demand for bread there cease to be isolated events separated by thousands of miles and become interconnected episodes in the "planetary village."

I was left with no doubt that the companies at the center of the grain distribution system are not only wealthy but important and very powerful. The time for them to stand up and take a bow is long overdue.

Merchants of Grain

Glenas, Inc., of Panama 1

"Grain is the currency of currencies."
—LENIN

It was late June 1975, and Parisians strolled a little more casually than usual past the bakeries, boutiques, and tiny art galleries on the Opéra district's rue Vignon. Thoughts had begun to drift from work to vacations at the beach and in the countryside. But on the fourth floor of Number 28, rue Vignon, the shipping broker Jean Lerbret and his associates were as busy and preoccupied as if it were still the middle of winter. The graying, crew-cut Lerbret intently dialed telephone numbers in Denmark and Norway. There was something about the bustle in the office—the hum and chatter from the bank of telex machines, perhaps—that hinted at a big business deal in the offing.

Lerbret reached a shipowner in Copenhagen. After a few pleasantries he came to the point. Some clients of his were interested in chartering freighters. He regretted that these clients had requested absolute confidentiality and could not be identified. However, Lerbret was prepared to put the good name and reputation of his half-century old family firm behind these particular individuals. They had deposited impressive financial guarantees at leading Swiss banks. Their credentials were impeccable.

The shipowner in Copenhagen was interested. Business was in a slump, and the Russian merchant fleet had once again been grabbing contracts away from Western shipping companies by offering to haul freight at discounts. Could M. Lerbret please give at least the company name of his clients?

"Glenas, Incorporated, of Panama," was Lerbret's laconic reply.

As Lerbret made these calls, his associates directed a flow of telex messages around the world. The messages announced that Glenas wished to hire medium-sized vessels for one to three years to carry dry, bulky cargoes to unspecified destinations. If possible, these vessels should be "Lakes fitted"—narrow enough to squeeze through the St. Lawrence Seaway into the Great Lakes and equipped with special gear to stabilize them in the locks. There was nothing unusual about this message tapped out from the obscure office in the rue Vignon. It was one of hundreds that arrived that day at the trading centers of New York City, Geneva, and Rotterdam and at the Baltic Mercantile and Shipping Exchange in London's St Mary Axe.

The Baltic Exchange, 231 years old in 1975, is a picturesque relic of imperial Britannic commerce. It has the look of an English gentleman's club that has been accidentally situated in a cathedral. Its soaring marble pillars support a high, domed roof. Uniformed doormen in gold-braided caps nod ceremoniously at the people who come and go. Groups of men huddle in conversation, while others walk arm in arm or doze in the adjoining library. The Baltic is a grand bazaar—the central brokerage for the world's fleet of tramp steamers—vessels that ply the oceans without any fixed routes. Representatives of charterers and shipowners meet on the floor of the Baltic Exchange to confirm deals involving tens of millions of dollars with no more than a handshake. On any given day at the Baltic, a Greek ship may find a cargo of French flour to carry to Egypt; an international copper company may locate a ship to haul its ore from Zaire to Philadelphia; an old tramp steamer out of Hong Kong may be consigned to a Japanese scrapyard; or a 50,000-ton tanker may be leased for twenty years. The Baltic is also a marketplace of information, one of the strategic listening posts in world trade. Economic recessions and recoveries are often first detected in the slackening or quickening of chartering activity there.

None of the dozens of cargoes handled by the brokers of the Baltic Exchange is more unpredictable than grain. A harvest failure in one country can presage a big grain deal—and big business for the tramp fleet. And in June 1975 some of the brokers read in the Glenas cable a clue to just such a development. "Lakes-fitted" vessels often are on their way to the wheat ports of Duluth, Minnesota, and Thunder Bay, Ontario, in the center of the North American wheat belt. But this was only guesswork. Only Jean Lerbret and a few of his associates knew for certain what the cargo and destination of the ships sought by Glenas was—and they were not talking.

There has always been a grain trade, ever since men began to eat bread.* The early civilizations of Greece and Rome imported wheat from their colonies, and Socrates himself recognized that "no man qualifies as a statesman who is entirely ignorant of the problems of wheat." From the fourteenth century on, Mediterranean merchants (well paid by the grand dukes of the coastal city states) organized relief shipments of wheat from northern Europe in times of famine. And in the eighteenth century, merchants gathered in the coffee houses of London to trade information about the prices of wheat from the feudal estates of Poland, east of the Oder River, wheat that flowed to London from the port of Danzig.

But it was not until the nineteenth century that the modern grain trade came of age. Southern Russia and North America became the great suppliers of wheat to the new industrial cities

* "*Grain:* the edible, starchy fruits of the grasses." That is a dictionary definition. In this book, I use the phrase "grain trade" loosely. Grain traders also deal in soybeans, a legume.

of England and the Continent. The Industrial Revolution, which drew tens of thousands of European farmers, peasants, and laborers into factory towns and away from their food supply, created an insatiable demand for wheat. And gradually, the international trade in basic necessities—in wheat for bread, in cotton for cloth, and in tallow for candles—overshadowed the ancient trade in luxury items for the rich (spices, ivory, silk, and indigo) that had been the principal activity of merchants until then. The growing international demand for wheat transformed the world's trade routes. Russian peasants hauled wheat in wooden oxcarts to Odessa, on the Black Sea, and California merchants loaded great clipper ships full of bagged wheat and sent them on 14,000-mile journeys around Cape Horn—all so that the new British workingman could eat wheat bread.

The first of the modern, long-distance grain traders were Greeks. This was not surprising. They had the ships, the connections in the Mediterranean ports, and the large, tightly knit clans that gave them advantages in a business where trustworthy partners (or cousins) were a necessity. When at the end of the eighteenth century the Russian empire reached down to the Black Sea and Odessa became a major port for exporting the wheat grown in the coastal steppes, the Greeks arranged the shipment of Russian wheat to London.

In the second half of the nineteenth century, however, these Greek grain traders were overshadowed by west European merchants, most of whom had originally been established along the Continent's commercial artery, the Rhine River. Leopold Louis-Dreyfus, born in an Alsatian village, completely dominated the Odessa trade by the end of the century. The importers and millers of Liverpool, which overtook London as England's major grain port, looked not just to Russia, but to North America, Argentina, India, and Australia for their wheat supplies—and the west Europeans slowly began to dominate the trade routes.

The five enormous companies that controlled the global grain trade in the summer of 1975 all had their origins in that period a century ago when the cities of Europe, and of England in particular, needed foreign wheat. By 1975, the founding families of those companies had meandered about and maneuvered all over three continents, surviving wars, famines, economic crashes, and revolutions, always moving, changing countries, trading their nationalities as well as grain, forming alliances with kings, queens, and Communist rulers, and disengaging when historical developments required it.

Yet the companies managed to stay in the shadows most of the time. Perhaps it was the ancient nightmare of the middleman-merchant that made them all so aloof and secretive—the old fear that in moments of scarcity or famine, the people would blame them for all misfortunes, march upon their granaries, drag them into the town square, and confiscate their stocks. And they had grounds for concern. The Fribourgs of Continental were twice uprooted from their home base by German armies, in 1914 and again in 1940. The Louis-Dreyfuses saw their Black Sea assets seized in 1917. The Cargills and MacMillans, heirs of the Cargill grain dynasty, were twice at the brink of losing everything. Whatever the source of their anxiety, their secrecy was part of their means to alleviate it, part of their knack for survival. Throughout most of this century the fact of the matter has been that most Americans have never heard of the companies that distribute and sell American grain all over the world. And the names are still, certainly, much less familiar than the names of the "Seven Sisters" of oil. There is Cargill, Inc., of Minneapolis; the Continental Grain Company of New York City; André of Lausanne, Switzerland; the Louis Dreyfus Company of Paris; and the Bunge Corporation—companies that all can boast, with Cargill, that "some of our best customers have never heard of us."

These five companies have grown, diversified, spread their operations to almost every continent and country so successfully that by the time most Americans heard of them for the first time, during the grain sales to Russia in 1972, the firms were among the world's largest multinational corporations. Cargill and Continental probably rank as the two largest privately held companies in the United States, and Bunge may be one of the largest in the world. Cargill's annual net profits from its worldwide operations exceeded those of Goodyear Tire and Rubber in 1974 and 1975, and its annual sales are greater than those of Sears, Roebuck. The companies have interests in banking, shipping, real estate, hotels, paint and glass manufacturing, mining, steel plants, cattle ranches, flour milling, animal feed processing, and commodity brokerage. Bunge has an estimated 50,000 employees, mainly centered in its paint, textile, food-processing, and milling plants in Argentina and Brazil, but scattered around the world, too. And the companies run their own intelligence services all over the planet—private news agencies that never print a word.

Grain provided the cash flow and capital for the postwar expansion of the five grain giants, just as oil financed the vertical and horizontal integration of the petroleum companies into uranium, coal, chemicals, and plastics. Mysterious and obscure as the firms may be, they are near-perfect stereotypes of the new global corporations that manage the distribution and processing of basic resources in the late twentieth century. Earlier in their history they had been middlemen-merchants—minor players in a colonial era when control of natural resources was one of the main ingredients of corporate power. The grain companies have never owned vast plantations, as United Fruit did in its heyday in Latin America; and they do not control "upstream" oil "taps," as Exxon does. The resource by which they live is grown by millions of farmers all over the world. But in recent years this lack of control over sources of raw materials has ceased to be a disadvantage. After 1960, most of the major multinationals surrendered some or all of their control of resources to increasingly nationalistic governments all over the world; yet the companies' power did not diminish. They had made themselves indispensable because of their control of the distribution systems, the processing plants, the technology, the capital, and the communications with buyers and sellers. The rubber plantations belonging to ten major tire and rubber companies, for example, grew only 15 per cent of the world's natural rubber in 1970; but these same companies consumed nearly 75 per cent of all natural rubber produced on the planet. This was a world in which tens of thousands of rubber farmers in Malaysia and Indonesia were growing rubber for half a dozen giant tire manufacturers.

A similar, if not identical, situation exists in grain. It is no disadvantage or sign of weakness that the companies do not produce grain. Quite the opposite. Farmers take the risks of falling prices, bad weather, and governmental policies that sometimes depress farm prices. The grain companies, one stage removed from the production process, can make money whether prices are rising or falling.

The Big Five are at the center of the global system by which grain is distributed and processed. The grain companies invest in shipping, grain elevators, communications, and processing plants—grain "refineries" which make wheat into flour, soybeans into cooking oil or animal meal, and corn into animal-feeding compounds or liquid sweeteners for soft drinks and ice cream. They also operate the grain "pipeline"—all the way from farmer to foreign consumer. Together, Cargill and Continental handle half of all the grain exported from the United States—and the United States exports half of all the grain in world trade (in some years, Cargill has even been the leading exporter of wheat from France, the world's third or fourth largest wheat trader). The Big Five dominate the grain trade of the Common Market; the Canadian barley trade; the South African maize trade; and the Argentine wheat trade. In the 1960s, these same companies expanded into trading in sugar, meat, and tapioca. And the directorates of these firms channeled money into facilities "upstream," closer to farms. Cargill runs 50-to-100–car freight trains full of grain from the interior of the United States to the ports. And the dollars circulating through the companies come in very large figures, or so it seems to anyone except perhaps an analyst used to the statistics of the oil industry. The companies dominated a trade in cooking oil, grain, and animal feeds with a value of $38.3 billion in 1974, according to United Nations figures.

Typically, the grain companies (like other big multinational corporations) see themselves as neutral in modern ideological and political struggles. They see their main interests as residing in a non-ideological, non-nationalistic world in which trade is unencumbered by regulations, and their lack of national identities distinguishes them from earlier merchant empires. There is no comparing the modern grain companies with firms such as Baring Brothers, the great British merchant banking house once described by Richelieu in the eighteenth century as "one of the six great powers of Europe" (along with France, England, Russia, Austria, and Prussia). Nobody doubted that Baring Brothers was British, and its Britishness in fact augmented its influence and prestige. It was a bold, independent but sensible extension of imperial power that would never have acted against the interests of the Empire. Today, only a few giant Japanese trading houses—Mitsubishi, Marubeni, Mitsui—are in any way instruments of their country's foreign policy. Modern grain companies, like other multinational corporations, have much blurrier loyalties. A company such as Bunge seems to have no nationality at all. It grew up in Holland in the nineteenth century, moved to Argentina, and in the 1970s its high command, the Born and Hirsch families, lived in Brazil and Spain.

What distinguishes the grain multinationals from their corporate contemporaries is their uniquely private structure. Seven families are all-powerful: the Fribourgs at Continental; the Hirsches and Borns at Bunge; the Cargills and MacMillans at Cargill, and the Louis-Dreyfuses and Andrés at the companies with those names. Members of these families not only own most of the stock of the companies, but also serve as board chairmen, presidents, and chief executives at each of them. It is as if the

Rockefeller family were still in absolute, day-to-day control of Exxon, or the Carnegies still dictated every major decision of U.S. Steel. In the grain companies, it is possible to observe a social and economic phenomenon of some historical note: a functioning oligopoly that has survived right into the contemporary, post-industrial age. Not that there are no family dynasties left in business: The Michelins still run the world's third-largest tire company; the Rothschilds still have their bank; Henry Ford still wields influence over his company; and a fourth-generation Weyerhaeuser rules the United States' largest timber company. But these are exceptions. The descendants of nineteenth-century business barons have for the most part drifted away to New York City or Palm Beach, or into other pursuits altogether. The Firestones are gone from their Akron, Ohio, tire company, and the Morgans no longer wield decision-making power over banks and railroads. Descendants of most of the colorful founding fathers and early go-getters have faded from the picture, though many of these families may still derive wealth from the companies.

But the grain families, like Greek shipowners, manage to stay in control. And every now and then, perhaps for the benefit of those employees who have been tempted to doubt their authority and staying power, they demonstrate it with a flair. When the prospering Louis Dreyfus company moved its Paris headquarters into a modern glass office building half a dozen blocks from the Arc de Triomphe in 1975, Pierre Louis-Dreyfus did not fancy the shade of blue glass that had been selected. On a whim, it was all replaced with a shade that more exactly suited his taste. That was Monsieur Pierre's prerogative. (When the company regrouped after World War II, it had interests in shipping and banking as well as grain; fortunately there was an able Louis-Dreyfus to head each of these divisions—Pierre, and his cousins Jean and François. Responsibility was divided among the three of them, a solution that was far more effective than a power struggle.)

At Continental, company headquarters is wherever Michel

Fribourg may be—whether that is his art-filled New York town house, his Paris apartment, his ski lodge, his home in Connecticut, or his hideaway in the Swiss mountains. Continental is a company that has always attracted virtuoso performers; it is said that there are "many egos but only one opinion"—that of Michel Fribourg.

Family control is absolute. But the succession is a constant worry, for the families remember what happened to the Bunges. The Bunges lost control of their company early in the century— there were no sons or heirs to fight for the survival of the dynasty (one of the Bunge brothers had five children, all daughters), so the Hirsches and Borns took control.

When the families began their long saga generations earlier, they could never have dreamed that grain would come to play such a central role in the affairs of nations as it did in 1975. The grain trade as a business involving billions of dollars and millions of tons of commodities a year is a recent phenomenon. Before World War II, the amount of grain that crossed borders, or oceans, seldom exceeded 30 million tons a year. By 1975, this figure reached nearly 160 million tons, a growth only slightly less spectacular than the growth of the oil trade. Countries such as Russia and India, which once exported grain, have become big importers. Developing countries of Asia, Africa, and Latin America have begun importing wheat on a major scale for the first time. Rice-eating people have acquired a taste for bread, and governments find it expedient to satisfy this taste. Bread has become the ideal food for the millions who have been migrating to the cities from the countryside, away from their traditional food supplies. One by one, countries have plugged into the global system of commercial grain-trading. By the 1970s, imported wheat was a costly factor in the trade of dozens of nations and one that often diverted foreign exchange from other uses, including investments in domestic agriculture.

In the richer countries, people copy the American diet. They eat more meat from grain-fed beef, hogs, and poultry, and less potatoes, bread, or rice. Trendy young Japanese consume "jyamba baga" (jumbo burgers) at "Macudonarado's" and affluent South Americans step into restaurants serving American-style fried chicken under giant plastic statues of the ubiquitous Colonel Sanders. Fast-food chains have gone international. These food habits all require vastly greater supplies of grain. By the early 1970s, *animals* ate up about as much of the world's annual harvest of wheat, corn, barley, oats, rye, and sorghum as humans did. Livestock and poultry in just two countries—the United States and the Soviet Union—consumed one bushel out of five of *all* this annual harvest of grain.

The *sources* of grain are considerably less diverse than those of other basic resources. A number of different countries have surpluses of oil, or bauxite, or iron ore. But grain surpluses are found in only a handful of nations, and the United States is always one of them. In agriculture, there is only one superpower. Iowa raises one-tenth of all the corn on the planet, and Kansas and South Dakota produce more wheat than all of Australia. American farmers are connected to Asians, Europeans, Africans, and South Americans by a moving belt of grain. One bushel of wheat out of two, one bushel of rice and soybeans out of three, and one bushel of corn out of four moves abroad. The grain flows in all directions. Ohio wheat is made into flour for Indian chapatis; Washington State wheat goes for Korean cookies; North Dakota durum wheat becomes yellow pasta flour in Italy and couscous in Algeria; Iowa corn feeds Europe's hogs and California rice fills Indonesians' supper bowls.

Americans, who moved off farms and severed their roots to their rural homes by the millions in the 1950s and 1960s, have been only dimly aware of the growing importance of their grain in the world economy. And they have felt comfortable in their prosperity. Most of them have assumed that technology, chemical fertilizers, and new hybrid seeds offer more or less permanent insurance against a recurrence of the Dust Bowl—that historical interlude, now receding in the national memory, when American agriculture was crippled by drought and the United States was forced to import wheat.

There is much for Americans to be proud of in their agriculture and in their generosity with food. American food alleviated misery all over the world after World War II. It fed starving people in Europe and Asia, and it was credited with building an economic bulwark against communism. Then the United States began shipping millions more tons of food aid abroad through the "Food for Peace" program. Dispensing this food seemed to satisfy a humanitarian impulse in Americans; in the Marshall Plan aid to Europe there was something of the old frontier tradition in which the more fortunate pitched in and helped the less fortunate when barns burned down. But there was always a strong element of self-interest and *Realpolitik* in this food aid. It helped to dispose of mountainous U.S. surpluses, and the food went mainly to nations with "friendly" governments. These fundamental aspects of the aid tended to be obscured by the rhetoric of politicians in Washington, who indulged the growing complacency and national *hubris* with assurances that Americans were "feeding the world."

The Russians understand the realities of food politics better than any other people in the world. They have been educated to this lesson by harsh, direct experience. Virtually none of the elders in power in Moscow is a stranger to the experience of actual starvation. People starved in Russia after World War I; they starved again in the Ukraine in 1932 and 1933 during the chaos created by forced collectivization of Soviet farming; and more soldiers and civilians perished from hunger in besieged cities in World War II. It is not surprising that harvests are front-page news in Soviet newspapers.

By the 1970s, starvation was no longer an imminent danger. After Stalin died in 1953, the Soviet government had allocated large sums of money to agriculture, with impressive results. Soviet grain production doubled between 1955 and 1972, rising from 100 million tons a year to more than 200 million tons, thanks partly to Premier Nikita Khrushchev's decision to order millions of acres of steppe in western Siberia settled and planted with wheat. Although production from this area was unpredictable, it added to the country's output.

But, as the Soviet leaders well knew, the truth was not so impressive as the statistics suggested. Soviet agriculture was extraordinarily inefficient. Russia's overall grain production lagged behind America's, and there were awesome difficulties in making the collective and state farms more productive. Thirty-seven million workers—almost one-third of the entire Soviet labor force—were still employed on farms in 1972, yet agricultural productivity lagged behind that of other countries.

And in addition to the structural and economic problems, Russian weather was a constant worry. Two-thirds of the country's grain acreage was in areas that could not depend on receiving sufficient moisture. The main gains in Russian agriculture occurred in just four years, 1969 through 1972, when a strong flow of maritime air from the North Atlantic resulted in more rainfall, warmer winters, and cooler summers, all ideal for growing crops.

The result of all this was fundamental: Russians ate less well than people in most other developed countries—less well, in fact, than citizens of neighboring Communist countries dominated by Soviet power. Six years after the Soviet Army's 1968 invasion of Czechoslovakia to put down Alexander Dubcek's experiment in "socialism with a human face," the conquered Czechs ate 173 pounds of meat per person a year while the conquerors consumed only 108 pounds. (Czechoslovaks looked so well-fed and prosperous that some of the occupying troops refused to believe that they had invaded a socialist country!)

The shortcomings of the Soviet food and agriculture system posed awkward strategic and political questions. In 1971, the Soviet Union had commitments to provide nearly 8 million tons of its own grain, or other countries' grain, to Eastern Europe,

Cuba, North Korea, North Vietnam, and Egypt. The leadership was caught between these imperial obligations and its commitment in the Ninth Five-Year Plan (1971–75) to improve the diets of the Russian people. Suddenly, its inadequate grain supply was a major weakness in the Soviet Union's ambitions to become the most influential and successful nation in the world. In other ways, it was a disturbing source of instability within its empire. Communist leaders in Russia and Eastern Europe were under increasing pressure to provide their people with a standard of living commensurate with their military and industrial development. That was demonstrated in the bloody rioting that occurred when the Polish government attempted to raise food prices before Christmas, 1970. In purely economic terms, the increases were justified. Polish food prices were heavily subsidized; there was no doubt that food really was underpriced. Polish agriculture had failed dismally to produce enough meat and grain to hold prices down; year after year, the Warsaw government had covered this up with food subsidies paid for out of its budget. But Polish dockworkers were not prepared to accept higher food bills, regardless of economic logic. And so Communist leadership in Warsaw agreed to withdraw the price increases after the infuriated dockworkers burned the party headquarters in Gdansk and their comrades in Szczecin seized the shipyards in that Baltic city.

Sometime between then and 1972, the Soviet government made a command decision to cover its grain deficit with imports and to continue increasing the size of Soviet cattle herds. This was in lieu of returning to the policy of austerity that had made Eastern Europe such a cold and forbidding place for most of the years since 1945. Whether the Polish riots were responsible for the Russian grain-buying spree in 1972 is not known, but it seems likely that there was a connection. If so, it was a striking example of global interdependence, for the Polish dockworkers' action was to give impetus to unprecedented inflation of American food prices.

Other events in 1972 in addition to the Russian grain purchases helped to drain the United States of its surpluses and send grain prices to their highest levels since 1917. Droughts occurred all over the world that year, and prices would have risen with or without Russian buying. But the surprise in, and the magnitude of, Soviet buying tipped the balance. As grain prices rose, there was panic and hoarding on a planetary scale. The effect of the Soviet buying was comparable to the quadrupling of oil prices by the OPEC cartel a year later.

The United States, curiously, was both a beneficiary and a victim of this "grain robbery." U.S. grain shipments increased from 34 million tons in 1971 to 82 million tons by mid-1975. U.S. earnings from its agricultural exports grew from $7.7 billion to $21.3 billion, and these exports helped to offset costlier foreign oil. But these developments were a two-edged sword that cut at the American economy. Higher grain prices meant higher food prices. Nearly $54 billion was added to the food bills of Americans between 1972 and 1975, the most rapid increase in a century. Poor Americans were especially disadvantaged because they did not have the option of making economies in other parts of the family budget. Their choice was a cruel one: eat less, or buy less nourishing products. For those low-income Americans in particular, the Nixon administration's arguments about American food exports' helping the balance of payments and trade offered little comfort. In the single year 1973, Americans paid almost $2 billion more out of their pockets for food as a *direct* result of the Soviet purchases the previous year. In January 1973, the month the Nixon administration chose to loosen its controls on retail food prices, the costs of beef, pork, and broilers were increasing at annual rates of 54, 62, and 62 per cent respectively, compared with normal rates of less than 10 per cent.

The land itself exhibited the scars of these developments in the grain economy. Along the North Carolina coast, Italian and Japanese investors bought tens of thousands of acres of marshy wetlands, cleared the trees with bulldozers and Caterpillar tractors, installed drainage ditches, and announced plans for "super-farms." The incentive was corn at $3.00 a bushel and soybeans at $6.50; the world needed more food. But environmentalists in that state expressed concern about the effect of the runoff of chemical fertilizers, pesticides, and herbicides on the fish and wildlife in the coastal waterways. Investors also purchased marginal farmland at the western edge of the Corn Belt in Nebraska and ordered fragile grasslands set to the plow. Groves of trees, planted under federal programs in the 1930s to prevent soil erosion, were bulldozed so that spindly irrigation systems that wheeled around a central well in 160-acre circles could move unhindered. The land irrigated by these watering systems was plowed, disked, and planted to corn. After the corn was harvested, the thin layer of topsoil blew away in many places, leaving gashes of dunelike sand in the fields of Nebraska.

All this raised the question of governmental control over American grain resources. The government had been operating under the complacent assumption that American food supplies were virtually infinite. For at least a quarter century, Americans had been conditioned to believe in a permanent surplus. Suddenly, unexpectedly, it was gone.

As the Nixon administration attempted to maneuver through the economic storm of unprecedented food price inflation, world food shortages, and a worrisome trade deficit, it was caught in a bind. By philosophical inclination, the Nixonians favored a minimum of government control and regulation. In June 1971, President Nixon had taken the step that made the big grain deals with Russia possible, quietly removing the requirement that exporters obtain licenses for these transactions, and by eliminating an earlier standing policy that a minimum of 50 per cent of the grain be shipped on American vessels. But the chaotic behavior of the grain markets made it difficult to stick to this antiregulatory position: The dollar was in trouble, the balance of trade and payments was worsening, and American economic hegemony was being questioned.

Moreover, Nixon's earlier decision left the United States exposed in another important respect. All through the surplus years of the 1950s and 1960s the Census Bureau and the Department of Agriculture had kept informal (and often conflicting) statistics about American grain exports. Nobody was worried about any "robberies." The problem was how to "get rid of the stuff," and accurate statistics on what was going on in the grain markets were not considered essential. In 1973, Congress finally did order the Department of Agriculture to start collecting more up-to-date trade figures. Companies had to report to the government sales of more than 100,000 tons of grain within twenty-four hours of making them. But it was not until October 1974, in the face of extraordinarily short food supplies, that the Ford administration tightened this procedure to require the companies to get *prior approval* of sales of 50,000 or more tons in a single day or 100,000 or more tons a week. Then, astonishingly, after so much grief in the matter of grain deals, this prior-approval system was terminated in March 1975.

At this point, then, the American government's knowledge of what the Soviet Union was buying was hampered. And at the same time its information about the size of Russian crops—which might provide at least clues to what the Russians might do in the markets—was also inadequate. The fact was that the American government had no real substitute for sending its own experts into Russian wheat fields for a firsthand look. And the Soviet Union was less than cooperative in permitting these inspection missions.

On June 19, 1973, Secretary of Agriculture Earl Butz and Soviet Foreign Minister Andrei Gromyko, in Washington, had signed an agreement on cooperation in agriculture. Article II committed the two countries to "regular exchanges of relevant information," including "forward estimation on production, consumption, demand and trade of major agricultural commodities." But the Russians subsequently refused to provide any such forecasts. They also refused to approve trip itineraries requested by visiting American crop-inspection teams, as provided for in the agreement. In the summer of 1974, for example, an American "spring wheat" survey team had to cut its visit short when Soviet authorities refused to permit the team to examine crops in several key growing areas of spring-planted wheat in northern Kazakhstan and the southern Ural Mountains. Agricultural attachés in Moscow were even more restricted. Their travel was limited to the Intourist routes that were standard for all foreign visitors. The attachés repeatedly asked to examine grain crops in the Volga River valley, for example, one of the farming areas plagued by variable output, but this permission was denied.

Starting in the summer of 1975, LACIE (Large Area Crop Inventory Experiment) was to use special infrared sensing equipment aboard two civilian satellites, Landsat I and Landsat II, to measure the light waves emitted from crops below; these photographic "signatures" were supposed to help specialists at the Johnson Space Center in Houston evaluate the condition of the world's wheat crop. But this technology was still in its infancy.

In February 1975, the condition of that distant Soviet wheat crop was the subject of a passing conversation in the White House mess between Under Secretary of State for Economic Affairs Charles Robinson and Alan Greenspan of the Council of Economic Advisers. As Greenspan consumed his chowder and crackers, he remarked to Robinson that the Russians were selling unusually large quantities of gold in Switzerland. "Something is going on, Chuck," he said.

Both men thought the Russians might be raising cash to buy grain. Robinson was concerned enough to mention this to Secretary of State Henry Kissinger, and Kissinger authorized him to convene an informal meeting to consider if and how the United States could exploit its agricultural advantage. But just as these discussions were starting, the prior-approval requirements were abandoned at the Department of Agriculture.

Wheat has been called a "desert plant" because of its stamina in extreme climates. It thrives along the edges of the Sahara Desert, in the Asian steppes, and in the prairies of North America. But there are limits even to wheat's endurance. About half the Russian wheat crop is planted in September and October of the year before it is harvested. The seeds of this "winter wheat" sprout in several days and send out tiny roots that require moisture to get established before the plants enter dormancy in the long Russian winter. Once cold weather sets in, the roots benefit from a blanket of insulating snow. Strange weather patterns over Russia in late 1974 and 1975 jeopardized the root systems of the early grain. There was no snow at all in some places, and irrigation equipment ran all winter in the Crimea.

In the final week of May 1975, several months after the Robinson-Greenspan conversation in the White House mess, but several weeks before Jean Lerbret's messages about Glenas, Inc., of Panama went out from his office in Paris, a thirty-four-year-old American drove a black Chevrolet hundreds of miles through the wheatlands of southern Russia and the Ukraine. Larry Panasuk, an assistant agricultural attaché at the American Embassy in Moscow, had grown up on a wheat and cattle ranch in Montana. Later he studied agriculture at the universities of Montana and North Dakota. Then he went to work for the Department of Agriculture and joined its corps of economists and agronomists assigned as agricultural attachés at American embassies abroad.

The Department of Agriculture's attachés once had been near the bottom of the caste system at the American Embassy in Moscow. They read the farm news in provincial Soviet newspapers, studied the statements of the Ministry of Agriculture, briefed visiting officials from American farm organizations, and sent reports back to Washington on the state of Russian crops. The glamorous work of the embassy took place in the political section, where foreign service officers analyzed Soviet diplomatic and military intentions and speculated on political alignments in the Politburo. Agronomy took a back seat to Kremlinology. But in the summer of 1972, the status of the agricultural observers in Moscow had suddenly changed. Their reports to Washington were read not only by the ambassador and the diplomats in the political section, but also by senior policy-makers in the White House. Information about Soviet crops was seen as vital economic intelligence with a bearing on the economic security of the United States.

Panasuk's knowledge of wheat and barley, crops that thrived in his home state, made him especially useful to the U.S. government in Moscow. Now, in late May 1975, Panasuk was on his way through southern Russia on a U.S. government mission to inspect the Soviet grain crop. When Panasuk set out from Odessa, he was aware of the difficulties the early Russian wheat crop had had. He had read the weather reports and the Soviet press. But as he traveled the Intourist route, Panasuk could observe only the fall-planted grain. Spring grain, a little more than half the total annual Russian wheat output, would not be ready for weeks. And in any case, most of this spring grain grew in areas to the east that were off limits to Panasuk and other American officials.

In Odessa, the weather was hot and sticky. Panasuk drove north to Kiev, where it rained, and then turned east. At the Ukrainian city of Kharkov, recent rainfall had been so heavy that puddles were standing in the fields. As Panasuk started south again, the rain resumed. The wheat that he saw growing along the road was in excellent condition—still green but nearly four feet high. When he returned to Moscow in early June, he cabled the Department of Agriculture in Washington: "The conditions for an excellent winter grain harvest continue."

Viktor Pershin, chairman of the Soviet grain-trading agency Exportkhleb, had no more precise knowledge of the size of the 1975 Soviet wheat crop at that time than Panasuk did. Pershin was a dour, humorless, stiff personality, but he was also tough and experienced; he had traded rubber and other commodities during a stint in the Soviet trade mission in London years earlier, and he was said to be a brilliant trader of diamonds as well. However, information in the Soviet bureaucracy is disseminated on a need-to-know basis and Pershin was not told what the conditions of the Russian crops were—only how much grain to buy or sell.

Pershin was a member of an organization that is nearly unique in the Soviet bureaucracy. Exportkhleb is the Soviet Union's grain company, and the people who work for it are unusually privileged. They travel abroad, dine in the best restaurants in Paris, London, and New York, are entertained by Western grain merchants. They have authority to make quick decisions based on conditions in the marketplace. In short, Exportkhleb operates like a Western grain company in many respects: When Russia has some "surplus" grain to sell, as it often did in the 1960s, men from Exportkhleb go to their friends in the Western companies. But Exportkhleb invariably is playing from a weak hand. The Soviet Union never really has a grain surplus. Any exports are a sacrifice to help political allies or earn foreign exchange. Still, Exportkhleb is adept at exploiting the commercial rivalries of the private grain companies. It knows that if Continental's price is not right, Cargill's might be. Also, the merchant companies provide Exportkhleb with information about global trends in the grain market, and give assessments of prices and grain supplies. In return, Exportkhleb gives favored companies an opportunity to bid for Soviet business.

Sometime in June 1975, Pershin received his instructions, and soon after that he picked up the telephone and dialed London. For all the other shortcomings of the Soviet economy, the telephone and telex service to Western Europe are excellent. A few moments later, his party came on the line.

"Patrick," said Pershin, "get to Moscow as quick as you can."

Patrick Mayhew is a merry-eyed Englishman, blond, well-tailored and full of boyish enthusiasm. If the Fribourgs, Borns, and Hirsches are the kings of the merchant business, men such as Mayhew are the knights. Mayhew is a salesman—but of a very glorious kind. Selling enormous quantities of grain for cash is his speciality, and it requires unusual talents. It is not like selling

Rolls-Royce engines. Grain has no brand name or trademark. Cargill's grain is the same as Continental's, and a merchant cannot approach a customer and say, "I am selling number two yellow corn, five per cent broken kernels," as if he were selling an expensive wristwatch with a known trademark and ten-year warranty. Anybody can acquire corn, so merchants have to resort to the oldest selling technique—they have to sell themselves. Personality, contacts, and connections sell grain. The best of the traders spoil their customers at expensive restaurants, take them on trips to country resorts, and rush to their side whenever they are called.

In addition to that, the traders need a good nose for knowing whether customers are serious or just fishing for information, and they have to have a good understanding of the technicalities: the depths of ports; the dates that rivers and waterways freeze; the quality of rail freight service and port storage in various countries; the ins and outs of insurance and shipping, not to mention the tangle of customs and tax regulations that affect the price of grain.

When it comes down to actually closing grain deals, poker skills are required. A penny a bushel in price can be translated into millions of dollars in a big deal. A trader out on his own in Algiers, Tehran, or Moscow has to know at what price his company can acquire grain and then not let himself get pushed beyond that point out of enthusiasm for getting the business. Traders who lack that restraint do not last long.

All of the companies have their star traders—men who are better paid than star athletes. Mayhew had earned his place among this select group with good luck and hard work. He had become acquainted with Viktor Pershin in London in the 1960s, when the Russians were selling British millers small quantities of their new, premium wheats from the cold, western Siberian steppes. Mayhew worked for a London grain company then. But he went to work in the late 1960s for Edward (Ned) Cook, president of Cook Industries, Inc., of Memphis, just as Cook was building his small family cotton business into an aggressive rival of the older, established grain firms. Mayhew never lost his boyish enthusiasm for his work. He still got excited when he thought about flying off to Moscow to talk grain, which is what he did that June of 1975.

As soon as his discussions with Pershin in the Soviet capital were over, Mayhew boarded the first available plane back to Western Europe. He took care to seem casual and he made no telephone calls to his home office until he reached London. Cook was preparing to take his son to summer camp when Mayhew reached him. "I can't talk on the phone," the Englishman told him. "Just pack your bags and get on the next plane."

Then Mayhew relaxed long enough to look at the London newspapers, which he had not seen for several days. One story in particular caught his eye. *The Financial Times* and other papers were carrying stories about rumored Russian grain purchases. The papers said that unidentified brokers at the Baltic Mercantile and Shipping Exchange had identified a company called Glenas, of Panama, as a front for the Soviet government in a rumored Russian plan to charter dozens of freighters to haul North American grain to the ports of Leningrad on the Baltic, Odessa and Novorossisk on the Black Sea, and Nakhodka on the Pacific Coast of Siberia. The first clue had been a Greek vessel called the *Hellas in Eternity;* the Baltic brokers had learned that the *Hellas* was to ply from the Gulf of Mexico to Odessa—a grain route—in August. They checked further. The *Hellas* was chartered to Glenas.

Cook could not get to Europe fast enough, Mayhew thought.

Pershin, meanwhile, was in contact with other European salesmen—buying American grain without even leaving Moscow. He reached Francis Turion of Continental, back from a weekend at his villa in Saint-Tropez; and Milan (Mike) Sladek, the Slovak-born trader who represented Cargill all over Eastern Europe and the Middle East. Sladek was an avid tennis player who carried his racquet with him on his travels. Tennis was an ice breaker, and some of his customers played the sport. But it was clear to Sladek that there would be no tennis for several weeks. The Russians did not play.

From that moment on, developments picked up speed on both sides of the Atlantic:

July 9: When Assistant Secretary of Agriculture Richard Bell stepped off a plane at Des Moines Airport he had no special business on his mind, except for the speech he was about to give at the annual meeting of the Iowa Corn Producers Association. But a messenger handed him a note from his Washington office that said, "Call Willard Sparks." Sparks was a senior adviser to Ned Cook, and Bell knew him well. Sparks now confirmed what Bell suspected: Cook had been summoned to Moscow and was leaving immediately.

Bell hung up and climbed into a government car for the one-hour trip to Mason City, where he was to give his address. It was high summer and the corn growing beside the roads was ramrod straight and emerald green—a good crop, thought Bell. No sooner had he arrived at Mason City than he was handed another message, this one instructing him to telephone Clarence Palmby, a vice-president of Continental Grain in New York City. Bell fidgeted as he waited for a chance to make the call. Finally, after giving his speech, he excused himself and found a telephone. Minutes later, he was talking to Palmby. "Our Geneva people have opened negotiations in Moscow," said Palmby, by which he meant Francis Turion. "At this stage it looks like five million tons of feed grains—four corn and one barley. We'll keep you advised." This was big news. But it was only an advisory. Under existing rules, Bell had no obligation to report it to other branches of the government.

July 10: Vice-president William Pearce of Cargill notified Bell, by now back in Washington, that his company was putting together a "team" of negotiators for Moscow.

July 12: President Ford held a press conference in Washington, at which he said that he had "no idea" about the size of any possible sale of grain to the Soviet Union. Farm prices had been declining, the President had vetoed higher price supports, and now the election was only a little more than a year away. "I think the fact that we can make one is a blessing and I hope we do make one," he said when asked about a sale.

July 15: Secretary of State Kissinger, in Cargill's home town of Minneapolis, defended Soviet-American détente in ringing phrases. "The world's fear of holocaust and its hope for a better future have both hinged on the relationship between the super-powers," he said. In its edition dated the same day, the *Milling and Baking News*, organ of America's flour, milling, and grain trade, disparaged the rumors emanating from the Baltic Exchange; there were "increasing doubts over the reliability or credibility" of the reports of Soviet grain buying, it wrote.

At that point, the Agriculture Department had predicted a Soviet harvest of 195 million tons, a shortfall from the planned 215 million tons, but still a respectable yield. But the Commodity News Service was reporting that the Russians had chartered an armada of thirty-nine vessels to haul grain, and Agriculture itself was becoming less sanguine. It dispatched an urgent cable to Moscow ordering the agricultural attachés to ask Soviet authorities for permission to reinspect important grain-growing areas.

July 16: The Department of Agriculture announced that Cook had sold the Russians 2 million tons of U.S. wheat and Cargill's Geneva subsidiary, Tradax, had sold another 1.2 million tons.

July 17: The Canadian Wheat Board announced a sale of 2 million tons of red spring wheat to the Soviet Union. At the same time, a spokesman for Continental denied to a reporter of the Commodity News Service that it had made any sales to Russia.

July 21: The Department of Agriculture announced that Continental had sold 4.5 million tons of corn and 1.1 million tons of barley, most of it to come from the United States, to Russia. This was a $640-million deal at prevailing prices, perhaps the largest single grain transaction of all time.

July 22: The department announced Cook's sale of another 1 million tons of wheat.

July 24: The Canadian Wheat Board reported selling 1 million tons of durum wheat to the Russians. By now the Soviet Union had bought 12.8 million tons of North American grain—more than in their first round of purchases in the "great grain robbery" of 1972.

By this time, the Agriculture Department had lowered its estimate of the Soviet grain harvest to 185 million tons. But department officials conceded such estimates were only "judgments." Soviet authorities approved only part of the itinerary of the American spring-wheat inspection team that arrived in Moscow the day after those revised estimates came out. Suspicions that they were covering up the real extent of the grain harvest's failure were strengthened by the Soviet Foreign Ministry's postponement of travel visas for members of a House Agriculture Committee delegation that had planned to visit Russian farms in August.

In the steamy July days in Washington, the highest economic planning body in the United States government, the Economic Policy Board at the White House, already had a fairly heavy summer agenda that included the financial condition of Pan American World Airlines, New York City's fiscal difficulties, foreign aid, the Law of the Sea, and the public's response to the new two-dollar bill. Suddenly, these concerns were put aside as the government riveted its attention on the grain markets.

To many, it all seemed like a painful reenactment of 1972.

When grain is exported, less is left behind. As the selloff of American stocks continued through July, prices of corn and wheat futures advanced in the trading pits of the Chicago Board of Trade. Consumer organizations and labor union leaders began to attack the administration's handling—or nonhandling—of the grain sales and warned that Americans would pay for this mismanagement with higher prices in supermarkets. Chairman

Arthur Burns of the Federal Reserve Board gave credence to these fears by saying on July 29 at a hearing before the Joint Economic Committee that the grain selling "frightens me." Two days later in Chicago, President George Meany of the AFL-CIO charged that the grain sales were a product of "a calamitous, one-way détente." The International Longshoremen's Association, with Meany's approval, announced its intention to boycott the loading of grain bound for Russia.

At the CIA, a task force was assembled to reevaluate the Soviet crop situation. The CIA's Bureau of Economic Research had been skeptical for a long time of the crop estimates the both the Soviet Union *and* the Department of Agriculture. The CIA felt Russia's grain estimates were biased, as well as padded by inclusion of water, weed seeds, and extraneous material.* It revised its computer model of the Russian agricultural situation to reflect more complete data on the previous winter's rainfall and soil moisture, and to utilize information in the first LACIE satellite pictures. The figures that emerged from the new model shocked even the CIA analysts. It appeared that Soviet grain had suffered not just a setback, but a calamity. The agency lowered its esimates to 165 million tons and left room for further downward revisions.

This new knowledge came late for President Ford. The merchant companies already had sold almost 10 million tons of American grain. The government's early warning system had malfunctioned. Once again, the United States was dealing with a *fait accompli* in the grain markets.

Beyond the immediate situation were other questions. Should private companies or the U.S. government control the disposition of American grain? Was it feasible for the government to

---

* The late Premier Nikita Khrushchev also was skeptical of Soviet agricultural estimates. He said Soviet bureaucrats' figures on crop yield reflected "wishful thinking rather than reality." In his view, Soviet statistical experts were "the kind of people who can melt shit into bullets." (*Khrushchev Remembers* [Boston: Little, Brown, 1974], p. 131.)

establish the same kind of monopoly over grain as the OPEC cartel had over oil resources? Should the laws of the market-place allocate American grain around the world, or was a more planned, bureaucratic system necessary in an era when the supply of grain was finite? What ends should the American grain surplus serve—the requirements of diplomacy, the incomes of domestic farmers, the needs of consumers, or the hopes of humanitarians? Would some kind of effective international control, such as international grain stockpiles, help to stabilize the world's grain economy?

That the questions were even being asked showed how much the world had changed from the time—so few years before—when America's food supplies had seemed boundless. Our perception of grain resources had been distorted by the glut. To recover a sense of proportion and perspective, it is necessary to go back in history to a time when grain held the key to industrial development in the modern era.

Bread and Dynasties 2

"Our business fills a great human
and economic need."
—LEOPOLD LOUIS-DREYFUS, 1912

One of the traders busily trying to sell grain to Exportkhleb in
that summer of 1975 was a short, husky-voiced man who usually
dressed in a rumpled pin-striped suit. If anybody had caught up
with Gerard Louis-Dreyfus on his travels and asked him what
made him run, he would not have said "profit" or "cash flow" or
"corporate growth," as most other businessmen would. He
might well have answered as had his great-grandfather Leopold,
the most spectacularly successful of the nineteenth-century
merchants of grain.

Satisfying "a great human and economic need" has been the
rationale for merchants through time. It has always justified
their explorations, adventures, and fortune seeking, just as it has
been said to excuse their wealth, opulent life-styles, and (from
time to time) exalted places in society. "Merchant princes"
moved in the company of the well born because they had proven
qualities of boldness, and skills in trade that were essential to the
perpetuation of the wealth and power of the nations in which
they lived.

At the end of the eighteenth century a human need requiring
the services of merchants developed on a scale that had never

been experienced before in history. The need was for bread. By 1800, England was a country that ran on coal and wheat; bread had become the established food of the Industrial Revolution, the staple of populations drawn away from their usual food supply on farms and in villages. British millers turned to the new American nation and imported flour from Baltimore and Richmond. Wheat and oats came from Sweden and Poland. But it was the surpluses that began to be produced in the remote hinterlands of the Black Sea that often made the difference between misery and sufficiency in Europe's crowded communities of urban workers.

The first masters of this early wheat trade were Greeks. Greek traders and shipowners had been active for centuries all across the eastern Mediterranean, where they also acted as agents for British and French commercial companies and manufacturers. Eventually, the most prominent of these adventurer-traders— families such as the Rallis—set up their own offices in London and took control of the British trade to and from Constantinople, Smyrna, and the Levant. From there it was an easy leap to Odessa, the new city that was becoming a wheat port at the edge of the Black Sea.

It was an odd Russian city, in many ways, less severe in its climate, architecture, and mood than most others. The polyglot merchant community, drawn there by wheat, gave Odessa in the early nineteenth century its special character as a somewhat rakish Riviera enclave in Imperial Russia. Along with the Greeks were Italians, Slavonians, Triestians, Genoese, French, Germans, Englishmen, and Spaniards. Italian, first spoken there by the Tuscan merchants who came to obtain grain for their native province, was the *lingua franca* of the city. Street signs in Italian as well as Russian pointed the way to broad, tree-shaded boulevards where the most successful of the wheat entrepreneurs built their villas.

The town had grown rapidly, encouraged in its expansion by Empress Catherine the Great, who had hastily tried to consolidate the southern territories won by Russia in its battles with the Turks in 1774. As the Turks were driven out of their strongholds along the Black Sea and in the Crimea, Catherine had invited colonists to settle the land. Russian landlords, aspiring to a lordly life-style, built manors and brought in serfs to farm vast acreages. Along with them came Swiss, Germans, Serbs, Bulgarians. In 1794, Catherine had founded Odessa. By the turn of the century, oxcarts full of wheat were clattering down the rutted roads through the bleak steppe to the port, first by the hundreds, then by the thousands, and finally by the tens of thousands. At the marketplaces, the peasants sold their wheat (and sometimes their oxen and oxcarts, too, for tallow, hide, and firewood) before returning to their villages.

There was little place for the surplus to go, except abroad. Odessa lacked flour mills or processing plants, and the sparse population of southern Russia did not require wheat in such great volumes as was coming off the estates and farms. This rising tide of wheat and oats out of the Black Sea region, managed by Mediterranean merchants, was the first major grain passage to develop from the bread revolution.

It was something quite new in human history. Grain, to be sure, had always been traded and distributed over long distances. Wheat had been on the move since the first primitive strains were cultivated in the Middle East in 7000 B.C. and began to spread slowly around the world. Wheat was carried to Egypt, to northern Mesopotamia and Iran—and then on to China and India. Migrating people and traders took it up the Danube River valley into Europe in the fourth millennium B.C. Somewhat later, traders traveling by sea in search of copper and tin brought wheat to Spain and Italy.

Russia in the twentieth century and England in the nineteenth were not the first great powers to experience food deficits. Neither Rome nor Greece was self-sufficient in ancient times. Roman landowners tended to give over their fields to sheep or cattle, leaving the empire dependent upon grain sent as tribute from its annexed or conquered territories: Sicily, Spain, North Africa, Gaul, Brittany, and Egypt. In the fifth and fourth centuries B.C., Athens often depended on the grain trade for its nourishment. Spartan armies invaded Attica in many summers and destroyed the wheat, barley, orchards, and vineyards. To Socrates, one mark of a statesman was the knowledge of how much wheat was needed to feed the population of Athens.

The grain trade then, and for many centuries afterward, depended on financiers ready to put up the money to buy the goods, a shipowner prepared to carry them, and a merchant-adventurer. The merchants of Athens (and of other Mediterranean ports later on) had little or no capital of their own. They accepted credit from bankers, chartered a ship, and often rode along on the dangerous voyages to be on hand to pay for the grain in person. This did not mean that the grain always reached its destination. Piraeus was called "thieves' harbor" because, rightly or wrongly, many of the merchants around it were suspected of "rascality and ill-will."* Along with the upright merchants were swindlers who diverted cargoes from their rightful destinations to ports where they commanded a higher price, regardless of the need for food supplies back home.

Much later, as European populations grew, Mediterranean merchants performed remarkable feats of moving grain to combat the recurring famines. Florentine merchants handled ten thousand tons of Sicilian grain a year in the fourteenth century. At the end of the sixteenth century, when Tuscany suffered famines, the grand dukes of Tuscany, Venice, and Genoa organized flotillas that brought tens of thousands of tons of grain from the Baltic and Black Seas; and ports such as Livorno (Leghorn) rose

---

* George Calhoun in *Business Life of Ancient Athens*. Calhoun describes a merchant-adventurer called Parmeniscus who bought corn in Egypt but en route home to Athens received a message from his partner, Dionysodorus, that grain prices were falling there. Parmeniscus sold the grain in Rhodes, and for a while, until his bankers got wise, he used the money borrowed from them to carry on a lively grain trade between Egypt and Rhodes.

to prominence as grain depots for the central Mediterranean. Merchants rose to such occasions, for mercy missions also turned a profit. But these were spectacular feats rather than the everyday work. The lifeblood of the early traders was the commerce in the superfluous luxuries for which the rich would pay: chocolate, coffee, tea, tobacco, spices, sugar, ivory, and indigo.

Until the late eighteenth century, familiar commodities—wheat for bread, cotton for cloth (most cloth then was made of wool), and tallow for candles—scarcely were traded internationally. Fernand Braudel estimates that in the late seventeenth century, no more than three bushels of grain out of every one hundred consumed in Europe were grown in another country. And even as civilization expanded, grain was usually cultivated, distributed, and consumed all within a few miles—within the distance that a farmer could haul his grain on an ox-drawn cart to the village mill. Snowy white bread—the "Queen's bread," as it was called when Maria de Medici ate it—was food only for the wooden bowls and pewter plates of noblemen and wealthy burghers. The poor ate mostly coarse gruels, soups, porridges, lentils, chick peas, and sometimes even "flour" from acorns.

By 1800, however, bread eating was on its way to being democratized. The milling technology for making fine, white flour free of hulls and bran had been introduced widely. France had founded the first school of baking, in 1780. Bread was a staple food for the workingman and his family, detached as he was from his old village or farm. Workers in Paris, London, and Manchester in 1800 paid half their wages for bread alone. Eating bread was a badge of attainment and social status. Once achieved, it was not easily given up, as governments invariably found when they took administrative measures to lower the quality of bread to conserve wheat.

It was no coincidence that the century in which bread eating finally extended downward to all elements of society in western Europe (even to paupers in the poorhouses and orphanages) was also the century of revolution. Riots in France in 1789 began in the towns, where bread was in short supply, and a reduction in bread prices was the result. An adequate wheat supply was, therefore, a prerequisite of social order and political stability. Towns and cities were filling up with people who had to live on the surplus. But often the only surplus was in the distant wheat-growing corners of the world.

This was the social and political imperative behind the rapid increase in the international cereal trade of the nineteenth century. By the middle of the century, Greeks were sending their sailing vessels beyond Odessa into the Sea of Azov to collect wheat that was being cultivated farther east, in the Volga River basin and even beyond, at the western edges of Siberia. Along with the wheat came oats for the horse population of London, barley for brewing and animal feed, and the hard durum wheat that produced the yellow flour for Italian pasta.

From the beginning, it was a wide-open, disorganized trade, requiring iron nerves. All the natural and human hazards that are present in the twentieth century were also evident in the early stages of the modern grain trade. The weather was a constant source of uncertainty. Droughts destroyed some crops, while in other years the harvest was so abundant that the farms lacked adequate manpower to cut, bind, and thresh it and transport it to market. One-third of the south Russian grain crop of 1845—the year of the Great Hunger in Ireland—was left in the fields because of lack of manpower to harvest it. Good crops in other parts of Europe could depress the prices of Russian wheat. The prices of wheat and barley at Danzig, the port for grain grown east of the Oder River in the lands partitioned to Poland in the 1790s, often set the wheat price in England. Also, there was competition from oats out of Sweden, where British merchants financed granaries with their own capital.

Government policies, ranging from embargoes to import duties, also created hazards for the early traders. Emperor Nicholas I forbade wheat exports during the Crimean War, for fear that the cargoes would fall into the hands of the enemy. This embargo caused a panic in Tuscany, which had come to rely on Russian grain, and wheat was imported into Italy from Spain to replace it.

All of these uncertainties affected price.

Odessa merchants usually shipped wheat to England without any idea of the price it would fetch when samples of it finally were laid out on tables in London's Mark Lane several months later. The grain was dispatched unpriced—"to arrive"—which meant that it often was floating on the high seas, en route to western Europe, without a customer. It was not even certain that the wheat could enter England, for import embargoes could be put on and taken off within a few weeks, depending on the price that British farmers were receiving for their own grain. The British trade laws of 1815, designed to protect home farmers, forbade imports of any wheat when the domestic price dropped below a fixed sum. Bumper crops, drought, flooding, poor harvest conditions, transportation breakdowns—these events in England, all beyond the control of the Black Sea merchants, nonetheless affected their fortunes, and those of the peasants and landlords on the steppes.

Information, good communications, and mobility could overcome some of the risks, and the Greeks set up an elaborate, far-flung system to reduce the hazards. Constantinople, on the Bosphorus, overlooked the sailing vessels passing from Odessa to the Mediterranean and thence to north European ports. Not surprisingly, it became an intelligence center for the wheat trade. From Constantinople, Greek merchants dispatched samples taken from the vessels overland to their London agents, who sold the cargoes direct to millers on the basis of the samples. When the captains put in at Cork or Falmouth, they received orders to proceed directly to the customer's unloading port. The Greeks excelled at this trade. They swarmed all over the Baltic Exchange, already then the clearing house for news about grain and shipping. The Greek presence even caught the attention of that omniscient observer of British economic institutions, Karl

Marx, who wrote in 1853: "How important . . . the Black Sea trade generally is becoming, may be seen at the Manchester Exchange, where dark complexioned Greek buyers are increasing in numbers and importance and where Greek and South Slavonian dialects are heard along with German and English."

From the mid-eighteenth century onward, Britain's farms had made heroic efforts to keep up with the increasing food demands of the growing cities and towns. Wheat cultivation spread rapidly across England (replacing rye in many places) as a result of improved farm equipment and farming methods. But although farm modernization progressed, England encountered the same experience that Japan and Russia were to know one century later. Agriculture could not keep up. In 1846, the British Parliament finally conceded defeat and repealed the protectionist Corn Laws.*

This was one of modern history's great political dramas, and it was made more compelling because of its background of human misery: the Irish potato famine that began when blight struck the potato fields in 1844. More expensive bread was the price that urban British workers had been paying for protection, but the system favored the interests of the farmers and landed aristocrats who made up the backbone of Prime Minister Sir Robert Peel's conservative party. In 1845, however, Peel decided that the starving Irish would have to be fed on foreign grain and that the impediments of the Corn Laws complicated this task. His decision to import American corn as a relief measure in 1845— "Peel's brimstone," it was called—was denounced for its potentially depressing impact on grain prices; but Peel felt that as long as the Corn Laws existed, such government relief was the only salvation for the starving. Peel succeeded in getting the repeal of the Corn Laws through Parliament, though it wrecked his political career and may not have helped the Irish. As the famine continued, with Peel out of office, free trade functioned in Ireland—on the export side. Cartloads of wheat, barley, and

---

* In England, "corn" refers to all grain.

oats moved steadily off the farms and into ports, past potato fields stinking and blackened by blight. It was not the grain trade that was at fault, but the social and economic structure of Ireland. Tenant farmers paid rent to their landlords with oats and wheat; many preferred to starve instead of perishing in ditches after being forcibly evicted from their hovels for non-payment of rent.

But Parliament, with its stroke of repeal, had changed the world. Repeal of the protectionist system had opened England to the wheat of all the world, created incentives for the settlement of vast territories across the oceans, and established the conditions for modern international trade, with new sea routes and modern trading empires.

It was not surprising that many of the new masters of this trade grew up in a narrow strip of western Europe extending along the Rhine River and, beyond, to Switzerland and Marseilles. The Rhine was Europe's greatest commercial artery. To the north were Antwerp and Rotterdam, two ports with access to the Atlantic Ocean. Along it, merchants, brokers, grain warehousemen, millers, and shippers functioned at Duisburg, Mannheim, Basel, and other trading centers. Barges carried flour and wheat in both directions. Its tributary, the Main River, reached toward southeast Europe—toward the Danube cities of Vienna and Budapest and toward the southeast European wheat basin. So it was natural that the Rhine and its environs would spawn more than their share of merchants. Of the five global grain firms that dominate the market today, three grew up in this crossroads of trade in the last half of the nineteenth century. The Fribourgs of French Lorraine, the Louis-Dreyfuses of Alsace, and the Bunges of Antwerp all went into the grain trade. A fourth dynasty began not far away. Georges André came down from his tiny Swiss mountain village of Sainte-Croix in 1877 and started a grain business at Nyon that was still thriving all over the world a century later.

It was also logical that many of the nineteenth-century traders, like the Fribourgs and the Louis-Dreyfuses, were Jews. European Jews, always a minority, were often prohibited from owning land or joining the army or civil service. They gravitated, understandably, to trade and finance. Jews were bankers and givers of credit; it was a natural step from giving farmers credit to buying their grain. Grain, the "currency of currencies," was good as gold in most times. Their close-knit family ties were also an asset in the grain trade, just as they were for Greeks, Quakers, and other minorities who prospered in the business. Grain trading was becoming a long-distance enterprise, requiring the confidence that some newcomer in the firm would not take advantage of a situation and run off with the money, or squander it speculating on his own account. It was prudent to keep things in the family as much as possible.

Little has been written about these old families, but it is evident from what knowledge we do have that many of the qualities that distinguish them today were already characteristic in their earliest days.

Georges André, in his early years, stayed put in Switzerland, letting his frugality and his talent for clever calculation do his work for him. The son of a watch assembler, he handled his business with all the serious attention to detail his father might have given to the springs of some delicate timepiece. He was a strict Calvinist who lived simply and austerely. When he died in 1942, at the age of eighty-six, he had never been in an airplane or owned his own automobile. But in him, as in many of his countrymen, there was more dash and daring than met the eye. His first successful venture was a shrewd speculation. Using some of his father's capital, he bought Russian hard durum wheat for macaroni and dumplings. The grain was unloaded at Marseilles and railed up to Switzerland. Swiss farmers did not grow "pasta" wheat, but there was a demand for it; André's Russian wheat undersold the bread wheat from Swiss farmers, and still made him money.

The Fribourgs, on the other hand, were a wandering, mysterious clan with a flair for a spectacular flourish. At the end of the eighteenth century, they lived in Metz, in French Lorraine. In 1813, Simon Fribourg was in Arlon, Belgium, running a small grain business. By 1870, Simon's grandson Arthur had moved to Antwerp and was building flour mills in Luxembourg and Belgium. In between, Simon's son Michel satisfied his wanderlust with a dangerous journey through the Balkans. In the 1840s, when there were food shortages in northern Europe, Michel Fribourg, carrying sacks of gold, went out on behalf of millers and importers to buy wheat in Bessarabia. He dodged highwaymen and armed Turks—and he came back with receipts for the grain. In the nineteenth century, the Fribourgs were still brokers—middlemen between importers and merchants. They earned commissions on grain sold on behalf of others who took the risks of owning grain. It was not until the next century that the Fribourgs' itinerant spirit and bent toward adventure were to assert themselves fully.

When Leopold Louis-Dreyfus started out in the grain business in 1850 he was not much different from the Russian peasants who were then carting their wheat to market in Odessa. Leopold, who had twelve older brothers, perceived that future opportunities on his father's farm in Sierentz would be limited. In 1850, at the age of seventeen, he piled sacks of locally grown wheat on a cart and set out for Basel, eight miles away across the Swiss border. The Swiss city, pinched into a crevice between France and Germany on the Rhine River, was a crossroads for the whole continent. The towers of its red-painted Gothic *Rathaus* looked out at barges plying the Rhine. And Leopold, mingling with the farmers, townsmen, and traders in the marketplace after selling his wheat, had his eyes opened to the world. Two years later, in 1852, he left home for good and established his own grain business in Basel.* Soon he also joined

* Louis Dreyfus headquarters in Paris uses "Sierentz" as its cable address to this day.

the stream of wandering merchants, extending his buying excursions to Bern, and later to central Europe.

It was natural that he was drawn eastward. Budapest, which got its wheat from the flat, rich plains of the Banat and the Vojvodina extending northward from Belgrade, was the flour-milling center of the world (though its supremacy was soon to be challenged by Minneapolis). Uprisings were rapidly driving the Turks out of the Danube River basin, and the rich peasantry of Moldavia and Wallachia (in what today is Romania) began to supply London and Liverpool, rather than Constantinople, with grain.

When Leopold reached Odessa sometime in the 1860s, the Greeks who had once dominated the business on the Black Sea were in decline. By then, new wheat sources in America had made the importers less dependent on Russian wheat and on the Greek merchants who controlled this source of supply. Larger volumes of grain, and the needs of merchants to own their own warehouses, docks, and ships in order to stay competitive, had increased the requirements for large amounts of capital. The British, French, and German merchants who began to take over in Odessa had the advantage of financial backing from their home banks. As the risks and hazards of the still speculative and volatile wheat trade grew, so did the need for credit to maintain liquidity when wheat markets were depressed—as they often were as more sources of wheat became available. British trading companies such as Ross T. Smythe and W. H. Pim expanded into Russia and the Balkans in this period. British merchant companies also laid off some of the risks of wheat by diversifying into insurance, land investment, copper, oil, lumber, cement, and salmon fishing in the western United States. Greeks had no such advantages, and when the wheat trade went global, their influence waned.

It did not help that English importers began, in midcentury, to complain of inferior quality in the Russian shipments. Sharp practices abounded among the merchants who operated in

Odessa in the interim period 1850–70 after the decline of Greek influence. One chronicler, Max Winters, wrote that "one can hardly say that one quarter of the traders have the desired moral qualities—or adequate capital." Russian wheat's reputation in Liverpool diminished. The middlemen in Odessa blamed it on the shoddy farming practices of newly emancipated (1861) serfs; the producers said that the merchants mixed dirt, stones, and worthless filler in the shipments abroad.

But Leopold Louis-Dreyfus assessed these difficulties as temporary. There was still a strong market for Russian wheat (Russia remained England's principal source for grain until 1874), and 1 million cartloads reached Odessa in 1866. With the completion of the railroads connecting wheat ports such as Odessa and Rostov on the Don with the hinterlands, Leopold foresaw opportunities for expansion. He invested the capital he had acquired through his own trading, borrowed from French financiers in Paris to purchase grain elevators, and sent his own agents to the countryside to purchase grain on the spot. In 1870, he began importing Russian wheat into Marseilles. Soon thereafter he was marketing grain through a network of offices in Hamburg, Bremen, Berlin, Mannheim, Duisburg, and Paris.

In the process, he left behind every trace of his humble origins in the muddy streets of his Alsatian village. He cut an imposing figure, with his sparkling eyes peering out above a large square black beard. In Leopold there was none of the peasant's humbling himself before his betters. Leopold was a self-assured merchant, with the air of an aristocrat. He must have been one of the most upwardly mobile entrepreneurs of his times. Leopold made a close friend of King Carol I of Romania, and he charmed as well the king's English-born wife, the poetess Carmen Sylva—so much so that he became a councillor at the Romanian court. It is not hard to see the reasons, in addition to his charm, why Leopold, together with a few other merchants, was so favored by Balkan royalty. Carol I depended on merchants to market Romanian agricultural products, particularly the Romanian corn that was the best and highest-yielding in Europe. To the king, agriculture was a source of wealth to be tapped to pay for the financial, industrial, and urban development to which he gave precedence.

The policy unabashedly exploited the peasants. There was nothing unusual about that. As in the case of coal, the other essential resource of nineteenth-century industrialization, the producers were the last to derive the benefits of the dirty work. It had been so in Poland and Ireland in the eighteenth century; it was so in Russia in the nineteenth century; and it was to be so, as well, in Argentina. In 1907, an embittered Romanian peasantry, driven by neglect and a desire for land, rose up in revolt, and before Carol I had regained control, 10,000 Romanians had died. Afterward, Romania continued to export corn. Three years before the revolt, in 1904, Leopold had named his first Black Sea vessel after his friend King Carol. He was rewarded with an appointment as Romania's consul in Paris.

Even when grain was grown under miserable or difficult conditions, it still served a "great human need." But the needs were changing in the final third of the century. Misery and hunger existed in west European cities, but they were not widespread. Europe was on a prosperity binge; the cafés of Paris, Vienna, and Berlin were full, and the French were so well fed that they made light of the Prussian siege of their capital in 1870—until they finally were forced as a last resort to give up their crepes, baguettes and patisseries and eat their house pets. As the world was to see in the next century, prosperity and affluence increased rather than diminished the dependence of many rich countries on outside sources of grain.

Without developments in technology, changes in demography, and alterations of economic institutions, Europe would not have been in reach of distant food supplies. The Industrial Revolution not only created a larger appetite for wheat and grain but also provided the wherewithal for merchants, farmers, and mariners to satisfy it. Mechanized, water-powered flour mills (replacing windmills in the late eighteenth century) made it possible to grind more flour. A steam-operated system for removing bulk grain from the holds of ships with a bucket lift was invented in America in 1843, and rodent-proof and weatherproof concrete storage silos replaced wooden warehouses and elevators at the end of the century. New canal and railroad systems opened up new wheatlands. Iron-hulled ships, stronger, larger, and more fire-resistant than the successful clipper ships and down-easters, appeared at the grain ports in the 1880s, and ocean freight rates declined steadily all through the century, so that distance became a minor factor in the cost of wheat. New farm machinery brought larger acreages under tillage for individual farmers. The transatlantic cable, laid in 1866, facilitated fast communication between the major supplier and the major consumer of grain in the last third of the century.

Leopold and his associates in the eastern Mediterranean benefited from the new efficiencies and from the new institutions streamlining the grain trade. In 1883, the Liverpool Corn Trade Association authorized "futures" trading, which meant that contracts could be bought and sold for grain to be delivered months later. When Leopold's agent bought grain from Russian peasants in the Black Sea hinterland, Louis Dreyfus agents in Liverpool were notified to sell similar quantities of wheat, at profitable prices, for future delivery. This "arbitrage" reduced some of the risks.

The commodity exchanges had begun in London in the eighteenth century as primitive "rings" or "clubs" that met in coffee houses to discuss the prices, shipping possibilities, and other details of trade in tea, tallow, hemp, and finally grain. Gradually, the exchanges became more formal institutions, with contracts, rules, and finally, futures trading that made it possible for members to fix prices months into the future. As milling became more sophisticated and more varieties of wheat became available from all over the world, millers needed to keep on hand dozens of different wheats for blending purposes. Since these wheats were harvested and shipped at different times of year in the northern and southern hemispheres, it was necessary to buy them in advance in order to keep a supply on hand through the year. The futures markets, the millers and merchants said, enabled them to do this without undue exposure to the risk of adverse price fluctuations.

None of these advances would have sufficed without the migrations that populated the empty plains and grasslands abroad and turned them to agriculture. America's wheat shipments to England were negligible until the Civil War, but as wheat rose on the new farms of California and the Plains, they increased sharply, until they overtook Russia's shipments in 1874. In 1873, with the opening of the Suez Canal, the first wheat arrived from India, after a push by British entrepreneurs to obtain a cheap, secure source of wheat under British control. The British envisaged India as a potential great source of wheat for the Empire. Industrial tycoons pushed railroads and canals into the Indus and Ganges river basins, where farmers had been growing wheat for centuries.*

At first, Australia did not seem nearly so promising a wheat source for British millers as India. In the waning years of the nineteenth century, it was still raw, untamed land, inhabited by fortune seekers who had been attracted to it by the discovery of gold in Victoria, and by desperadoes looking for adventure and quick riches. Sheep farming had predominated in the first part of the century, and wheat took hold only slowly; it was still necessary to import wheat from Chile and India to feed the shifting population. But as new drought-resistant strains of wheat ("Purple Straw") were introduced, wheat growers pushed

---

* Peasants in British India unknowingly made a major contribution to the prosperity of North America. They had patiently developed a wheat that could ripen quickly between Indian monsoons. The seeds developed by these poor peasants subsequently were used in adapting Marquis wheat, which became Canada's premium grain, to the short, northern growing season of the prairies.

out into the dry, marginal, inland wastes, and wheat began to flow from Australia to Liverpool.

By the 1880s, this wheat from Australia mingled with wheat from California, the Great Plains, the Argentine Pampas, and the Ganges on the docks of Liverpool, Hull, London, Bristol, and Glasgow. In 1883, *The Economist* waxed almost poetic in describing Britain's heavy dependency on other sources of wheat:

People think of the old days when the British harvest really fed the British people. Now we have to go further afield. A good wheat harvest is still as much needed as ever to feed our closely packed population. But it is the harvest already turning brown in the scorching sun of Canada and the Western States—the wheat already ripe in India and California, not the growth alone of the Eastern counties and of Lincolnshire, that will be summoned to feed the hungry mouth of London and Lancashire.

The two merchant houses that were most adept at exploiting these developments, Bunge and Louis Dreyfus, could not have been more different. By the time Leopold left the mud of Sierentz behind, Bunge was already an established merchant company with an illustrious name. The Bunges had come down to the Continent from the island of Gotland in the early seventeenth century, when King Gustavus of Sweden was spreading his military power into Denmark and Estonia. The émigrés split into three branches: Bunges in Russia became scholars and jurists, while in Germany the descendants performed brilliantly as intellectuals, Lutheran clergymen, and civil servants; in Holland, Bunges were drawn to commerce. By the time that Charles Bunge moved company headquarters from Amsterdam to Antwerp in 1850, Bunge had been trading in hides, spices, and rubber from Dutch overseas possessions for a century.

Charles's two sons—Edouard, in Antwerp, and Ernesto, who emigrated to Buenos Aires in 1876—established a dual merchant monarchy straddling the Atlantic Ocean. Its ubiquitous operations were to earn Bunge a sinister nickname in South America:

"the Octopus." In Antwerp, Edouard, like Leopold Louis-Dreyfus, also had a king for a friend, but his king was far more powerful and considerably more useful to a merchant than Carol I of Romania. The Congo Free State, established in 1885 as the personal domain of King Leopold II of Belgium, was created to satisfy the ruler's fervent desire for a foreign colony. Edouard Bunge was the king's broker and a royal business associate who administered economic and commercial activities in one of the ivory- and rubber-producing regions. The conditions under which the king exploited these resources were criticized abroad for their harshness. Edouard's role in this aspect of the Congo trade is murky. But whatever Edouard may have had to do with Congolese exploitation, his royal ties undoubtedly helped cement the Bunge company's position in northern Europe.

Ernesto, meanwhile, was seeking to establish a Bunge trading monopoly over the grain that began to move out of the ports of the Plate River in Argentina. He had reached Argentina just as the empty grasslands of the Pampas were being transformed into one of the world's wheatlands. These lonely fields had been unfarmed since Spanish *conquistadores* first came upon them in the sixteenth century. They had been left instead to Indians and to *gauchos*, to pursue wild horses and cattle across them. It was a desolate and unpromising landscape, broken only by a gnarled tree or the low flight of a flamingo.

As long as the rangy cattle of the Pampas were used for hides, tallow, and tough, salted meat, the natural grasslands provided a very adequate pasture. Prosperous Europeans and Englishmen wanted juicy steaks, but their palates were too refined to eat the tough meat of Argentine range cattle. But in the 1880s, it became possible to ship cattle to Europe, on the hoof or as frozen carcasses. It was the incentives to raise beef for European tastes that indirectly made Argentina a great wheat-growing country, for beef animals needed forage and alfalfa, these needed farmers to grow them, and farmers needed a cash crop—wheat, corn, or maybe wool.

At this time, a few families with *estancias* of a million acres or more controlled most of the Pampas and, with it, the financial resources and political power of the nation. They had no intention of working the land themselves, so they invited European farmers in as tenants to fence the open fields and cultivate hay and alfalfa for the animals. These tenant farmers came from Ireland, Germany, and Switzerland, but mainly from the Italian provinces of Lombardy and the Piedmont. They traded the farms and sunny vineyards of Europe for the harsh environment of the grasslands. The Pampas were fenced for Shorthorn, Hereford, and Black Angus stock, and the old *gaucho* culture was supplanted by dirt farming. The soil was unexpectedly productive and rich. The new tenant farms raised corn for England and the Continent, wool for Belgian and French carpet factories and textile mills, and wheat. To pay their rents, the farmers sold their wheat to the agents of Leopold Louis-Dreyfus and Ernesto Bunge.

In the United States, wheat farmers fought battles against the railroads and grain warehousemen whom they thought exploited them, and they won some concessions through the courts. In Argentina, recourse to such action was out of the question. Most of the tenant farmers had no land of their own, and less power. The grain production and merchandising system favored the huge landowners, the railroads, the exporters, and the grain exchanges in Buenos Aires and Rosario. The railroads, financed in part by British capital, could set whatever rates they wanted and could provide freight service at their convenience.

The two European exporting companies and several smaller ones were also in a position to dictate prices. The companies linked Argentina to the world wheat economy; and when there were profits to be made, the growers were usually the last to get them.

It was said, some years later in Argentina, that "Bunge gives the farmer his credit, sells him his seed, and buys his grain. And when the crops are in, Bunge sells the farmer the rope to hang himself." This comment only slightly exaggerates the power of the Argentina grain exporters in the late nineteenth century. Farmers sold their wheat to *acopiadores*—country storekeepers or millers—many of whom were virtual agents of the export houses in Rosario and Buenos Aires. From Bunge and Dreyfus came the funds that enabled the *acopiador* to advance money or seed to farmers before the harvest. The exporters, in effect, established the price for the crop, and they did this on the basis of their exclusive knowledge of the price (fixed to wheat's gold value) in European markets. Any disputes over prices and contracts were settled through the arbitration procedures of the Comisión Arbitral de Cereales, a board that was strongly influenced by the export firms. In some cases, Dreyfus and Bunge dealt directly with the farmers through their own rural agents, thus cutting out the *acopiadores* and increasing their own profits. A final exercise of control was the requirement that farmers sell their grain bagged. The bags were made from precut pieces of jute that entered the country duty-free and then were sold at inflated prices to the farmers. To protect this system, stiff duties were levied on ready-to-use, imported bags. Bunge pioneered in the import of raw jute from India to Argentina and thus profited in several different ways from the bagged-wheat trade.

The companies wasted no time investing grain profits in more durable fixed assets. Bunge channeled its profits into flour mills, paint plants—utilizing the abundant supply of Argentine linseed for oil bases—and textile mills employing local cotton. By the turn of the century Bunge's Argentine operations outstripped those of the parent company in Antwerp.

Ernesto Bunge had formed a partnership with his brother-in-law, Jorge Born, who had emigrated with him. In Argentina, the company went under the name Bunge y Born. But the firm grew so fast that more help was needed. In 1897, the partners brought in a group of German traders, including a Mannheim Jew by the name of Alfredo Hirsch. Hirsch became president of Bunge y Born in 1927, and remained president for thirty years. Hirsch had joined Bunge as if he were entering the priesthood. While he accumulated *estancias* of his own, as part of a personal fortune, he was in some respects as austere and frugal as Georges André, over in Switzerland. In his final years, he suffered from painful rheumatism and was confined to a wheelchair. He rejected the treatment that doctors said would cure him, for it would have involved an extended recuperation. Time away from Bunge was time ill spent.

As Leopold Louis-Dreyfus's empire grew to encompass Russia as well as Argentina, the United States, Canada, and all of Europe, he too needed help. But Leopold had three sons, Louis, Charles, and Robert, and he was able to follow the merchant precept of keeping control in the family. Leopold sent Charles to manage the company facilities on the Black Sea in the 1890s. And by the time of World War I, the Louis Dreyfus company was nothing less than a produce merchant for all of Europe, a wholesaler of grain that purchased enormous quantities of wheat, corn, barley, and other crops from farmers or small middlemen in Russia, the Balkans, Canada, the United States, and Australia and delivered it to small customers on the European continent, in Berlin, London, Rome, Antwerp, Brussels, and Rome. The food deficit was growing, as industrialization continued and populations grew, and Leopold had an organization on three continents that served the "great human and economic need."

England more than sixty years after repeal of the Corn Laws was the greatest market for food the world had ever seen. Its own farmers were producing only enough wheat to feed their countrymen for eight weeks a year. The remainder floated steadily toward Liverpool, Hull, Bristol, and London month after month over the seven seas. In 1914, there were 5 million tons of wheat arriving by sea. As the world turned and the harvests swung across the planet, the sources of the wheat changed. In March the shipments began arriving from Argentina and Uruguay; in April, from Australia; in June, from Africa and India; in

August came the fall-planted wheat from Russia and America; and in November, the spring-planted wheat from Canada. Huge flour mills were situated at major ports.

The Louis Dreyfus company's Paris headquarters, in a renovated nineteenth-century mansion on a handsome square near the Paris bourse, gave a sense of the firm's imperial reach. In the traders' cramped working quarters, coded messages arrived by transatlantic cable from New York, to be quickly deciphered for the information they contained about the price of wheat offered from various ports in various months of the year. Elsewhere in the building, Leopold Louis-Dreyfus managed his affairs in opulent surroundings. To an awed visitor in those premises, the great merchant looked confident, kindly, and patriarchal, with no hint that this was the son of an Alsatian farmer. His office, a huge drawing room with high ceilings decorated in the First Empire style, was stately. Behind a polished desk sat the founder himself, eyes clear and penetrating, peering out from above a crisply cropped beard. Business associates came and went, bowing from the waist. In 1915, Leopold died, leaving the business in the hands of his two surviving sons, Charles and Louis. His legacy to them was a merchant empire unsurpassed except perhaps by Bunge. The family dynasty was secure and well positioned for a century in which Russian grain would play no less a role in the fortunes of the merchant families than it had in the preceding one.

Grain Barons 3

"I saw the wheat running in rivers."
—ANTHONY TROLLOPE IN CHICAGO, 1861

"Take the robber corporations and shake them
all to Hell."
—GRANGER NEWSPAPER, 1870s

Europe's insatiable appetite for wheat in the nineteenth century coincided with the heyday of the business entrepreneur in the United States. So it was not surprising that the spread of wheat cultivation into the prairies and the inland valleys of California called forth a cast of speculators and capitalists worthy of the era of the "robber barons." California had its Isaac Friedlander ("the Grain King"); the milling industry of Minneapolis had the Washburns and the Pillsburys; and the whole Midwest became a vast Monopoly board for the most successful of the grain warehousemen, William W. Cargill and his rival Frank H. Peavey ("Grain Elevator King of the World").

The wheat business was as rough and ready as railroading or oil, as the fluctuating fortunes of those early grain barons show. Friedlander died in 1878, only a year after losing the fortune he had amassed cornering wheat and sailing vessels in San Francisco. After Will Cargill's death in 1909, his Midwest empire only narrowly avoided bankruptcy and liquidation as a result of speculative investments made by a Cargill son in an irrigation project in the Montana wilds. Fortunes made and lost, rivals outsmarted and bankrupted, opportunities seized—this was the natural order of business. All of the wheat and flour men were in search of the American dream—growth, expansion, wealth— and they pursued it unrelentingly. When Cadwallader Washburn's Minneapolis flour mill exploded in 1878, in the worst milling accident in American history, "the governor"* came straight to the smoldering, body-littered wreckage, summoned his advisers, and paced off the dimensions of a new mill, which he announced on the spot would be the most up-to-date ever built in the United States. This kind of resilience, this kind of betting on the country's future, was a common characteristic among the early capitalists of wheat.

Like other aspects of the American dream, the wheat business often promoted progress and economic exploitation simultaneously. Wheat provided the economic incentive for the settling of the prairies; it gave value to the land homesteaded by landless immigrants; and it helped to finance the extension of the railroads across the continent. However, wheat was also the cause of a fierce economic struggle played out according to the harsh rules of nineteenth-century capitalism.

Wheat was the main cash crop, and therefore the main source of accumulating agricultural wealth as the frontier moved west. Wheat profits were, therefore, up for grabs. There were as yet no great international markets for such crops as corn and oats, but there was for wheat. Corn was consumed by frontier farmers and their families in the form of corn bread, corn pone, and corn whiskey, and fed to hogs and to the horses, mules, and oxen that broke the sod and pulled the wagons and harvesters. But trade in corn was hindered by the absence of an efficient method for se-

* Washburn served as governor of Wisconsin in 1872 and 1873.

parating the grain from the cob (a problem that was not overcome until the cylinder-type corn sheller became available in 1902). Oats was not a marketable crop, either. It was grown everywhere in the United States; and was too light, requiring too much space in railroad cars for its weight, to be moved economically to distant markets.

Grain prices were wheat prices in the new territories, and it was wheat that Trollope saw "running in rivers" when he visited the granaries of Chicago in 1861. At the time, the nearby farmlands of Wisconsin and Illinois were still the main wheat-producing areas. But as rising land values encouraged more intensive forms of agriculture in these two states, the frontier pushed west and wheat spread to Minnesota, the Dakotas, western Iowa, and Kansas.

Before the railroads caught up with the pioneers, the settlers found that their fortunes depended completely on the markets and merchants in river towns. For a Minnesota farmer in the early 1860s, the closest place to sell wheat might be a 150-mile trip away over forest trails and rutted paths menaced by robbers and Indians. The elements were another obstacle. Wheat farmers with ox-drawn carts battled the cold and floods on the way to market towns, and Minnesota newspapers regularly reported the names of wheat farmers who had frozen to death alongside their carts on these journeys. When the farmer reached his destination, he had no guarantee that he could sell his wheat for a price that seemed fair to him.

The grievances of the settlers were real. But their problems often stemmed as much from the economic structure of the wheat business as from the greed of individual entrepreneurs. Wheat prices were established in Liverpool, Buenos Aires, Karachi, Odessa, Antwerp, and Marseilles, not just in Chicago and New York. Ultimately, Americans had no control over the price of wheat in the towns along the Mississippi River, or in Chicago.

Given this fact, margins of profit had to be extracted "upstream"—along the railroad lines and at the storage terminals in the interior. In the struggle among farmers, merchants, millers, and exporters for their share of the wheat price that was determined in world markets, the advantage always went to those who controlled the storage and transportation of grain. This was the decisive factor, as well, in the ability of the grain barons to amass fortunes.

Nowhere was this more evident than in California, which rose to prominence in the world wheat trade after the Gold Rush, long before wheat grew in large quantities in Kansas or the Dakotas. Wheat thrived in the Sacramento and San Joaquin valleys. Once the gold fever abated, the more enterprising newcomers to California made this discovery. They staked out ranches and began growing wheat as a permanent and (they hoped) reliable source of income. The soil, climate, and topography of the inland valleys, as well as the large ranches, were well suited to the "desert plant." As railroads began to penetrate more deeply from San Francisco, the volumes of marketable wheat increased. It soon turned out that wheat could be as speculative as gold in California.

The problem, of course, was that the main domestic market for this wheat—the eastern cities of the United States—was not accessible. The transcontinental railroads had not crossed the Rocky Mountains in the 1850s, and although New York, Baltimore, and Boston could be reached by sea, those markets already were well supplied by the rivers of wheat from the Midwest. Foreign export markets therefore became an urgent necessity for California wheat growers and merchants. At first, British and American merchants newly arrived in San Francisco shipped some wheat to Australia, China, Alaska, South America, and the Sandwich Islands. But as the volume increased, it was clear that only England could absorb the surpluses. So it was that "rural California and mercantile San Francisco became almost a colonial appendage of Victorian Britain [recognizing] no economic overlord save Liverpool."[*]

By 1870, California had become so dependent on the English market that it used a British measurement (the cental: 100 pounds) instead of the bushel, and it was said that there were only two subjects of conversation on the wheat ranches: the weather in California and the price of wheat in Liverpool. "California No. 1" was one of the standard varieties traded by the merchants and millers at the Liverpool Corn Trade Association in the 1880s.

The California wheat trade that evolved with Europe in the 1850s was one of the most remarkable feats of commerce in history. The distance to Liverpool was 14,000 nautical miles, a treacherous route around Cape Horn that took four to five months. Naturally, the tendency developed to overload the huge sailing vessels—clipper ships and down-easters—that made the journey (it was not economical for coal-burning steamers to make so long a haul). And from the outset, control of the ocean shipping was the key to control of the trade overall. Control of the shipping was, in fact, the secret to the inordinate power and influence of Isaac Friedlander, one of the century's most audacious commodity speculators.

Friedlander was a German-Jewish immigrant who grew up in Charleston, South Carolina, and went to San Francisco in the 1849 Gold Rush. He was a six-foot-six, 300-pound giant of a man whose figure, striding around the docks of San Francisco, was an awesome though familiar sight. In 1852, he made his first fortune—not in gold but in flour. The adroit German cornered most of the available flour supplies and forced up the price at the expense of the gold miners, who paid more for bread. Friedlander invested some of his profit in the first flour mills built on the

[*] Rodman Paul, "The Wheat Trade Between California and the United Kingdom."

West Coast. He lost most of his fortune in more speculation several years later, but by 1858 he was back in business, exporting wheat to Britain and Australia.

As the trade with England began to pick up, Friedlander positioned himself to control the incoming ships and the outgoing wheat, thereby taking the California grain markets into his own hands.

Friedlander quickly grasped the importance of ocean shipping in the cycle of harvesting and marketing California's grain. There was no regular European steamer service to and from San Francisco in the 1850s and 1860s, as there was from Atlantic Coast ports. Vessels had to be chartered, since the four- and five-masted sailing vessels would not call at San Francisco without a guaranteed charter for the run to England. Friedlander developed a system for estimating the size of the California crop and booking the required number of vessels to haul the wheat. He had the financial backing of San Francisco bankers, who were eager to put the city on world trade routes. Friedlander's agents and intelligence sources fanned out through California each spring to collect estimates on crops. Then, Friedlander would charter the needed sailing vessels early in the season. As the size of the coming harvest became more widely known, freight rates rose. If someone had the temerity to challenge Friedlander's monopoly, he would bid up the cost of tonnage to exclude all competitors until he completely controlled the shipping needed to haul the wheat crop.

At the same time that he chartered vessels, he also bought wheat from local merchants, who in turn had a strong hold over wheat farmers. Farmers put up their crops as security—this was often their only way to obtain loans from urban bankers. These loans gave bankers and middlemen-financiers the power to force the crop to market whenever the time was propitious for them. When the crops came in to the San Francisco docks, Friedlander sold the wheat to representatives of foreign export houses and then provided these companies with the shipping required to move the grain.

Friedlander's hold over the wheat trade made him an obvious target in the 1870s for the Patrons of Husbandry (the Grange), the agrarian reform movement that fought for regulation of the railroads and grain warehousemen across the country. Friedlander's access to capital led the California *Patron*, the Grange's organ, to call him "the money king as well as the grain king." However, the Grange's only determined effort to break his power, in 1873–74, failed when the British agent the Grange picked to market its wheat overchartered shipping.

In 1877, Friedlander himself overchartered vessels and went into bankruptcy. A year later, he died while attempting another of his comebacks. His demise was unmourned by the Grange, which claimed that Friedlander "used his power with such a merciless hand that farmers would receive no more for a large crop than for a small one. He had the wheat growers so completely under his control that even with larger crops, farmers were growing poorer and poorer, year by year."

The Grange did not know it in 1878, but California's days as a great wheat exporter already were numbered. Like the rest of the country, California suffered the effects in the 1880s of low prices due to competition in its overseas markets from such new producers as Canada, Argentina, India, and Australia. California was able to stay in the wheat trade mainly because the increasingly large and economical sailing vessels reduced freight rates. In 1891, the four-masted *Shenandoah*, driven by a spread of two acres of canvas, left San Francisco with 5200 tons of wheat, the largest grain cargo on record up to that time. But the appearance of the spectacular vessel was a glorious epitaph. California wheat exports dwindled rapidly. By the end of the century the conversion of many wheat holdings into irrigated plots for other crops was well under way, and the California wheat trade was fading into history.

Across the plains and prairies of the Midwest, however, wheat grew and grew.

The endless prairies became the nation's last frontier after the Civil War. There had never been anything like prairie farming in the whole history of agriculture. The first farms of America had been hacked out of eastern forests so thick that the sun never broke through the canopy of foliage, and it took a man a year to "ring" the trees, push them over, pull out the stumps, and clear a couple of acres for corn. But in the Midwest, one settler wrote, "you could aim your team west and plow in a straight line until you were an old man—and you still wouldn't be out of the prairies!" There were sinister hazards—fire, rampaging buffaloes, and tornadoes—but once those were overcome, the thin topsoil, mixed as it was with "gumbo" clay that clung to a farmer's boots, produced an excellent yield of wheat.

The new labor-saving machinery available to farmers made the cultivation of these large acreages possible. McCormick's reaper made its appearance in 1831, and John Deere began making steel plows six years later. Other weird-looking metal contraptions (such as the spidery "New Yorker self rake") were also revolutionizing farming practices. In 1837, it took 148 man-hours to plant, cultivate, and harvest an acre of wheat; in 1890 it was down to only 37 hours.

The government and the railroads offered inducements to settle, and after the Civil War the states west of the Mississippi River filled up with young war veterans eager for the freedom and opportunities of the frontier; immigrants from Europe; and eastern farmers disillusioned with a long series of depressions back home.

However, the very productivity of the new lands was often the settlers' worst enemy. Surpluses were a problem as early as 1860 in Minnesota, where the entire prosperity of the two-year-old state depended on finding outlets for surplus agricultural products. The development of Minneapolis as a major flour-milling center, rivaling or surpassing St. Louis, Buffalo, Liverpool, and even Budapest by the 1880s, helped to solve this surplus problem and make the upper Midwest one of the great wheat centers of the world.

This development was hastened by the competition for dominance between two families that came to Minneapolis from New England in the 1860s—the Pillsburys and the Washburns. Neither had any extensive experience in milling; good instincts apparently drew them to Minneapolis, a village becoming a city with scarcely any transitional period as a town. In 1863, when the Chippewa Indians ceded the Red River Valley, more excellent agricultural land became available, and Minneapolis's population rapidly increased. Its main milling asset was the Falls of St. Anthony on the Mississippi River, considered by the Sioux Indians to be the shrine of a great spirit and by Pillsbury and Washburn to be the potential source of power for mills to grind the new wheat produced in the state. By the end of the decade, flour had surpassed lumber as the city's main manufactured product.

By 1866, when Cadwallader Washburn began building his six-story stone "B" mill at the Falls, he was already rich and prominent. He was an American of Jeffersonian breadth: patrician, politician, patriot, interested in everything. A biographer described him as "a kind of universal genius of business enterprise, the archetype entrepreneur who laid his hands on any project that could turn him a profit but who touched all his interests with a fastidiousness that allowed the dictates of idealist and patriot to dominate those of the man of affairs."*

Descended from a long line of Massachusetts Puritans on both sides of his family and raised in Maine, Washburn left the East in 1839 and made a fortune in pine, mineral, and agricultural lands in Wisconsin territory, was elected to Congress, and reached the rank of major general in the Civil War cavalry—all before getting seriously involved in the Minneapolis company that was the ancestor of General Mills.

* James Gray, *Business Without Boundaries: The Story of General Mills.*

Charles Alfred Pillsbury was young (twenty-seven) and inexperienced when he arrived in Minneapolis and purchased a small interest in a mill at the Falls in 1869. But he was energetic and had the backing of his uncle John Sargent Pillsbury, who already had extensive lumber, real estate, and hardware interests in Minnesota. By 1872, the Pillsburys had increased their holdings in the milling business and were actively organizing the purchase of wheat and the extension of railroads into the surrounding countryside.

Great as their waterpower asset at the Falls was, the Minneapolis millers had several serious problems to overcome. The first was that their flour was worthless without good railroad connections to eastern markets. Initially, Minneapolis products went downstream to St. Louis and thence east by rail; the Northern Pacific Railroad reached Minneapolis in 1862; but regular service to the east from Minneapolis did not begin until 1871.

The second problem, a technical one, was worse. When Washburn and Pillsbury began work in Minneapolis, milling was still a dirty, imperfect business employing stone millstones of the kind that had been used for centuries. The millstone, crashing down on the wheat berry, was a crude instrument, but effective enough in dealing with the soft-kernelled wheats that grew east of the Mississippi River. The white flour could be separated from the bran fairly cleanly. Millers, bakers, and consumers liked the white texture of bread from this flour. But as wheat cultivation moved west, farmers planted harder-kernelled wheats, which stood up better in the cold, continental climate. In northern latitudes such as Minnesota and the Dakotas, the fall-planted wheat could not survive the winter, and wheats with even harder kernels (some varieties of which had migrated from Russia, Germany, and Scotland) were sowed in the spring. The Minneapolis millers had difficulty dealing with these hard wheats. As the millstones came down on the flinty kernels, the kernels cracked and left specks of bran in the flour, discoloring it. For this reason, Minnesota spring wheat sold at a discount of ten cents a bushel in the 1860s. Washburn and Pillsbury, therefore, began an urgent search for methods that would eliminate the disadvantage of Minnesota flour. The financial stakes were very high. Washburn was the first to succeed, with the help of a French-trained engineer by the name of Edmund La Croix.

France and Hungary possessed the most advanced flour-milling technology in the world at the time, and European experience, such as La Croix had, was an invaluable asset for American mill planners. The reputation of Hungarian milling was especially awesome, for Budapest's mills were the most elaborate in the world. It was said that these mills, drawing on the wheats that grew in the Banat, along the Danube River, were capable of producing as many grades of flour as there were social classes in Hungary. They ranged from the premium, milky white *Kaiserauszug* (Emperor Extract) to the rich dark, inferior grades for the bread of the poor and the lower classes.

The trouble with both the French and Hungarian milling systems was that they required large amounts of manual labor. The system of separating the product into dozens of different grades of flour fit for the bread of separate social strata was inappropriate for the United States, which had a single food standard. Inferior flours still made up half of French production before 1850; substandard flour financed the elaborate system that made it possible for the French and Hungarian mills to produce superior white flour also, for those who could afford it. One Hungarian mill produced eighty-four different flours, all requiring individual handling.

Washburn put La Croix to work in the B mill in 1871, with instructions to develop a more efficient system for purifying flour. A year later, the "new process" was in place. La Croix's system functioned with moving sieves passing over delicate jets of air that suspended the clean, lighter flour while the heavier impurities were whisked away from underneath it. This air separation system, refined many times over, is still in use in American mills.

In the milling community at the Falls of St. Anthony, proprietary information of such momentous value could not be kept secret for long, and Washburn's method soon leaked out to Charles Pillsbury via an employee who switched to the rival company.

The results of this relatively small, obscure technological improvement were felt across the whole upper Northwest and insured the prosperity of the region for years to come. The "new process" milling reversed the economic position of Minnesota flour on the bakers' scale of preferences, not only in the United States but in England as well. Once it could be sold as a white product free of impurities, Minneapolis flour became the premium flour of the United States. The reason was that the spring-planted wheats of Minnesota and the Dakotas, ripened as they were in the dry, sunny climate, contained a higher percentage of protein, or "gluten," than soft eastern wheats. This was an advantage of enormous economic significance. Gluten gives flour the capacity to absorb water and, when yeast is added, to rise. To bakers this meant that hard, spring wheat flour produced more loaves per pound. To consumers, the benefit was bread that tended to stay fresh longer.° Minnesota flour was soon in demand not only in New York but also in London and Liverpool. The profits of Pillsbury, Washburn, and other Minneapolis millers rose accordingly. In 1871, profits had averaged 50 cents a barrel; by 1874, they were $4.00 to $4.50 a barrel.

For all the economic advantages of the new process, milling was still a dirty and dangerous business—more so, perhaps, than

° The delicious, distinctive-tasting French bread has the disadvantage of staling quickly—thus the French housewife's frequent trips to the bakery and the existence of 40,000 decentralized bakeries in that country. The reason is that French bread is made mainly from soft wheats short on gluten. British, Dutch, and German flours are blends of soft wheat and hard, high-protein wheat and tend to make bread that keeps longer.

ever, since volume increased and productivity often took precedence over safety. The noise, the heat, the thick flour dust, and the sweetish smell made the mills as unpleasant to work in as coal mines. And the danger of explosions from spontaneous combustion or sparks was a constant threat.

At six-thirty in the evening of May 2, 1878, a loud noise was heard all over Minneapolis and people saw a firebolt rushing upward, followed by clouds of thick black smoke. The Washburn A mill was wrecked, eighteen men were buried beneath it, and nearly half the city's milling capacity had been destroyed. Washburn, in go-getter style, seized the opportunity to build the world's most modern mill on the site of the blackened ruin. He summoned a Vienna-trained milling engineer named William de la Barre and dispatched him to Europe to gather all the latest intelligence about milling. American millers had been interested since the early 1870s in Hungarian "roller" milling, a technique that utilized porcelain rollers rather than millstones to break the wheat kernels. The process performed the operation with repeated gentle blows on the kernel instead of pulverizing it with one grinding. De la Barre knew of this, as well as of Gustav Behrn's exhaust system for ventilating mills. But de la Barre still needed more up-to-date information and he set out for Europe on a mission of industrial espionage. An atmosphere of intrigue surrounded his trip. Mills in Switzerland, Germany, and Austria refused to admit him. In Budapest, finally, he slipped into a mill disguised as a workman, studied the equipment carefully, and emerged with the information he needed. Back in Minneapolis the stolen Hungarian technology was copied and improved on—with the use of chilled steel rollers instead of porcelain ones.

Pillsbury and his associates had also been traveling in and out of Hungary on similar missions, and despite the Hungarians' attempts to keep their techniques secret, Pillsbury obtained several rollers, brought them back to Minneapolis, and installed them in his mills. Pillsbury, in 1879, ordered a six-story mill built that was to be even larger than the Washburn facility. But disaster also dealt his plans a setback when, in 1881, an explosion and fire leveled many of Pillsbury's mills, killed four persons, and injured and burned others.

The hectic growth in Minneapolis milling is evident in the fact that the volume of flour produced there increased from 850,000 barrels in 1875 to 5 million barrels in 1885—despite the two disastrous explosions. By now flour milling was one of the most profitable businesses in the Midwest, thanks to the improvement of milling technology, the rapid expansion of wheat growing, and the advancement of the railroads. Wheat was the mainstay of the Midwest's new economy. The mills needed prodigious amounts of it.

The millers wasted no time insuring that they, not the farmers, got the primary benefits of the increased value of wheat that resulted from the milling improvements. The Pillsbury and Washburn families took the lead in organizing a buyers' cartel of sixteen of the eighteen Minneapolis mills. The Minneapolis Millers Association, incorporated in 1876 and lasting until 1885, exercised its power along several of the railroad lines that had begun to run out from Minneapolis like spokes of a wheel. Although the association could not fix the price of wheat at the grain elevators along all the lines, it was arbitrary in its grading and pricing of the farmers' grain in some places.

Still, the millers did not have everything their own way, for they often found themselves at odds with other powerful interests. Minneapolis had to compete for its wheat against such cities as Duluth, Green Bay, and Milwaukee, and that competition often brought them into conflict with the bankers, railroads, and warehousemen who had a vested financial interest in promoting grain traffic to those cities. The best spring wheat grew along the route of the Northern Pacific Railroad, but for a time, the road favored traffic to the Great Lakes port of Duluth over traffic to Minneapolis. Minneapolis did not establish a direct railroad route to the eastern seaboard until 1888, when the Soo Line linked up with the Canadian Pacific, making possible through service to Boston.

As the railroads reached west across the Mississippi, they took an active hand in the wheat business. They needed wheat traffic to supply them with freight, and they used all kinds of devices to stimulate the business—for example, lowering freight rates at grain collection points where there was competition from other nearby railroads and raising them stiffly elsewhere. Favoritism, under-the-table dealing, and inequity were the rule of thumb in the Midwest wheat trade.

It was in these difficult conditions that Will Cargill and Frank Peavey accumulated their fortunes—by collecting and shipping the farmers' grain.

Will Cargill was a short, stocky man with soft, round eyes. Like Leopold Louis-Dreyfus, he was the son of a farmer. In 1865 (when Leopold was just beginning to do business in Odessa) Will was still pushing a plow on the Wisconsin farm of his father, a retired Scottish sea captain. When the Civil War ended and the frontier began to expand once again, Will bought a railroad ticket to the end of the line and then purchased a small interest in a small wooden grain elevator in Conover, Iowa.

It quickly became apparent, however, that the one-crop wheat economy would develop north of Iowa, so Will and his brother Sam began in about 1870 to build or buy grain elevators along the Southern Minnesota railroad. Financing was not a problem: Banks in Milwaukee were eager to invest in the grain trade so as to increase the business that moved through their city; with some of this Milwaukee money and some capital from his father, Will began playing Monopoly across southern Minnesota and Wisconsin. The financial panic of 1873 had sent many elevator operators into bankruptcy and Cargill bought them out at distress prices. In 1874, Will moved to a picturesque Victorian mansion overlooking the Mississippi River at La-

Crosse, Wisconsin. From this base in LaCrosse, he pioneered the system of "integration" that made his company a major power in the Midwest.

Cargill created a "moving belt" of grain that transported wheat from small countryside depots all the way to Chicago, and he hauled coal back through the same system. The cooperation of the railroads was essential for his schemes. Will Cargill's plans hinged on the building of a large grain terminal at Green Bay to serve the Great Lakes; but for the depot to be successful, it was necessary to get a railroad spur built across the Green Bay peninsula, so that grain could be moved to Milwaukee when the lakes were frozen. Cargill persuaded the Green Bay and Western and the Chicago and Northwestern railroads to share in the cost of building the Green Bay depot and the connecting link of railroad spur. This small rail route was so strategically placed that Cargill sold it later at a substantial profit. Cargill used his moving belt to haul coal back on his own steamships from Milwaukee or Chicago and sell the coal to farmers through his own retail outlet at LaCrosse.

Meanwhile, Will's brothers Samuel and James expanded Cargill's elevator holdings along James J. Hill's Great Northern railroad line west of Minneapolis, and into the Red River Valley as far as North Dakota. While Will worked with the bankers and dreamed up new schemes, Sam handled the day-to-day operations from Minneapolis with the same uncompromising toughness that still characterized the Cargill company a century later. A glowering man with a thick mustache, Sam was so intimidating that when he barked an order to an employee to go to St. Paul, the hapless man was halfway there on a streetcar before he realized he had forgotten to ask the reason for his mission.

Frank Peavey's elevator system, which began a little later, eventually outstripped even that of the Cargills. But not much is known about the maneuvers he used to establish his holdings; very little is written down, and the company's history depicts Peavey as a bland, kindly soul who enjoyed helping newsboys get a start in life—surely not the driving entrepreneur who established one of the largest nineteenth-century business conglomerates in the United States.

Peavey, a tall, bearded man with deep-set hawklike eyes, reached the Midwest in 1865 from his home in Maine, where his father had prospered in the coastal shipping and sawmill business. Peavey worked for a while as a messenger for a Chicago grain firm (where he developed a phobia against speculation in grain futures) and later invested in a farm-implements company in Iowa whose factory burned down. In 1874, Peavey got his start as an independent grain man working for the Minneapolis Millers Association in Sioux City, Iowa. Peavey impressed the millers with his ambitious plans to divert wheat from Iowa to Minneapolis. He then convinced officials of the Chicago-St. Paul-Minneapolis railroad to permit him to extend his line of grain warehouses all the way from Sioux City to St. Paul. That line became the nucleus of Peavey's holdings. In 1886, one year after he established his headquarters in Minneapolis, Peavey constructed one of the world's largest grain terminals in Minneapolis at a cost of $3.5 million. The Minneapolis millers continued to be Peavey's biggest customers, even as he extended his network of collection facilities west along the Union Pacific, Northern Pacific and Great Northern rail lines.

Installed on the West Coast, with his own one-million–bushel elevator at Portland, Oregon, Peavey attempted another logistical coup in 1895, when he shipped Oregon wheat to Liverpool in a little over thirty days. The cargo was taken by sailing vessel to the Isthmus of Panama, transported in open rail cars across land, and loaded onto another vessel. The grain arrived in England in reasonable condition despite its exposure to sun and rain in the tropics, but the experiment did not make money and Peavey discontinued it. The West Coast grain business was still transacted in 100-pound sacks, and Peavey became discouraged with this practice, too cumbersome a method for his liking. Three years later, Peavey's firm sold the Portland terminal.

It was not only the millers who were plagued by fires and explosions. By the late 1890s, insurance premiums on a single large wooden grain terminal sometimes ran $150,000 a year, a very large sum in those times. Most grain men believed that silos had to be made from wood because of its "give." It was commonly believed that a concrete tank holding grain would explode or crack when grain was drawn from the bottom. But Peavey proved these experts wrong in 1899 by building an eighty-foot-high experimental grain silo at the outskirts of Minneapolis. This edifice, nicknamed "Peavey's Folly," was such a major breakthrough that even *The New York Times* reported it: "a mammoth elevator of a style of construction novel to this country."

The European masters of the grain trade and flour business were beginning to be impressed. In 1900 representatives of the Russian tsar invited Peavey's son-in-law to Moscow and St. Petersburg to discuss the possibility of a joint venture that would modernize grain handling on the Siberian railroad route. The project did not materialize, but the Peavey delegation took the opportunity to look at concrete grain warehouses in Romania. Some of them probably were used or owned by Leopold Louis-Dreyfus and his firm. The Peavey people were impressed.

At his death, in 1901, Peavey's business stretched across the United States. He operated four of the largest steamships on the Great Lakes and had extensive interests in railroads, banking, land, and a piano company. Most of all, though, as the obituaries put it, he was the "Grain Elevator King of the World."

Elevator men like Peavey and his associates also were active north of the border in the new wheat country that was opening up in the Canadian provinces of Saskatchewan and Manitoba. The Canadian-Pacific Railroad ("the Great Colonizer," it was called) reached the Pacific Ocean in 1885. It had a charter that included tax concessions, rate privileges, and 25 million acres of land for "resettlement." Canadian wheat acreage began to increase dramatically near the end of the century, as the railroad network was extended and new wheat varieties spread. Peavey's heirs were in at the start of this boom, contracting in 1906 to build fifty elevators along the Canadian Pacific railroad line in Saskatchewan. Thirty of these were built before the crop of that year was even harvested.

There was always some semblance of competition for the farmers' wheat at the grain-collection points along the railroad tracks. In some cases, there was more than one elevator. And "floaters"—representing millers, Great Lakes steamship owners, and eastern brokers—did ride out to meet farmers on the market roads, jumping on their carts, sampling the wheat, and offering a spot price. But often this "competition" was more perfunctory than real. By the early 1880s, Cargill and another LaCrosse firm, Hodges and Hyde, controlled 525,000 bushels out of the 920,500 bushels of elevator capacity on the Southern Minnesota railroad. In her book *The Wheat Market and the Farmer in Minnesota*, Henrietta Larson has noted that even after the two firms formed different companies, "they did not compete seriously" and "their attempt to keep up the appearance of competition was often so ill concealed as to make farmers suspicious."

By 1895, Peavey, Cargill, and a third company, Northern Grain, owned almost all the grain storage capacity in Duluth, the port at the far western end of the Great Lakes that was strategically situated to handle the grain of the upper Midwest. Central grain terminals such as those in Duluth were very profitable, as was seen whenever their balance sheets were brought to the knowledge of the public. Between 1883 and 1889, for example, two large terminals in Minneapolis (Empire Grain and Minnesota and Northern Grain) averaged annual returns on capital investment of 40 per cent and 30 per cent respectively, rates that make the era of the "grain robberies" seem like a time of thin margins.

The lot of any small-town businessman who wanted to compete with the big "line companies" such as Cargill or Peavey, without the support of some big railroad company, was never an easy one. The line elevators along the Great Northern, Soo, Northern Pacific, and Minneapolis and St. Louis railroads, Ms. Larson writes, "could not afford to compete among themselves and tried to prevent others from competing, and no small independent elevator could withstand the methods of lines bent on destroying him."

The consolidation process also moved ahead quickly in milling. By the end of the century, virtually all the milling capacity in Minneapolis was owned by the Pillsburys, Washburns, Crosbys,* and the Northwest Consolidated Grain Company.

In many cases, both the millers and the warehousemen interlocked with railroad companies or, in some cases, owned their own railroads. Will Cargill's ventures in railroading in the Green Bay peninsula contributed to his fortune, and the Cargill family established a close enough rapport with the tycoon James J. Hill to obtain favored positions for Cargill elevators all along Hill's Great Northern Railroad west of Minneapolis to the South Dakota line. Peavey, likewise, was sitting on the boards of two railroad companies when he died. One of the most important rail lines into the wheat country out of Minneapolis was named after Pillsbury, and *The Minneapolis Tribune* commented that this line gave the Minneapolis millers "practical control of the wheat grown in the Northwest." Cadwallader Washburn promoted the Soo Line that by 1888 gave the millers a through route to Boston, bypassing Chicago, and he was one of the builders and stockholders of the Minneapolis and St. Louis Railroad.

---

* Consolidation was expedited by a short-lived British takeover of Pillsbury's mills in 1889. The syndicate combined them with the mills of Cadwallader Washburn's brother, William D. Washburn, to form the Pillsbury-Washburn company. Meanwhile, another Maine Yankee, John Crosby, had become a partner of Cadwallader's in the newly constituted Washburn-Crosby Company. In 1889, another outsider, James S. Bell, became president of Washburn-Crosby; in 1928, his son, James F. Bell, took over. Minneapolis milling really has been dominated by just four families: the Washburns, Pillsburys, Crosbys, and Bells.

The impression that many farmers and smaller merchants had of being at the mercy of powerful economic monopolies was anything but modified by the shenanigans that took place year in and year out at the Chicago Board of Trade, where speculators and gamblers vied with each other to corner the wheat market. The Board of Trade, which was created in 1848 at the instigation of Chicago's merchants, soon became a sort of international symbol of the worst elements of American free enterprise: greed; the cycle of riches and ruin, boom and bust; corruption. There was an orgy of speculation and market manipulation during the Civil War. The Board printed rules governing trading in 1869, but abuses of all kinds continued—fraud, bribery of telegraph operators to obtain confidential information (until coded messages were used), and the spreading of false rumors to influence prices. Outside the trading floor at Jackson and La Salle streets, bucket shops, not much different from bookie joints or other gambling establishments, flourished.

The first big "corner" came in 1888. In May of that year, government crop reports predicted a wheat shortage, and prices rose moderately. B. P. ("Old Hutch") Hutchison began buying September futures in August. Hutchison received and paid for much of the wheat in September, and started buying December futures. As it became apparent that the Midwest had suffered a major crop disaster and that European crops were also "short," the price of wheat rose from $1.00 to $2.00 a bushel between September 22 and September 29. Hutchison controlled a substantial amount of all the wheat in Chicago, or deliverable to it, for long enough to extract profits of up to $1.00 a bushel in the course of selling it to millers or speculators with commitments to deliver wheat in Chicago.

Then, in 1897, a 28-year-old Harvard graduate by the name of Joseph Leiter launched what the *Chicago Tribune* called, with its usual flair for understatement, "probably the most gigantic and sensational attempted coup in the history of modern commerce." Leiter was a young man of charm and good fortune, and a carefree romantic to boot. He once talked of buying the Great Wall of China, and he had sailed his own yacht around the world. His millionaire father was Levi Leiter, the cofounder of Chicago's Marshall Field department store. Leiter entered the trading pits of the Board of Trade like a light-haired young Lochinvar with the aim of cornering all the wheat in America. For a while it seemed that fortune would smile on him. With $1 million of his father's money, he began buying wheat futures. The Indian and European wheat crops had been poor, and Chicago prices rose steadily above the price at which Leiter had begun accumulating the wheat. Leiter kept buying, leaving the sellers with larger and larger commitments to deliver this wheat in Chicago.

The man on the spot was Philip Armour, whose family's fortune in the city's meat and grain business rivaled that of Leiter's. It became a point of pride, as well as a question of money, to put Leiter in his place. Armour directed huge quantities of wheat into Chicago, and as the Great Lakes routes from Duluth and Canada began to freeze, he kept the waterways open for his vessels by dynamiting passages through the ice. Armour met all of his commitments, and the price of spring wheat from Minnesota and the Dakotas fell to under $1 a bushel. Leiter held on through the spring, and wheat prices again rose, from 90 cents a bushel in January to $1.83 a bushel in May. But Leiter was too greedy and refused to take his profits and quit. In June the federal government predicted a record wheat crop and wheat prices collapsed, leaving Leiter holding enormous quantities of overpriced wheat. He lost almost $10 million, which his father paid by selling or mortgaging his Chicago real estate.*

---

* Nigel Nicolson's *Mary Curzon* (New York, 1977) adds a curious footnote to this episode. Joseph Leiter's sister Mary married George Curzon, later to become Lord Curzon, Viceroy of India. The couple had figured on the help of Leiter money to finance the expenses of that post, but as a result of Joseph's losses, only $3000 of Leiter money was available. Curzon almost turned down the job.

These episodes caused a public clamor for reform at home and abroad. The German government was so appalled by the developments across the Atlantic that it banned "futures" trading from the Berlin Exchange in 1897, and traders, merchants, and speculators there had to move their business to Amsterdam and Liverpool.

Yet there were reasons why the Board of Trade survived all the attacks and barbs of its critics. The board, after all, had replaced a system that was even more chaotic. Before the Chicago exchange opened, farmers who hauled their grain over plank roads to the raw, new city often had to go from merchant to merchant to find a buyer, sometimes to no avail. Sometimes, after the harvest, when the grain converged on Chicago, there was so much of it that it had to be dumped into Lake Michigan, and later, shortages would develop. There was no organized system for spacing the marketing of crops out over the year. Futures contracts gave traders, millers, merchants, and exporters an incentive to sell grain at different times all through the year, with the price at time of delivery guaranteed, and this in turn provided incentives to hold grain in storage. Moreover, the fact that there was a public price for all to see in Chicago reduced the chances that merchants could cheat the farmers. True, the markets were often manipulated—but often to the benefit of farmers. During Leiter's attempt to corner the wheat market, hundreds of Midwest farmers lit candles for the man who was helping to raise the price of wheat with his buying spree.

The grain exchanges that existed by the end of the century in Winnipeg, New York, Buenos Aires, and many European cities were a sign that the grain business was achieving a global organization and integration. The exchanges were connected by the new high-speed international communications equipment; the grain trade was the first great international business to make full use of this new technology and of all the modern logistical systems that reduced the size of the planet in the twentieth century.

Still, the monopolies and the grain exchanges made easy and often justifiable targets for reformers, populists, and radicals. In the 1870s, farmers felt that railroad companies, grain elevator owners, bankers, farm implement dealers, commission men, and speculators all were flourishing while they often failed to get a fair return. Typical of this sentiment was an article in a Swedish-language newspaper published in the Midwest in 1883: "When our people arrived in this free country, took land on the prairie, dwelt in sod huts and endured hunger and sickness in the thought that they might become their own master, it was only to become slaves under the president of one or another railroad company. We escaped from one slavery only to be soon under another which is more unbearable now when the spirit of freedom has been awakened in us."

The hard, lonely life on the vast prairie contributed to the farmers' profound sense of isolated helplessness. Settlers had to contend with grasshoppers, tornadoes, rampaging buffaloes—and a silence deeper than that in midocean. "The Great Plain drinks the blood of Christian men and is satisfied," wrote O. E. Rölvaag in *Giants in the Earth,* his pessimistic novel of madness overtaking a prairie family. Yet difficult as it was for such families to comprehend, they were anything but isolated. They were, in fact, part of the world economy, and that very fact was sometimes the real source of low grain prices.

After the Civil War, the prairie farmer, the sharecropper on the Pampas, and the immigrant farmer in southern Australia were linked with factory workers in Berlin, Paris, Hamburg, and Liverpool. Most of the time, this interdependence was extremely advantageous for the United States. Wheat was part of the patrimony of the New World. Dollar-a-bushel wheat was a worthy goal, not just for farmers but for the whole country. Europe's wheat requirements spurred the rapid development of the Midwest and was a source of American well-being and prosperity. Exports of wheat and flour rose steadily, from $60 million in 1870 to $200 million in 1898. This trade provided a permanent transatlantic connection, and sometimes (as in the case of San Francisco) added American ports to the trade routes of the world.

America became a crucial source of food for Europe whenever its harvests failed or war and politics disrupted its supply lines. European importers hurried to America during the Crimean War in 1854, again during the Franco-Prussian War of 1870, and once more at the end of that decade when crops failed all over Europe. Visiting America, Trollope felt that "in the corn lands of Michigan, and amid the bluffs of Wisconsin, and on the high table plains of Minnesota, and the prairies of Illinois, God prepared the food for the increasing millions of the Eastern world as also for the coming millions of the Western." * Another, less obvious side of this was that the aggressively marketed U.S. grain exports cut into the exports from Russia and must have affected the prosperity of the Odessa wheat regions.

Interdependence worked both ways, of course. American agricultural prosperity also could be affected adversely by political decisions and natural occurrences beyond the control of anyone in the United States. It was particularly frustrating for independent-minded Americans to recognize that, where wheat prices were concerned, they did not control their own destiny. "Would to God [our legislators] would rise to the present emergency and deliver the American farmers from one of the most unjust, unfair and crushing burdens," wrote Ivan Michels in a report to the United States Senate in March 1886. The "unfair burden" was the competition that American wheat was meeting from Indian grain exports in the British market—a situation that American politicians claimed had been rigged by an artificial sterling/rupee exchange rate. And when in 1879 Chancellor Otto von Bismarck imposed stiff duties on grain imported into Germany, the reason was political: to help the grain-producing Junker landlords on whom his political support depended. Even

* Anthony Trollope, *North America* (London, 1862).

then, a century ago, agricultural trade had become a matter that was far too important to be left to the grain traders.

The barons did prosper from the growth of the American grain business, but their investments and innovations also helped to create the most efficient system in the world for producing and distributing grain. The system was streamlined not only by advances in agricultural technology but also by the rapid adaptation of the new technology of communications and transportation and by flexible new institutions, such as the futures markets. Chicago offices were flashing prices to the hinterland by wireless in the 1880s. Ports such as Chicago, Milwaukee, Boston, Baltimore, Philadelphia, Galveston, and Portland, Oregon, were becoming more and more efficient in grain handling. The building of the Erie Canal in 1825 had made it possible for Midwest grain to reach New York City by water, via the Hudson River. Railroads subsequently brought larger quantities of Canadian and American grain to the Hudson River piers of lower Manhattan and Hoboken. In 1874, the New York Produce Exchange abandoned the old system of buying grain in parcels and lots and adopted a system of commingling grain of like grade and quality, certifying ownership through warehouse receipts which were as good as money. The system vastly expedited the handling and storage of grain. At the turn of the century, ocean liners of American and European shipping lines did a lively grain business out of New York and Boston, sometimes using grain as ballast on passenger vessels, and at other times hauling grain back to Europe on the same ships that had transported European emigrants to America.

In the farmers' fights with the "interests" to get their fair share of the benefits of these efficiencies, both the courts and the government came (if slowly) to the side of the farmers. The oppressive feudalism that prevailed in Europe and in the Argentine Pampas never took hold in the American grain belt. The 1862 Homestead Act heeded rural demands for "free soil" by opening up large tracts of public land for settlement on 160-acre plots. It was a commitment to the family farmer. In that same presidential term, Abraham Lincoln established the land-grant college system and created the Department of Agriculture, steps that helped regionalize the nation's educational infrastructure to the benefit of the farm states of the Midwest. With its landmark decision in 1876 in *Munn* v. *Illinois*, the Supreme Court established the right of the states to regulate private grain warehouses (and, by implication, other private corporations such as the railroads). Eleven years later Congress passed the Interstate Commerce Act. In 1902, Congress tightened restrictions against railroad "rebating"—the practice by which the roads subsidized favored grain companies and kept their control over the wheat economy.

To the north, in Canada, farmers also made some progress in their demands for a better deal from railroads and grain merchants. The Manitoba Grain Act of 1900 provided for regulation of grain dealers and for increased competition at shipping points. Subsequently, a federal agency took over the job of assigning boxcars to grain collection points, and in 1912 the Canada Grain Act established mandatory federal grading of grain to prevent merchants from cheating farmers.

In America, the foundations of the future grain power had been constructed by the time of World War I—and in an epochally American way: with opportunists, go-getters, technical efficiency, and crude exploitation, but also with a sense, conveyed especially by the immigrants arriving in the Midwest, that it was still better than anything that had been left behind.

4   Living by Their Wits

"We have survived by working with our wits."
—MICHEL FRIBOURG

Long after managers and organization men had taken over the
command of the new twentieth-century corporations of oil, automobiles, and manufacturing, the international grain trade was
still a refuge for merchant-adventurers. To become an international grain trader in the early part of the century, it was not
necessary to have huge amounts of capital, big grain depots,
ships, and thousands of employees. What was needed was credit
(to cover the margins and storage costs), a telephone, personal
connections, and a sound knowledge of the technical intricacies
of trading. But financing and expertise were not enough by
themselves: Success called for charm, good instincts, luck, and
audacity—the qualities of the gambler, salesman, and entrepreneur rolled into one.

None of the century's grain merchants fit this mold better
than the brothers Jules and René Fribourg, who founded the
Continental Grain Company in France in 1921 and built it into a
far-flung enterprise rivaling Bunge and Louis Dreyfus. The Fribourgs performed brilliantly during the most hectic period the
grain trade had ever known. War, panic in the grain markets,
inflated wheat prices, depression, unprecedented government

intervention in farm economies all over the world, and the Dust Bowl—this was the tumultuous sequence of events between 1914 and 1940 through which the Fribourgs maneuvered, changing countries and finally changing continents, but always managing to keep a step ahead of ruin and build their fortune.

World War I, which sent the Fribourgs on their wanderings, completely transformed old patterns and routes of the grain trade. In the years before 1914, Russia was the world's largest wheat producer and exporter, and British India was an important supplier to Europe. After the war, Russia became caught up in civil war and revolution, and India's growing population finally began to absorb its surplus grain. Neither country's wheat was ever again a significant part of Europe's food supply. The United States had been a major grain exporter since the Civil War, but it always had stiff competition for foreign markets; trailing Russia, Argentina, and Canada in wheat exports; lagging behind Russia, Romania, and India in the barley trade; and falling second to Argentina in corn shipments. After the war, with its competitors no longer major factors in the markets, the Western Hemisphere became the primary source of grain for Europe.

The old patterns changed slowly. War between Turkey and Bulgaria in 1912 interrupted Balkan grain shipments to western Europe, but only briefly. By 1914 the immediate threat of hunger and starvation among civilians in territories occupied by the Germans in northern France and Belgium was allayed by American relief shipments organized by the Commission for the Relief of Belgium, headed by Herbert Hoover. Western Europe was not seriously in need of food until 1916, by which time submarine warfare had taken its toll on shipping and the Dardanelles were closed, permanently blocking Russian and Romanian cereal shipments to western Europe. In the same year, the German army captured the Romanian wheat crop—much to the chagrin of the Allied powers, which had taken the precaution of buying it. Argentine and Australian grain was out of reach much of the time because what scarce merchant vessels were around could not be spared for such long voyages.

The French and British governments then turned in considerable panic to the United States, and their need for grain set off a furious wave of buying in the American grain markets that lasted through 1917. The heavy European purchases sent the price of U.S. wheat to an unprecedented $3.17 a bushel in May 1917, one month after the American declaration of war on Germany.

The war period was marked—as wars frequently are—by plenty of profiteering and speculation. Grain trading was especially hazardous after August 1914, when the futures market of the Liverpool Corn Trade Association shut down (it was too risky trading foreign wheat for future delivery that might never get past German U-boats), but as the risks increased, so did the opportunities for windfalls.

One of the North American traders who cashed in was a six-foot-six, 300-pound Canadian by the name of James Norris. Big Jim Norris had come down from Canada some time after 1910 and worked for a while as a telegraph operater in Chicago before he got some supporters to help him buy several Midwest grain elevators. Then Big Jim plunged into the trading business. He was a one-man grain company. When the United States declared war on Germany in April 1917, Norris's elevators were full of corn that Big Jim had acquired to fill an order from Germany. Now delivery of grain to the new enemy was precluded and Big Jim's contracts were voided—much to his good fortune. He was free to sell his stocks at the higher prices that prevailed after the state of belligerency was announced. In the 1920s and 1930s, Norris pyramided his assets through investments in hotels, real estate, bank stock, and railroad bonds. Big Jim became a legendary figure as he strode around Chicago, followed by a crowd of admirers or favor-seekers, or as he stepped onto a scales for one of his periodic "weigh-ins."

The wartime controls that President Wilson and Congress imposed on the grain trade in August 1917 halted the sort of opportunities that had originally come Norris's way. The Food Administration Grain Corporation, under the direction of Herbert Hoover, took over the sale of grain to the Allies and the allocation of foodstuffs to the American armies abroad. Congress fixed the prices of spring wheat from the upper Northwest at $2.20 a bushel, and the Allies bought their wheat through their own Wheat Export Company in New York City. It was all government-to-government. The United States, Britain, and France had effectively made the grain trade into a public utility.

Meanwhile war proved to be a boon to American agriculture. Farmers received unprecedented prices for their products, and the United States and Canada emerged as the dominant factors in the world grain markets. U.S. wheat shipments increased from 4 million to 9 million tons between 1913 and 1921, and in the latter year U.S. grain exports earned more than $1 billion—one dollar out of every eight it took from abroad.

The United States plainly was the place for an up-and-coming grain merchant to be, and it was to New York City that many a European merchant-adventurer headed after the war. Governmental controls did not last long after the conflict was over in Europe. The United States decontrolled prices in 1920, and the Grain Corporation was completely disbanded two years later. The French and British governments also withdrew from the grain business, and the old private system of moving grain across the Atlantic from the grain depots on the Great Lakes to the millers in Liverpool and Antwerp resumed.

There were plenty of grain merchants competing in those days, for it was still a cash-and-carry business, and the new, free prices provided plenty of chances for sharp-witted speculators. An exhaustive Federal Trade Commission study of grain companies operating in New York City in 1920 and 1921 revealed that some companies' earnings (as a percentage of their capital

plus bank accounts) ran as high as 448 per cent in 1920 and 641
per cent in 1921 (although some operations did report losses of
up to 20 per cent).

It was such opportunities that Jules and René Fribourg saw as
they looked out at this transformed world from London, in the
aftermath of the war. The brothers had hurried to the British
capital from Antwerp in 1914, one step ahead of the invading
German army. The departure must have been a traumatic one.
The North European grain port had been the base of the Fribourg family for three generations. In Antwerp, with its deep-
water harbor and canal connections to the Rhine and the markets along it, the Fribourgs had prospered for almost a century.
As long as Belgium stayed out of European political conflicts,
the grain men of Antwerp flourished. Belgian neutrality had
suited the Fribourg grain business well in the Franco-Prussian
War, when the family firm worked with both sides. Later, Fribourg money was invested in flour mills. But "Fribourg Frères,"
the company that Jules and René ran in Antwerp, did not satisfy
the ambitions of the young brothers. It was only a brokerage
firm; the Fribourgs were not yet international merchants. Bitter
as the flight to England must have been, it gave the brothers an
opportunity.

When the Fribourgs reached London in 1914, the British government had not yet taken over the grain trade and the brothers
made a quick profit speculating on Australian wheat shipments
to England. At the time, wheat cargoes at dockside in Australia
could be purchased for as little as $100 a ton, considerably less
than the selling price in England. The margin was due to the risk
that grain ships bound for England might be attacked and sunk
by German submarines. But once the cargoes had safely passed
the German hunters and were in sight of England, the wheat
could be sold for $120 a ton.

Even after the establishment of government controls over the
grain trade, the merchants still had work to do in London, Paris,
Washington, and New York—advising governments, handling

the details of shipping and logistics, supplying information and technical expertise. They could also make money. As a European merchant who lived through those times noted, "The Allies bought huge quantities—and there were no taxes, good margins and small expenses!"

For the Fribourgs, this was much more exciting than brokering grain for others had been in the Antwerp days. And it may have been these experiences in London that persuaded them to become grain merchants in their own right. But both of them had personal reasons for raising their sights. Jules was aristocratic, self-confident, businesslike, and eager. René, a dapper, twinkly-eyed man with a fuzzy mustache, was an inveterate collector of art objects, a hobby that required resources even beyond the means at the family's disposal at the end of the war. In 1920, the brothers went to Paris and opened a small firm in the rue de Moulin with the name Compagnie Continentale.

The direction in which the Fribourgs moved probably was preordained by the realities of the grain business at that time. It was true that the war had dealt several setbacks to Bunge and Louis Dreyfus, the great, dominating world grain companies. Allied purchasing agents in New York City and Washington had "blacklisted" Bunge from participating in the North American trade with Europe during the war because of the company's alleged pro-German sentiment. Louis Dreyfus had been unceremoniously chased out of its old Black Sea strongholds in 1917. The company lost grain elevators and a naphtha plant—assets said to be worth more than $10 million.

Still, for all that, the two old grain houses remained preeminent. In Argentina, the two companies (along with a Belgian company named De Ridder and Georges André's Argentine subsidiary) monopolized the cereal trade out of Buenos Aires, Rosario, La Plata, Paraná, and Santa Fe. Bunge had its own grain elevators and its own flour mill—a contribution dating from the reign of Alfredo Hirsch. More than a thousand agents of Louis Dreyfus could be found dotted throughout the Argentine countryside at harvest time, buying corn, wheat, barley, and oats from local middlemen or sharecroppers. (This was an almost embarrassingly profitable business for grain traders and landlords. Many of the sharecroppers were unskilled, ignorant peasants only recently arrived from some of the poorest farmlands in Europe. Rather than let their grain rot in the late autumn weather, they sold it to the European buyers who drove out to the mounds of freshly threshed grain and golden straw in Model-T Fords.) In Argentina, Bunge and Louis Dreyfus were thus very much in control. And the outlook for ambitious newcomers was not much better in the Balkans, another important source of surplus grain. The Balkans were almost perennially in a state of political ferment and change, which meant that the situation was less than conducive to foreign investment. Still, Romania was one of the world's largest producers of corn. The crop, which had been introduced by Turkish traders centuries earlier, did well in the warm summers of the lower Danube basin. But the Romania government had put down a peasant rebellion in 1907 at the cost of enormous bloodshed; the clamor for land reform had led to the breakup of the old feudal estates; and the country's agricultural system was in flux. (Some European importers claimed that the quality of Romanian corn had deteriorated.) Bulgaria was just as dubious a proposition. The peasant leader Alexander Stambulisky, who came to power briefly in 1923 promising major reforms, was overthrown and tortured to death by monarchist police before he could act. But experience in Balkan armies had politicized many a young peasant and opened his eyes to the world. Returning soldiers wanted bread, a food they had developed a liking for in the army. Now bakeries opened in towns and villages all over Romania, and this meant that less wheat was available to exporters and merchants. The returning war veterans also wanted land—and a better deal from the monarchs, landlords, and grain merchants. In Yugoslavia, similar peasant movements occurred after the war, and proposals were made even for a "Green International" uniting all the European peasantry into a political force for change and reform. (The idea made little headway.) None of these developments boded well for a stable agriculture and a growing Balkan grain trade.

There was another reason for any newcomer to be wary of Balkan investments. The Louis-Dreyfuses were still in firm control of the lower Danube. The family continued on excellent terms with the Romanian monarchy, a connection that must have been to their mutual advantage: The royal family wanted to sell Romanian corn, barley and wheat; the Louis-Dreyfuses wanted to trade it in western Europe. After Leopold Louis-Dreyfus died, the old connections continued. His son Louis succeeded him as Romanian consul in Paris. Braila, the main Danubian downstream port, was a Louis-Dreyfus stronghold. At Constanta, at the mouth of the Danube, foreign wheat traders, already conspicuous by the diamonds glittering on their fingers and clothing, crowded into the local theater to watch the only play in its repertoire: Molière's *The Miser*. The Fribourgs decided to look elsewhere. It was the United States to which the brothers turned their attention.

The Fribourg family already had the essential connections with the major customers of the growing American international wheat trade—the millers and importers all over the European continent. And their rivals Bunge and Louis Dreyfus had tended to shun the United States because of the difficulties of operating "upstream," where Canadian and American businessmen like the Cargills and MacMillans controlled the grain elevators, transportation and shipping. But in 1921, the Fribourgs sent Frederick Frohman to Chicago with instructions to open a small office near the Board of Trade and sent another associate, a dour German by the name of Jules Isaac, to New York City. Starting with capital of $50,000, Isaac began buying cargoes of American grain.

The Fribourgs were affluent, but they needed partners in their new venture at the outset. They gave a one-third interest in the new American company to two other grain brokers they had known in Antwerp, Jean and Alfred Goldschmidt. But by 1924, the Fribourgs were doing well enough to buy out the Goldschmidts, increase the capital of the New York company to $300,000, and send one of the shrewdest grain men in the world to represent them in New York City.

Joseph Feuer, the new Continental chief in New York, was short, bald, and potbellied, with red-rimmed eyes, a duck-bill nose, and thick lips—an ugly sight until people became better acquainted with him and discovered his charm, fertile imagination, and breadth of experience. Feuer was the epitome of the worldly European grain trader who dominated the international merchant business between the wars. He had been born in Poland, spoke half a dozen languages, had worked in the Danube grain business in Romania, had run his own grain firm in Antwerp (where he knew the Fribourgs), and had traveled widely in Argentina. His only shred of national identity was his Polish passport, which, with the loyalty to country that only an émigré Pole can express, he refused to trade in for American papers.

Feuer wasted no time building up an organization that stretched across North America all the way to Vancouver. Continental men penetrated to St. Louis, Kansas City, Winnipeg, Duluth, New Orleans, Galveston, and Montreal. It was a question not only of the Old World finally confronting the New World on its own turf—the turf that had always belonged to Cargill, Peavey, Norris, Armour, Pillsbury, and Washburn—but also of an upstart European company often besting the likes of old Europeans like Bunge and Louis Dreyfus in their own tactical and strategic games. The Fribourgs and Joe Feuer, it quickly became apparent, were more mobile than the older European companies. One winter in the late 1920s Continental's men in Vancouver ran rings around Bunge and Louis Dreyfus, purchasing wheat from Manitoba and loading it aboard ships just as the Great Lakes were beginning to ice over. Continental's grain moved out into the Pacific as Canadian grain was blocked by the freeze in the port of Thunder Bay, Ontario. Soon after that, the company pulled another tactical coup, anticipating and exploiting an unusually early movement of American winter wheat down the Mississippi River to the Gulf of Mexico.

It was just such good timing and logistical expertise that determined profits in the grain trade of the 1920s. The broad cycles of the grain trade, it was true, were predictable. Europe, the great wheat market, drew from its own freshly harvested supplies throughout most of the fall and early winter. Shipments from North America were slow at that time of year, except for the high-protein Canadian and Minnesotan spring-planted wheat that European millers needed to mix with their own protein-deficient wheat. Argentina entered the world wheat markets in January and February, when the Southern Hemisphere's summer wheat harvests began. The Argentines were notorious price cutters, and as long as there was Argentine wheat available, Louis Dreyfus, Bunge, André and De Ridder could usually sell their European customers Argentine wheat cheaper than anything they could offer from North America. The export companies based in New York kept "winter books" on the Great Lakes—grain stowed aboard vessels or in port elevators ready to move to Europe as soon as the waterways unfroze.

But within these cycles, there were always a multitude of variations that made the grain trade a risky business. An unusually dry, hot summer in Europe could add protein to European wheat and reduce the requirements for early shipments of North American protein wheats. When the Great Lakes froze each fall, merchants had to be ready with cargoes of late-harvested spring wheat out of the open-water port of Vancouver. And then, of course, exact dates of freezes in the Great Lakes and in the canals and barge routes could not be known in advance, and the logistical complexities of moving grain from Duluth in Minnesota or Port Arthur and Fort William in Canada were enormous.

Arrangements had to be made with elevator companies, barge lines, steamship companies, and insurance men in two countries. Grain could be put on 7000-ton steamers, shipped to ports on Canada's Georgian bay, unloaded onto railroad cars bound for Montreal, and reloaded onto ocean steamers. Or it could be shipped by an even more complicated route through the Welland Canal at the eastern end of Lake Erie, west of Niagara Falls, where it was transferred onto small "canalers" for the 326-foot drop through the locks between Lake Erie and Lake Ontario.

Feuer directed these operations from a malodorous office, heavy with the stench of stale grain samples, on the second floor of the New York Produce Exchange building at 2 Broadway, off Battery Place. In the span of just a few years, the Produce Exchange had become one of the principal centers of the international grain trade. It was a place that seemed perfectly to incarnate both the glamor and the grubbiness of the business at this stage in its historical development. The setting, across the way from the Customs House and within sight of the harbor, was romantic. (Many a trader who had just bungled away more money than he could afford to lose spent his lunch hour in Battery Park, feeding the pigeons and consoling himself with the thought that the world was bigger than the seedy interior of the Produce Exchange.) Inside the squat, red-brick building, traders organized the exportation of Canadian and American grain to Europe. The Produce Exchange was a world market for corn, wheat, rye, barley, oats, and even hay for the dwindling horse population of Manhattan. The efficient overseas distribution of the New World's food surplus depended on deals made here. But the lofty purpose of this task—the feeding of Europeans—was seldom apparent at the Produce Exchange, a place given over to the free-for-all of commerce.

To an aspiring young grain man arriving on the floor for the first time, the place "looked, sounded and smelled like something between a railroad terminal, a midway and a monkey house."* In those days before computers and telex machines, grain shipments were arranged on the spot by brokers, commission men, exporters, shipping agents and insurance men, all pushing and shoving, sending messengers on errands, and keeping one eye on the blackboards on which clerks recorded the latest Chicago grain prices arriving by Morse code.

The many European accents at the Produce Exchange conveyed the polyglot international flavor of the grain business in the 1920s. Europeans dominated everywhere. The Russian revolution and the first threats of Fascism and organized, armed anti-Semitism had dislodged many European merchants, and they wandered to America. The accents of Russians, Armenians, Romanians, Greeks, Dutchmen, and Lebanese mingled with those of Americans at 2 Broadway.

Typically, the New York office of Louis Dreyfus was directed by a triumvirate consisting of the Swiss-born Fernand Leval, the Viennese-born Leopold Stern, and the Armenian-born Jacques Kayaloff. Stern had joined Louis Dreyfus soon after the Paris company opened its New York office in 1907. Leval had got his start in the grain business riding around Belgium selling seed samples to farmers for the company's office in Antwerp; Louis Dreyfus sent him to the United States after the war. Kayaloff, who came later, had had an even more romantic past. He had served in the Armenian army that battled the Turks in the Transcaucasus after the end of World War I, had escaped from Bolshevik Russia and using the name of his father (then head of a tobacco syndicate in Moscow) had landed a job at Louis Dreyfus in Paris. These three men were the main European opposition for Feuer and his men.

The grain business was still a wide-open free-for-all when the FTC investigated the business in 1920. It found that three

* John Houseman, *Run-Through* (New York, 1972).

houses—Louis Dreyfus, the Bunge subsidiary P.N. Gray & Co., and the British firm of Sanday*—did 30 per cent of the business—but that thirty-three other companies divided up the other 70 per cent fairly evenly.

It was the financial structure of the business at that time that gave the grain trade many of its distinctive qualities. Credit, not capital, was still the foundation of the business, much as it had been in the days of the merchant-adventurers serving the Athens market twenty-four centuries before. It was not necessary to be rich to challenge the established grain companies: Shipping and insurance could be contracted for once grain was purchased and a customer had been found. Credit and quick wits were what enabled Continental to grow as rapidly as it did in the 1920s; and the same qualities made it possible for newcomers to pop into the business all the time. Much of the storage capacity at the grain ports of Boston, Baltimore, New York, Philadelphia, Galveston, and New Orleans was owned not by international merchants at all, but by domestic businessmen. To the New York exporters, good communications, connections, and knowledge of the European markets were what counted most.

The FTC study revealed that the companies were making their substantial profits mainly with borrowed money. "In the business of exporting grain as conducted at the present time in this country, there is very little fixed investment in plant, almost all the funds being in liquid form and in large proportion generally borrowed," the FTC reported. Twenty-six companies handled 40 per cent of the nation's wheat exports in 1921, and half of the $50 million they used in the business was borrowed. Their earnings on this $50 million were $11 million, a

---

* There are several reasons why British firms such as Sanday, Ralli Brothers, and others lost out to the European and American firms. One is that powerful British millers such as Rank's took a direct hand in the trade themselves, eliminating the middlemen. Another reason may be that British tax laws and currency controls made it difficult for these firms to survive in the competitive, fluid grain markets.

return of slightly more than 20 per cent for the funds employed.

Thus, the grain trade was still a low-overhead business, even though millions of dollars were involved. Money was made from turnover. It was common for the companies to turn over their stocks of grain twenty or thirty times a year. This gave the companies large net profits on rather small investments.

Since large infusions of capital were not required to enter the grain game, outside stockholders or shareholding partners were needed less than they were in the oil business, for example, or in manufacturing. The grain companies were able to finance their own growth and remain small, compact, family-controlled businesses. Their main assets were not their products or their holdings but their connections and their experience. These were some of the factors that gave the business its cliquish character. Loyalty was demanded, and defections to other companies were viewed as acts of betrayal. Nepotism flourished, because family members were considered to be more trustworthy than outsiders. Louis Dreyfus traders signed pledges that they would not go to work for a rival grain company for at least six months after leaving, so as not to give away the company's tactics and strategy.

A promising young man who announced his intentions to leave a grain company was treated as if he were slightly mad. Men from the firm would contact the young man's parents to convey grave warnings that their son seemed about to stray from the certain path to success. Senior officers would invite the would-be rover to long, solemn luncheons in fine restaurants to persuade him of the error of his ways. When all efforts failed, he was shunned as an ingrate. The international grain trade grew up as a calling with its own codes, hierarchies, and traditions: secretive, closed and tribal.

That was the way it was up to October 1929, when the bottom dropped out of the wheat market. After that, the grain trade was never the same again.

They saw it happening on the floor of the Produce Exchange that Black Thursday. Wheat futures lost a tenth of their value in two hours and kept dropping. The clerks manning the blackboards that recorded the price of futures in Chicago and Winnipeg lost track of what was happening and gave up trying to record the downward trajectory of the market, leaving the shaken traders to hover around the ticker tapes and to listen powerlessly to the ceaseless jangle of telephones. It was all perfectly logical. As the financial boom had progressed all that summer, the spiraling stock prices affected commodities, and speculators put their money into wheat futures. Wheat became overpriced, given world requirements, and the grain companies knew it. Yet they had no choice but to buy wheat at the inflated prices in order to keep their regular customers in Europe supplied.

After the disaster, they had to carry hundreds of millions of bushels of wheat at high precrash prices. Worried, impatient creditors collected their debts before the New York traders could collect from their European customers. The Produce Exchange was like the scene of a funeral. Day after day, traders trooped to bankruptcy proceedings to settle up with their creditors. The crash wiped out many smaller, undercapitalized companies. There seems no doubt that the crash of 1929 contributed to the concentration of the grain trade in the hands of a much smaller number of rich, economically powerful firms—the survivors of Black Thursday.

What had happened? There had been too much wheat and not enough money to buy it, that much was certain. The deeper causes of this situation were much more complicated.

Instability—the very thing that had made the unregulated world commodity markets so appealing to speculators and merchants all through the 1920s—had ravaged the agriculture upon which so much of the North American and European economies depended. The entire decade had been a speculator's hayride. The volatility was apparent in commodities other than wheat.

Brazilian coffee, Japanese silk, Cuban sugar, Argentine corn, Mexican silver, and Chilean nitrates—all experienced fluctuations similar to the kind that hit wheat markets in the 1920s. And behind each of the "boom and bust" statistics were hardship and misery for farmers and peasants all over the world.

In 1920, most officials in Washington had assumed that the wartime and postwar farm prosperity would continue indefinitely. They were quickly proven wrong. That year, the same one in which U.S. price controls on wheat were removed, prices plunged. European governments had anticipated a poor harvest on their side of the Atlantic and had overbought from other sources. When they realized that their own harvests would be good, they dropped out of the markets. U.S. government purchases of $20 million worth of corn for the relief of Russian famine strengthened grain prices, but only temporarily. In 1921, Nebraska farmers burned corn for fuel, and the prosperity of the previous decade faded into memory.

North American wheat farmers were thus adversely affected by the recovery of European agriculture. And changing dietary habits at home were not helping matters. Americans were eating less bread and more meat, poultry and dairy products. Flour consumption declined from an average of 230 pounds a person per year at the turn of the century to 200 pounds in 1920. (Not even the introduction of sliced wheat bread in the New York City market in the early 1930s could reverse this trend!)

So the situation of American wheat farmers had hardly been good before 1929. Afterward, it steadily worsened, and grain farmers were tragically affected all over the world. Overproduction and glut became the curse of farmers, and they lost their markets one by one. In the Danube grainlands, moneyless farmers were isolated in their villages and on their farms. American wheat prices fell to 50 cents a bushel in Kansas City in 1932, and corn sold for as little as 32 cents a bushel in Chicago. The mood in America's farm country was sullen and rebellious. Protesting farmers burned their grain, dumped their milk, slaughtered their livestock, and in one case dragged a judge from his courtroom during a farm foreclosure hearing and threatened to hang him on the spot if he did not stop the proceedings. (He refused, but the farmers spared him the lynching.) Western Canada's one-crop wheat economy was even harder hit.

The problems confronting American agriculture were fundamental and long-term. The international political and economic structure of agriculture was also changing but the U.S. government seemed to have no policies to deal with this. The terrible impact of unstable world commodity prices caused other governments to take action, however. France suspended import duties on wheat as bread prices rose, but the uneasiness caused by reliance on foreign food sources had the more likely effect of encouraging protectionism in European agricultural policy. The most striking example of this new trend was to be found in Italy, where Mussolini announced a "wheat battle" in 1925. The dictator had in mind an "operation independence"—in food. The Italian government increased tariffs on imported wheat, initiated programs to encourage Italian farmers to produce more, established import quotas, and ballyhooed all this with demonstrations and propaganda campaigns. By the early 1930s, Italy had become the third-largest wheat producer in Europe, after Russia and France, and its output of wheat was 60 per cent above what it had been in 1922.

Throughout the Depression years Europe continued to be the main market for the world's grain. But the drive for self-sufficiency did not let up, and protectionist sentiment was stronger than ever. European governments, already embittered over America's efforts to collect its war debts, were infuriated when Congress passed the Smoot-Hawley Tariff Act in July 1930, setting duties on foreign imports at all-time highs. They retaliated with stiffer duties on American farm imports. Meanwhile, Nazi propagandists, undoubtedly concerned about Germany's reliance on imported foreign wheat, began extolling rye bread's alleged ability to give Germans "the strength and endurance of the Nibelungen," and maligning wheat bread for "weakening the fighting will" of the Kaiser's losing armies in World War I.

Some campaigns for self-sufficiency were surprisingly effective. In 1932, experts at Stanford's Food Research Institute thought there was no likelihood that Japan would reduce its importation of wheat for making noodles, a popular food in Japan. Three years later, to the astonishment of the experts, Japan had increased its home wheat production by 60 per cent and achieved self-sufficiency. (These phenomenally successful food production campaigns tend to be forgotten amid today's talk that the world is running out of food.)

Farm organizations and politicians had all perceived in the turmoil of the 1920s that the agricultural crisis was broader and went further than the crooked commodity exchanges or filthy, powerful meat-packing houses about which the farmers so noisily complained. But under the presidencies of Harding, Coolidge, and (to a lesser extent) Hoover, the government was unenthusiastic about interfering with the grain trade or with the agricultural economy. These presidents were all proponents of limited government, believers in laissez-faire, and devotees of price as the great regulator of international economics. The trouble was that they closed their eyes to the fact that other nations had begun to discard these notions and that, increasingly, the American farmer stood alone in a world in which many important factors in his life had changed. The grain trade now had become so large that it could affect fundamentally the economies of dozens of countries, and more and more governments were inclined to give some protection to their farmers.

The Harding and Coolidge administrations had given little thought to fundamental adjustments in agricultural policies. There was no serious consideration of reducing farm output, or finding ways to increase the buying power of consumers of food at home or abroad. Instead, the aim of congressional efforts to help farmers was to increase agricultural exports. Senator George Norris of Nebraska proposed, in 1921, that a government corporation be set up to buy surplus farm products and sell them abroad on credit. And from 1924 to 1928, five bills were introduced by Senator McNary of Oregon and Representative Haugen of Iowa to establish a similar government corporation to sell the surplus at world prices. The bill was twice vetoed by Coolidge, with the approval of Hoover.

The Depression forced governments all over the world to change course radically. And the 1930s marked a turning away from seventy-five years of a light governmental hand in the grain economies. It was a decade that saw more governmental intervention in the grain trade than there had been since the repeal of the British Corn Laws in 1846. The decade produced the New Deal farm programs; the Canadian Wheat Board, a quasi-governmental monopoly that replaced many functions of the private grain trade; comparable government boards in France, Norway, Italy, and the Netherlands; government-to-government agreements regulating the grain trade. In 1932, the governments of Canada and Great Britain established stringent rules over their grain transactions. Britain gave a preference of 6 cents a bushel to the wheat of Canada, which had Dominion status. (The trade preference ended in 1938.)

The United States came out of the 1930s conditioned to farm price supports, wheat export subsidies, and farm programs that regulated the amount of acreage planted to certain crops.

The movement toward farmer power in the form of farmer-owned cooperatives received government support in both Canada and the United States. In the United States, the Grain Terminal Association was established as a powerful business arm of the National Farmers Union to collect grain from members of the NFU and market it in competition with the private grain trade.

In Canada, cooperative "wheat pools," originally formed by farmers in Alberta, Saskatchewan, and Manitoba between 1924 and 1926, gained strength. The question of pools versus the private grain trade had been a political issue across the Canadian

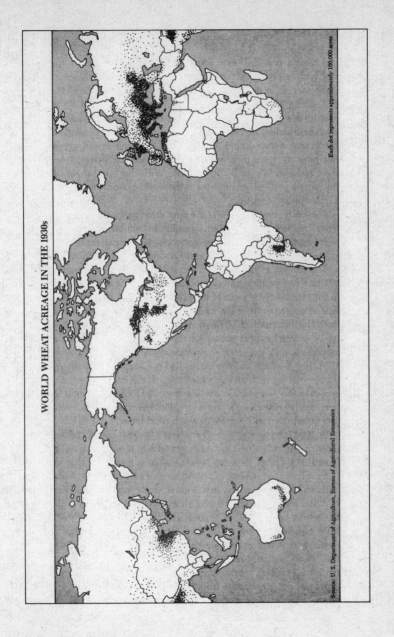

WORLD WHEAT ACREAGE IN THE 1930s

Each dot represents approximately 100,000 acres

Source: U. S. Department of Agriculture, Bureau of Agricultural Economics

prairies in the 1920s and had helped give the Progressives control of parliament in the early part of the decade. The near collapse of the pools and their central selling agency in the Depression strengthened the drive in the prairies for a compulsory marketing board that would displace the grain companies. In 1930, 1500 farmers stormed the legislature in Saskatchewan demanding a wheat board. That effort did not succeed. But pressure from farmers finally persuaded parliament to establish the Canadian Wheat Board in 1935. With that, the wheat of one of the largest producing countries in the world came under the control of a quasi-public agency.

The early 1930s also saw the first attempt to stabilize the global wheat markets by concerted international action. Representatives of eighteen European countries met with representatives of the United States, Australia, Argentina, and Canada in London in August 1933 and approved a plan for an international wheat agreement. Henry Wallace had in mind an "ever normal granary" that would put an end to the instability by a world stockpile, or reserve, that would accumulate when prices were low and be released when prices increased too fast. The International Wheat Agreement of 1933 established country-by-country export quotas for the 1933 and 1934 harvests and also agreed on a 15 per cent worldwide reduction of wheat acreages in 1934. But Wallace and the others had not bargained on the complexity of policing such an agreement, or on the imperatives of national greed. In the first year, Argentina exceeded its export quotas by 1 million tons of wheat, and efforts to make the acreage limitations stick also failed. By 1935, the IWA was a dead letter.

In 1934, the great "rivers of wheat" flowing out of the American prairies suddenly dried up. As it turned out, it was the tragedy of the Dust Bowl, rather than the New Deal farm programs, that unexpectedly solved the problem of unsold surplus grain. Farmers had planted millions of acres to wheat in marginal, sandy farmlands in World War I. When severe droughts finally hit in 1934 and 1936, the ecology was too tender to survive the dryness and the wind. Tons of thin topsoil were blown away by winds that carried dust as far as the Atlantic Ocean and dirtied windowpanes in eastern cities. From 1934 to 1936, the "river" actually reversed itself briefly. New York merchants imported 1.7 million tons of wheat to supply East Coast flour mills that could not obtain supplies from the Midwest.

All these developments changed the grain trade and the character of the grain business beyond recognition.

In one sense, the intervention of governments restricted the freedom of the merchants. Bureaucracy and speculation, it was clear, did not mix. For example, when Canada and Britain signed their preferential arrangements on wheat in 1932, the agreement also stipulated that Canadian grain had to originate in Canadian ports to qualify for the preference. (The preference went to Canadian grain as long as it was offered for no more than six cents above competing grain.) This made it difficult for New York merchants to bring Canadian grain through Buffalo and other American Great Lakes ports because it was difficult to prove that the cargo was Canadian.

The new conditions were not favorable to the old hand-to-mouth speculators and plungers who darted around the Produce Exchange. The high volumes that had been the bread and butter of the traders were down. Prices were much more stable, profit margins on each transaction were minuscule, and there were government regulations, stricter tariffs, and preferences to deal with.

On the other hand, for the companies with the capital, the international connections, and the facilities to have weathered the Depression, the opportunities were still considerable. There had always been a grain trade and there always would be—only henceforth the imperatives of success would be different. There was place for gadflies, but the power of the better capitalized, older, established firms was greatly strengthened. The grain trade began to become a modern industry, much closer to railroading, or shipping, or even the oil business than to the old merchant-adventurer craft from which it was descended.

In the new conditions, capital *was* important. It was useful to have upstream grain elevators, where the government would store grain it purchased under price supports. An efficient network of barges, railcars, and ocean-going vessels under company control could shave pennies off transportation and storage costs and make the difference between survival and ruin in the sluggish markets of the time. As volumes and turnover slackened, the premium went to companies with marginal advantages in moving grain from inland to ports where world prices prevailed.

The inevitable consequence was that grain business fell more and more into the hands of a small oligopoly of giant companies. Events in the 1930s speeded the trend toward concentration, consolidation, specialization, and industrialization. And the companies that saw this coming emerged dominant.

One of them was Continental. Since 1928, the Fribourg brothers and their man Feuer in New York had quietly been penetrating the United States interior by buying or leasing inland facilities. Jules Fribourg's instructions to Feuer, relayed from Paris, were straightforward: "Don't bother to look at them—just buy them!" He was referring to grain elevators, and Feuer had done his bidding. Feuer's friends were to say later that the Pole had been like a Greek shipowner buying up vessels at bargains when prices were depressed. In the late 1920s the onset of the Depression in the wheat country had reduced the value of elevators, and Feuer bought some then at distress prices. In 1928, Continental leased an elevator in St. Louis. Two years later the company leased a major Galveston terminal owned by the Southern Pacific Railroad. In 1931, in the depths of the Depression, Continental opened a Kansas City office and bought strategically situated elevators in Kansas City, Toledo, and Nashville.

Bunge and Louis Dreyfus were less aggressive in their acquisitions. At Louis Dreyfus, the seizure of the Black Sea assets had instilled caution about acquiring fixed assets that could not be moved in the event of political trouble. Bunge's surplus capital tended to go into diversification. The Hirsches and the Borns were unfamiliar with the United States, and in any case they preferred to put the company's money into banks, flour mills, textile plants, and other enterprises, mainly in South America but in Asia and Europe as well. Still, both of the European companies also began to buy inland elevators.

But North American companies continued to dominate, and many medium-sized grain-elevator companies flourished between the wars. Under the direction of the Heffelfinger family, Peavey in Minneapolis moved more into milling. Pillsbury and General Mills were also in the grain business, owning elevators and barges, but mainly to supply their own flour mills. Other companies such as Norris's, Rosenbaum, and Armour concentrated on grain trading—though only in the American interior. Of all these, Cargill grew with the most relentless, purposeful sense of direction.

The death in 1909 of the founder, Will Cargill, had for a while thrown the company off stride. Will died a rich man, but his son William Cargill had sunk a lot of money into unwise outside investments—a vast irrigation project in Montana and a railroad that was said to start nowhere and end nowhere. This was a time when the fever of American expansion infected many young men who had a little money to play with. Old Frank Peavey himself had visions of what later came to pass: great dams in the Rocky Mountains to catch the snow-melt and store water for western farmers. Before his death Will Cargill had taken a trip up to Montana to look at the irrigation project that was draining his company's money. He discovered that his name was on paper floating all over the West. Appalled, he returned home, caught pneumonia, and died. The result was that creditors, when they heard of the outside investments, began clamoring for payment. For the seven years 1909–16, Cargill hovered at the brink of bankruptcy. A creditors' committee sold off holdings in land and timber; property in Mexico and British Columbia was written off.

The power struggle that ensued was a clan war between the Cargills and the family of John MacMillan, the young man who had married the girl across the street in La Crosse—Will Cargill's daughter Edna. The MacMillans triumphed in this battle and gained control of the Cargill company. (The Cargills to this day maintain a toehold, though. James and Margaret Cargill, two of Will's grandchildren, are 10-per-cent stockholders—perhaps because their father Austen was helpful to the MacMillans during the feud—but William was bought out with $25,000 in cash, some gold railroad bonds, and notes of $250,000.)

By the time the Europeans were encroaching in the Midwest, the Cargill Company was galloping ahead, with John MacMillan firmly in the saddle. He was a sound, sober man with a streak of stubbornness that had been useful during the fight against bankruptcy and was valuuable in rebuilding the Cargill organization across the Midwest. The company was still mainly a regional firm, provincial by the standards of the far-flung European merchants. But the MacMillans and Cargills in Minneapolis could not ignore the changes all around them. In about 1919, a large Buffalo wheat broker leased space of his own in Duluth and began buying spring wheat from the samples at the Minneapolis Grain Exchange; he then sold it to exporters in New York and Montreal. This invasion cut into Cargill's sales to the East Coast, and MacMillan retaliated. He set up a sales organization in New York in 1922. Cargill's elevator, shipping, and communications system then reached from the center of the continent to the Atlantic seaboard. In 1929, it also opened an office in Argentina to obtain quick, accurate information on South American wheat prices.

What exactly happened to Cargill during the crash of 1929 is one of the company's best-kept secrets. There is not a word about its Depression troubles in *The History of Cargill, 1865–1945*. But presumably Cargill was squeezed just as other merchants were, and before it could rebuild its capital. There was a new creditors' committee, and Cargill hired John Peterson, vice-president of Chase National Bank, to guide it through this new, difficult period.

Peterson, who had enough Scottish blood in his veins to feel comfortable with the MacMillan clan, was an all-around "Renaissance man" with an inquisitive mind. He had been Phi Beta Kappa at Brown University; had worked as a banker in Antwerp; and was interested in physics and plant genetics. Peterson had ideas, and he helped to shape Cargill into the international giant it became over the next quarter century.

As the grain trade stagnated and prices fell in the 1930s, the MacMillans and Peterson continued to put Cargill money into the basics of grain transportation and storage. It was unglamorous but smart. They formed a subsidiary to build barges for hauling soybeans and corn down the Mississippi River; that put the company into the shipping business. They also built a huge, 10-million–bushel storage depot in Omaha with an unconventional, tabernacle-shaped roof that followed the slope of the grain. And when Cargill heard that the Albany Port Authority was negotiating with a Canadian syndicate to build a grain terminal on the upper Hudson River, officials rushed to Albany, made a proposal on the spot, and obtained a long-term lease on a huge new elevator. The facility was paid for by the Port Authority and built according to Cargill's specifications.

The goad behind all these expansionary moves was MacMillan's son, "John Junior," an engineer with a brilliant, quirkish mind in which imaginative ideas that revolutionized the grain trade coexisted with impractical fantasies. He once had a scheme to build huge, steel-hulled grain ships powered by gigantic sails that would be raised and lowered by motors and operated by a single crewman at a console.* But he also de-

---

* This idea was not wholly fantastic. Economical, four-masted, steel-hulled sailing vessels carried grain cargo from southern Australia to England in the "grain races" until German submarine warfare ended this tradition in 1939.

signed and built integrated barge- and towboat-units that locked into place to form a single bow, thereby putting a maximum payload through the locks and canals of the Great Lakes at a minimum cost.

The company's trading operations were directed, predictably enough, by a European, one of the few to penetrate the inner circle of the clannish Scotsmen of Cargill. Julius Hendel was a Jew from Belorussia. He joined the rock-ribbed Scottish firm in the late 1920s and set to work tutoring the provincial Americans in the ways of arbitrage, futures trading, and grain shipping. Hendel had come from a long line of brokers and grain merchants in his home village of Sloutzk, and in native instincts as a trader he was a match for Joseph Feuer at Continental. Hendel gave classes to the young traders at Cargill, taught them how to sense the subtle fluctuations of supply and demand, how to operate across the American agricultural chessboard, how to employ the stratagems and tactics of the modern trade. It was years before Hendel broke Minneapolis's anti-Semitic social barriers and was allowed to dine at the prestigious Minneapolis Club, citadel of the city's business, civic, and academic establishment. But at Cargill, Hendel's talents were always deeply appreciated.

Hendel, Peterson, and MacMillan Junior were the threesome that gave Cargill a reputation for being one of the toughest and most uncompromising companies in the Midwest. Cargill did not back down when it was challenged by competitors, by the government, by customers, or by anybody else. This stubborn strain was typified in its long and bitter fight with the Chicago Board of Trade, in which Cargill's buccaneering spirit also came out clearly. Part of the trouble went back to the Dust Bowl. Corn was a scarce commodity in September 1937. The 1936 crop had been a failure and the new crop would not be harvested until October. Cargill began buying up corn for delivery in September. As supplies dwindled, Cargill's suppliers had trouble obtaining enough corn to fulfill their sales contracts to the Minneapolis firm. The Chicago Board of Trade ordered Cargill to sell some of its own corn to relieve the "squeeze," but the company refused, claiming the sale would collapse prices and cost it $2 million. Faced with this defiance, the Board halted trading in September corn futures and expelled Cargill's representative from the trading floor. The "shorts" who owed corn to Cargill were ordered to pay it the going price of $1.10½ a bushel. Secretary of Agriculture Henry Wallace charged that Cargill had tried to corner the corn market. The ousted company used independent brokers to do its floor trading, and when the dispute was finally settled and Cargill was invited back, John Junior spurned the offer. It was years before Cargill again sent its own men back to the floor.

The incident did little to diminish Cargill's cockiness. Cargill officials were to say later that they had learned an invaluable lesson that would help them greatly over the years. By using independent brokers on the floor they could keep their trading activities even more secret and increase their advantages.

Incidents like that showed that the grain business was not for widows and orphans. It was becoming more and more an industry. Not that there was no place for the occasional enterprising, out-of-pocket merchant. Frederic Hediger, for example, the son of a small-town caterer in Switzerland, came to the United States in 1937 and founded Garnac. Garnac became one of the major American-based grain companies, thanks largely to its close (and closely guarded) financial connections with André in Switzerland. Hediger had started in the grain business in Antwerp, working for André. The United States was in the depths of the Depression—and the Middle West was suffering the worst ravages of the Dust Bowl—when Hediger arrived in New York; after establishing financial links with André, he began importing flaxseed from Uruguay, India, and Argentina. (Staten Island and New Jersey in those days were paint manufacturing centers, which depended on a steady supply of flaxseed oil for the mixes.)

Hediger's own experience showed that outside financial backing and capital was essential in grain. In 1933, Jules Fribourg

had made a trip to the United States and ceremoniously purchased a million tons of wheat from the Federal Farm Board and
resold it in Europe. It was one of the largest purchases in history.
It was not something that the New Dealers, then struggling
with the wheat surplus, forgot quickly. And it spoke volumes
about the magnitude of money in the grain business as well as
about the progress of the Fribourg fortunes.

The stagnation of the American markets in the 1930s was a
disappointment but not a disaster for the Fribourgs and the
Louis-Dreyfuses in Paris. When North American grain supplies
dried up, the companies imported barley from Iran and North
Africa, soft wheat and corn from Romania, and a steady stream
of wheat, corn, meat, linseed, and flaxseed from Argentina, the
leading grain-exporting country of the 1930s. War and disorder
provided opportunities as well as problems. Profit margins were
unusually large because the hard-pressed customers did not have
time to seek competitive offers, and the commodities were
highly perishable. (During the Spanish Civil War, the Fribourgs'
well-connected agent in Barcelona sold the Republican side
large quantities of dried beans and peas from central Europe and
the Balkans.)

Outside the United States, Continental developed as a far-
flung, polyglot organization, full of merchants of different nationalities recruited by the Fribourgs. (The company was hon-
eycombed with Egyptians, most of whom were related to each
other.) Continental was already a global company that, on any
given day, was trading wheat from Manitoba or rubber from
Vietnam.

Louis Dreyfus, the other Paris-based company with global interests, was also thriving. Leopold Louis-Dreyfus's son Charles
had died in 1929, leaving his last surviving son, Louis Louis-
Dreyfus, in charge. The Louis Dreyfus company, which had entered the shipping business in 1905, was now focusing on its
boats. Leopold, who had his own ideas about transportation,
dispensed with the old coal-burning craft and built and bought

new diesel vessels. He did not see why others should get rich carrying his grain, and he had merged the grain and transportation functions to add profit margins in the Odessa trade. By the early 1930s, the firm's independent shipping operations had become one of its biggest money-makers. Most of the vessels that the family built between 1933 and 1938 did not carry grain. They were elaborately outfitted with the technical specifications for handling many different kinds of cargoes. Leopold's grandson Pierre soon became the big shipping enthusiast of the family. Grain, he believed, was here today gone tomorrow, but ships were permanent assets. Pierre hired one of the best naval architects in Europe, an Italian by the name of Procacci, to design the most modern vessels he could devise. The family soon had at its disposal a small fleet of diesel vessels capable of doing 14 knots, equipped with on-board cranes, and each bearing the name of some family member. The *Jean L-D* (1936), the *Louis L-D* (1936), and the *François L-D* (1938) were the envy of other shipping companies.

The prestige of the Paris grain families, the Fribourgs and the Louis-Dreyfuses, had never been higher. Georges André might choose to keep his growing wealth discreetly hidden behind a veil of Swiss frugality, but this was Europe between the wars, a time when indulgence was in style. André's counterparts in Paris were enjoying life unashamedly. Jules Fribourg purchased a large, garden-studded country estate near Paris, in addition to his city home, and he lived the life of the French gentry. On weekends, friends from all over Europe filled his country home. When he was not busy with grain deals, he amused himself raising champion race horses for the purses at Longchamps, Auteuil, and Saint-Cloud. His shy, quiet son, Michel, was sent off to be educated properly at the exclusive Janson de Sailly high school in Paris.

For Jules's brother, René, the good fortunes of Continental meant a chance to satisfy his extravagant tastes. While Jules lived like an aristocrat and collected American grain elevators,

René lived like a Medici and collected gold snuff boxes, Louis XV and Louis XVI furniture, and porcelain fit for the tables of Versailles. René had fallen in love with eighteenth-century France, and his exotic Paris apartment expressed the fullness of his passion. He possessed artifacts of extraordinary value, and invited friends to share the enjoyment of his opulence, dining off period china, drinking wine from the Clos de Vougeot vineyard (in which he had an interest), and toasting his chef with champagne.

Meanwhile, the Louis-Dreyfuses mingled with the wealthy and celebrated in the world of politics, the press, and the aristocracy. In Paris it was said that the Louis-Dreyfus family was the model for Colette's novel *From the Window*. Louis married a Florentine baroness; his brother Charles married the daughter of the editor of the newspaper *Le Temps*. (When Charles died in 1929, his widow married Henri de Jouvenel, the French senator and later French ambassador to Mussolini's government.) Louis preferred the limelight to the shadowy grain world upon which the family fortune rested, and he plunged into politics; he became a deputy in parliament and later a senator from Nice. When his friend Maria, the British-born queen consort of Romania, traveled to America, Louis followed. His newspaper, *L'Intransigeant*, was a popular right-of-center publication, and he filled it with splashy pictures and a society column by his son François, a notorious Paris bon vivant.

There had never been a better example of the feudalistic structure of the grain trade than the 1930s, when the contrasts between the poverty of those upon whom the whole system depended—the farmers—and the prosperity of the shippers and processors were probably the greatest in history. For the latter, it seemed almost too good to be true. And it was. The grain trade felt the chill of impending disaster before most other businesses. In Chicago, Buenos Aires, and New York, the network of old European émigrés and Jews talked among themselves about Germany's unusually active grain buying. In the winter of 1937, ships loading grain for Hamburg at the Plate River in Argentina were busier than usual, so much so that a delegation of Louis Dreyfus officials soon called on French government officials to express alarm at German grain stockpiling. Hitler's grain buying had become a "Beethoven crescendo," one trader recalled.

The German invasion of France threw the grain companies and the families into confusion. Shortly before the Wehrmacht marched on Paris, several executives had come over from Continental's office in New York to plan an escape route for the Fribourgs. But they had neglected to obtain entry papers into the United States for the family. As the Wehrmacht hurtled toward the French capital, Jules and René assembled their families and a coterie of close friends (including a diamond merchant and Jules Fribourg's personal physician) and set out by auto convoy for Bordeaux. No ships were available, and the convoy continued south to the Spanish border at San Sebastian. The cars were left behind, and now the Fribourgs crossed the border on foot, before finding a trail to take them the rest of the way.

Michel Fribourg, Jules's son, had been spending the summer working at W. H. Pim Co., a grain brokerage in London. Pim's dispatched a rusty, 9000-ton, family-owned freighter to Lisbon to rendezvous with the wealthy refugees. At Lisbon there were difficulties with papers. Jules did not want to wait for American visas and the group climbed aboard and ordered the captain to sail for the Dominican Republic. Ten days later, the ship arrived in Santo Domingo carrying its strange cargo of wealthy Europeans.

It was months before the Fribourgs were permitted to enter the United States to take triumphal charge of the successful American company that was waiting for them. As René Fribourg organized bridge games and Jules chafed at the delays, Continental men came and went, briefing them on world grain news and lobbying with Jewish refugee organizations in Santo Domingo to speed up the paperwork.

Jules Fribourg never saw his beloved France again. He died in

America in 1944, and power over the family grain company passed to René and to Jules's son Michel, then an enlisted man in the army of his new country, the United States. Not only was Continental firmly established in the United States and ready to take advantage of the new, American era in the history of the grain trade, but René's art works, which had been left behind in Paris in the hasty departure, came through the war unscathed. A German general had occupied his home, and the Wehrmacht officer was so appreciative of the cooking of René's chef that he gave his personal protection to the collection.

The Louis-Dreyfuses did not have a powerful American organization to flee to. The New York office notwithstanding, Paris was the center of the family's life, and of the company's empire. It could never be otherwise. The Louis-Dreyfuses were Jews, but they were deeply and patriotically French. In 1870, Germany had defeated France and the Alsatian homeland of Leopold had gone to the victors. Alsatians were given a choice of remaining in an Alsace under German control or becoming French citizens, and Leopold had chosen France. He had moved his base to Marseilles and then to Paris and vowed never to return to Alsace until the Germans were repulsed. Now, in 1940, when the Germans invaded, the entire dynasty was threatened along with the home base. It was the most difficult moment in the history of the family.

For one thing, Louis was dead, killed in a horse and carriage accident just before the invasion. The firm was now being run by his sons François and Jean and his nephew Pierre. As the Germans drove toward Paris, the family left its estates around Paris in the care of non-Jewish neighbors and sold half a dozen of its ships to a Paris bank. Notwithstanding the traditional family skepticism about fixed assets, the Louis-Dreyfus empire had other properties to worry about. Those in the United States were also in jeopardy, for as soon as the Germans invaded France, the Treasury ordered all French assets in the United States frozen. There was nothing for the Louis-Dreyfuses to do but negotiate with Leval, Stern, and Kayaloff in New York to devise a solution. The New York partners were American citizens by this time, and the cousins in Europe hastily worked out an arrangement for them to take control of the Louis Dreyfus holdings in a fifteen-year trust. The Louis Dreyfus company became Leval and Co., and the Louis Dreyfus name did not appear again in New York until 1955.

The cousins did not leave France immediately. They made their way to Marseilles, then under the control of the pro-German Vichy French authorities. In early 1942, Jean and François finally left for Argentina. Pierre, a short, wiry, Chaplinesque man, stayed on. Thanks to his secret contacts with the Free French and the British in the immediate aftermath of the German occupation, Pierre managed to get almost all the remaining Louis Dreyfus ships out of France and into British ports. (The details of how some of these vessels came into British hands are murky. One version is that British naval intelligence picked up messages between the company office in Marseilles and company vessels at sea—and that Pierre planned it that way.) Soon after that, Pierre joined the French underground that was smuggling enemies of Germany out of France through the Pyrenees. On December 18, 1942, a month after Hitler had liquidated the Vichy government and completed his occupation of France, Pierre followed the same escape route. Thereafter, with British help, Pierre, practically penniless, made his way to England, where he joined the air force of the Free French under General Charles de Gaulle.

In Paris, the German army grabbed the Louis Dreyfus headquarters on the rue de la Banque. In a cynical stroke, the building was designated as the Reich's Office of Jewish Affairs in Paris, the headquarters for the "final solution of the Jewish problem" as it was to be implemented in occupied France.

Rendezvous at Château Laurier   5

"I remember hearing about a graduate of the prestigious Timiryazev Agricultural Academy who took a job as a floor polisher rather than as an agronomist or animal husbandry expert on a collective farm. Why? I was told he could make much more money being a floor polisher than an agronomist. That's shameful! It's the kind of stupidity which will lead to inefficiency and irresponsibility."
—NIKITA KHRUSHCHEV, in *Khrushchev Remembers*

The United States emerged from World War II as the preeminent grain power of the world. In the beginning, it was not a position that Americans had sought or even anticipated.

The Department of Agriculture and the War Food Administration, which controlled the grain trade, allocated food, and regulated domestic food supplies through rationing, had underestimated postwar grain requirements. Policy makers, remembering the glut and the collapse of wheat prices after World War I, had followed a "bare shelves" policy in the war years; even before the war ended the government sold off most of its surplus wheat stocks for animal feed and promoted the conversion of grain to "gasahol" as a fuel for vehicles.

But in the 1940–45 war, European and Asian agriculture had been devastated. The farms of France, Italy, and Germany were in far worse condition than they were after World War I, and millions of hungry people in bombed-out cities were shivering and begging GIs for chocolate.

It took all the ingenuity of America's agricultural planners and farmers to rise to this war-weary, unhappy occasion. The government quickly began making loans to Europeans so that they could buy food, but it was not at all certain that the United States could in fact provide the necessary surpluses. To do this, the government sucked grain from every rural crevice, offering farmers premiums and bonuses, and restricting domestic flour-milling so as to free more grain for export.

In the end, the food was there. The United States supplied half the world wheat trade from 1945 to 1949. Food shipments to Europe and Asia, under the auspices of the United Nations Relief and Rehabilitation Agency (UNRRA) and the Marshall Plan, made life somewhat more bearable for hundreds of thousands of people in China, Japan, West Germany, the Ukraine, Belorussia, Hungary, the Balkans, Korea, the Philippines, and the Dodecanese islands. American food was credited with preventing famine in urban Austria, rural Greece, and rural Yugoslavia.

It was clear that the food enhanced American political prestige in Europe, and that the economic stability which the food provided served to shore up Western Europe against the threat of Soviet territorial expansion and Communist political gains. How serious a threat this really was is a matter that historians will continue to debate for years, but there is no doubt that American food was a political "plus" for the Western allies. It created a psychological atmosphere, a European psychological division that remains to this day: austerity in the East; affluence and plenty in the West.

Oddly enough, this period when America emerged as the one unchallenged agricultural superpower was not a particularly glamorous one in the grain trade. The companies had to function more like public utilities than like the swashbuckling merchant firms of earlier days. To be adjuncts to a vast governmental food distribution system was profitable, to be sure, but the companies' freedom was hampered by the fact that the government really ran the show—first directly, through the War Food Administration, and later indirectly, through its relief loans to the Europeans.

Both the companies and the U.S. government had a strong interest in a return to the prewar commercial system. The mountainous surplus of unsold grain that appeared in the Midwest beginning in 1948 was a constant political headache for Washington. And the companies also were eager to be free of the heavy governmental embrace. They had a vested interest in freer grain markets, which would permit them to capitalize on their transportation, communications, and information systems and to exploit price swings.

Opportunities for developing new commercial markets were limited by the poor state of foreign economies; America was overproducing, and stable prices made for dull grain markets. In this situation, almost all the major companies began expanding and diversifying in new directions, where the opportunities for profits seemed somewhat greater than in the business of trading grain.

Pierre Louis-Dreyfus, never enamored of the grain business in any case, threw his energies into rebuilding the decimated fleet of his family firm. Pierre was a war hero when he finally returned to Paris. He had become a pilot for the Free French and flown tactical bombing missions over France, attacking V-1 rocket sites and other targets in France and Germany. Now he wore the cherished Compagnon de la Libération, an order bestowed on less than a thousand Frenchmen who served with de Gaulle. These were credentials that were useful as he went about trying to rebuild the old prewar empire of Louis Dreyfus.

There were still two shipping companies, Louis Dreyfus in Paris and its British affiliate, Buries-Marks, in London, but not many ships, and all of them were prewar tonnage. But the family name was still good at banks. With 20 per cent down, banks would loan money to build new vessels, and there were also a few bargains around in naval surplus. Pierre picked up an engineless hull that had been seized as a prize of war in a north European harbor, had it fitted out, called it *El Gaucho*, and made it the first of the L-D ships to fly the Argentine flag. He purchased several other surplus vessels and added them to what remained of the prewar fleet—several diesels and an aging Baltic timber ship. In 1953, Pierre had four new ships built in France.

Everything in the newly emerging company was divided according to family responsibilities. While Pierre managed the shipping side, cousin Jean handled grain, and cousin François concentrated on banking.

Georges André, in landlocked Switzerland, had also plunged into shipping during the war, and his company was no longer exclusively a grain concern. At the outset of the war, André had continued to import grain into neutral Switzerland from Garnac in the United States: The grain was moved to Genoa, later to Lisbon, where it was sealed and transshipped to Toulon and from there to Switzerland by rail. The difficulty was that neither Allied nor Axis shipping was available after 1940, so André had his own ships built. After the war, more were added and soon the Lausanne grain company was one of the largest, if not the largest, maritime powers in Switzerland.

Bunge had come through the war relatively unscathed, but immediately after the war political developments in the home base of Argentina helped to nudge the company closer to the United States. Soon after President Juan Perón began his first term in office in June 1946, he made clear that the private grain companies were in for hard times. Perón intended to finance the industrialization of Argentina with proceeds from grain exports, and this meant getting control of the trade. Perón's government began doing what the companies had been doing for years—buying from the farmers cheap and selling the grain abroad for all the market would bear. But the profits, instead of going to a few wealthy families, went to investments in industry—and to Perón's own bagmen. The opportunities for Perón's "profiteering" were enormous. There was a real grain shortage in 1946 and 1947, as the United States attempted to crank up its own sputtering grain output. In October 1947, *The Washington Post* described Perón as a "sort of international blackmarketeer." The Argentine government was buying wheat from Argentine farmers for $1.25 a bushel and reselling it to war-torn countries in Europe for $5.00 to $6.00 a bushel.

By 1948, Perón had tightened his government's grip on the grain trade by establishing the Argentine Institute for the Promotion of Trade (IAPI), thereby formalizing the monopoly over the cereal trade for the purpose of raising money for industrialization.

Given these restrictive new arrangements in Buenos Aires, Bunge turned elsewhere. The company already had flour mills, textile mills, paint plants and soybean-crushing installations beyond its Argentinian home base, and it now began to put more money into Brazil, where the political climate was more favorable. It also reached into the American interior, buying two Midwest grain-elevator companies that gave it terminals and lines of country grain depots.

Louis Dreyfus, wary of fixed investments, was slower to position itself in the nation's grain system, but in 1962 the company took over a 5-million-bushel depot in the Gulf port of Pascagoula, Mississippi. Jean Louis-Dreyfus himself came over on the flagship *François L-D* and entertained the awed employees in a stateroom decorated with art masterpieces. For a few hours, as they sipped champagne and ate cream puffs, the harbor people got a whiff of the opulence of their remote employers.

Of the Big Five, however, Cargill and Continental were best situated to take advantage of the new American era in the grain trade. They had the most invested in inland grain terminals, port depots, and storage facilities. Much of the food aid moving in unprecedented quantities to Europe went through these facilities. Big Grain, it was clear, could make money from government programs and subsidies as well as Big Oil. Cargill and Continental were paid for storing government grain; and government subsidies stimulated exports.

At Continental, a three-man regency was in control while young Michel, the late Jules Fribourg's son, learned more about the business. (René had become interested more in his art collection than in the grain business, but he held the title of chairman of the board.) The regency was suitably international, for Continental was still a sort of United Nations of the grain business. The triumvirate consisted of the Dutch-born Willem Schilthuis, the German-born Julius Mayer, and Eugene Bissell, an American. Continental under these three continued to grow, but Cargill was expanding faster and with the same deliberate steps that it had followed in the 1930s. The company had diversified, too. It became a shipbuilder in World War II—a natural extension of its barge building, which had begun earlier. Cargill built eighteen naval tankers and four ships for the army at installations at Albany, New York, and on the Minnesota River. (One of the Albany vessels survived two torpedoes.) By 1949, Cargill owned or leased 35 per cent of all the space on Great Lakes vessels, and nearly one dollar out of every five the company earned came from activities other than grain trading.

But Cargill stayed close to agriculture, commodities, and transportation in its new undertakings. Dazzling new ventures had gotten it into trouble in 1909, and John MacMillan Jr., his brother Cargill MacMillan, and John Peterson vowed to keep the company's expansion orderly. In 1945, Cargill went into the soybean-crushing business and also acquired Nutrena Mills, a large manufacturer of high-energy, protein-packed animal feeds made from corn. Corn and soybean processing were to become the agricultural glamor industries of the 1950s and 1960s, and Cargill entered on the ground floor. In 1947, Cargill opened a $2-million grain-storage and processing plant in Puerto Rico.

The following year, it went into a joint venture with the Rockefeller-backed International Basic Economy Corporation, building grain elevators in São Paulo and Paraná, Brazil. This was territory that had long belonged to Bunge, and Cargill was signaling that the real battle to divide up the world had begun.

At first Cargill had moved gingerly.

It had taken nearly a century for Cargill to move out into the world dominated for so long by the Europeans, but when John Junior and his brother Cargill MacMillan finally ordered it done, they took two steps that put them ahead of all their competitors. They organized an overseas subsidiary in Geneva, and they built an enormous grain elevator at Baie-Comeau, Quebec, a remote, ice-free port at the mouth of the St. Lawrence River. In 1955, a Cargill delegation led by Peterson went to Europe to assess setting up an offshore affiliate. A year later Cargill established Tradax, in Geneva. (One of those helping to set up shop was Pearsall Helms, a ten-year veteran of Cargill, whose brother Richard Helms later became director of the CIA.) Tradax became one of the world's largest grain companies in its own right.

In 1959, Cargill and Tradax began moving grain to Europe through the company's new, multimillion-dollar grain elevator at Baie-Comeau. Company barges delivered Great Lakes grain and backhauled iron ore from Labrador. The efficiencies cut the expense of getting grain to the Atlantic and enabled Cargill to shave 15 cents a bushel from the cost of delivering Midwest grain to European buyers. The facility also made it possible to continue loading ocean vessels long after the ice had closed the Great Lakes grain traffic to the competition. With that, Cargill was launched abroad with considerable advantages in the global grain chess game.

All these developments in the companies took place against a single, inescapable backdrop: the agricultural surplus that began to develop in the late 1940s. It was the surplus, more than anything else, that encouraged the companies to branch out into new enterprises and endeavors where they got a better return on their investments. The surplus made for dull markets and extremely thin margins, and the zip went out of the business. It was a time when traders had to fight for a quarter of a cent a bushel, and this situation indelibly stamped and indeed altered the essential character of the companies.

John Berry, who worked for Bunge in New York City in the 1950s and subsequently quit and became a newspaperman, remembers the grain trade then as grindingly hard, detailed work completely devoid of glamor. It was Berry's first job out of college and it was a rude introduction to the working world as the company battled for every nickel: "Bunge at the time was run like a European company—new boys were apprentices who were ordered about by the older traders. We addressed the traders as 'Mister.' In the six months I worked there I never once heard my boss say 'please' to my partner or me. It was always, 'Get me Zurich!' or 'Get me cables!' Europeans were in charge, and several were brilliant—but without any apparent soul. One of them had a mind like a calculator. He could put together the various figures in his head—price of corn at the country elevator, transportation to New Orleans, Louisiana (NOLA), up the port elevator, storage, down the elevator into the ship, freight to Rotterdam. All this in his head."

The companies felt shackled: The grain trade was becoming not much more than a service business, which eked out a living on "costs plus commissions."

In the United States, the government was as eager as the companies for a change that would finally enable the nation to sell its monstrous surpluses for cash. The surplus was a stone around the neck of every president who came into office. But a return to the old, laissez-faire ways of the 1920s was unthinkable, even to Republicans committed to the ideology of free markets. The New Deal had brought the government permanently into agriculture, and for good reason. Agriculture was too fundamental to the national well-being, to the economy, to food prices, to the nutrition of school children, and to business to be left to the whim of the private markets. The Department of Agriculture, by 1950, had become a vast planning agency that reached into every rural county of America with credit, crop insurance, scientific advice, and farm programs that controlled how much farmers grew and how much they received for their grain. The Republican Ezra Taft Benson, President Eisenhower's secretary of agriculture, called his job a "monster," and branded the farm programs a "sordid mess." But the farm bloc had political power, and not even Benson could dismantle the New Deal. Presidential politics in the 1950s was as often as not farm politics; the farm bloc helped to elect Truman in 1948, and it added to Eisenhower's plurality in 1952. One American in five still lived on a farm in 1950. Gordon Roth, writing in *The Nation* of April 18, 1953, declared that "farmers in the upper Midwest wheat country will decide whether Congress stays Republican or goes Democratic in 1954."

The government was locked into a system in which farmers consistently produced too much grain, and got paid for it, while the outside world had too little money to absorb the excess. Various developments at home contributed to this unnatural glut. Gasoline had replaced oats as the main "fuel" used in agricultural operations, freeing millions more acres of grainlands for cash food crops. Corn yields increased rapidly with the advent of new chemical fertilizers and hybrid seeds. Yields went from an average of 50 to 75 and finally, in the late 1960s, to nearly 100 bushels an acre. American demand soaked up some, but not all, of this extra grain. The ready availability of a seemingly inexhaustible supply of cheap corn helped to make the United States a nation of steak eaters. The beef animals from which Americans cut their juicy, marbled steaks consumed a ton of corn or more before they went to the slaughterhouse. These steers were truly "hides stuffed with corn." In a sense, this was and is a wasteful use of grain. It takes seven pounds of grain to add one pound of weight to a beef animal, and two and three pounds of grain, respectively, to do the same job for chickens and hogs. But America had lots of grain, and a food system grew up that made it possible—even economically necessary—to run as much grain as possible through livestock. The United States became hooked on steak because of cheap corn.

The American appetite for more meat and poultry also was the incentive for the postwar "soybean miracle." Until the 1920s, soybeans were hardly grown at all in the United States. The USDA didn't keep track of plantings, since most farmers grew the nitrogen-rich plant to plow under later to enrich worn-out soil. But livestock men discovered that the yellowish bean was a sort of protein pill. Its 40 per cent protein content was twice that of beef and fish, three times that of eggs and eleven times that of milk. Mixed with corn in the diets of cattle, hogs, and poultry, the meal from crushed soybeans speeded up the weight-gaining process, reducing the time and expense of fattening animals. America was blessed. It had the ideal soil and day-length for growing the light-sensitive miracle beans.

To strategists at the USDA, Cargill, and Continental, the solution to the surplus problem was self-evident. It was to get people in other countries to eat the way Americans did. A global economy in which millions of rice-eaters in Asia were converted to wheat bread was one that absorbed some of the perennial U.S. wheat surpluses. And a food system in which affluent countries bought billions of dollars of U.S. corn and soybeans to feed their beef, hogs, and poultry every year was one that helped the American balance of payments and trade.

Few questioned the profound economic and political implications of such a new matrix of dependency on the United States. Once the United States began to push its grain into other countries, rationales were found. Bread was nutritious; well-rounded diets including meat produced taller, stronger Asians; food imports combated food inflation in the economies of developing countries and freed labor and capital for industrialization; America had "natural advantages" as a food producer for the world.

For better or worse, the encouragement of maximum U.S. exports was momentous in its long-range economic, diplomatic, political, and social implications. Many peoples that became accustomed to bread after the war did not live in climates suitable for growing wheat. If they were to continue eating bread, they had to import their flour or wheat. Conquerors have always influenced the cultures and life-styles of the vanquished, but seldom in history have they changed the food and meals of the defeated, as America did after World War II. The Japanese wheaten food had always been noodles, and wheat bread was almost unknown when General Douglas MacArthur began importing wheat into the occupied nation in 1946. The wheat, in this case, was often baked into bread to feed school children and civilians. It was the first mass exposure of the Japanese to this Occidental delicacy, and they liked it. In Taiwan, President Chiang Kai-shek gave a helping hand by having his propagandists announce that "wheat eating is patriotic."

The American diet did not, of course, spread around the world only because a few bureaucrats wished it to do so. The overflowing populations of Asian and South American cities could most easily be fed with wheat, just as the European industrial workers were in the nineteenth century. But U.S. officials did their part. The Department of Agriculture's representatives took a broad view of their "market development" mission. In Korea, they promoted biscuits for which the "soft" wheat of the Pacific Northwest was perfectly suited. In Japan, they organized campaigns to get Japanese school children to wash their hands more frequently—in the interest of better sanitation, but also of the U.S. tallow industry. The USDA sent frozen broilers to Ger-

many as part of government-financed food shipments, and soon
the succulent birds were turning on restaurant and grocery store
spits all over the country.*

But it was Public Law 480, passed by Congress in 1954, which
gave the U.S. government a perfectly designed tool for disposing
of the surplus. P.L. 480 organized the dribs and drabs of food aid
into a permanent fixture of farm policy and of foreign policy as
well. It became one of the most durable pieces of legislation ever
passed by Congress.

P.L. 480 is now such an accepted part of the agricultural and
diplomatic landscape of the United States that it takes an effort
of imagination to recall that there was some opposition when it
was first proposed. Shipping American food abroad to help war-
torn nations or to prevent famines was one thing. A permanent
welfare program for the world was something else. Many conservatives and southern Democrats were philosophically opposed to foreign aid. Corn and cotton congressmen were worried
that if U.S. food were too readily available, farmers abroad
might shift their own production out of food grains into exportable crops that might compete for foreign markets against
American commodities.

But a permanent food aid program had appeal that far out-
weighed the reservations. It appealed, of course, to most of the
farm bloc, which realized that the program would enable farmers to keep getting paid for growing surpluses. Senator Hubert
H. Humphrey saw a mixture of humanitarian and ideological
(not to mention agricultural) benefits. It would, he felt, add a
"new, positive, humanitarian force into the world ideological

---

* The Germans became addicts of the broilers and soon began to develop
their own broiler industry. This was to result, in the early 1960s, in the first
serious economic confrontation between Europe and the United States since
the end of the war: the "chicken war." The Europeans put up high tariffs to
protect their new broiler industry, and U.S. broilers could not get in. The
Americans lost the battle but the American corn industry won the "chicken
war": the European broiler producers fed their birds U.S. corn and soybeans.

struggle." It would be a "simple, Christian, humanitarian approach to better world understanding." Foreign-policy hawks also were attracted. Secretary of State John Foster Dulles was an outspoken advocate of food aid to drought-threatened Pakistan in 1953: He was impressed with the "martial spirit of the people" and with what he believed was their strong anticommunism. He reminded Congress that Pakistan controlled access to the Khyber Pass—which guarded the route from the Soviet Union to South Asia. Food to Pakistan made foreign-policy sense.

The P.L. 480 finally passed by Congress in 1954 was worded broadly enough to satisfy all the various supporters of food aid. The aid was to promote the foreign policy of the United States, combat hunger, and dispose of surpluses. But in its early years the last provision was the main rationale for the program.[*]

In the first years, an average of one bushel of wheat in four and one bushel of rice in five ended up going abroad with P.L. 480 financing. In 1959, a particularly bleak year for the grain trade, four out of five dollars' worth of wheat exports and nine out of ten dollars' worth of soybean oil exports were so financed.

P.L. 480 was advertised as an aid program for foreign countries, but above all it provided assistance to American farmers and the grain trade. Foreign governments received authorizations from the U.S. government to purchase, with American loans, certain quantities of American farm commodities; and the foreigners handled the actual transactions, contracting with private exporters to obtain the goods. But payment for these goods actually went straight from the U.S. Treasury to commercial banks in the United States and then to the private exporters—as soon as they presented documents certifying that the commodities were loaded aboard ship. The foreign governments had the

---

[*] Later, Secretary of Agriculture Freeman was to stress market development and combating hunger. Under Jimmy Carter, the program was nudged toward supporting agricultural development abroad.

obligation to repay the loans, but the terms provided grace periods and long maturities.° Essentially, the system was that agricultural commodities left the country, but the money stayed home.

In effect, P.L. 480 made the U.S. government the principal American financier of the grain trade. This was not an ideal situation for the companies. Cargill took the lead in advocating policies that would lessen the governmental role and the reliance on artificial devices such as P.L. 480 to stimulate trade.

Cargill's William Pearce, a lawyer who headed the firm's public affairs department, began showing up frequently in Washington to press for changes in regulations—changes that often seemed technical but might nonetheless involve millions of dollars. Pearce worked to persuade the Agriculture Department to put surplus government grain up for sale inland, as well as at the ports. This helped Cargill and the USDA. Cargill could offer more for the U.S. grain and still make money because its superior transportation facilities enabled it to cut costs "upstream."

Another time, Pearce checked in with Senator Humphrey when the company had trouble with a new regulation pertaining to foreign subsidiaries. "Now that you say it sounds unreasonable, it sounds unreasonable to me, too," Humphrey told Pearce; the regulation was modified.

In 1962, Cargill was caught up in the drafting of a major piece of farm legislation that was to affect both farmers and grain companies. It involved price supports and export subsidies on feed grains (corn, barley, sorghum, and oats)—a seemingly mundane issue that involved billions of dollars. In January 1961, when President Kennedy took office, the country had such a

---

° Initially, foreign governments could repay these "loans" with their local currencies. The United States accumulated vast accounts of such currencies as Indian rupees and eventually wrote all or some of the money off. The problem of how to get rid of the money occupied officials in Washington in the 1950s and 1960s.

large surplus of corn on hand that it was feared there would be no place to store it if there was a large crop that summer. The new administration's emergency measure had offered farmers a minimum $1.20 a bushel for their corn if they agreed to plant 20–50 per cent fewer acres of the crop than they usually did. Most farmers and economists considered the program, which reduced government costs and government stocks of grain, a success, but Cargill officials felt it was a "disaster." They maintained that the price support of $1.20 a bushel priced American corn out of world markets. This meant that corn could only be exported with a government subsidy—if it could be sold at all.

In early 1962, Cargill's new public policy committee of senior executives instructed Pearce to seek changes. Pearce consulted the Cargill wheat trader Melvin Middents and these men drafted what later was nicknamed the Middents Plan. Price supports were to be reduced to world levels and the export subsidy on corn ended; farmers would get a government check to make up for the lower supports. This was, in fact, the outline of the measure that emerged after Pearce's intensive lobbying in Washington with the administration and with key senators such as Humphrey.*

The episode was indicative of the Kennedy administration's approach to the farm problem. It stressed trade over aid handouts. This approach called for more grain exports for cash, and it enlisted the aid of the companies.

While the Middents Plan was being adopted, there was another sign of the new aggressive course, this one involving the nation's wheat trade with Japan. Until Kennedy took office, America's global wheat policies had been fairly relaxed. Canada and the United States, which overwhelmingly dominated the wheat trade, coordinated their policies and their international

---

* Corn was supported at $1.07 a bushel in 1963, and farmers received another 18 cents a bushel in cash from the government.

pricing. In effect, they were a two-nation wheat cartel that saw its long-term interests served by keeping prices low enough to discourage other countries from growing more of their own supplies or, worse still, going into the wheat-exporting business themselves. But the advent of P.L. 480 had other wheat-producing countries charging that the United States was "dumping"—as indeed it was. During the 1950s, the State Department received complaints from Canada, Argentina, New Zealand, Denmark, Mexico, Uruguay, Australia, Burma, Italy, and Peru about American wheat-trading practices. But it was not until the early 1960s that the United States abandoned the "Mr. Nice Guy" role completely. The first clues were the Kennedy administration's decision to do something about the Canadian takeover of Japan's wheat market.

The first American wheat shipments to Japan had gone as postwar relief. After that, Japanese ate steadily increasing amounts of wheaten products. The average consumption rose from 30 pounds of flour a person a year before World War II to almost 90 pounds a person by 1955. By then, Japan was importing 2.3 million tons of wheat a year, half of it from the United States. After P.L. 480 in 1954, the USDA accelerated its dietary proselytizing, sponsoring school lunch programs, training for bakers, and department-store exhibits that introduced the Japanese to such American foods as pancakes.

Of all the new wheat products circulating in Japan, bread was the most popular. But because of the pattern of the Canadian and American wheat trade, this began to create serious problems for the United States. For many years, the soft-kernelled "white wheats" that flourish east of the Cascade Mountains and in the Columbia River Basin in the state of Washington had produced an ideal flour for Japan's noodles, biscuits, and cakes. But this low-protein wheat was less suitable for making bread flour. For that purpose, Japan imported high-protein Canadian wheat from Saskatchewan and Manitoba. By 1960, as bread-eating continued to gain popularity in Japan, Canada was outselling the United States two bushels to one.

The Americans were at a disadvantage. The American bread wheats grow in the belt of prairies that run from Texas to North Dakota—distant from West Coast ports. Moreover Vancouver had the benefit of government-subsidized railroad rates for grain. Alarm spread at the USDA, and plans were prepared for an American counterassault. The federal Commodity Credit Corporation moved some of its stocks of Midwest bread wheat to the West Coast and offered it for sale to the private grain companies at prices competitive with those in Vancouver, and the government invited Japanese bakers and millers to the United States to show them the excellent qualities of these Midwest varieties. The USDA and private lobbyists pressed for, and obtained, lower freight rates for grain shipped by rail to the West Coast. Simultaneously, the State and Treasury departments increased pressure on Japan to pare down the size of its trade surplus with the United States by "buying American."

By 1962, this pressure began to yield results. The Japanese government issued directives to its Food Agency to purchase more American bread wheat and in 1963, U.S. wheat sales to Japan increased by 70 per cent. The Food Agency announced that it would divide its wheat imports equally between the United States and Canada as a concession to Washington. (The Americans, for their part, were going out of their way to keep their new customers across the Pacific happy. When Japanese importers complained that one shipment of wheat was infested with weevils, the U.S. government paid the damage claim.)

The Johnson administration delivered the *coup de grâce* to the Canadians in 1964. Henceforth, it made clear, the U.S. wheat trade with Japan would receive generous enough government subsidies to insure that not a single bushel of Canadian wheat would ever reach the Asian country at below the U.S. price. The Japanese wheat market belonged to the United States.

During the whole postwar period, there had been only casual discussions at the USDA of Russia as a potential market for American surpluses.

Russia had lived a life of extreme economic isolation between the two world wars. Its new rulers, struggling to put their ideology into practice across the vast reaches of the world's largest country, had neither the money nor the inclination to develop its economic relations with the West. They turned a sullen, suspicious face on capitalists in Western Europe and America. The New Economic Policy, which allowed for traces of liberal "market" practices, was abandoned and with that the country sank into a long period in which Soviet accomplishments were achieved through harsh policies of austerity and self-sufficiency.

The men who directed the Revolution did not assign a priority to agricultural development. They were contemptuous of the peasantry and of the kulaks, whom they viewed as reactionary and backward. When Stalin finally launched his program of agricultural collectivization in 1928, he did it with a pitiless disregard for either the human or economic costs. As people starved by the thousands in the Ukraine in 1932, 1933, and 1934 and kulaks were killed or shipped off to Siberia, grain production stagnated.

From their vantage point in the West, the grain companies watched developments in the Soviet Union after the second war with interest. Events were beginning to force the Soviet leaders to devote more of the country's resources to agriculture. Although starvation disappeared, Soviet farming was not a success, and food was a perennial problem. Production, distribution, and quality were poor.

Some analysts in the companies believed that as the Soviet Union recovered from the war and invested more capital in agriculture, it eventually would emerge as a grain power once again, competing with the United States, Canada, and other surplus-producing countries for world markets. Less plausible was a second possibility—that Russia would abandon its attempts to be self-sufficient and turn to the West for grain. The self-sufficiency notion was embedded in Soviet policy—for reasons of pride, security, and economics. Becoming dependent on the West for a resource as basic as food would not fit the Soviet Union's views either of itself or of its historic position as a food-exporting country. If anything characterized the Soviet Union since the Revolution, it was its economic isolation and its determination to survive on its own. It was a Yugoslav Communist politician, Svetozar Vukmanovic-Tempo, who had told American officials in Washington in the late 1940s that his countrymen would rather eat grass than accept help from the West with strings attached. The same sentiment had characterized Soviet policy through virtually all its history.

Soviet agricultural policy in the 1950s and early 1960s fit the self-sufficiency tradition. Under Premier Khrushchev, agriculture finally did receive priority treatment. Khrushchev fancied himself something of a farmer. He was fascinated by American agriculture, by its successes in developing hybrid corn, and by the impressive accomplishments of American farmers such as Iowan Roswell Garst, with whom he visited and became friends.

Khrushchev's greatest agricultural achievement was helping to make the decision in 1953 to plow the "Virgin Lands" of southern Kazakhstan, in Siberia, and plant millions of new acres of wheat there. Politically and economically, this was an enormous, risky undertaking. The Siberian steppes were deeply isolated, remote from European Russia, and unimaginably vast. The weather was freezing cold in winter and boiling hot in summer. Day and night a westerly wind blew unrelentingly at 15 knots across the wastes. The proposed wheatlands were without roads, grain-storage facilities, or housing for workers.

The scheme was opposed by Stalin's old foreign minister V.M. Molotov as "premature and expensive." But Khrushchev prevailed, and his dream of opening up the Virgin Lands came true. By 1960, 55 million new acres had been added, most of them between the Ural Mountains and the Ob River. Russian grain production increased steadily, and her selling agents began to move around the capitals of Western Europe, peddling their new "SKS 121" (No. 2 grade Southern Kazakhstan spring wheat), along with the traditional "431" winter wheat from European Russia.

In fact, there was a lively, continuing communication between the Western merchants and the agents of Exportkhleb, the Soviet grain-trading monopoly. Russia had always managed to export a little wheat to earn foreign exchange, even in the 1930s, and in the 1950s these exports were small but steady. The International Wheat Council in London listed Russia as one of the world's *exporters*, even though the Soviet Union did purchase grain from time to time in modest quantities from Canada and France when Soviet harvests were poor or when Soviet flour mills needed certain qualities of wheat that were unavailable at home. Several of the companies had Russian-speaking employees who traveled regularly to the Soviet Union or who entertained the Soviet agents when they came West to sell grain.

The capitalist and Communist grain men shared that special camaraderie of specialists. Some continuity to the great days of the Odessa trade was provided by the presence on the Exportkhleb staff of at least one former Russian employee of Louis Dreyfus. At Continental's office in Paris, the contact man with Exportkhleb in the late 1950s and early 1960s was Gustav Meeroff, a half-Russian who looked suitably capitalist in his black suits, hats, and topcoats. Meeroff was a specialist in the "switch," an intricate maneuver in which goods instead of cash are bartered for grain. Meeroff helped arrange elaborate swaps of Soviet commodities for goods of other countries. In the process, he earned profits and Russian good will for Continental.

Jacques Lang, Louis Dreyfus's man in London after the war, was another natural "Russian connection." A gifted linguist, Lang had quickly picked up the language from his Russian wife, whom he had met when he was interned in Shanghai by the Japanese in World War II.

These men all had access to Leonid Matveev, the director of Exportkhleb. Matveev had given up a career in engineering to become a grain trader. He was correct, gentlemanly, and a bargainer of legendary patience and stubbornness. The Soviet Union's grain exports were a small but precious source of foreign exchange, and Matveev did his best to get top dollar, pound, or franc for them. His only real advantage was that he alone knew what the Soviet Union had to buy or sell. It often was an advantage that offset the Russian's vulnerable negotiating position. Often as not, political or economic considerations that the Western merchants could never guess motivated Soviet buying or selling—an urgent need to raise money for machinery purchases, perhaps, or a decision to increase the number of livestock receiving corn or barley rations.

Surprise was useful in his arsenal of stratagems. Western merchants were sometimes awakened in the middle of the night by one of Matveev's local men saying into the telephone: "I have a hundred thousand tons of SKS One Twenty-one—do you want it? Let me know by noon." There would follow frantic telephone calls to millers or cables to New York, Chicago, or Liverpool seeking the latest price quotations. At noon, the merchant would appear at the appointed hotel bar with a bid—only to discover that several rivals already were sipping Scotch whisky with the Russian, after having submitted high offers.

The particular telephone call that was one of the first signals of a new era in the postwar global grain trade came sometime in early summer of 1963. It was a call from Matveev to Patrick Mayhew, then an energetic and determined young grain man employed by the Ross T. Smythe Co., in London. Mayhew had worked hard on his Russian connections. As a result of his diligence, the Smythe firm rivaled Louis Dreyfus as the leading merchandiser of Soviet wheat to British millers by the end of the 1950s. Louis Dreyfus's Lang and Mayhew were long-standing friendly competitors. There were times when, maneuvering to get control of a *tranche* of Soviet wheat, they would vie in the pubs and hotel lobbies of London with all the intrigue of Sherlock Holmes and the chief detective of Scotland Yard.

In that early summer of 1963, Mayhew felt that he had been tapped for the role of Sherlock Holmes. In advance of the Russian harvest, he had sold 400,000 tons of Russian wheat to English customers. This was so much, in fact, that British authorities had questioned him about possible Soviet grain "dumping" in England. All it took was one telephone call from his friend Matveev to deflate him. Matveev told Mayhew that the big deal was off. But Matveev did not hang up. Instead of buying Russian wheat, he asked, how would Mayhew like to *offer* wheat to the Soviet Union?

Behind this question, with its implication that the Soviet Union was going into the markets to *purchase* grain instead of exporting it, lay a significant policy shift by the Politburo. Although Khrushchev boasted of Russia's agricultural accomplishments and devoted much time to farm matters, the fact was that Russia still had a major food problem. Not only that, it was a food problem that already had exploded into violence, although this was not known in the West. A year before military units and tanks had to be called out to put down strikes and demonstrations against increases in the price of meat and butter in the town of Novocherkassk. The strike had spread through the huge locomotive works, picked up support from school children and housewives, foundry workers and shopkeepers. Slogans appeared on the works: "Down With Khrushchev!" and "Use Khrushchev for Sausage Meat!" Soldiers fired into a crowd, killing seventy or eighty people; blood ran in rivers in the town square. Subsequently, the families of the killed and wounded were deported to Siberia.[*]

Whether Novocherkassk had anything to do with persuading

---

[*] Aleksandr I. Solzhenitsyn wrote in *The Gulag Archipelago,* 3 (New York, 1978), that "without exaggeration, this was a turning point in the modern history of Russia."

the Politburo to authorize grain imports on a large scale for the first time since World War II can only be guessed at. According to Solzhenitsyn, as a result of the incident, six members of the Central Committee, including Anastas Mikoyan and Frol Kozlov, flew in to the area. (At one point, the crowd yelled, "Let Mikoyan come down here! Let him see all this blood for himself!") It was, in any case, a clear demonstration of the menacing situation prevailing in Russia's food economy, and of the political dangers of skimping on food imports.

Mayhew, of course, was unaware of any of this, but he knew something important was now in the works. His first hope was that he just might be able to persuade his American client, the Peavey Company in Minneapolis, to take the Russians up on their offer.

The Louis Dreyfus's virtuoso trader Lang, who had been summoned to Moscow about that time, also became aware of a sudden shift in the Soviet mood. He had gone to the Soviet capital prepared with bids to buy some of the small Russian corn crop (another Khrushchev agricultural project). But the Russians were not selling, and Matveev told Lang that the wheat crop had "drawn a blank." Lang may have been the first to know. Before he went home, the Russians used him as broker in their *purchase* of 200,000 tons of wheat from Canada.

Soon after that, Matveev himself flew to Canada and began to talk with officials of the Canadian Wheat Board in Winnipeg. To most of the world that pays attention to grain, this did not seem unusual. The Soviet and Canadian governments at that time handled transactions under the broad terms of a bilateral grain agreement. The Russians agreed to make purchases of certain quantities of Canadian wheat in return for guarantees that this grain would be available when needed. The most recent agreement had expired in 1962, and it was logical for Matveev to be in Canada negotiating a new one. But Lang and Mayhew now knew that bigger things were under way than new government protocols. Both traders hastened separately to Ottawa. When they arrived in early August, Matveev was still in Canada, but he had moved his talks with the Wheat Board to Ottawa's Hotel Château Laurier, a vintage, 500-room relic on Parliament Hill, where William MacNamara of the Wheat Board and Matveev were incommunicado in an upstairs suite for days. Sometimes MacNamara stumbled out of the room, rushed to the hotel bar, downed a whiskey and muttered, "It's big!"

Mayhew did not doubt that it was, but he was having great difficulty interesting his American clients at the Peavey Company in selling U.S. wheat to the Russians. At the headquarters of the Minneapolis flour-milling company, the high command was jittery. Peavey was, by then, mainly a flour and food company, and it only dabbled in the grain trade. And Peavey officials felt that selling grain to Russia was an unusually sensitive and politically risky maneuver. Mayhew was told that a commitment of any kind was unthinkable without U.S. government approval. However, the Peavey officials authorized a contact with the Russians, and they dispatched their grain division chief, Eugene Bissell,* to Ottawa on condition that he travel incognito and that he not spend the night in the same city as the Russians. Bissell flew to New York, bought a ticket under the name "Mr. Adams" and flew to Montreal, where Mayhew picked him up and drove him to see Matveev at his hotel suite in Ottawa. Bissell gave Matveev a thorough briefing on the American, free-enterprise grain-trading system and returned to Minneapolis without having made or obtained any commitments. There was nothing left for Mayhew to do except to return to London.

However, Lang and several Louis Dreyfus associates from New York City stayed on in Canada, and at some point they slipped into Matveev's suite and began negotiating privately to sell him grain and flour. It was a moment that Lang had awaited eagerly all his working life. He was fluent in Russian, his pol-

*Son of Continental's Eugene Bissell, who left that company in the early 1950s.

ished European manners conveyed trustworthiness and integrity, and Matveev was in a buying mood. When Lang and his colleagues were done negotiating, they had sold the Russians 1.3 million tons of Australian wheat (on behalf of the Australian Wheat Board), as well as large quantities of French wheat and West German flour.

The world knew nothing of this when Canadian Foreign Trade Minister Mitchell Sharp announced on September 14 that Canada had sold the Soviet Union 6.8 million tons of wheat at a price of nearly $500 million.

This announcement was a watershed in the history of the postwar grain trade—in the history, even, of the Soviet Union itself. The grain crop had failed, but this time Russians were not being asked to tighten their belts. Khrushchev was doing what other rich countries like Japan were doing: covering the deficit with imports. It was at one and the same time a mark of Soviet self-confidence and insecurity—self-confidence because the Russians were accepting the fact that they were rich and strong enough to import without compromising their independence, but insecurity because the factors contributing to the decision included events such as those at Novocherkassk. Henceforth, the Soviet Union would be the "X" factor in world grain markets.

It is not difficult to imagine the consternation south of the border. Canada had found this tremendous outlet for its surplus, but the United States still had not sold a single bushel to the Russians.

This was particularly annoying to Secretary of Agriculture Orville Freeman, who had made such efforts to reduce the surplus and put American agriculture on a sounder footing. Yet for all his efforts, agriculture was still the "mess" that Freeman found it when he took office, though for reasons opposite to those in Russia: In America there was too much grain. A billion bushels of unsold grain were being stored in American stocks when Sharp made his announcement. This grain had been acquired under the price-support system. When farmers could not sell their grain, they had the option of pawning it to the government. They received a one-year loan with their grain as collateral—the number of bushels times the government support level. If prices had not improved at the end of the one year, they forfeited their grain but got to keep the loan.

It was a costly system. Once the government took over the grain it had to pay grain companies to store it. The farm agency's budget of $7 billion a year was more than twice the combined expenditures of the State, Labor, Justice, Commerce, and Interior departments, and a vast bureaucracy of 96,000 people ran the farm programs. The Department of Agriculture had become a huge government planning agency. The depressing thing was that it seemed all but impossible to turn this situation around. *Time*'s cover story on Freeman in April 1963 well illustrated this prevailing sense of pessimism:

Hope, springing eternal, argues that the farm mess will somehow, some day, just go away. Maybe the growth rate of the U.S. population will catch up with farm output, perhaps export markets will open up and swallow the surplus. But projecting present trends, the Agriculture Department foresees farm capacity running ahead of population growth until 1980 and beyond. Any export markets for U.S. farm goods may well narrow in years ahead: Europe's Common Market, customer for nearly half of U.S. farm exports, is building a tariff wall against agricultural imports.

It is easy to understand the frustration of the Americans when they learned of the huge Canadian sale. Canada, it was plain, had no political hangups about its grain trade with the Russians. Sharp made no distinction between Communists and others when he noted that Canadians were "conscious of their responsibility to those who need our food throughout the world."

It was not so simple in the United States. The Soviet Union was the adversary, and there were powerful political constraints against closer economic relations, let alone against feeding Russian people. Grain trade with the Communists could not be separated from politics in the American context. This was not even one year after the Cuban missile crisis, which had brought the superpowers to the brink of nuclear war. Americans were still building fallout shelters in their basements and backyards. Berlin was still a world danger point, and many in Washington believed that the Russians were behind the nagging Communist insurgency in Southeast Asia.

Anti-Soviet attitudes were strong enough across the conservative spectrum, but they could be found elsewhere, too. The American labor movement was relentlessly anticommunist, and so were many liberal Democrats. Senator William Proxmire of Wisconsin called the huge Canadian grain sale "an inexcusable case of trading with the enemy, for the enemy's benefit, in our cold war with the Soviet Union." Senator Paul Douglas of Illinois called it a "direct blow to U.S. foreign policy that damages the best hope of overthrowing Russia and China through revolution from within."

Other voices spoke out in favor of modifying American policy on this issue, which had been dead set since 1948. Republican Senator George Aiken of Vermont observed drolly that he "couldn't recall a single case in history where people have been starved into democracy." And, of course, the farmers were all for feeding the Communist nations. When Senator Douglas and Secretary Freeman showed up at a Midwest farm rally, Freeman dared the senator to ask for a show of hands on the issue of selling grain to Russia. Douglas, convinced that few would be for it, took up the challenge. But when he asked how many favored selling the grain, a sea of hands surged up. Douglas began to have second thoughts.

President Kennedy also wanted to make a change. Not only was he convinced that there was support for it beyond the farm bloc, but he also saw an opportunity to broaden the relationship with the Russians and lessen the tensions of the Cold War.

He believed he had authority to permit the sales. In 1962, Congress had extended the Export Control Act for three years.

The act directed the President to prohibit exports that "would make a significant contribution to the military or economic potential" of nations threatening U.S. security. Kennedy felt the wording was general enough to permit Russian grain sales, but he worried about the political reaction. He was haunted by fears of being outflanked on the right. Richard Nixon, his recent opponent, publicly opposed selling the Russians grain. Kennedy also was uncertain of the reaction of the American labor movement. The pro-Soviet elements in the labor movement had long since been purged and labor had become one of the supporting pillars of the postwar foreign policy of the Cold War. Kennedy feared a backlash. What if union labor refused to load the grain for shipment to Russia? To forestall labor criticism, Kennedy decided to sweeten his decision to issue wheat-export licenses for sales to Russia: Half the grain would have to be transported on American vessels; Kennedy proposed to pay for labor's support for a "soft" policy on grain sales with seagoing jobs for American merchant sailors.

Kennedy's decision, on October 9, 1963, to authorize the sale to Russia of up to 4 million tons of wheat and flour opened a new chapter in the postwar relations of the superpowers and helped to prepare the American electorate for the later steps that President Nixon took in expanding economic relations with the USSR. But this decision was almost an anticlimax to the events that had been taking place at the Château Laurier. The news of the huge Canadian sale had set off a frantic scramble by grain men from all over the world, converging on Canada, and what then ensued was perhaps the closest thing to a summit conference that the grain trade had ever seen. They came, the merchants of grain, from Minneapolis, Memphis, New York, and Europe, seeking the favors of the Communist official in his suite beneath the green copper towers and turrets of the castlelike hotel. The merchants, unaccustomed to being at such close quarters, eyed each other uneasily around flower pots, past the languid couples swaying in the hotel's afternoon tea dance, and around the native Indian totem pole in the lobby, an object that never ceased to attract the curiosity of the Russians.

There was Ned Cook, whose father ran a thriving cotton business in Memphis, padding around the corridors in slippers, sniffling from the flu. There was Michel Fribourg of Continental; Frederic Hediger of Garnac; Leopold Stern up from Louis Dreyfus in New York City; Walter B. (Barney) Saunders and Robert Diercks of Cargill.

At first, it had been thought that the traders might form a cartel to sell American grain under the same exclusion from antitrust law that enabled the great oil companies to cooperate abroad. And indeed, Minneapolis soybean dealer Burton Joseph, of the I. S. Joseph Company, had hastened there with Freeman's approval* to explore this possibility. For several nights, while the discussions were going on between Joseph and Matveev, the leading lights of the grain trade crowded around a table at the hotel like all-night poker players, debating the shares their companies would have in the new grain-selling consortium. But the old wariness and suspicions soon prevailed. Cargill dropped out, to go it alone with the Russians. So did Continental and Bunge. The Aramco of grain never got off the ground.

Of all merchants at the Château Laurier, none was more determined to succeed in the quest for Soviet favor than Michel Fribourg.

Fribourg and his collector-uncle René had inherited control of the firm when Michel's father, Jules, died in 1944, but Michel had not inherited his father's power or authority over the merchant house. At first he was painfully shy, relatively inexperienced in the grain business, and uncomfortable with his father's old associates in New York. He had not been close to his

---

* Joseph's wife, Geri Joseph, was then Democratic National Committeewoman, a power in Minnesota politics and a friend of Freeman's. In 1978, she was appointed ambassador to the Netherlands.

father. And to the men of the world who bustled about Continental's Manhattan offices, Michel seemed too intellectual and reserved for the tough, competitive world of grain. He read French classics, enjoyed painting, and seemed hesitant and withdrawn in comparison with his aggressive father and life-loving uncle. Soon after the war, his Swedish-born wife died, leaving him to care for their adopted son, and Michel withdrew further.

As Fribourg slowly mastered the business, he gained confidence, remarried, had four children, purchased an elegant town house on Manhattan's East 73rd Street, and decorated it with French furniture and paintings by Modigliani, Pissaro, Pascin, Chagall—and the vivid, colorful canvases of amateur Michel Fribourg. In the basement was a wine cellar with 1500 bottles of fine vintages.

But Fribourg's reserve stayed with him. There would be meetings when minutes of silence passed as Fribourg struggled to find the precise words to express some point. Yet the reserve and aloofness of "MF," as associates began calling him, was sometimes an asset. It kept him above the rivalries and intrigue that always were brewing in the middle echelons of the company. Fribourg followed the management technique of "divide and rule"; he often appointed two men to key positions, gave them equal authority, and kept them guessing.

His talent for mastering corporate intrigue was enhanced by his skill in the grain business. To their surprise, the traders in New York began to learn that Michel Fribourg was more his father's son than they had thought. Underneath his retiring, polished manner, Michel Fribourg was a risk-taker who enjoyed the hazardous, speculative side of the grain trade. To Fribourg the gambler, the Soviet Union was a potential jackpot. He must have thought of it with some of the same sense of anticipation as his father Jules and uncle René when they turned to America in 1920.

Fribourg's brother-in-law, Bernard Steinweg, ran Continental's grain division in New York. Steinweg had turned out to be a skilled grain man himself. But for the Russian mission Fribourg selected a Dutchman still in his twenties. Ben Nordemann had risen rapidly in the company hierarchy, exploiting quick wits, a driving ambition, and an instinct to go for the jugular. (Some years later, an official of the Department of Agriculture who had known Nordemann was to say that the Dutchman had such a fearsome reputation for outdoing competitors that "the hair bristled on your neck when he came into the room.")

On October 5, Nordemann flew to Canada in search of the Russians. He traced Matveev to Winnipeg, where the actual talks on a new Soviet-Canadian trade agreement on grain finally were going on. Matveev was not available. So Nordemann hung around the airport until Matveev and his entourage checked onto a plane. The Dutchman hastily booked himself onto the same plane, wangled a seat next to the Russian, and attempted conversation—a difficult matter since Matveev spoke no West European language, and Nordemann did not speak Russian. Nordemann did succeed in getting an appointment in Ottawa, which Matveev kept. But by then, there was not all that much to discuss. President Kennedy's linkage of grain sales to business for American merchant vessels had created a snag: American shipping rates were the highest in the world, and for the Russians to have grain carried on U.S. vessels amounted to a heavy surcharge. As badly as the Russians needed grain, they were not ready to pay a special price.

Not that the Russians lost interest. Matveev came down to Washington in late October. Nordemann saw him again, as did other American grain merchants. Matveev listened with interest to their explanations of the U.S. system, of its futures markets, ports, grain routes, and grain companies. But there was no interest in grain as long as the requirement that half of it move in U.S. bottoms made it so prohibitively expensive.

It was Continental that finally broke the ice. It may have been Nordemann's brainchild, or perhaps Fribourg's, but in any case, it required the assurances and cooperation of the U.S. government. (Later this resulted in some charges of government favoritism toward Continental.) The scheme relied on the government's taking steps to give the Russians a special bargain on one kind of wheat so that the cost of buying the rest would balance out to what all the wheat would have cost without the high shipping costs. Export subsidies had been the USDA's main tool for keeping U.S. wheat moving abroad since 1949, and these subsidies helped to break the impasse on American grain sales to Russia in 1963.

Wheat had been a drug on world markets since 1949. Most of the time world prices were lower than American prices, which were supported by the U.S. government. Since grain companies could hardly make money selling grain for less than it cost to obtain it, the government had to compensate them to keep the exports flowing from American ports. These compensations were the difference between wheat prices inland in the United States and the gateway price at which foreign customers would buy it at the ports. When grain companies sold grain, they also registered for the compensation, which changed as prices varied at home and abroad. When the USDA wanted to "dump" wheat, or underprice Canada in the Japanese market, it only had to increase the compensation. This enabled the companies to sell U.S. grain at world prices, or even at discounts.

Nordemann was intimately familiar with these subsidy arrangements. He knew, for example, the special system for setting compensations on durum wheat. Durum wheat went mainly to Algeria, Morocco, and Italy, for couscous or pasta; since it was a small market there was no knowledge of world prices at USDA, and the export compensations (subsidies) were fixed instead in a complicated bidding system. The government had wide latitude, and Nordemann figured that in the Russian case, if USDA offered a big enough compensation on durum, it would wash out the extra costs of shipping larger quantities of milling wheat. Continental's idea meant that American taxpayers would be subsidizing the American merchant fleet and, to lessen the effect of the subsidization, also giving the Russians a discount on durum—all so that the sale of grain to Russia could take place.

It was to be another of those occasions when the virtues of "free trade," so often extolled by grain men, just had to be momentarily set aside. But Freeman and Kennedy wanted to act; and they approved the scheme. With a green light from Washington, Nordemann and Continental's Roy Folck° hurried off to Moscow to see Matveev. Now the unresolved question was whether the Russians would agree to buy enough durum to wash out the high shipping costs. (This meant a lot of durum, and Russians were growing tired of noodles, which is what the durum would be used to make.) It was Christmas week when the two arrived, and the negotiations dragged on.

On New Year's Eve, Matveev hosted a festive lunch for the visiting merchants and, in typical Russian fashion, began with a toast. It was an unusual one: Matveev quoted the Americans a price for 350,000 tons of durum wheat, announced that there would be no further discussion of business, and sat down. The Americans gulped down their food, went through the requisite toasts and conversation, and raced to catch a plane back to the United States.

Fribourg was skiing in upstate New York. Afterward he was to say that each time he looked at the snow he thought of Russia and wondered about Nordemann and Folck. When the two men arrived back, they reported to the USDA, and Freeman and Commerce Secretary Luther Hodges reached the new President, Lyndon Johnson, at his ranch in Texas. The President had to give final approval. This obtained, the USDA calculated the durum subsidy once again and told Continental's people they had a deal.

The government said later that the additional subsidy com-

° Then president of Continental's subsidiary Allied Mills, and later chairman of the board of Continental.

pensation was only $1.7 million—a small price for opening up a market such as Russia to U.S. farm products. But there was more trouble ahead. Continental's total sale was a million tons. In early February, Cargill followed suit with a sale to Russia of 750,000 tons of U.S. wheat. But by then, Continental was claiming difficulty in finding available American ships to transport the cargos, and it went back to the government for more assistance. This time, it turned to the federal Maritime Administration, the government agency which was handling the shipping side of the grain deal. On February 12, the Maritime Administration conceded some of Continental's claims about unavailability of U.S. vessels and let it reduce its usage of American tonnage by 120,-300 tons.*

When Theodore Gleason, president of the International Longshoremen's Association, learned of this development he erupted with a dockworker's brawling fury. It was obvious, he said, that Freeman, Hodges, and the Continental people were in cahoots to cheat U.S. merchant seamen. Teddy Gleason had a flowery description for the government's waffling on the 50-50 shipping promise, which *Newsweek* quoted: "the characteristic pose of two-faced panderers and their scarlet women caught *in flagrante delicto.*"

To the government and the grain trade, this did not sound like poetry, though officials had to give Gleason credit for a gift for

---

* Apparently the Russians bought the wheat "delivered" at Soviet ports. This way, Continental had opportunities to make additional profits on the shipping but it also had to comply with the 50-50 requirement. This it found difficult to do. On January 29, it asked the government to waive 281,000 tons of the U.S. flag quota. Continental claimed that no American vessels were available within the shipping schedule. Continental succeeded in chartering another 97,000 tons by February 6. But it rejected seven other vessels and was having trouble making the quota. The Maritime Administration told the company to reinstate four of the seven rejected vessels but granted the company a waiver for 120,300 tons. Only on March 11, after the labor complaints, did the Commerce Department announce an end to waivers.

colorful imagery. After this outburst, Hodges went to see the labor people, took more of the same abuse, but finally worked out a peace: There would be no more waivers.

The U.S. government had had its first lesson in how political fingers could be burned when they touched the grain trade.

Fribourg himself went to Moscow for a triumphal visit soon after the problems were ironed out. Matveev threw a cocktail party for him at the old National Hotel, which was almost as much of a relic as the Château Laurier. Fribourg had come to Russia wearing a fine platinum watch, a gift from his wife. In one of those characteristic Russian gestures, Matveev suggested a trade of watches; it would put a comradely seal on the grain deal. It was an old Russian custom. Fribourg hesitated. He did not want to part with his timepiece, which he treasured. But he handed it over. In the grain trade, good will sometimes has to go before even sentiment.

In a sense, the grain deal was Khrushchev's epitaph. His political and economic problems were multiplying, and though he was not to blame for the manifold failures of Russian farming, it did not help his weakened position to have gone to the West to buy food for the Russian people. Not surprisingly, there is no mention of either Novocherkassk or the Matveev mission to Canada in his memoirs. He does, however, describe what must have been one of his last official trips, one that took him through the vast agricultural project to which he had given his blessing a decade earlier. He could not restrain his pride as he toured the Virgin Lands:

Everywhere I went I saw fields of wheat stretching as far as the eye could see. The wheat fields rolled like waves in the wind. And everywhere there was the sweet smell of good, honest sweat. . . . The farmers laughed as they toiled in the fields. They were happy because they knew that they were laboring for the good of their country—and because a rich harvest meant high incomes for them. I saw that villages had sprung up; there were simple but cozy houses with children playing and flowers growing in front of them.

He could have been describing the plains of Kansas—except for one thing. In the American Midwest, "a rich harvest" of grain still meant only problems.

Leopold Louis-Dreyfus, founder of the company that bears his name.

Left: François Louis-Dreyfus with his wife, circa 1953.

Below, left to right: Continental's Michel Fribourg, Vice-President Harold Vogel, and Fribourg's brother-in-law Bernard Steinweg of the Grain Division.

Opposite: Michel Fribourg, of Continental, with his wife, 1972.

Above, left: William W. Cargill, the founding father.

Above, right: The late John H. MacMillan, Jr., of Cargill ("John Junior").

Right: Whitney MacMillan, now chairman of the board of Cargill.

Opposite: Ned Cook, in Geneva, shortly before losing $80 million.

Earl Butz (seventh from the left, with glasses) and the Russian grain men, July 1972.

U.S. Department of Agriculture

"Cram It Down Their Throats" 6

"This is by all odds the greatest grain transaction in the history of the world. And it certainly is the greatest for us."
—SECRETARY OF AGRICULTURE EARL BUTZ ON
GRAIN SALES TO RUSSIA, JULY 1972

For a moment, in early 1964, it seemed that Russia would be the answer to America's farm problems. Cargill and Continental had been quick off the starting mark with shipments to the Black Sea. That same year, Nordemann, Continental's indefatigable Dutchman, sold Matveev 50,000 tons of bagged rice. (The Russians worried about the American labels on the 100-pound bags, but they needed the rice, and they accepted it.) The following year, 1965, was another poor crop year in Russia, and Nordemann sold Matveev 90,000 tons of American soybeans.

But that was that. The Soviet-American grain trade slowed to a trickle, then stopped. On the American side, the labor movement was ideologically biased against selling grain to the Communists; in practice, the maritime union's insistence that American vessels be used made further deals prohibitively costly.

On the Russian side, it was not at all clear that the purchases in 1963 and 1964 were part of a new pattern. Soviet grain imports dwindled subsequently, and most Americans soon forgot about the political flurry over grain sales to Russia.

When the grain trade with Russia finally did resume years later, it was under spectacular conditions that affected every American and that no American could ignore. The "grain robbery" of 1972 was one of those economic events that, like the OPEC oil embargo the following year or the repeal of the Corn Laws more than a century earlier, can truly be said to have changed the world.

To this day, the search continues for a "smoking gun" that might conclusively prove criminal collusion between the U.S. government, the companies, and the Russians—or any combination of the three. Certainly it is clear from the record that there was bureaucratic mismanagement bordering on negligence. Numerous congressional reports have said this.

Official claims of ignorance as to the magnitude of the sales are particularly suspect in light of CIA reports that, though never before made public, clearly indicate that the agency had detailed, current information on the status of the trading and had forwarded this crucial data to the USDA.

But the real negligence of 1972 had as much to do with longstanding policies as with the conduct of officials in power. When the Russian "robbers" came to jimmy open the door of the American granary, they did not find it bolted and secure. They found the Americans pushing from the other side.

The compelling factors behind American food exports have shifted frequently throughout this century. Humanitarian considerations, diplomacy, and economic self-interest—all have been present at one time or another and often together. During World War I, Americans paid higher prices for food so grain could be exported to the Allies. After that war, food was shipped to Germany and to Russia, in part to relieve suffering, but also to support prices and get rid of surplus pork and grain at home. After World War II, the nation sent food to Europe and Asia even though stocks were dangerously low at home. The motives were humanitarian, but there was, as well, an element of *Realpolitik* in buttressing weakened countries against communism. The overriding priority in the Eisenhower years was the disposal of the surplus.

In the 1960s, new conditions emerged. Stronger strains of diplomatic and economic self-interest became evident in American grain policy. Food was used more freely as a diplomatic "carrot," and the emphasis on dumping surplus crops wherever they could be disposed of was replaced by the priority of selling grain for cash. Trade replaced aid as the dominant impulse driving grain exports. And the USDA embarked on an aggressive and at times ruthless campaign to carry out this objective.

The companies and the government now had a common interest in increasing exports. Oil companies do not make money bottling up petroleum reserves underground, and grain companies cannot make a living storing unsold grain for the government. As American exports of wheat, corn, and soybeans grew, so did company profits. When Cargill quadrupled its volume of American grain exports between 1955 and 1965, its sales rose from $800 million to $2 billion and its assets increased from $40 million to $100 million. In 1963, the year before the first Russian sales, Continental's annual sales also exceeded $1 billion.

However, the situation still was far from ideal from the companies' point of view. The federal government was still deeply involved in subsidizing the grain trade. In 1963, the year of the Château Laurier drama, the government provided the financing for $1.5 billion of the country's total agricultural exports of $4 billion. By then, P.L. 480 had generated nearly $1 billion each in sales for Cargill and Continental.

It was true that these sales might not have been made if the U.S. government had not put up the dollars. This was federal money that was transferred to farmers and companies. The grain companies were as willing as oil companies to accept subsidies. But they yearned for more freedom. Cargill had "merchant teams" that specialized in trading various commodities, but as long as prices fluctuated by only a few pennies a day, companies such as Cargill could not fully exploit their worldwide communications and information systems.

The Kennedy administration had vowed to end the annoying surpluses, and Secretary of Agriculture Freeman had a mandate to accomplish this task. The food giveaways of the 1950s had not done the trick, and cash markets were developing too slowly to absorb the surplus. Now, by the mid-1960s, a new set of pressures had arisen: American military aid, tourism, foreign assistance, and the cost of stationing and arming several hundred thousand U.S. soldiers in Europe and Asia were all straining the resources of the American superpower. There was growing concern about the United States' balance of trade, the balance of payments, and the dollar; and demands were made on the European allies in NATO to shoulder more of the costs of defending Western Europe.

The operation against Canada in the Japanese market had provided a taste of the policy response that Freeman and Kennedy adopted. It was significant for it marked the end of postwar cooperation between Canada and the United States in wheat markets. Few had spoken out loud about a wheat "cartel," but the fact of the matter was that almost since the end of World War II, Canada and the United States had fixed the world price of wheat: Both countries were plagued by surpluses and both feared dumping by the other; the Canadian Wheat Board and the USDA cooperated to make sure that neither country suffered unduly. This was the easy-going policy that Freeman ordered abandoned in 1964. Henceforth, the floating American wheat export subsidies set daily by the USDA were to be pegged high enough so that American wheat would always be a good bargain for customers abroad. The government paid grain companies a large enough subsidy for every bushel they shipped so that companies could offer U.S. wheat at a discount from prevailing world prices. The subsidies came out of the federal budget; the trade-off was that the more wheat was shipped abroad, the less the government spent to store unsold surpluses and the more foreign exchange came back into the country. The United States set out to grab away markets from Canada and other competitors. Officially, this was called "making American agricultural products more competitive abroad." Privately, officials acknowledged that the objective in foreign markets was to "cram it down their throats."

It is worth examining the changes that took place in the food system of just one country—Iran—to see how the new agricultural policy functioned throughout the world. The relationship between resources and global demand was slowly shifting, influenced, as it was, by expanding urban populations, better diets, higher incomes, and rising expectations all over the world. The changes were dramatically evident in Iran.

Until a decade ago, Iran had imported only small amounts of grain. Its population of 30 million people lived off home-produced meat and crops. Mutton, goat, and to a lesser extent veal and beef accounted for most of Iran's red-meat consumption. And Iranian farmers grew more than 1 million tons of barley a year—nearly enough to feed these animals. Wheat (the largest grain crop) was amply available, so that bread was plentiful at low prices. Food imports were growing, but modestly. The United States sold only $24.6 million in food there in 1965, the largest item of which was soybean oil for cooking.

Agricultural attaché Charalambos Stephanides and his staff operated a low-key program of "market development" that consisted, among other things, of trying to interest food vendors at the Tehran bazaar in buying American rice. The attaché and his aides would disguise U.S. rice in unmarked paper bags, slip down to the bazaar, and ask the vendors to try it. After the local merchants had incorrectly identified it as coming from a remote region of Iran, the American officials came on with a strong sales pitch, to try to persuade importers to purchase U.S. rice. They told the importers that they could have full confidence that it would be accepted in the Iranian markets.

In 1967, with all apparently going well, a problem arose unexpectedly for the American agricultural representatives in Iran: Russian sunflower oil displaced American soybean oil as the main imported shortening and cooking oil. Politics apparently had little to do with this change. The Soviet Union and several other East European countries had been "dumping" the sunflower product abroad at cut-rate prices for years, to the detriment of producers of olive and almond oil in Italy and Spain, and of U.S. soybean-oil companies. When Iran began pumping natural gas to the Soviet Union in the 1960s, the Russians offered their sunflower seed oil as barter payment. The Iranians accepted.

The Iranian market was not one that the U.S. soybean-oil industry was prepared to surrender. At home, this basic American cooking ingredient was perennially in surplus, mainly because of other developments then taking place in agriculture. As American livestock and poultry inventories expanded, the demand for high-protein meal from crushed soybeans had grown, but there was no corresponding growth in the market for soybean oil, the other by-product of the crushing process; in some years 95 per cent of American soybean-oil exports were subsidized by the P.L. 480 program.

To Stephanides, the prospect of losing one of the few overseas markets for this American soybean oil was distressing. He proposed to Washington that the Soviet dumping be countered by offering Iran U.S. government credits to buy American soybeans: "Once our soybeans become indispensable to Iran's seed-crushing industry, it will be difficult if not impossible to find another substitute. . . . Once we get into this market with our soybeans, no one can get us out," he wrote home to the USDA.

There were difficulties with the idea of shipping unprocessed beans rather than oil. It would not help the U.S. industry, then awash in oil. But the officials in Washington were intrigued.

They drew up an action plan for retaking the Iranian market with offers of P.L. 480 loans. To receive the loans, the Americans selected Bank Omran—a Tehran financial institution with unusual connections. Omran, as it happened, had been created in the 1950s to administer the Shah of Iran's imperial lands after he returned them to the nation. Its ties to His Majesty the Shah were close. In 1961, it was incorporated into the Shah's Pahlevi Foundation, and his former civil adjutant was put in charge of it. At the USDA, Omran was usually referred to as "the Shah's bank."

Once Omran entered the picture, Stephanides' difficulties miraculously disappeared and the possibility of selling not just soybeans but also the troublesome soybean oil opened up. The general who purchased food for the Iranian army once had been a "staunch fighter against imports of U.S. soybean oil," according to Stephanides. The general even had a notion that soybean oil could lead to sterility in his troops. However, for reasons that are not clear, the general had become a convert and agreed to purchase the oil imported by Bank Omran for army kitchens. Between 1968 and 1973, "the Shah's bank" purchased 89,500 tons of soybean oil valued at $26.6 million, much of it with P.L. 480 credits. By 1975, total Iranian purchases of the American soybean oil reached a record $117 million. The Soviet Union's sunflower oil disappeared from army kitchens, homes, and restaurants, and the American soybean once again was king.

Meanwhile, another threat to American exports to Iran arose—Australian and Canadian wheat was penetrating the Iranian market in larger and larger volumes. (Australian wheat had the advantage of lower shipping costs.) Once again, a decision was made in Washington to use subsidized loans to counter the competition. This time, the USDA loaned Omran about $25 million at P.L. 480 terms to purchase wheat; the P.L. 480 wheat purchases began in 1970. (Stephanides, continuing his lobbying in Tehran on behalf of American commodities, suggested that the government purchase an additional million tons of wheat to keep on hand for "security reasons"—presumably as a military stockpile for wartime. However, this proposal was not accepted.)

Although the U.S. government financed these P.L. 480 wheat sales, the Iranian authorities did their buying from the international grain companies exactly as if they were regular commercial transactions. This contributed to a sense at the American Embassy that the companies were working on behalf of the United States, that they were part of the "team" that was helping to sell American farm products to countries abroad. When traders from Continental and Cargill dropped by to see Stephanides, they were treated like friends from back home.

One of the regular callers at Stephanides' office was Milan (Mike) Sladek of Tradax, Cargill's Geneva subsidiary. Sladek worked out complicated deals in which almost no money changed hands yet Tradax made a profit. Tradax would deliver grain to one country, accept another product as payment, deliver it to a third country, and receive more local products as payment for that. Finally, it would sell those last products to a country in Europe for currency.

In the early 1970s, Stephanides learned something that distressed him. Sladek also was selling *Australian* wheat to Iran. The old Minneapolis company Cargill was now the exclusive agent of the Australian Wheat Board for selling grain to Iran. Stephanides thereupon refused to provide Sladek with any more briefings, and (according to Cargill) began to view the company with hostility. In 1972, the dispute between Stephanides and Sladek came to a head over a large rice sale to the Iranian Army. In the bidding, Tradax and an American rice cooperative (Riceland Foods of Stuttgart, Arkansas) were contenders. Tradax won the contract to deliver American rice, which it planned to obtain from a larger American shipper. Then, in early February, the American rice shipping company (Connell Rice and Sugar, of Westfield, N.J.) complained to the Agriculture Department that Stephanides had advised the Iranian government that Tradax was an "unreliable supplier"; as a result, the New Jersey firm complained, the government had canceled the contract, and Connell was going to lose business. USDA's Ray Ioanes cabled Stephanides:

IF THIS HAS BEEN DONE YOU ARE IMMEDIATELY TO NOTIFY IRANIAN GOVERNMENT THAT TRADAX IS A REPUTABLE INTERNATIONAL TRADING FIRM FOR WHICH YOU HAVE NO BASIS TO QUESTION THEIR RELIABILITY AS A SUPPLIER AND THAT ANY EARLIER INFORMATION YOU SUBMITTED IS WITHDRAWN. YOU SHOULD ALSO REQUEST GOVERNMENT OF IRAN TO REINSTATE CONTRACT TO TRADAX IF IN FACT IT WAS CANCELED DUE TO YOUR ACTION. . . .

In a reply sent several days later, Stephanides denied that anyone from the American Embassy had condemned Tradax. Rather, he said, an official of the Iranian Army food agency ETKA had informed him that Tradax's local representative was an "unscrupulous and dishonest businessman with whom ETKA did not desire to deal":

BARGAHM (OF ETKA) CLAIMED TRADAX WELCOME COMPETE FOR ETKA BUSINESS ON BASIS PRICE AND QUALITY BUT HE COULD NOT ENTERTAIN BID BY A LOCAL CROOK.

Stephanides said his representations on behalf of Tradax had been fair and equitable.*

Although the USDA in Washington took Cargill's side, there were many indications that it was concerned, even panicked, about a potential decline of grain exports to Iran. Back in the United States food prices were rising and funds appropriated for

---

* Cargill Vice-President William Pearce wrote to me that the USDA cables "do not correspond with the facts. We are convinced that Stephanides counseled that Tradax, and not its agent, was not reputable. . . . At the time, Iran favored imports of Australian wheat for which we were exclusive agent. Stephanides in his zeal to promote U.S. commodities came to regard Tradax with great hostility, despite what before was a warm and helpful relationship."

P.L. 480 bought a smaller volume of commodities than at any time in the previous twenty years. As the squeeze continued into 1973, an interagency task force suggested that the P.L. 480 credits to Iran be terminated. This notion was strongly resisted at USDA.

Stephanides had received information from his Iranian sources that Canada had secretly offered to match the American credit terms for wheat sales and to build a huge grain elevator for the Iranians at the port of Bandar-e Shahpur as an additional concession. Turkey also had approached the Iranians about selling wheat. The USDA's Frank McKnight warned that if Bank Omran could not obtain additional P.L. 480 wheat, Iran might seek "other sources." McKnight strongly remonstrated against the cutbacks. It was the oil price increases imposed by Iran and the rest of the oil cartel that finally resulted in termination of the P.L. 480 aid to Iran.

USDA had good reason to be optimistic about the future of American grain exports to Iran. In the previous ten years, drastic changes in the structure of the country's food system and the makeup of food consumption had made the country a virtual agricultural protectorate of the United States. By now, about a quarter of all the grain used in the country originated in the United States; new agribusiness methods had been introduced that required machinery and chemicals from the United States; large poultry and dairy industries relied on American corn and soybeans, and wheat bread had become more popular. In a decade, the average annual per capita wheat consumption of Iranians increased from 118 kilograms to 173 kilograms, thanks mainly to a sharp rise in U.S. wheat imports. Iran, which spent only $15 million on American wheat ten years earlier, had become a $325 million customer by 1975.

For reasons that are not entirely clear, Iran's own production of barley declined sharply after 1970—just at the moment when Iran was introducing a modern broiler industry requiring animal feeds. It is possible that many farmers switched from growing barley to growing wheat and rice because of high prices for the latter commodities. USDA officials attribute the shortage of barley in commercial markets to the fact that Iranian pasturelands had been so overgrazed that farmers fed more barley to their sheep, goats, cattle, donkeys, and camels.

Whatever the reason, Iran turned abroad for feed grains. This was as the USDA had hoped. The Americans stipulated in the P.L. 480 agreements that some of the proceeds from selling the wheat and soybean oil in Iran would be used to set up dairy, poultry, or livestock operations that would "facilitate the utilization of *additional* U.S. agricultural commodities." The bilateral agreements further stated that project funds were not to be used for any purpose that would produce Iranian commodities *for export.*

Iran, in effect, had surrendered to the United States a good deal of its agricultural sovereignty.

The USDA even won a contractual right to meddle in Iran's internal agricultural affairs. The United States had the right (under P.L. 480 agreements) to review Iranian domestic farm projects financed by proceeds from the sale of these same P.L. 480 commodities on the local economy. Iran agreed to allow seven U.S. specialists into its Ministry of Agriculture "to help establish government policies and influence the performance of the Ministry of Agriculture for years to come." Iran also was expected to buy farm equipment and breeding animals from the United States as a sign of its gratitude. As Stephanides noted in 1973, "The sooner John Deere company establishes itself in Iran, the sooner it will control much of the needed agricultural projects." One angry communication from the USDA to Stephanides demanded to know "why did they purchase Israeli cattle with the first loan after telling us they decided U.S. cattle were good investments *even at higher prices?*" On another occasion, Bank Omran's director apologized profusely to American officials for purchasing South African corn rather than American corn in one particular transaction. By 1975, Iran was buying so much

American food that ports of the Persian Gulf were clogged with grain ships that were obliged to wait for weeks before unloading their cargoes.

Iran had money to pay for all this grain because of the increased revenues it was by then receiving for its oil. However, it was but one place where the drive was on to open new markets for American farm products. Throughout the 1960s, the USDA worked closely with Cargill and other grain companies to establish Asian poultry industries, baking industries, cattle-fattening yards, and fast-food chains—all of which absorbed U.S. grain. In 1968, a USDA official proposed a "seminar" with Cargill executives to discuss improving the "competitive position of U.S. corn in Taiwan."

As long as markets kept expanding, as long as countries such as Iran were converted to the American way of eating, there was hope that the surplus would be reduced. But, invariably, it was slow going. The pressure to sell grain was almost always more powerful than the pressure to hold it off the market. The downward pressures on world prices were evident in the unhappy history of the 1967 International Grains Arrangement.

The IGA was the most significant attempt yet made to stabilize world wheat prices through concerted international action. The first such attempt had been made in 1933. It produced an International Wheat Agreement, which was undermined by governmental maneuvers in producing countries and by the Dust Bowl. In 1967, international trade negotiations were under way in Geneva, and the Johnson administration was pressured to "do something for agriculture." It responded by signing the IGA, which fixed a floor on world wheat prices, using No. 1 Manitoba wheat as the reference, at $1.95½ a bushel. (Representatives of the grain companies, and some USDA officials, argued that this was too high—that the current prices were inflated because of the decline in U.S. stocks resulting from recent massive relief shipments to India.)

Within eighteen months, the IGA had indeed collapsed. The United States, Australia, and other countries had undermined the price floors by increasing export subsidies administratively. The Canadian Wheat Board tried unsuccessfully to hold the line, but rapidly lost customers, and its share of the world wheat market declined from 25 per cent in 1965 to 17 per cent in 1968. Prime Minister Pierre Trudeau urged President Nixon to salvage the IGA, but Nixon declined. Eventually, Canada dropped its own wheat price to $1.70 a bushel.*

An even more serious problem for American wheat farmers than competition from Canada was the farm policy of the European Common Market.

In 1962, the six original members did away with their old trade barriers and agreed on a "common agricultural policy"—the CAP. Though it was warmly endorsed by the American State Department and the Pentagon as a contribution to European unity and the security of Western Europe, the CAP quickly became the bane of officials at the USDA who were trying to increase U.S. grain exports.

CAP created a free market in the Six for wheat, rye, and feed grains, and it erected a system of floating duties on farm imports, to prevent foreign wheat from underselling grain produced by Common Market farmers. This was a time when President de Gaulle was at the peak of his power and petulance, and CAP made important concessions to France. France was an agricultural power in its own right, with a surplus problem similar to that of the United States. CAP enabled France to sell its surplus wheat to the other five Common Market countries without having to fight competition from Canada and from the price-cutting

---

* Canada also had other problems. English and European bakers, caught in a squeeze between rising costs and controlled bread prices, turned to new baking processes requiring less of the high-protein, premium wheat that is Canada's speciality. Canada reacted slowly. The United States, Russia, and Australia all began offering protein guarantees of their wheat several years before Canada, which did not do so until 1971.

Americans. The high duties of the CAP left the Europeans free to pamper their farmers with a generous price-support system. It was intended that European millers would turn to the United States and Canada only when European surpluses were used up or when they needed for their grists high-protein wheats that were not available on the European continent.

It would be difficult to overestimate the political importance of CAP as a postwar European achievement. CAP became the region's most significant step in the direction of that elusive goal: economic integration. And there was a strong social as well as political content to the policy. The high domestic farm price supports kept money flowing to rural areas and encouraged a more gradual exodus of rural populations to cities than occurred in the 1940s and 1950s in the United States. There were still 16 million people working on European farms in 1962. Planners thought it was important to bring these workers into other sectors of the economy only as fast as there were jobs, houses, and schools to accommodate them.

To be sure, the CAP's protections were devised under strong political pressure from farmers and their powerful organizations, such as the French cooperatives and the West German Bauernverband, which negotiated with governments for income guarantees and price supports. Farm strikes occurred when the governments or the organizations of grain users refused to meet these demands.

Critics argued that the CAP was expensive, wasteful and responsible for high European food prices, and in terms of pure economics, they had a point. The high European price supports did encourage overproduction and wasteful farming practices.* Landowners in France's wheat-growing regions of the Beauce and the Brie cultivated and fertilized grain crops as if they were

---

* Forty per cent of Common Market dairy farmers have less than ten cows, and French wheat price supports are targeted near $5.00 a bushel, compared with $3.10 a bushel in the United States.

raising roses, not the "desert plant." Wheat yields of 3300–4000 kilograms a hectare were common, compared with typical yields of 1300–1700 kilograms a hectare in the American Midwest.

The subsidies, in addition to helping wheat growers, also encouraged French farmers to raise more corn, which also enjoyed the protections of the CAP. Cargill and other seed companies soon began selling more hybrid corn seed in France. This was a new development. Corn had once flourished in Europe mainly in Romania, but soon a French "corn belt" stretched from the Pyrenees northeast nearly to Belgium.

The CAP gave advantages to French grain growers. Yet it did not substantially worsen the terms of trade for non-European suppliers. France and West Germany both had had national tariffs and duties to protect their farmers before the CAP went into effect. In any case, Europeans were becoming so rich and prosperous in the 1960s that their meat and poultry diets required far more grain and soybeans than their own farmers could provide. So Europe continued to be America's largest cash customer for agricultural commodities all through the 1960s. Europe spent almost $2 billion on agricultural products in 1971 and transatlantic agricultural trade went lopsidedly in favor of the United States. U.S. corn exports to Europe increased and soybean exports doubled after the advent of CAP. The Europeans noted that protectionism was a two-way street: The Americans maintained duties against European dairy products, while American soybeans were not even dutiable under the rules of the General Agreement on Tariffs and Trade (GATT). Europe's climate and soil, unsuitable for growing soybeans, condemned the continent to a permanent deficit in vegetable protein that could be made up only by imports.

Nevertheless, the USDA and Cargill, in particular, viewed the CAP with bad-tempered hostility. Dislike of the CAP was a badge of manhood in the middle ranks of the USDA bureaucracy, much as intolerance of communism was a test at the Pentagon. At the USDA were to be found the "CAP cold warriors"—the most zealous critics of European farm policy. In Minneapolis, critics of CAP framed their criticism with more finesse and sophistication—cleverly using the argument that the policy was not in the interests of Europeans, that the Europeans needed to be "saved" from an expensive, inefficient policy that wasted resources, that it was bad government and bad economics to allow inefficient farmers to continue to operate. This, at least, was Cargill's public argument. What was more, Cargill and the USDA were in a position to do something about the CAP—or at least to try.

The man who directed the campaign against the CAP at Cargill was William Pearce, vice-president for public affairs. Pearce had never traded grain in his life. He was a lawyer who believed in a public stance for Cargill—this in one of the world's most secretive businesses. Pearce believed that a skilled corporate advocate had to fit narrow self-interest into a broader public policy framework. He felt that the grain trade was changing, that it needed public advocates as much as the oil business did, that governmental regulations were pinching more and more; he would become the "Mr. Outside" of the grain trade. Pearce was no CAP cold warrior, no ordinary Washington lobbyist, and certainly not a typical grain man. In fact, Pearce fit in so well that some people mistook him for a high-ranking official.

In 1964, Pearce became president of the Feed Grains Council, a Washington-based industry group that worked to promote U.S. grain exports. In 1967, he was an observer at the trade talks in Geneva. Pearce also lobbied against the price formulas in the International Grains Arrangement and later testified against the IGA in the Senate. (Pearce argued that the high price levels would eventually discourage exports and adversely affect farmers and the USDA, not to mention Cargill.) Soon after that, Pearce obtained a membership in the Council on Foreign Relations in New York, where he rubbed elbows with the foreign-policy Establishment, and he also saw to it that Cargill kept up its connections to national political figures in both parties. He was a personal friend of Minnesota Senator Walter Mondale and he helped raise money for Senator Humphrey's campaigns.[*]

In 1970, Pearce embarked on a new project. He organized a grain-trade pressure group in London to persuade the British government to "insist on major reductions in the price levels of the CAP" when negotiations on British entry into the Common Market reached the technical stage of deciding on Britain's financial contribution. This *ad hoc* international lobbying organization was named the Trade Information Bureau. Pearce worked to enlist as many of the major grain companies as he could. Gilbert Vigier, president of Garnac in New York, was chairman; other members represented Bunge, Louis Dreyfus, Cook, and several agribusiness firms. But Continental was notable by its absence. Pearce called on Fribourg in his Paris office and invited him to join, but the chief of Continental had never been enthusiastic about Pearce's public presence in the otherwise secretive grain trade, and moreover, he was a Francophile: He loved France, French wine, and French people. The TIB wanted to bring about an end to the privileges of French farmers. It was implicitly anti-France. Fribourg declined to join.

Others in the grain trade were also bothered by the TIB, even including some in Cargill and Tradax. Tradax was beginning to dominate France's grain trade, so the people who worked for the multinational in Europe had quite different interests from those of Minneapolis. State Department officials were also nervous. "You know that European unity is more important to us than your grain exports," an American ambassador told Pearce. Less than convincingly, Pearce assured him that the grain trade also favored European unity and did not oppose British entry into an expanded Common Market. But he noted that Britain had been America's best grain market since the Corn Laws' repeal in

[*] John McGrory, head of Cargill's legal department, was a power in Minnesota politics in the 1960s. He was chairman of the Third District, Republican party, which includes Minneapolis.

1846; the companies only wanted to get Britain into Europe on terms that would not be ruinous to them.

The TIB took several more steps in the summer of 1970. It hired the American public relations firm Hill and Knowlton to survey the attitudes of European "elites"—journalists, lawyers, clergymen, and other opinion-makers—toward EEC farm policies. The Hill and Knowlton survey reached a disappointing conclusion—that there was no sentiment in favor of changing these policies. Undeterred, the TIB hired Harald Malmgren, a Johnson-era White House trade expert and a private consultant since 1969. Malmgren personally visited many of the men in the "shadow cabinet" of the British Labour party to warn them of the grave effect that an unreformed CAP would have on England's economy should Britain join the Six. A TIB paper written and circulated by Malmgren warned of "heavy new burdens on the British balance of payments," increases in the costs of food imports, large contributions from the British budget to the CAP bureaucracy in Brussels, "upward pressure on wages and labor costs from high food prices," and "damage to the competitive position of British industry at home and abroad." To align its farm policies with those of the other members, the TIB paper warned, Britain would have to increase its domestic wheat price supports by 46 per cent. In a crescendo of activity, Pearce and Malmgren brought Senator Humphrey to England to address a meeting of the prestigious Trade Policy Research Centre.

By early 1971, Pearce was involved in yet another project, a major study for the Nixon administration on the United States' role in the world economy, to be carried out by a presidentially appointed but unofficial commission chaired by Albert Williams of IBM. The Williams Commission Report became a White Paper outlining policies for strengthening the dollar and improving the balance of trade and payments. Pearce wrote large segments of it. The report, arguing that agriculture was the nation's ace in the hole for reestablishing America's international economic position, recommended that the United States "vig-

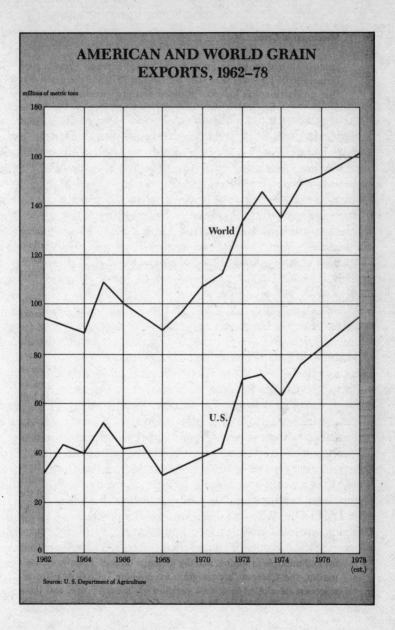

AMERICAN AND WORLD GRAIN
EXPORTS, 1962–78

millions of metric tons

World

U.S.

1962 1964 1966 1968 1970 1972 1974 1976 1978
(est.)

Source: U. S. Department of Agriculture

orously assert its agricultural interest in bilateral discussions at the highest political level with all parties to the proposed enlargement of the European Community. The need for lower grain price supports in the Community is especially urgent and should be given primacy in our negotiations." This was of course identical to what the TIB was proposing.*

The Washington and Minneapolis preoccupation with Europe reflected a perennial American concern about surpluses. But surpluses were, in fact, the overriding problem for agricultural planners in most industrial countries. Europe had what the Germans called the *Butterberg*—the "butter mountain" that resulted from subsidies to dairy farmers. Japan had a huge rice surplus—a consequence of exorbitant subsidies to rice farmers and of the substitution of bread for rice in the national diet. Farm surpluses tended to occur in rich, industrial nations, where farmers had powerful, well-organized lobbies, rather than in developing countries, where farmers usually were weak and underrepresented. This was true in the world wheat economy. Because of their surpluses, the United States, Canada, Australia, and Argentina all had programs for reducing wheat acreage. Canada paid farmers $6.00 for every acre they fallowed in 1970 and the result was that production was halved. "Planned scarcity" worked. The combined wheat production of those four major exporters declined from 80 million to 60 million tons in 1968–70. Only France's farmers kept growing more wheat in that period.

The reasons for complacency were understandable. World food production expanded steadily, if undramatically, in the 1950s and 1960s (with the exception of the Indian drought years of 1965 and 1967). Food prices were stable, and stocks were plentiful. There were nearly 200 million tons of grain stockpiled

* The TIB was unsuccessful. When Britain entered the Common Market on January 1, 1973, it did not attach any technical conditions or insist that the agricultural policy be modified.

on farms or in government granaries in 1970—a two-month supply.

Economists who kept track of agricultural statistics saw a number of positive indicators. For example, the world's two most populous countries, China and India, were agricultural success stories of sorts. The droughts in India had been devastating, and the food-grain deficit had to be covered with massive imports from the United States, but Indian grain production rebounded quickly after that. Food-grain output increased by more than 10 million tons in two years, thanks primarily to the introduction of high-yielding wheat varieties in the Punjab, Haryana, Rajasthan, and Uttar Pradesh states. In grain trade circles, there was talk of India becoming a significant food exporter again, as it had not been for more than half a century. Surpluses of corn, basmati rice, and sugarcane were building up in warehouses. In 1971, the government in New Delhi asked the United States to halt P.L. 480 shipments because of storage problems. Despite the impression in the outside world left by the relief shipments and by the pictures of hungry beggars in Calcutta, India ranked third or fourth in the world in wheat production.

During the 1960s, Chinese farming recovered miraculously from the initial chaos of communization and the Great Leap Forward. Grain production increased at a rate of 4 per cent a year, one of the fastest growth rates in the world. By 1970, China had become the world's largest food-grain producer, with an annual output of 240 million tons of rice and wheat. The government mobilized hundreds of millions of peasants to build tube wells for irrigation, reclaim land, expand multiple cropping, and dig drainage ditches. Following Mao's maxim, the Chinese "stored grain everywhere." Chinese plant researchers developed their own varieties of "miracle" rice, and thousands of rural workshops began turning out farm implements, tools, and small, lightweight tractors that reduced some of the field work and freed rural people for other tasks.

Partly because of the advances in new seeds, irrigation, chemical fertilizers, and new farming methods, the annual wheat output of developing countries rose from 50 million to 80 million tons during the 1960s. There were, however, three fatal flaws in the logic of experts who believed that a world food supply balanced on the side of surpluses would continue indefinitely.

In the first place, the positive developments notwithstanding, some saw signs that agricultural productivity was leveling off. Hybrid seeds already were used by almost every American corn farmer, and additional doses of nitrogen fertilizer did not substantially increase the yields. Scientists were stymied in their quest for wheat hybrids or for corn varieties that could extract their own nitrogen requirements from the soil through root nodules, as soybeans do. In the absence of such corn species, enormous quantities of nitrogen fertilizer derived from natural gas were still necessary for high outputs. Raising crops costs more and more money and energy.

In India, lack of irrigation limited further growth of food production. Dry-land farming was always risky in India because of the unpredictable rainfall, and while irrigation from surface (river) sources was the best hope for expanded wheat production, the costs of installing it were high. Also, no less an authority than the Central Intelligence Agency took early note of the negative social and nutritional effects of the introduction of new high-yielding wheat species in India in the 1960s. "Benefits have been unevenly distributed," it said; landlords often demanded higher rents or a larger share of their tenants' crops as soon as wheat production increased. The CIA also noted that the shift away from the coarse grains that are a staple in the Indian diet to new strains of wheat "reduced the quality of the Indian diet," since the new wheat varieties tended to be low in amino acids, the components of protein that are essential to human metabolism.

In the second place, there were large surpluses, only because an estimated one human being out of ten on the planet did not have enough money to pay for adequate food. Assuming that wealth went on being unevenly distributed, hunger and malnutrition might persist indefinitely. But it was questionable that this status quo, which condemned hundreds of millions of people to hunger, would be tolerated indefinitely.

The third factor that warned against complacency was that demand for grain to feed animals had been growing steadily. Rising incomes put more money into people's pockets for buying food. Millions of families "stepped up" to diets that included more bread, meat, and poultry—a development that of course the USDA had promoted as improving the standard of living and benefiting American agriculture and the American economy. Livestock and poultry rather than people became the main market for American grain, and the soybeans and corn ranked with jet aircraft and computers as the country's major exports. As more countries aspired to this grain-based diet, the need for grain increased.

It was precisely the American dietary model that the Soviet Union began to follow in the 1960s. It became the policy of Leonid Brezhnev's government to maintain steady growth in the livestock sector. Brezhnev was determined to put more pork and poultry onto Russian dinner tables. And with that, the problem of Soviet agriculture was internationalized; for Russian agriculture could not possibly produce enough grain to support that policy indefinitely.

The trouble was that Soviet agriculture, improved though it was since the 1950s, was still a dismal failure by Western standards. The collective and state farms were inefficient for all kinds of reasons—poor transportation, inadequate incentives, investments in the wrong places, the rural "blahs." The weather was also a constant problem, always making wheat production in the Virgin Lands of Siberia an uncertain undertaking. Harvest failures, when they occurred, were usually colossal.

Western specialists in animal nutrition also were puzzled by the Russian livestock-feeding formulas, which seemed to be

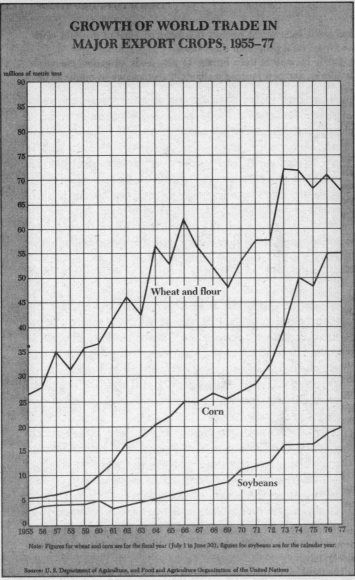

GROWTH OF WORLD TRADE IN
MAJOR EXPORT CROPS, 1955–77

millions of metric tons

Wheat and flour

Corn

Soybeans

Note: Figures for wheat and corn are for the fiscal year (July 1 to June 30); figures for soybeans are for the calendar year.

Source: U. S. Department of Agriculture, and Food and Agriculture Organization of the United Nations

short on protein. American nutritionists believed that adequate protein, in the form of meal from crushed soybeans, fish, or oil-seeds (such as cottonseed), speeded up animals' weight-gaining. Although the Russians grew sunflowers, an oilseed that was rich in protein, their feeding mixtures lacked "wallop."

The agricultural planners in Moscow certainly were trying to improve the diets of their countrymen. Between 1968 and 1971, there was a 40 per cent increase in the use of feed grains in Russia, and livestock herds expanded. If there were any doubts left about the wisdom of this policy, they probably disappeared in 1970 when Polish workers rioted in Gdansk and Szczecin in an East European version of Novochevkassk, but with quite a different ending. The regime had increased food prices just before Christmas in a bewildering piece of timing. The demonstrators made clear they were dissatisfied with all the general conditions of life, from housing shortages to the lack of red meat and good-quality food. Wladyslaw Gomulka was replaced as head of the Polish party and for a while "consumerism" became the slogan all over Eastern Europe. The Soviet leadership took note; more funds were allocated for housing and agriculture in the Ninth Five-Year Plan.

There was nothing to suggest that the Russian rulers intended to meet the agricultural targets with massive food imports—that corn from the United States would be needed for the continued buildup of the beef herds and hog populations. But by 1971, the handwriting was on the wall. The Russians turned to their friends in the Western grain companies.

Continental had never lost touch with the Soviet grain authority after that first big sale in 1964. Fribourg was one of those who felt the Soviet Union would one day be forced to resume its imports of U.S. grain; he became an advocate of better economic relations with the Communist countries—for the sake of peace and the grain trade.

The Continental-Russian connection was not new. People like Meeroff had been building good will with the Russians for years;

Continental had even taken a young Exportkhleb man into its Paris office as a trainee for a while in the 1960s. Until 1963, however, the Russians had always viewed Louis Dreyfus as the Tiffany of the grain trade, mainly because of the French house's old Russian connections. But when Matveev had reached the United States for his first visit in 1963, he found a Louis Dreyfus operation that was less aggressive than in some other parts of the world. On the other hand, the mysterious, aristocratic Michel Fribourg of Continental was just the kind of archetypal capitalist who perfectly fitted the old communist stereotype and had the same strong personal authority as did the people at the top of Soviet bureaucratic hierarchy. When Soviet officials dealt with Fribourg they knew they were in touch with the man who made the decisions.

The Russians had good rapport, as well, with the international cast of characters that peopled Continental. Francis Turion, Nordemann's understudy in Paris, was French, more flamboyant than the Dutchman but just as gifted a trader and salesman. Neither Turion nor Nordemann spoke Russian—interpretation and translation were handled by Gregoire Ziv, a Russian émigré who was in charge of Continental's customer relations—but language was seldom a barrier when Turion was negotiating. In such situations he gave vent to his Mediterranean temperament, waving his hands as if he were conducting an orchestra, and letting his voice rise excitedly. Turion sold wheat everywhere, even in Albania. Finding a new customer in unlikely places was what both the tireless Nordemann and Turion excelled at. Their talents included the requisite understanding of the technical details—of the loading facilities, depth of ports, shipping schedules, grain quality, and, of course, the arcane language of grain contracts—but above all, they were relentless salesmen, always looking for the grain trade's ultimate scoop: new business. Michel Fribourg chose these restless two as his special friends in Continental's organization; when he showed up in Paris, the three of them would sometimes don old sweaters and go to dine in a bistro like three Parisian boulevardiers on the prowl.

The major difficulty in expanding grain trade with the Russians was still the plum that Kennedy had thrown out to the unions in 1963 in the form of a guarantee that American ships would carry half the grain. No sooner was the new Nixon administration voted in than Continental began lobbying to get the old Kennedy policy modified. Nixon had been one of the most outspoken critics of the first grain deal, but he was considered to be a pragmatist, and Continental quickly tested his administration's position on the issue.

In December 1968, a month after the election, Turion sold the Russians 400,000 tons of corn. (December always seemed to be a lively month for grain merchants in Moscow.) Turion knew the corn could be obtained in Argentina, but he got an option from the Russians to deliver U.S. corn if the government changed the 50–50 vessel requirements. Then the company began to play a middleman role in Washington, pressing for changes while keeping the Russians informed.

It was the new assistant secretary of agriculture, Clarence Palmby, to whom Continental turned. Palmby had been professionally associated with the grain trade for a long time. Since 1961, he had been executive vice-president of the U.S. Feed Grains Council, which promoted feed grain exports by helping countries set up high-technology poultry and livestock industries. Most of the companies were represented on the Feed Grains Council. Pearce had been president, and he (and Cargill) had helped Palmby get the job. Palmby had a son working at Cargill and he also knew Fribourg well. Fribourg had approached him about working for Continental, but Palmby went to work for the government instead. His ambition was to be secretary of agriculture.

Palmby is a folksy, ruddy-faced man with jet-black hair and the build of a badger. He quickly became the most influential official at the USDA during the tenure of Nixon's first secretary of agriculture, Clifford Hardin, former chancellor of the University of Nebraska and a man less experienced than Palmby as a Washington insider.

Soon after Palmby came into office, Continental officials informed him that the Russians were eager to buy corn from the United States "on a continuing basis"—for cash and without any subsidy of any kind. Palmby passed this intelligence on to Hardin, who wrote a memorandum to President Nixon reporting what Palmby had said and adding his understanding that the initial purchase would be 300,000 tons. Hardin said that such sales "would serve the best interests of the United States." Hardin then made a plea for Nixon to revoke the major obstacle: the 50-50 American-flag shipping requirement. He noted that it had been imposed "as a matter of policy, not as a matter of law," and that the policy discriminated against a single country—the Soviet Union—that had great potential as a U.S. grain customer.

Turion was still hopeful about a quick policy shift when he went to Moscow in the first week of May 1969. Again Matveev told him that the Russians wanted to buy grain on a regular basis, and invited Fribourg himself to visit the Soviet capital in July. Nordemann, in reporting this to Continental's Washington representative, Sam Sabin, was intrigued enough about the possibility of a breakthrough to tell Sabin that if there were to be a policy change, "it would be highly desirable for Continental to have some advance notice of a final decision." At this point, Continental and Palmby were concentrating on the problem, and Nordemann's letter was made available to the assistant secretary. But Nixon was not yet ready to move. On June 3, Palmby told Continental that there would be no change of the maritime policy for the time being. Continental had made a strong pitch, without success, but the company had enhanced its reputation with the Russians as an American firm that could get its message through all the way to the President of the United States.

It was the fundamental changes in America's monetary and

economic situation, rather than any corporate lobbying, that turned Nixon around. The nation's balance of payments deficit, the weakness of the dollar (all the developments that had caused Nixon to name the Williams Commission) weighed on the President. And on June 11, 1971, his administration announced an end to the licensing of grain exports to Russia and China and to the 50-50 provisions on grain cargoes instituted by Kennedy.

But there was no rush on the part of either the companies or the Russians to close any big deals. A government announcement was one thing. Loading grain on ships was another. Officials do not load vessels, only workers do, and the position of the labor unions became a matter of intense, behind-the-scenes negotiations in the months ahead. The day before the announcement, Henry Kissinger, then the President's national security adviser, called in Teddy Gleason, still president of the longshoremen and just as much a tough dockworker as ever. Also invited was Jay Lovestone, international affairs director for the AFL-CIO. Lovestone's name was synonymous with resolute anticommunism, and the Lithuanian-born labor ideologue viewed the current rulers of the Soviet Union with enmity. Gleason's feelings toward the Russians were scarcely more sympathetic. "Let the Russians go to hell! Let 'em starve," he had shouted in 1964. But times had changed. Seagoing jobs on American merchant ships were at a twenty-year low. And as the union officials recognized, 50 per cent of nothing is nothing.

Recollections of what happened at the meeting with Kissinger differ. The labor officials say they indicated the unions would not load the ships if any deals were made under the new conditions that abandoned quotas for American-flag vessels. But government officials say there was "no fuss." Nothing had been settled, but at least the unions had not made more than a pro forma protest.

The following month, July, Fribourg went to Paris and met Exportkhleb's chief, Nikolai Belousov. (Matveev had since been reassigned to a sinecure in Beirut to wait out retirement, but even there Western grain men visited him, still treating him as the doyen of the Soviet grain trade.) According to Fribourg's own account, he hit it off with Belousov, a florid, temperamental man with a liking for vodka and bourbon.°

That October there were more high-level contracts. Belousov came to New York for meetings with Fribourg (Nordemann was getting ready to go into business on his own and did not participate), and Erwin Kelm and other Cargill officials joined Tradax experts in serious negotiations in Moscow. The problem was still the question of shipping. Would the unions load Soviet-bound vessels?

Fribourg met at least once with Gleason, and President Nixon discussed with Hardin and other cabinet officials various ways to clear the hurdles. The final agreement was reached in meetings in early November involving White House adviser Charles Colson, Paul Hall, president of the Seafarers International Union, and Andrew Gibson, head of the Maritime Administration.

As it was, the unions were in a weak position to make demands, and they went along, agreeing to load Russian-bound grain on the strength of not much more than mere assurances that the administration would intensify efforts to get U.S. vessels a share of the business once a regular Soviet-American grain trade was established. The Nixon administration had incongruous words of praise for union "statesmanship."

As soon as the obstacles were cleared away, the companies moved quickly. Within a few weeks, Continental and Cargill, ahead of everybody else as usual, sold a total of nearly 3 million

---

° According to one account, which may refer either to this meeting or to a subsequent one that year, the two men had good reason for rapport. After Paris, they carried on their discussions in the south of France. The story has it that the Russian grain group, booked into a hotel in Nice, became noisy, and were asked to leave. Fribourg came to the rescue by inviting them all on board his chartered yacht and whisking them out to sea. A violent storm came up and the ship nearly foundered off Corsica. All the while, presumably, the passengers were stoically discussing grain prices and shipping costs.

tons of U.S. corn, oats, barley, and sorghum to Russia. (In true multinational fashion, Continental also supplied the Russians with corn from Mexico, Argentina, and Thailand.)

The Russians were not looking for wheat to make bread; they were looking for corn (or if corn was not available, wheat would also do) to feed livestock. Acting Secretary of Agriculture J. Phil Campbell said that if the Russians kept expanding their herds and hog populations, they would need still more. In fact, there was good reason for officials in Washington to be intrigued by what was happening. The Soviet Union had had bumper grain crops in both 1970 and 1971; yet their traders bought 7.8 million tons of grain worth half a billion dollars. If they bought that much in good harvest years, what would happen when the inevitable occurred—when Russian harvests failed?

Even given America's need to redress the trade and payments deficit and strengthen the dollar, the administration's lifting of all controls over grain sales to the Communists was a drastic step. It ran contradictory to the Nixon-Kissinger policy of linking sales of technology to Soviet concessions in other areas. (Administration witnesses had testified before Congress that the President opposed the expansion of trade with the Soviet Union until agreements had been reached on a wide range of other Soviet-American problems. Among them, the Americans claimed the Russians still owed $1.3 billion in World War II Lend-Lease repayments and that a satisfactory settlement was a condition for improved economic relations. At the time, Soviet-American trade came to a paltry $200 million a year.) But it also seemed to Kissinger, who had followed developments closely, that grain was an important, if not crucial, bargaining chip in any subsequent diplomatic talks with the Russians.

On January 31, 1972, Kissinger wrote to the secretaries of State, Commerce, and Agriculture that "one of the possible areas for increased trade with Russia relates to agricultural products and Commodity Credit Corporation outlets." Kissinger said that Agriculture should "take the lead in a new public discussion." He followed this up on February 14 by directing the USDA to begin work on a "negotiating scenario" that would include the opening of a U.S. credit line to the Russians for the purpose of buying grain.

In their contacts with Continental, the Russians had frequently mentioned their desire to enter into a long-term arrangement with the United States, but they had never suggested this should be based on credits. They bought the feed grains for cash in 1971, and as a subsequent CIA report was to make clear, the Russians had "no major difficulty" raising money to pay for grain imports. It was possible for them to raise "$1 billion or so" by gold sales, or by a combination of gold sales and borrowing in the Eurodollar market. (In the first half of 1972, South African gold sales declined sharply, enabling the world gold market to absorb larger-than-usual Soviet sales at a price of $65 an ounce.)

But Kissinger was plainly more than a little interested in establishing a grain linkage to détente. The perennial efforts of the farm bloc and the USDA to sell more grain converged with his desire to engage the Russians on as many fronts as possible, to create linkages between economics and politics, and to give the Soviet leadership a long-term vested interest in continuing their "dialogue" and "relationship" with the United States.

Not that there is anything to suggest that either Kissinger or the President perceived grain as having a mysterious or mystical power in the new relationship. Kissinger knew little or nothing about the grain trade, and his knowledge of Soviet agricultural difficulties was superficial. The United States needed to sell grain, and the Russians wanted grain and U.S. technology, but these needs were overshadowed by the military and strategic issues then requiring the attention of the superpowers. Both nations had an enormous stake in slowing down the arms race and reducing the danger of nuclear war. This had the highest priority. The United States also had short-term reasons for pursuing détente. The Kremlin was the principal supplier of arms and economic aid to North Vietnam. It had influence in Hanoi, and its cooperation therefore was considered crucial in extricating the American ground force from South Vietnam. Given the Soviet Union's agricultural situation, the Kremlin's interest in grain must have been more intense than either Kissinger or Nixon realized.

From the point of view of the grain trade, the moment could not have been more opportune for these issues to be coming to a head in Washington. The trade's influence in the capital had never been greater. Palmby was at the USDA and beneath him were several officials who had worked for grain companies or related businesses. Then, in November 1971, at about the time of Cargill's and Continental's feed-grain sales to the Russians, Bill Pearce came to Washington. His work on the Williams Commission had been widely recognized and he was becoming well-known in the foreign-policy Establishment as an expert on trade. Now Nixon appointed him to a White House job as deputy special trade representative, with the rank of ambassador. The other deputy was none other than Harald Malmgren, whom Pearce had hired as TIB's consultant.

At about this time, Earl Lauer Butz also arrived in Washington, to take over from Clifford Hardin as secretary of agriculture.

Even before he was sworn in (Senate confirmation came by a close vote of 51 to 44), Butz made news. The occasion was an interview he gave to Nick Kotz of *The Washington Post* during which he remarked that farmers should "adapt or die." Crude as his choice of words was, Butz was simply stating the credo he had always followed: that American agriculture was changing and farmers must either adapt to the changes or get out of farming. Butz had grown up on a farm in Indiana but he had not become a farmer. Now he represented the conservative wing of U.S. agriculture.

In the years since Butz had left his farm, an average of 2000 farm families had been leaving the land a week, and agriculture had come to be dominated more and more by the most efficient of commercial farmers. They were still family men, but some of them now lived in town, in big ranch houses with barbecue pits, and commuted to their spreads. The cash flow of many farmers exceeded $1 million a year. The most successful of them read *The Wall Street Journal,* dabbled in the commodity markets, ran a seed business on the side, and hired consultants to provide them with financial advice.

This group of large commercial farmers was part of Butz's constituency, as was agricultural business—the economically powerful bloc of farm-chemical companies, implement dealers, hybrid-seed companies, millers, food processors, retail food chains, railroads, Midwest banks. Butz himself was a charter member of this crowd: He had been a member of the board of Ralston Purina, an international company that produced animal feeds, pet foods, and other processed commodities.

Butz's base was Purdue University in Lafayette, Indiana. Purdue produced good agricultural scientists and technicians, but it was a bastion of conservatism during the time in the late 1960s and early 1970s when Butz and a few other professors were in control there.°

Butz first came to Washington in the 1950s as an assistant secretary of agriculture under Ezra Taft Benson. His political philosophy had not undergone any fundamental changes since then. He believed that supply and demand should regulate markets and that the government should use a light hand. Farm price supports should be kept low to discourage farmers from produc-

---

° A government official who studied at Purdue in the late 1960s said that "Butz and a few of his cronies ran the university. They wanted to work with the top 10 per cent of commercial farmers. They weren't interested in things like rural poverty or small farmers."

ing more food than customers would buy, but at the same time
commercial exports should be promoted vigorously. Butz's heart
did not bleed for consumers either at home or abroad. He
wanted higher prices for U.S. farm products.

The developing diplomacy with the Soviet Union gave Butz
one of his first major assignments as secretary. He headed an
agricultural delegation to Moscow in April with instructions to
make an offer of credits. By this time, the first signs had emerged
that early Russian grain crops had not come through winter
well. G. Stanley Brown, the U.S. Embassy's agricultural attaché
in Moscow, cabled Washington about the "precarious" soil
moisture in Moldavia and southern Ukraine, a "dust haze" over
Rostov-on-the-Don, and water so low on the Don River—in
wheat country around the Black Sea—that piers had been extended into the channel to permit steamers to dock.

If the Russians were "hurting," however, they did not let on to
Butz and Palmby. They were, in fact, notably cool to the U.S.
offer of loans for buying food. The Americans offered a credit
line of up to $500 million in return for a binding Soviet commit-
ment to purchase a minimum of $750 million in grain over three
years. At the then prevailing prices, the American offer would
have involved minimum Soviet purchases on the order of 12
million tons of grain spread over three years. Deputy foreign
trade minister M. R. Kuzmin was interested in a long agreement—perhaps up to ten years—but he balked at the 6⅛ per
cent interest rates attached to the American credit terms; he had
in mind interest of 2 per cent—the P.L. 480 rate. Butz called his
attention to the fact that the Russians bought Canadian wheat
for cash and hardly qualified for "food aid." But the Americans
left their offer open and the Russians continued to sniff at the
bait. There was nothing secret about the offer. Butz talked about
it at a press conference. And although Palmby quit a few days
after returning to Washington and went to work for, of all companies, Continental, it was hardly likely that Palmby knew more

about what the Russians were up to than the New York grain company. But it certainly looked odd in the light of what later happened.

(Pearce, when he heard of this, made a last-ditch effort to keep Palmby on board for the government. Would Butz be willing to name Palmby to a new superposition of deputy secretary? Pearce asked the secretary of agriculture. Butz had no objection, and Pearce obtained approval from higher up. But it was still necessary for Butz actually to request Palmby to stay on with the new title. Whether Butz did so or not is not clear. In any event, Palmby went.)

At that point, any "grain deal" still seemed conjectural, much as Kissinger and Butz may have wanted one. Nixon had discussed grain with President Podgorny and Prime Minister Kosygin when he went to Moscow, but this had proved inconclusive. Differences still remained on the credit terms, the length of the Soviet commitment, and shipping arrangements. Then, on June 27, the U.S. government received an unmistakable signal of new developments. In the United States, crop estimates are released on the tenth of each month; in the Soviet Union, the estimates come out on the twenty-fifth. The figures on June 25 must have been alarming, for on June 26, the State Department received an urgent request to issue visas to Belousov and other Soviet grain and shipping specialists. Belousov and his men arrived in Washington on June 28 and checked into the Madison Hotel.

Kuzmin and other Soviet trade officials were already in the country when Belousov arrived. On June 29, several of them went over to the Department of Agriculture and said without advance warning that they were ready to accept the American credit offer and wanted to work out final details. Only Butz, USDA General Counsel Claude Coffman, and Assistant Secretary of Agriculture Carroll G. Brunthaver (Palmby's replacement) knew of this, and Butz told them to keep the information confidential.

It was clear to the companies right away that the Russians

were in a hurry. Belousov began calling grain merchants almost as soon as he checked into the Madison. Bunge, Cook, and some others were notified along with, predictably, Continental.

It also was obvious that unprecedented quantities of grain were going to be involved. Fribourg's brother-in-law Bernard Steinweg, just in from Paris (Fribourg was still in Europe), was asked to provide a price for *4 million tons of wheat and 3 million tons of corn.* With so much money at stake, the Continental officials hardly dared let the Russians out of their sight. The new vice-president, Clarence Palmby (then still in possession of a house in the Arlington suburbs), was called in to take the Russians sightseeing in Washington over the weekend, and Continental's customer relations man Ziv took them shopping and looked after them. The Russians allowed themselves to be taken under the wing of their friends from Continental.

To the Continental officials who nervously awaited the arrival of Fribourg from Europe, it was clear that everything depended on the government, just as it had in 1963. In this case, they had to know from the USDA whether the government would continue wheat export subsidies—the compensation for the difference between higher domestic and lower world prices—even as they sold the Russians vast quantities of U.S. grain.

At the time of the Russian approaches, the gateway price of U.S. wheat at major ports was an average $1.63 a bushel, the equivalent of $60 a ton. This was the world price—the price at which American grain could compete for foreign customers. When priced above that, American wheat lost out to Canada, France, Argentina or Australia—and perhaps even to small exporters such as Mexico and Sweden.

Inland, U.S. wheat did bring a higher price. U.S. farmers had the benefits of price supports, which guaranteed them a market—the government—even when prices abroad were lower, as they had been most of the time since 1949. But the government used the subsidies, or compensations, to maintain the competitive gateway price. The government paid the grain companies the compensations so they could buy costlier U.S. wheat inland and sell it for less on world markets. The grain houses registered for the compensations and collected the money as soon as they could show with documents that they had made a sale. These export compensations had been the underpinning of Orville Freeman's whole aggressive export drive.

Steinweg and the other merchants knew that as soon as their agents in the Midwest began buying grain to meet enormous Russian commitments, prices inland would go even higher. But as long as the government kept paying the subsidy, they had no problem—except for the government. As domestic wheat prices rose farther above $1.63 a bushel ($60 a ton) subsidies would increase. This was a crucial safety net. But if the government refused to continue the subsidies, the companies would be dangerously exposed. They would be committed to fixed-price sales to the Russians in a volatile world market of rising prices and with no government insurance policy to compensate them for the cost of acquiring grain that had suddenly become very expensive in heartland America.

On the Monday following the week when the Russians had arrived in Washington, Steinweg and a contingent of Continental officials showed up at the USDA to see Palmby's replacement, Carroll Brunthaver. Brunthaver was a Palmby protégé. He had headed the international trade committee of the National Grain and Feed Association, another grain trade group. Although he had been a Korean War jet pilot, he was a nervous type of man, and he was new to the job. Now he found himself in the middle of the most momentous events in postwar agricultural history.

Brunthaver's reaction to Steinweg and company was casual, to say the least. Steinweg testified later that he told Brunthaver that at that very moment the Russians were in New York City, looking to buy 4 million tons of milling wheat, 500,000 tons of durum, and some corn. It was not necessary to be a star grain trader to figure quickly that grain worth a quarter of a billion dollars was under discussion. But Brunthaver was in a hurry—late for a luncheon with Butz and the Pakistani ambassador—and he testified that he had not heard any specific amounts from Steinweg. The meeting ended without definite word on continuation of export subsidies. But that afternoon, with Steinweg back in New York, Brunthaver called him and assured him that the government would stand by the $60-a-ton gateway price for American wheat.

This removed the only remaining obstacle to the deal. The moment that Continental had been waiting for for eight long years had arrived. On July 4, Fribourg finally returned from Europe. He had been vacationing in Spain and looked splendid. He went straight to the Russians' $175-a-day suite at New York's Regency Hotel and completed what quite likely was the largest grain transaction in the history of the world. Again, the Russians' main interest was in animal feeds: They bought 4.5 million tons of yellow corn, 3.65 million tons of hard, western bread wheats, and another 350,000 tons of soft wheats.

There is reason to believe that the Russians had gone with Continental not merely out of habit but also because Fribourg was able to offer them a bargain on top of a bargain. Rumors had it that he had sold them the wheat at $1.10 a ton less than the $60 a ton export price*—a "slight counter margin," Fribourg called it. Continental probably figured it could recover the discount by speculating on the government wheat subsidy. This was permissible, and quite common in the grain business. Companies could book subsidies in advance of shipping their grain, or they could make their sales and book the subsidy later. In the latter case, they were speculating that U.S. wheat prices would rise farther above world prices, increasing the size of the federal subsidy needed to get U.S. wheat moving into offshore markets.

---

* That would have meant a price of $58.90 a ton loaded aboard ships in New Orleans. The Japanese, who bought later in the year after prices had advanced, paid an average of $81.90 a ton.

With Continental entering the U.S. wheat market for 4 million tons of wheat, it was hardly likely that U.S. prices would decline. Still, Fribourg showed his mettle and nerve in those hours. Big numbers did not scare him. And he had gained an enormous tactical advantage. He *knew* the Russians had bought at least 8.5 million tons of grain. This was intelligence that in itself was worth millions of dollars. He had what is called a "full book"— the equivalent in the grain trade's game to being a queen up in chess. There was an additional plum: Continental's ship-chartering subsidiary, Stellar Navigation Company, was booking the foreign-flag vessels required to move the grain to Russia.

The U.S. government took another six days before it announced, on July 10, that the Russians had accepted its credit terms and would buy $750 million in grain over three years. Neither Butz, Brunthaver, Nixon, nor Kissinger said that Belousov *already* had purchased that much grain, or close to it. If high officials knew that Belousov already had purchased that much, they didn't give a hint of it. On the day the White House issued its announcement, Cargill sold the Russians 1 million tons of wheat and Louis Dreyfus sold them 570,000 tons. The next day, July 11, Cook Industries of Memphis sold Belousov 600,000 tons of wheat. On July 20, the Russians went back to Fribourg, who by then had canceled further summer vacation plans. Fribourg sold them another million tons of wheat.

The final *tranche* from Continental seemed to have satisfied them, for the following day, July 21, Belousov and the Exportkhleb people departed for Moscow via Amsterdam to await the July 25 crop report and further instructions. They already had commitments for 11.85 million tons of grain—about one-third of what the United States normally sold abroad to *all* countries in a single year.

There was to be little rest for the Russian team, however, for on July 27 (two days after the Soviet crop reports showed further deterioration) there was another urgent request for visas. On

July 29, Belousov arrived back in the United States and began another frenetic round of buying. By August 9, he had purchased an additional 1.75 million tons of corn, 100,000 tons of barley and 100,000 tons of sorghum from Continental; 1.5 million tons of wheat from Louis Dreyfus; 300,000 tons of wheat and 1 million tons of soybeans from Cook; 1 million tons of wheat from Cargill; and 350,000 tons of wheat from Garnac.

It is conceivable that the U.S. government was surprised—even astonished—at the magnitude of the Soviet transactions, though any careful student of Russian agricultural and food policy could have foreseen that substantial increases in the country's grain imports were coming. Possibly no one, either in the grain trade or in the government, had *advance* knowledge of the size of Soviet purchases. One knowledgeable person told me that Continental itself was fooled—that Continental believed it alone was making the sales, at least in the initial stages, and that is the reason the company was so severely "squeezed" on the ship-chartering arrangements it had made through its Stellar subsidiary. (This informant said that Stellar was caught "short" on ships as shipping rates rapidly moved up due to active chartering by other companies that had sold grain to the Russians. Fribourg still refuses to discuss details of the ship-chartering arrangements Stellar made with the Russians.)

It is true that the companies themselves misled certain government agencies in this period. Under the law that existed at the time, companies using the grain futures markets were required to report their trading to the Commodity Exchange Authority at the USDA. They had to provide evidence that they were not exceeding certain limits on speculation established by Congress. (The limit on wheat speculation, for instance, was 2 million bushels.) When this reporting system functioned properly it could provide clues to developments in the grain markets. But in 1972, it did not function properly. The CEA subsequently charged that Continental "willfully" violated the regulations by submitting incorrect reports, and that there also had been misreporting that summer by Garnac (André's U.S. affiliate), Louis Dreyfus, and Bunge.

It is true as well that the Nixon administration was preoccupied with the forthcoming presidential election, with the developing Soviet-American détente, and with its first nervous responses to the bugging incident at the Watergate. Even so, it is inexplicable that the American public was not informed in detail of the size of the sales before that finally happened.

Steinweg swore that he mentioned Continental's initial sale of 4 million tons of wheat during a telephone conversation with Brunthaver on July 6, two days after the transaction in the Regency Hotel. Yet Brunthaver could not recall any such specifics. Neither could Earl Butz, who told Senator Jackson's Permanent Investigations Subcommittee that he was unaware of the dimensions of the Soviet purchases until September 19, when Palmby gave details of the sales at a hearing of a House agriculture subcommittee.

It is evident from two now-declassified CIA reports prepared in the summer of 1972 that the government *did* have details of the Soviet transactions with the companies.

One of these is dated *August 11*, and was issued by the CIA's directorate of intelligence. Stamped "confidential," it was sent with a buckslip to Brunthaver and to the USDA's general counsel, Claude Coffman:

In July and early August the Soviet Union negotiated further purchases of unprecedented quantities of grain from U.S. companies. These new contracts, taken together with additional orders for Canadian and French grain, place total purchases for fiscal year 1973 at more than 20 million tons.

Neither the public nor the U.S. farm community had this precise knowledge of the behind-the-scenes developments this early. The disclosure that came closest was issued on August 9, two days before the date on the CIA report. The USDA issued a statement "estimating" that the Soviet Union "will purchase" $1 billion worth of grain from private dealers. By then, of course, grain with a value at or near that already had been committed. In the absence of hard information from the government, the public and the press depended on unsubstantiated rumors. Beginning in mid-July a man identifying himself only as "John Smith" of *The Financial Times* of London began calling Reuters news agency and the trade publication *Southwestern Miller* (now *Milling and Baking News*) with remarkably detailed reports on the location of Belousov and his men and the size of their purchases. Inquiries revealed that there was no John Smith at *The Financial Times*—only a literary editor by the name of Smith who knew nothing about commodities. Did "John Smith" work for the CIA? The Chinese? A rival grain company? Any of them could have had a political or commercial interest in publicizing the Russians' activities.

On *August 31*, an even more detailed report, this one classified "secret," was delivered by buckslip to Brunthaver.

Total [Soviet] grain contracts with all countries for delivery during FY 1973 now total 24.2 million tons worth almost $1.5 billion, three times the quantity imported in FY 1972 and more than twice the amounts bought after the disastrous harvests of 1963 and 1965. A recent contract for one million tons of soybeans [this referred to a sale by Cook on August 4] to be used for livestock feed and vegetable oil, brings total purchases of grain and soybeans to about $1.6 billion. *These imports of grain will be largely from the United States—17.5 million tons*—with the remainder from Canada, France, Australia and Sweden. . . . Negotiations reportedly are continuing for additional contracts.

There is no great mystery about how the CIA had obtained this information. The companies gave it to them. Over the years the agency kept in close touch with the grain houses. Its own Washington-based "domestic collections branch" checked with merchants returning from trips abroad and even asked them to complete forms reporting on trade information. There was, in fact, a steady interchange between the agency and officials in *dozens* of multinational companies, whose information about all the most vital developments affecting the economies of countries often was far more accurate and complete than that of any government agencies. To the CIA, the multinationals were an informational gold mine.

But the information was valuable only insofar as it was used to serve the public interest. In the case of the 1972 grain sales, the CIA passed on the information to the proper authorities. It could hardly be blamed if the officials chose to ignore it or conceal it, for whatever purposes. The CIA reports prove that the government had accurate current information on the state of the transactions.

Palmby received much bad publicity about his switch to Continental in mid-negotiation, so to speak. It was to come out later that he had had discussions with Fribourg about the job with the company as early as that January. He had purchased an apartment in New York, using Fribourg as a reference, even before he went to Moscow in the official delegation to negotiate government credits to the Russians. However, the credit offer was common knowledge. Palmby's own inside knowledge could not have benefited Continental. An FBI investigation subsequently cleared him of any criminal conflict of interest. Traders who worked on the Continental first team in that period scoff at suggestions that he helped them. They view him, with some bemusement, as a politician.

As for Pearce, he also denies any detailed knowledge of what was going on between the companies and the Russians. Pearce says that he "did not go into government to suit Cargill's interests, and I wasn't involved in Cargill's business while I was in Washington." But he never completely lost touch with Cargill. In 1973, Pearce enlisted the help of his former understudy, Cargill's public affairs official Robbin Johnson, to draft material for part of President Nixon's message to Congress on the trade expansion bill—the administration's major legislation for liberalizing trade. Pearce visited Cargill a number of times while he was in office, including the summer of 1972. It was a jittery time at Cargill, what with Jackson's investigators on the trail of all the companies. In January 1974, Pearce left the White House job and, after mulling over other job offers, returned to Cargill.

Whether more timely disclosures of what had happened would have modified the Nixon administration's policies indeed is questionable. It would have forced the government to stop its subsidizing of wheat exports, and it would have given farmers advance warning of price increases. But the push was on to sell grain—and this had been the policy since 1948. Twenty-four years of single-minded policy could not have been turned around overnight. American grain had been cheap all those years, too cheap for the liking of the farm lobby, and another aspect of the government's policy—not all that different from the Arabs' on oil—had been to hold down production in order to get the price up to where it thought it belonged.

As it happened, the gravest miscalculations and a series of chance circumstances found the American government charging hell-bent into a new era of resource scarcity. In 1971 and 1972, the world experienced a series of agricultural catastrophes: severe drought in Africa; a rice crop failure in Korea and other parts of Asia; and a decline in the anchovy catch (which provides protein-rich meal for livestock feeding) off Peru. Nixon devalued the dollar in 1971, and this made U.S. grain more of a bargain to foreigners than it already had been. And then came the Russians.

Until 1972, the international grain trade had been growing, slowly and inconspicuously, but not alarmingly. Between 1950 and 1970, U.S. wheat exports increased from 10 to almost 20 million tons and corn exports from 2.5 to 12.5 million tons. Soybeans, scarcely a factor at all in the country's trade after the war, rivaled corn shipments. Then, between 1971 and 1975, the increase in the international trade nearly equaled the growth in the whole previous postwar period. Global trade in wheat, corn, rice, sorghum, barley, oats, and rye grew by 50 per cent (from 114 to 157 million tons), and America covered most of the increase.

The terms of trade also swung dramatically in favor of the U.S. economy. Most of the post-1972 exports were for cash. Cash customers, and trade, took precedence over aid. The volume of foreign food aid was cut back in 1973 and 1974 because of domestic shortages. In 1971, government programs financed $1.1 billion of the United States' total $7.6 billion in agricultural exports. Two years later, in 1973, only $863 million out of a cash-value total of $17.6 billion for all farm exports was financed by the federal government.

Once the deed was done, there was an eerie quiet. Moscow was experiencing a particularly dry, hot summer. The peat bogs outside the Soviet capital caught fire and as they burned out of control, smoke sometimes drifted over the Kremlin. In the Great Plains, the companies that had sold grain to Russia began purchasing crops—gingerly at first, then with abandon as rumors of the "grain robbery" circulated.

Suddenly, the United States was hemorrhaging grain. Monumental tie-ups and traffic jams occurred as thousands of freight trains full of grain converged on the Gulf Coast ports of New Orleans and Houston.

In mid-1972, the U.S. wheat stocks stood at a comfortable 23.5 million tons. A little over a year later they had dropped to just under 7 million tons. (Between mid-1972 and mid-1974, the world stocks of all grain declined by 40 million tons.)

The sea-change in the global food economy was only partially the doing of the Russians. Worldwide affluence had increased the demand for imported grain; so had dietary changes in dozens of countries; and so had the needs of rulers abroad for enough imported grain to pacify swollen urban populations. These developments had been taking place slowly, but when grain prices began to rise, customers panicked and many nations bid up the price. Since they arrived in the markets after the devious Russians, they paid more.

This was what the market-development zealots at USDA and the grain companies had wanted for more than a decade. Prices of all grains rapidly rose above the government support price, placing the markets firmly in the hands of the commercial grain trade. Now the American price—the price shouted out at the trading pits of the Chicago Board of Trade—was the price for the whole world. On the electronic board that records prices and price trends, a line across various commodities in various delivery months read like this: UP . . . UP . . . UP . . . UP . . . UP . . . UP . . . UP . . . UP . . . UP . . . UP. There was no longer any need to bolster American farm prices. The days of soggy world wheat markets were over. U.S. food commanded top dollar, and the customers included every nation in the world.

The policy had succeeded, all too well.

For quite some time, there was still some of the old agricultural *machismo* in evidence in parts of the government.* Butz

---

* The message that the situation had changed was slow in getting out to some regions of the USDA. Conditioned for twenty-four years to fighting the surplus, the department was slow to adjust. It kept pushing for more exports to Iran, South Korea, and other "developing" markets. In August 1972, as the big Russian sales became known, Canada delivered an *aide-mémoire* to the State Department in which P.L. 480 loans to Portugal for buying surplus U.S. corn were strongly protested. Canada claimed Portugal's economy did not warrant food aid and that the credits interfered with Canada's commercial sales there. Spanish corn growers in Galicia, Asturias, and Extremadura complained to their government that U.S. corn imports by Bunge, André, and other companies were putting them out of business. Two bushels out of three of corn were imported. Meanwhile, the USDA hailed the growth of the Korean cookie industry. The agency reported that the use of U.S. wheat for making biscuits had increased by 80,000 tons in a year. It noted with approval that U.S. companies planned to build bakeries in Korea to produce a "luxury line" of cookies.

bragged that the American farmer was the "man of the century." He talked of "getting the government out of agriculture," and took credit for the rising farm prices as he whistle-stopped in the Midwest, even though it was Kissinger, the scholar of Metternich's time, and Palmby who were the real architects of the grain deals of 1971 and 1972. But that was the good news. For American consumers, there was plenty of bad news.

The year 1972 had been a presidential election year, and President Nixon was determined to put a lid on inflation. He had attempted to do this with a wage and price freeze in the summer of 1971, clamping the seal on powerful inflationary pressures boiling in the economy until after his victory. Then he relaxed controls and let events take their course. Food prices immediately rose sharply. The consumer price index had gone up only 3.4 per cent before December 1972; beginning in February 1973, it began rising at two and three times that rate. The impression began to spread that President Nixon had lost control of the American economy.

The dollar, among other things, was under worse pressure abroad. In February, Nixon was forced into another devaluation, the second in fifteen months, and this action only increased inflationary fears. The following month, Nixon responded to housewives' demonstrations by putting a ceiling on red-meat prices, but by June, wholesale food prices still were up 19 per cent above January and on June 13 Nixon reimposed price controls. By this time, the U.S. and world economies were in the final throes of a gigantic boom, and demand for food and everything else was strong. This was the summer of shortages—including shortages of beef, which cattlemen and packing houses held back hoping for still higher prices later.

Cattle feedlots were among the first places to feel the squeeze from higher corn and soybean prices. The owners tried to cut their costs by paying local ranchers less for the 450- to 650-pound steers coming off grassy upland ranges. But many of the ranchers sold these young animals to slaughterhouses instead; so the large quantities of beef with a "grass-fed" label coming to supermarkets in the summer of 1974 really were a result of higher corn prices. There was a sudden (though temporary) shortage of the juicy, marbled corn-fed steak which had become part of the American way of life. Cheap steak was a luxury that depended on a cheap and abundant supply of corn.

The high corn prices affected the price of bacon even more swiftly. The rising cost of corn was like a death sentence for millions of hogs. Many Corn Belt farmers decided in late 1973 and 1974 to sell their grain at premium prices rather than feed it to their hogs. The hogs—a record 81 million of them—went to market. Included in this slaughter were large numbers of sows. For a while the price of frozen pork bellies (from which bacon is cut) declined as all that meat came to market. Later, however, when fewer sows produced fewer new litters, the nation's "hog factory" had been depleted, and by the end of 1975, retail bacon prices reached a record $2.16 a pound—50–75 cents above the 1971 level.

The increase in the price of corn reverberated farther. Wheat is almost as good an animal feed as corn, and many farmers fed it to their livestock and dairy cows. That made U.S. wheat costlier to millers and to customers overseas.

On June 27, 1973, the U.S. government intervened in the American grain trade for the first time since right after World War II. The administration, plainly panicked by soaring prices of U.S. soybeans, ordered a temporary embargo on the exportation of this commodity. It was remembering the basic truth: When grain is exported, less is left behind. Soybean prices, which had tripled in a year, began to slide slowly downward. Cost of Living Council director John Dunlop applauded the embargo for "putting the dinner table of the American consumer first." But the world was more a global village than Dunlop was admitting. The embargo struck a blow at Japan, which relied on soybeans as a staple of its food system. It was months before the Japanese got over the "soybean shock." The embargo was not fully removed until September.

In mid-July, Nixon again loosened the price freeze, with the result that prices of wholesale farm products (such as meat) jumped 20 per cent. By the end of 1973, consumer food prices had risen 20 per cent overall in one year and the total cost of living index was up 8.8 per cent—although only at the very end of the year was the impact of OPEC's oil price increase felt. The inflation was worse than anything the nation had endured during the Korean or Vietnam wars. But by that time, distraction was being added to economic mismanagement. The Senate Watergate Committee had learned that all the conversations in the Oval Office had been taped. Nixon was fighting for his presidency.

In June 1973, Senator Jackson called Palmby back to Washington to testify about his role in the 1972 grain sales and had a little fun with the man who had once wanted so badly to be secretary of agriculture. Jackson asked Palmby if the 1972 sales to Russia had affected the price of bread:

Palmby: It had an impact on the price of flour and to the extent that the flour price could be passed on to the baker—
Jackson: How do you make bread without flour?
Palmby: But at times flour has been under price controls.
Jackson: Did it have an impact on the price of meat?
Palmby: That along with other export movements, yes.
Jackson: Poultry?
Palmby: Of course.
Jackson: Eggs?
Palmby: Yes.

For the grain companies, this was an embarrassing moment to be earning unprecedented profits. For more than a quarter century, the companies had been yearning for more volume and more freedom of movement. Now they had both. As prices of both grain and oil rose, the postwar systems that had protected both the grain industry and the oil industry were dismantled. Import quotas against foreign oil were abandoned and the export subsidies for domestic wheat were likewise suspended (after expenditures of more than $4 billion since 1949).

This was what the grain companies had all been waiting for. In 1971–72, Cargill's earnings after taxes were $19.4 million. The next fiscal year they jumped to $150 million. Worldwide the company earned $886 million after taxes between 1970 and 1976. This was money that now was available for expansion and growth. Cook Industries, a newcomer in the big leagues of grain trading, did spectacularly well in its first business with the Russians. Its earnings for the year ending May 31, 1973, were $47 million. Two years later, Cook's earnings had tripled. Almost overnight, the grain business had become glamorous and lucrative. Young men just out of college lined up for jobs, and veteran traders were rewarded with large bonuses. Cook paid his top strategists and traders, Willard Sparks and Christopher Parrott, $500,000 and $400,000 respectively in 1976. The payroll records of Louis Dreyfus show that a 1973 bonus of $1.2 million went to Phillip McCaull, the company's top grain trader. Louis Dreyfus was generous to others as well. Two others got bonuses of $750,000 each. Serving "a great human need" had become a most rewarding activity.

7

"Big Grain"

"We're just a little old grain company in the woods."
—CARGILL OFFICIAL

By the time of the "grain robbery," it had been years since any of the merchant firms was a "little old grain company in the woods." "Big Grain" had grown and diversified into dozens of other activities, just as "Big Oil" had. This was in the nature of corporate growth. But it still remained part of the companies' code to stay invisible, to conceal their wealth and their power as much as possible. Cargill boasted in its brochures that "99 per cent of our customers have never heard of us." It was said at Continental that Fribourg would "rather lose a million dollars than get his name in the papers."

None of them was more mysterious than Bunge, the South American giant that had overtaken its Antwerp parent firm in size and influence early in the twentieth century. The late Alfredo Hirsch, the Mannheim-born Jew who came to Argentina and helped Jorge Born and his partner Ernesto Bunge make "the Octopus" into a modern conglomerate, abhorred publicity, hated propaganda, and resisted advertising. Bunge, according to one of the Borns, was "a private company about which nobody knew and nobody could speak." To Bunge officials, "public relations" meant keeping Bunge out of the limelight.

This policy of obscurity was evident from the fact that hardly any of the scores of Bunge companies carried the Bunge name. There was Grafa (textiles); Alba (paint); Aguilar (mining); CEA (canning); Sulfacid (chemicals); Molinos Rio de la Plata (milling); Sanbra (Brazilian cotton and oilseeds); and (in agriculture) Induco, Iris, Cifas, Cosufi, Saima, Comega, and other companies with interests in Argentine agribusiness and farming.

It was always an occasion when, in recent years, the modern rulers of the Bunge empire, president Jorge Born II and vice-president Mario Hirsch (Alfredo's son), made their infrequent public appearances. When Hirsch came to cattle shows to judge champion bulls, it was, as an acquaintance recalled, "like Pablo Casals approaching his cello," and all eyes were on the great man. Hirsch and Born were *caciques*—men of influence. They and members of their families owned *estancias* with tens of thousands of acres. But the public knew not too much more about them than that they ran the Octopus from "the House"— the company's pseudo-Florentine headquarters on the Avenida 25 de Mayo in downtown Buenos Aires.

Then, on the morning of September 19, 1974, a terrifying incident on a downtown street in Buenos Aires showed how hard it was becoming for the food companies to stay in the shadows, to conceal their riches and their power in the new epoch of well-publicized grain deals and unprecedented prosperity. A strike force of Montoneros—members of the Argentine youth movement who claimed to be the only true followers of the ideas of the late President Juan Perón—swooped down and kidnapped Jorge and Juan Born, forty and thirty-nine years old respectively, grandsons of the founding partner of the company and heirs apparent to its power and fortune.

Even in a country that is hardened to kidnappings, random assassinations, and police torture, the daring raid was unusually spectacular. It occurred in heavy morning rush-hour traffic, as the Born brothers were being driven to work in two cars, with bodyguards. Urban guerrillas had made the streets of Buenos Aires dangerous for corporation executives, and the Born family thought it had taken adequate precautions. But it had not reckoned with the elaborate tactics of the Montoneros.

As the cars with the kidnap victims moved down the Avenida Libertador, "policemen" and "telephone repairmen" waved the cars into a side street. The moment the cars had been diverted, these disguised Montoneros let traffic through again. Once the company cars had been decoyed out of the mainstream of traffic, the guerrillas struck ferociously. Two heavy station wagons rammed the Ford Falcons carrying the brothers and blocked the only exit from the side street into which they had been led. Gunfire was exchanged. As Juan Born sprang from his car, guerrillas tackled him and forced him into a getaway vehicle where Jorge already was held. Then the escape vehicle sped off, leaving behind a fatally wounded company driver and the Bunge executive Alberto Bosch.

After the kidnapping, Bunge withdrew behind an even more impenetrable wall of secrecy. Even the kidnappers' demands were kept secret. There were meetings between the Borns and the Hirsches, and the families met with government officials to discuss the situation and to devise a strategy. The families were part of Argentina's economic establishment—part of the economic class that was threatened by the revolutionary objectives of the Montoneros. To give the Montoneros money would be to finance an enemy.

In Paris, Bunge company representatives held meetings with representatives of the Montoneros. But the first solid clue that the families were engaged in serious bargaining came only in March 1975, a full six months after the kidnapping, when the guerrillas released Juan Born. Though unharmed, he was exhausted and near emotional collapse; he had been subjected to a long, secret trial on charges of being "an enemy of the Argentine working class." Soon he dropped out of sight and was reported to be resting in a clinic in France.

Then, on June 18, several Buenos Aires newspaper reporters received telephone calls from Montonero contacts inviting them to a clandestine press conference at which there would be an "important announcement." The reporters were picked up in automobiles at prearranged locations, blindfolded, and taken on a zigzagging ride to a house in the northern Buenos Aires suburb of La Lucila. When their blindfolds were removed they saw two men seated at a table underneath a large Montonero banner with its symbolic "P" cradled by a flower bud and a machine gun. One of them was Mario Firmenich, the dark-haired, collegiate-looking leader of the Montoneros. The other was a nonchalant-appearing Jorge Born, his delicate features set off by a trimmed black beard and mustache.*

It was instantly clear that the apparently composed Born was to be released—but as a stupendous price even for Bunge. Firmenich said that the company was to pay the Montoneros $60 million—a sum that he noted was equivalent to one-third of the annual Argentine defense budget at the prevailing dollar/peso black-market rate.† The $30-million-a-brother sum was the largest known ransom since President Kennedy had authorized payment to the Cuban government of $67 million in food and medicine to obtain the release of 1113 Bay of Pigs invaders. Bunge money was to finance the regime's intrepid adversaries for years to come. Jorge Born, it was later learned, had personally instructed his Montonero captors how these funds could be raised from various Bunge subsidiaries in Europe. (The transfer of the money to Montonero bagmen caused difficulties with foreign exchange officials in several countries.)

Bunge agreed to other terms as well: the distribution of an additional $1 million of free food to poor people living in Argentine shanty towns; the placement of busts of Juan and Eva Perón in all Bunge plants and installations, together with the inscrip-

---

* Jorge Born showed himself to be a man of *sang-froid*, then and later. After he was freed and a Bunge limousine had picked him up, Born worried aloud whether his servants would have prepared his home for his unexpected arrival.

† The $60 million ransom figure has never been disputed by the company.

tion "Violence in the Hands of the People is Justice"; the purchase of full-page advertisements in newspapers all over the world explaining the Montonero political ideology, including the Perónist slogan "Only the People Can Save the People."

All this already gave some rare clues to the wealth of the Bunge company, but a Montonero report on the secret trial and testimony of the brothers provided more details.

Predictably, it stressed the dark side of the company's activities in Argentina. Argentine presidents consulted Mario Hirsch before selecting cabinet ministers or establishing economic policies. Bunge money was funneled into Argentine politics. A former economics minister had advised Bunge how to evade a law that limited grain-warehousing monopolies inland. But alongside the recent disclosures in the United States about corporate bribery, company slush funds, and political activities of multinational companies abroad, those disclosures seemed almost tame.

What was most startling in the Montonero report was its documentation of Bunge's vast reach, of its extensive influence over the Argentine economy, and of its evident capacity to affect the direction of the country's development through investment decisions made by a handful of unknown corporate directors. The report gave the nickname "the Octopus" new shades of meaning.

Bunge companies produced 40 per cent of the nation's paint—a strategically important product—and were the largest suppliers of paint to local makers of American and Italian vehicles. Bunge subsidiaries made one-third of Argentina's tin cans and one-fifth of its textiles. It was integrated backward, forward, and sideways—into vegetable and fruit farming, cotton trading, and soybean and tomato processing. In addition to its more traditional activities, Bunge and its related companies had also formed partnerships and joint ventures with European drug and chemical companies such as Bayer and BASF to produce chemical products in Argentina. Some 20,000 workers were employed in Argentina alone in the company's industrial and processing plants. And Bunge also had interests in banking, timber, mining, and resort properties.

That a firm that once simply traded ivory, hides, grain, jute, and meat in the nineteenth century had become a major industrial conglomerate in the twentieth is more logical than it may seem at first. Especially since World War II, there were new opportunities for the trading houses to integrate and diversify, to become great industries in their own right. There were also a number of strong incentives for them to develop in this way.

Before World War II, grain processing meant mostly flour milling, but in the 1950s and 1960s a whole new system of modern agriculture grew up in the wealthier countries around processed feeds for the mass production of poultry, hogs, and beef. This spawned a new industry at the center of the grain economy: the processing, or "refining," of corn, milo, barley, and soybeans into feeds ready to serve to cattle in feedlots or to poultry in confined chicken "motels." This was a business ready-made for the big grain houses. Unlike the early wheat traders, who tended to act as agents for established flour millers, the modern grain houses could move unimpeded into a new line of business. This was true as well for the other food-processing industries that became essential to the food system after 1950. Alert grain companies saw their opportunity and took it. By the middle of the 1970s, Cargill was listed by the United Nations as the twentieth largest food-*processing* company in the world; it dominated the glamorous new soybean industry, leading the nation in the volume of soybeans processed into animal feeds and oils for margarine, mayonnaise, and cooking.

Cargill also held a dominant position in an industry that stands at the far edge of food-processing technology—"wet milling," which converts corn into starch, corn oil, sweeteners for soft drinks and bakers' mixes, and high-protein poultry feed. By the late 1970s about 6 per cent of U.S. corn production was going into ultramodern wet mills costing tens of millions of dollars, and Cargill predicted that it would have a milling capacity of 100,000 bushels a day by 1980.

There were several strong incentives for this diversification. It was one way to reduce the hazards of cycles in the grain markets. Margins were often thin in grain trading—so thin that Louis Dreyfus considered abandoning the grain business in the 1960s—and processing widened profit margins. As supplies tightened, many companies foresaw stricter regulation over the trading side of the business and therefore sought to diversify into industrial sectors less subject to controls. Finally, the grain traders complained that they did not benefit from the tax breaks lavished on the oil companies and other big industries. Cargill estimated that its effective tax rate on worldwide income in fiscal 1975 was a respectable 37.4 per cent—compared, the company said, with 10.3 per cent for Chase Manhattan Bank, 16.7 per cent for the Weyerhaeuser timber company, and 20.6 per cent for Westinghouse.*

All these factors encouraged the companies to spread the risks and to invest in related ventures such as shipping, banking, transportation, and agribusiness. Big Grain became somewhat less dependent on trading wheat, corn, and soybeans—just as Big Oil was becoming less than 100 per cent dependent on its revenues from petroleum.

The scope of Louis Dreyfus's interests, for example, and the breadth of its ambitions were evident in a July 23, 1976, letter from its president, Gerard Louis-Dreyfus, to his staff:

---

* Cargill did not come out so badly in comparison with some other companies, however. Exxon's worldwide tax rate was 73.4 per cent for 1975. This included royalties paid to foreign governments and reflected the repeal of the depletion allowance for oil and gas in 1975. Other major companies had effective worldwide tax rates of: 47.1 per cent (General Motors); 47.1 per cent (ITT); 44.1 per cent (Union Carbide).

Louis Dreyfus is today in a wide variety of businesses as diverse as restaurant operations in France, irrigation systems in the Middle East, hotel ownership in Brazil, glass manufacture and wood products fabrication in South America, and office building development in the United States and Canada. We have diversified and will continue to do so where opportunities are found which can be integrated into and supportive of our existing activities.

The president announced that it would be company policy to "enter into new areas of commodity trading as well as to broaden our base in the agribusiness world," and he wrote about "our rapid expansion, both within existing lines of business and in new areas of endeavour." This letter was a sign of the new, upbeat mood; other companies were already moving in a similar direction.

Continental still derived 85 per cent of its sales revenues from grain, but it, too, had been diversifying. Or rather, Fribourg had been. It is never easy to distinguish where Fribourg's financial interests end and those of Continental begin. The family and corporate interests are really inseparable, as was made clear in a cover story on Fribourg that appeared in *Business Week* in 1972:

There are at least 100 companies under the Fribourg corporate umbrella, and new ventures in many new markets are being added regularly. American housewives buy Fribourg's Oroweat bread, his Polo Food frozen dinners, and his Hilbun chickens, which are fattened with his Wayne feed. Pets eat Ful-O-Pep animal food. Industrial plants and private homes are located on Fribourg's vast real-estate holdings in such places as France, Morocco, Switzerland, Staten Island and Long Island. Some 50,000 head of cattle graze on Fribourg's Argentine *estancias*, covering 250,000 acres, and Argentine supermarkets are supplied by Agricom, his food distributorship. Latin American farmers plant hybrid seed bought from a Fribourg company. When they harvest the corn or wheat, they bring it to a Fribourg county elevator. There are modest Fribourg construction joint ventures in Europe and South America. In Spain, skiers schuss down mountains at two Fribourg resorts that are in early stages of development. And in California, carpenters hammer nails manufactured in a Fribourg plant.

Note how often the words "his" and "Fribourg's" appear. The article accurately depicts the personal nature of Continental's activities.

Actually, Fribourg had to be prodded constantly by his advisers and consultants to embark on expansion. And Continental still lags behind Bunge, Cargill, Louis Dreyfus and André in this regard, perhaps because Fribourg's first love is the grain trade. However, in 1965, one year after his coup in the Russian wheat sale, he did set Continental on a course of acquisition. That year, Continental obtained control of a processing company, Allied Mills, through a tender offer for its stock. And in 1970, Allied bought the agricultural products division of Quaker Oats. That brought Continental into the broiler, egg, and canned dog-food business and, most important, gave it soybean-processing facilities. Allied did not miss out on the harvest of profits after 1972. Between 1972 and 1973, its earnings leaped from $1.22 to $6.14 a share, and earnings quadrupled from $3.2 million to $16.6 million, mainly because of large profits in soybeans. As the profits rolled in, Continental built or expanded flour mills overseas; bought most of the remaining stock of Allied Mills for $10.4 million; invested in cattle feedlots in Texas; purchased a West Coast seed company; acquired a bakery; built a soybean-processing plant in Liverpool; entered the metal-trading business; and bought more barges and upstream elevators. Continental had the same policy about acquisitions as Cargill, its Minneapolis rival: They should all be financed from cash within the organization or by borrowing from banks. There could be no thought of raising capital by issuing stock to the public.

Impressive as all this was, it was not nearly so spectacular as the growth and expansion that was taking place at Cargill. Even though Cargill is the world's largest grain-trading company, only half its revenues come from this activity. Cargill is active in dozens of other commodities, including sugar, copra, flaxseed, salt, and lead. It is an agribusiness conglomerate in its own right—a very active salesman of seeds, breeding chickens, and fertilizers. And it is America's fourth-largest processor of soybeans. Cargill is also a farmer; it owns two cattle feedlots in the Southwest and an 820-acre research farm in Minnesota.

There was an audible gasp and a breathing-out in Minneapolis on the morning of December 21, 1973, when a Cargill advertisement in *The Wall Street Journal* reported that the company had net sales of $5.2 billion, net income of $107.8 million, and a net worth of $352.4 million for the previous fiscal year. The gasp was because Cargill had never before made public such information about its finances. The disclosure was required in connection with Cargill's bid to take over the stock of Missouri Portland Cement. (The bid was dropped after the Federal Trade Commission announced its intention to issue a complaint that Cargill's acquisition of 18 per cent of the shares may have been anticompetitive. Cargill, by this time, had fifteen full-time attorneys on its legal staff to work on this kind of problem.) The breathing-out was caused by the sheer size of the numbers and what they told about Cargill. The sales figures were big—bigger than those of all but a few American companies. This was not so surprising. In a trading business, total sales are less significant than profits. But the profits of $107.8 million on net worth of $352.4 million—about 33⅓ per cent—instantly made Cargill the envy of every corporate treasurer in the country.

The money that rolled in after those figures were disclosed made the company look even more impressive and left a healthy surplus available to be channeled into new investments. Between 1970 and 1978, Cargill bought two steel companies; Ralston Purina's nationwide turkey-processing and marketing facilities; Texas- and Kansas-based flour companies with their own lines of grain elevators; 137 grain elevators in Canada; a solid-waste disposal plant in Delaware; a Memphis cotton company; and a Nevada life insurance firm. It also entered the coal business;* built plants to produce high-fructose corn syrup (the soft-drink sweetener of the future); opened new grain-handling facilities in Duluth, Minnesota, and Baton Rouge, Louisiana; and expanded its soybean processing at home and abroad. The bill for all this was somewhere in excess of $300 million.

There is a relentless logic in the way the company has expanded. "Cargill grows like a tree," an official said. It was not a bad description. Most of its investments have some connection to agriculture, bulk commodities, trading, or transportation. These are the main branches of the Cargill tree.

In the 1950s, when Cargill's grain barges came back empty from trips to the Gulf Coast, Cargill began filling the barges with rock salt for the return trip up the Mississippi River; then it developed its own salt mine at Belle Isle, Louisiana, and later began producing evaporated salt in Kansas. Soon it was selling salt—for family dinner tables, cattle licks, meat packing, and highway de-icing—from twenty outlets in the United States. Cargill's specialty was commodities: so in 1972, Cargill purchased a metals company and sent its Cargill people to New York to begin their transactions in the futures exchanges. Cargill traders bought lead concentrate from Australian mines, shipped it to smelters in Mexico, and sold the product in the United States. Cargill had made steel barges since the 1930s: so in 1974 it bought the two small steel companies mentioned earlier, for the purpose of processing scrap into specialty steel. Cargill used a great deal of energy in processing and transportation: so in 1976, it announced its intention to buy a coal mine in Ohio.

In 1978 Cargill's acquisition spree took it into a section of the U.S. food economy that has a critical effect on every American's

---

* This was a throwback to the days of Will Cargill's coal business in La-Crosse, Wisconsin, but on a much larger scale. Cargill formed a partnership to lease coal reserves within fifty miles of Manchester, Kentucky. Cargill's main role is to be in marketing the coal.

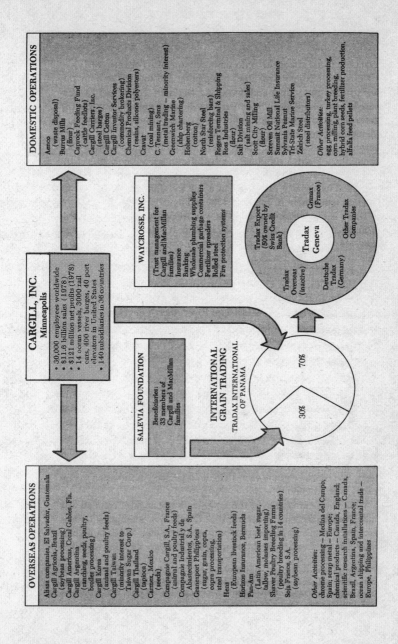

DOMESTIC OPERATIONS

Aemco
(waste disposal)
Burrus Mills
(flour)
Caprock Feeding Fund
(cattle feedlots)
Cargill Carriers, Inc.
(steel barges)
Cargill Cotton
Cargill Investor Services
(commodity brokering)
Chemical Products Division
(resins, silicone polyesters)
Cravat
(coal mining)
C. Tennant, Sons
(metal trading — minority interest)
Greenwich Marine
(ship chartering)
Hohenberg
(cotton)
North Star Steel
(reinforcing bars)
Rogers Terminal & Shipping
Ross Industries
(flour)
Salt Division
(salt mining and sales)
Scott City Milling
(flour)
Screven Oil Mill
Summit National Life Insurance
Sylvania Peanut
Tri-State Marine Service
Zelrich Steel
(steel distributors)

Other Activities:
egg processing, turkey processing,
corn milling, plant breeding,
hybrid corn seeds, fertilizer production,
alfalfa feed pellets

CARGILL, INC.
Minneapolis

- 30,000 employees worldwide
- $11.6 billion sales (1978)
- $121 million net profits (1978)
- 14 ocean vessels, 3000 rail cars, 400 river barges, 40 port elevators in United States
- 140 subsidiaries in 36 countries

WAYCROSSE, INC.

(Trust management for Cargill and MacMillan families)
Insurance
Banking
Wholesale plumbing supplies
Commercial garbage containers
Fertilizer spreaders
Rolled steel
Fire protection systems

SALEVIA FOUNDATION

Beneficiaries:
33 members of
Cargill and MacMillan
families

INTERNATIONAL GRAIN TRADING

TRADAX INTERNATIONAL OF PANAMA

30%   70%

Tradax Export
(50% owned by
Swiss Credit
Bank)

Tradax
Overseas
(inactive)

Deutsche
Tradax
(Germany)

**Tradax
Geneva**

Granax
(France)

Other Tradax
Companies

OVERSEAS OPERATIONS

Alisaa companies, El Salvador, Guatemala
Cargill Agrícola, Brazil
(soybean processing)
Cargill America, Coral Gables, Fla.
Cargill Argentina
(ranching, seeds, poultry,
broiler processing)
Cargill Korea
(animal and poultry feeds)
Cargill Taiwan
(minority interest to
Taiwan Sugar Corp.)
Cargill Thailand
(tapioca)
Carmex, Mexico
(seeds)
Compagnie Cargill, S.A., France
(animal and poultry feeds)
Compagnie Industriel y de
Abastecimientos, S.A., Spain
Graneport Philippines
(sugar, copra,
copra processing,
steel transportation)
Hens
(European livestock feeds)
Horizon Insurance, Bermuda
Pan-Am
(Latin American beef, sugar,
tallow, molasses importing)
Shaver Poultry Breeding Farms
(poultry breeding in 14 countries)
Soja France, S.A.
(soybean processing)

Other Activities:
chrome processing — Medina del Campo,
Spain; scrap metal — Europe;
chemical products — Canada, England;
scientific research installations — Canada,
Brazil, Argentina, Spain, France;
ocean shipping and intercoastal trade —
Europe, Philippines

food budget: meat packing. It paid $67 million in cash for MBPXL, of Wichita, the nation's second-largest beef processor and one equipped with the latest technology to serve America's ever-growing appetite for beef. In this system steers enter the slaughterhouse as live animals and exit in boxes containing chilled cuts ready for restaurants and supermarkets. Some of those cuts are made from the 175,000 cattle the company fattens at its Southwest feedlots each year. Americans were eating Cargill steaks, made from Cargill animals, fattened on Cargill corn grown from Cargill's hybrid seeds.

Cargill did not invariably make good corporate decisions, of course, though it sometimes seemed to its rivals that it did. In the late 1950s, the company had had the idea of building a soybean-processing plant in Norfolk, Virginia. This seemed like a wise move at the time, since Midwestern soybeans could be processed there and sold as meal to the expanding broiler industries of Georgia, the Carolinas, and Maryland's Eastern Shore; or the beans or meal could be exported if prices abroad were better. Railroad rates—always a crucial factor in the grain trade— intervened, however. The Southern Railroad began offering incentives to ship Midwest soybeans to mills in the South, putting the Norfolk plant at a competitive disadvantage.

All the while Cargill was, of course, expanding abroad, with much of the same logic and almost always following the same rule, staying close to what it was good at.

Cargill headquarters in Minneapolis is, in fact, the global command post for a multinational commonwealth of 140 affiliates or subsidiaries in 36 countries. Cargill's money may be made thousands of miles away; but the decisions are made in Minneapolis, or rather, in the woods outside it. In 1978, the company moved 900 employees into a tiered, tent-shaped office building with 350,000 square feet of space in Wayzata, fifteen miles outside Minneapolis and a seven-minute drive from Lake Minnetonka. Top executives continued to work in what is commonly called "the castle," a 63-room replica French château close to the new building. (Cargill purchased the mansion from the Rufus Rand family in 1944.) The location afforded unique privacy. It was not visible from McGinty Road, from which it was reached by a long, winding street through thick evergreens.

It seemed an odd place to locate the headquarters of a grain company. Inside were thirteen fireplaces and sixteen tiled bathrooms. Outside were lush lawns. Its most castlelike properties were the steep, gabled roofs. But the mansion was skillfully reordered according to the principles of Cargill efficiency. Soybean price quotations soon flickered over an electronic board in a former living room, and communications and telex machines were crammed into what looks like a butler's pantry. In another room, a map dotted with tiny flags pinpointed the weather all over the planet. There in the Minnesota woods, Cargill operates its own foreign office, gathering information, keeping in touch with its emissaries in dozens of countries, channeling money into many parts of the world, and assessing the impact of political, financial, and economic developments on Cargill's foreign relations. This is the seat of the "government of Cargill," which is like no government in the world.

In country after country, the Cargillian pattern of investment, carefully built around bulk commodities, agriculture, and transportation, is evident, and it parallels the company's expansion in the United States.

In the Philippines, for example, Cargill started small and just grew and grew. In 1947, Cargill had a dock in the coastal town of Iligan on the large southern island of Mindanao,* where it collected copra from the surrounding islands.

---

* The southern Philippines has since become a mecca for multinationals. U.S. companies own sugar and pineapple plantations. The Weyerhaeuser timber company has come and gone after cutting down thousands of tropical hardwoods on Minda-nao and Basilan; and Goodyear, Goodrich, and Firestone also operate plantations in Mindanao and other islands. But Cargill is still ranked as one of the foreign companies with the most extensive interests in the Philippines.

Copra—dried coconut that is processed into coconut oil for use in certain products such as margarine—was plentiful, and Cargill either bought the material at its dock or sent its own fleet of small coastal vessels around the islands collecting it. Business in Philippine agricultural exports picked up for Cargill in 1965 when the company went into the sugar business and began purchasing Philippine sugar and molasses in small lots direct from planters and brokers and selling to importers in the United States, Iran, Hungary and Japan. In 1970, Cargill stopped sending copra to San Francisco for processing, as it had been doing for twenty-three years, and began performing the function in a small plant in Iligan. This was a time when the government was pressing for "Philippinization," and for a larger Philippine share of the profits from the raw materials that foreign companies were taking from the country. But it was not bad business for Cargill. Costs of processing were lower in Iligan than in San Francisco, and at the time, the United States gave the Philippines a preferential duty on coconut oil, so the oil always competed effectively in the U.S. market with other vegetable oils. Cargill-owned or Cargill-leased vessels that were not used in the sugar or copra trade hauled steel from a small Philippine-owned steel plant in Iligan to Manila.

The advent of poultry industries in the Philippines and in such rice-eating countries as Taiwan and South Korea provided new opportunities for Cargill. The company not only sold more feed grain and soybeans for broiler chicks, but also became deeply involved in the agricultural economies of these countries. The new industries did not develop as small poultry farms but as modern, American-style operations utilizing imported laying hens, multimillion-dollar feed-compounding plants, and advanced egg- and broiler-processing technology.

Cargill did not invest directly in the Philippine broiler industry, but its interests there are considerable. The present climate, under President Ferdinand Marcos, is favorable to foreign investment, but local entrepreneurs still control the poultry-feed business—up to a point—as members of the Philippine Association of Feed Milling, Inc. Exact information about PAFMI's operations is not easy to come by, but reliable sources say that PAFMI companies own nearly half of all the broiler chickens in the Philippines and contract with local farmers to raise another quarter from eggs or chicks until they are full-grown birds ready for duty as laying hens or fat enough for slaughter. In other words, only a quarter of the broilers in the Philippines are bred, hatched, and raised by independent poultry farmers.

In this situation, Cargill operates through a PAFMI member, Universal Robina, a company owned by a local business family of ethnic Chinese origin, the Gos. Under a franchise arrangement, Cargill's majority-owned Canadian subsidiary, Shaver Poultry, supplies Universal Robina with laying hens or chicks from its hybrid lines ("Shaver Starcross 288," "Shaver Starbro," and so on). The Gos' company either multiplies the eggs of these chickens or contracts with local farmers to have this done. These hybrid lines are good for only one generation, for chickens grown from the eggs of the Shaver stock lose their distinctive qualities. So when one generation has been used, Universal Robina goes back to Shaver for more.

In what must be one of modern agriculture's more amazing lessons in global interdependency (or, less charitably, the global dependency on huge multinational companies), a Shaver computer in Galt, Ontario, regularly calculates the most economical feed ration for the chicks under the care of Universal Robina and its contract farmers, and it telexes this information to the Philippine company.*

---

* Poultry feed can be made from various nutrients, including rice hulls, tapioca, or citrus rinds, but the most important ingredients in modern feeds are soybean meal and corn. The figures suggest that somebody is getting very rich indeed off the U.S. corn sold to the Philippines. However, it may not be Cargill. American corn in recent years has been imported through a government monopoly, the National Grain Agency, headed by a close friend of President Ferdinand Marcos named Jesus Tanchanca. An American businessman

The Philippines is no isolated example of Cargillian growth. Elsewhere, where the political and economic climate has been clement, Cargill has followed the same pattern. Cargill Taiwan Corp., a subsidiary, supplies "less than 20 per cent" of Formosa's total compound feed requirements, but Cargill's business there is also impressive—and apparently secure. A government-owned public corporation, Taiwan Sugar, has a 40 per cent interest in Car-Tai. Car-Tai sells corn and other commodities to Taiwan Sugar, which distributes them or has them processed on the local economy.

In 1969, Cargill established a Korean company to produce poultry feeds from American corn and other ingredients. (Ralston Purina had been in Korea since 1967 doing similar things.) Cargill used the proceeds from the sale of the corn-based poultry feeds to pay for a feed mill, hatcheries, commercial chicken houses, broiler production, and egg and broiler processing. Koreans were trying at the time to develop their own domestic strain of broilers, but Cargill believed that "the Korean poultry farmer becomes a more efficient producer when he uses our strain." The government made difficulties. It clamped on foreign exchange restrictions and blocked importation of the breeder-chick parent stock of the Shaver subsidiary. But eventually, the difficulties were cleared up and Cargill got its way.

It is worth returning for a moment to Cargill's activities in copra and sugar in the Philippines because an important point about the evolution of the grain companies is involved. This is that lateral integration into commodities other than grain has been one of the most fruitful forms of company expansion.

---

who was in the Philippines in 1978 learned that imported corn sold on the local economy for $4.10 a bushel, compared with $2.30 a bushel in the United States, a difference of $72 a ton. When he asked Tanchanca why the Philippines didn't grow its own corn, Tanchanca replied with a laugh, "My friend, it is just too expensive to grow corn in the Philippines."

Dozens of companies trade in wheat and corn, although the trade on a world scale is dominated by the major houses. But there are many fewer companies in copra, and none of them has financial resources or facilities remotely comparable to Cargill's. And then it was natural for Cargill to branch into Philippine sugar, given its experience in that country. Worldwide, Cargill's share of the international sugar trade in fiscal 1974 was only 3 per cent. In that year, its sugar sales were $118 million and profits were only $3 million, a paltry sum for a company of Cargill's size. But in the Philippines, Cargill is much more dominant in the sugar trade than the global statistics suggest.

Cargill's entry into the tapioca trade a few years ago is a good example of the multinationals' economic Darwinism—of their capacity to grow right around the regulatory and tariff obstacles put in their path by government authorities. Cargill people themselves point to the tapioca brainstorm as an example of the company's commitment to free trade and efficiency.

Tapioca, made from the chopped, cooked roots of the cassava plant, is used not only in a pudding fed to young children, but also as an animal feed. The grain companies' interest in tapioca is that it is not subject to the duties of the European Common Market as, say, corn is. European farmers don't grow cassava and don't require stiff duties to protect them against imports.

When animal-feed producers in Europe figured out that they could substitute tapioca in their feed mixes for quantities of dutiable imported corn, demand for tapioca increased rapidly. Cargill, alert as ever, responded quickly. It set up a tapioca terminal at a special dock in Thailand and began loading tapioca "chips" onto vessels bound for Europe. Today the Europeans import about 4 million tons of tapioca annually in what is largely an unregulated trade, and Cargill is one of the major suppliers.

Louis Dreyfus had similar success recently when it went into the meat trade. In 1971, the company hired Jean Pinchon, who had been chief of staff and agricultural adviser in the French government of former premier Edgar Faure. Pinchon took charge of diversification, and Louis Dreyfus soon formed a partnership with Jean Doumeng, a French Communist entrepreneur whose political allegiances had always put him in a good position to participate in the growing food trade between France and Russia. Louis Dreyfus began buying meat in Argentina, Canada, and, of course, France, and selling it in other European countries. The attractions of the meat trade to an international merchant were evident. Most governments control their agricultural economies through price supports, stockpiles, production quotas, and tariffs on grain crops. But they let the prices of livestock fed on this grain move somewhat more freely. Provided the trade stays within the import quotas, the prices can fluctuate and margins can be wide. By 1975, Louis Dreyfus was trading 1 billion francs' worth of meat and livestock a year.

The companies, meanwhile, slid as easily into shipping as they did into agribusiness and exotic commodities.

To some degree, they all followed the precept of Leopold Louis-Dreyfus, which was to carry the grain yourself instead of paying somebody else to. French shipbuilding owes a considerable debt to the postwar activities of the Louis-Dreyfus family. As Pierre rebuilt the family fleet after the war, it troubled him that other governments were more generous to their shipping industries than the French government was. When, in 1958, Pierre's wartime commander-in-chief Charles de Gaulle came to power, he determined to try to persuade his old comrade in arms to do something about this. Here was France, aspiring to prestige and reasserting its independence, but without a first-rate shipbuilding industry.

Pierre finally had a chance to raise the issue with de Gaulle. "France can do without a shipping industry," he began acidly. "After all, Belgium does perfectly well without an automobile industry."

De Gaulle's face clouded over. "I think I get your point," he said.

Soon after that, massive French government subsidies began

to revive French shipyards, and the subsidies helped Pierre and his shipping partners speed up the growth of their tonnage. Louis Dreyfus now owns twenty ships ranging in size from a few thousand tons to 124,000 tons (and all bearing the name of some member of the Louis-Dreyfus family) and leases many others to carry cargoes as diverse as liquefied natural gas and grain. L-D's rivals are not far behind.

On any given day, vessels owned by Cargill or leased by its chartering subsidiary, Greenwich Marine, may be hauling Chilean wine to California, Brazilian beans to the Adriatic, or pig iron from Canadian ports to Houston. And André owns half of all the merchant tonnage under a Swiss flag, and has more on charter.

Michel Fribourg's shipping investments are among his most profitable. In 1969, the family took a 12.9 per cent interest in the Overseas Shipholding Group, a public company controlled by the Recanati family of Israeli banker-entrepreneurs. OSG owns and operates forty-six ocean-going bulk cargo vessels, flying both American and foreign flags. Fribourg's timing, right before the boom in Soviet-American grain trading, was superb. All but five of the company's American-flag vessels have participated in this trade. OSG's vessels have carried 20 per cent of the grain transported to Russia aboard U.S.-flag ships. American government maritime subsidies to OSG for its work in the Russian-American grain trade came to more than $10.5 million a year in 1973, 1974, and 1975. Continental sold the grain; ships in which Fribourg had an interest transported it, and the government paid a subsidy to boot.

If the grain business was a half-brother of the shipping business, it was also a close relative of banking and finance. In a sense, the companies were like giant banks. Enormous amounts of cash flowed through their treasuries. Warehouse receipts, which represented grain in company inventories, were accepted as negotiable financial instruments at most banks. Grain was excellent collateral, since bankers could keep tabs on its value at all times simply by checking the futures quotations in the daily newspapers. As a retired trader for Continental said, "I used to go to the bank and say, 'Can I have one hundred million dollars?' The answer was always yes." (Defaults are extremely unusual in the big-time grain business. A loan officer for one major New York bank confided to me that in thirty years of financing the grain trade, he had handled only one default, involving a barge-load of corn.) By the 1970s, the companies all had lines of credit in eight or nine figures at dozens of banks (Cargill's lead bank was Chase Manhattan). Cargill headquarters in Minneapolis operated as a bank for its worldwide organization and its subsidiaries. As of November 1977, Cargill had investments in and loans outstanding to subsidiaries and affiliates totaling more than $754 million. It was using at least forty-three banks, with an open line of credit for at least $300 million in *unsecured,* short-term borrowing.*

The decision of the Louis-Dreyfuses to enter the banking business in Paris after the war turned out to be one of the shrewdest that the family made. François, who was put in charge, proved to be a brilliant financier, and the timing was excellent. The Fifth Republic's devaluation of the franc and priority to a sound financial system—as well as European prosperity in general—

* In the booming commodity markets of the 1970s, the big grain houses all went into the commodity brokerage business. They set up their own brokerage subsidiaries and began taking orders from members of the general public who wanted to speculate in the commodity futures markets. Since the companies themselves are among the largest buyers and sellers of futures contracts, based on their own information and on their own requirements for grain, it seemed to some that this was conflict of interest. Customers of ContiCommodities (Continental's brokerage subsidiary) might be speculating against traders of the Continental Grain Company. But the government permitted this and the Commodity Futures Trading Commission, which regulates the exchanges, found nothing improper. One advantage to the companies was that banks counted money on deposit on behalf of brokerage clients as part of the balance of the grain companies. This, in turn, increased the credit available to the companies.

initiated a banner period for French banking. The Louis Dreyfus bank grew more rapidly than most and became the fifth-largest commercial bank in France.

At André, trading grain seemed almost secondary to the financial opportunities this trading provided. In classic Swiss style, the firm functioned as a sort of central bank for its associated companies all over the world. As the founder of André's American affiliate, Garnac, once said, "André helped us. Without their finances we couldn't have made it—and without us they had no connection here in the United States."

During postwar European reconstruction, and the subsequent economic development outside Europe, André had a talent for putting together intricate deals involving money and commodities. It created a subsidiary called Finco, which began working out schemes for trading with East European, African, and Asian countries that had many needs but few dollars with which to pay for them. Chase World Information Corporation's *Newsletter* describes Finco's specialty as "opening up trading opportunities usually denied to less adventurous traders through the use of unconventional methods." It was all done with paperwork, as the *Newsletter*'s further description showed. André's Frederic Schenk, a former banker, explained what was meant by "unconventional methods": "Arranging intricate and complex business deals with East European and developing countries involving compensation, barter, triangular contracts, switch financing and cooperation transactions. This might involve shipping Swedish precision tools to Rumania in return for a shipment of canned meat, which is then sold to an Indonesian importer against payment in convertible guilders in a Dutch bank."

Georges André, the boss of the old family company, says that Finco is one of his proudest achievements. Using the Swiss advantage, André has sold Indian mushrooms to France and Bangladeshi shrimp to the United States in exchange for consumer goods for which no dollars were otherwise available. In effect,

André runs a sort of mail order house for the world from the banks of the Lake of Geneva.

Fribourg has also dabbled in banking and finance, but with somewhat less success than his shipping investments. A decade ago, for example, Fribourg decided that big banks were taking over international finance, and he jettisoned two small ones he owned in Paris and Zurich, although he kept a 35 per cent interest in a Lausanne finance company, Société Continentale de Gestion Financier S/A (Fribgest). But Fribgest was in deep trouble by the end of 1970—one of the first of those seemingly unshakable Swiss financial institutions that turned out to be built on sand. It had made some bad real-estate deals in Greece, Portugal, Spain, and Italy, tried borrowing Eurodollars to make its mortgage payments, and fell behind. Its creditors shut off the loans, Fribgest voluntarily declared bankruptcy, and its creditors, including Fribourg, were $80 million in the hole. Worse still, the other major Fribgest stockholder, Banque de l'Indochine of Paris, blamed Continental for the failure. Several unpleasant exchanges between Continental and Banque de l'Indochine followed. Fribgest's creditors finally agreed to repayment over ten years.

8 Merchants of Grain

"The families are all basically paranoid.
Wouldn't you be?"
—FORMER CARGILL MAN

The kidnapping of the Born brothers was the worst shock that
any of the grain families had received since the war. It was one
of those sudden, unexpected turns of fortune of which the families all lived in partial expectation. The Borns and the Hirsches
had worked hard at being accepted in Argentina, yet many Argentines still thought of Bunge as a "foreign" company, so accustomed were they to big international firms coming from
somewhere else. Still, Mario had his status as a local cattle expert, and his sister Leonora was transcending the commercial
milieu to become a leading patron of art and music, principal
supporter of the Amigos de la Musica, and, until her death in
1974, a friend of young Argentine artists as well as established
ones from Europe and North America.

The families did their best to blend in. Alfredo Hirsch, father
of Mario and Leonora, was a believer in this. He had arrived in
the country at the end of the last century when Buenos Aires was
a haven for world Jewry. But Hirsch's children became Catho-
lics. Mario collected crucifixes and became an advocate of cultural and religious assimilation. One former Bunge official, a
Jew, tells the story of meeting Hirsch once in Paris and being

242

questioned about religion. "Have you become a Catholic?" Hirsch asked him severely. When told no, Hirsch noted pointedly, "This is a Catholic country."

Wanting to blend in, to keep a low profile, is a natural enough instinct in the grain business for the families have never felt beloved by the larger society. From the merchant-adventurer days on down to the present, they have been middlemen, suspected by their customers and their suppliers alike of shaving pennies on every bushel. Successful merchants quickly learned that it was unwise to go around sporting wealth very ostentatiously— all that did was confirm the worst notions about merchants as greedy profiteers.

So the kidnapping could not have been more disastrous. It embarrassed the Born family acutely with the army, the police, and the government that was fighting the Montoneros; it called attention to the families' wealth; and it forced the company into the limelight. Bunge performed acts of expiation—it financed a slick documentary extolling investment opportunities for foreigners in Argentina, and Mario Hirsch came to Washington to be present for the film's showing. But it would be years before Buenos Aires would be safe, if it ever would be. Mario Hirsch left hastily for Madrid, took a suburban house with a guard, and traveled incognito. The Borns moved over the border to Sao Paulo, Brazil.*

Traumatic as it was, however, the kidnapping was, in a sense, a tribute to their dynastic staying power. Outside consultants and professional managers have been brought in—the first breach in family absolutism. And the need for capital to finance continued growth even forces the families to think the unthink-

---

* In March 1978, almost three years after the release of the Borns, Edouard Bunge's grandson, Baron Charles Bracht, a Belgian millionaire with interests in wools and other international commodities and a minor shareholder in Bunge, was kidnapped. His body turned up later in a garbage dump near Antwerp. Police said money probably was the motive. The Montoneros denied involvement.

able—to consider issuing stock to the general public. Then, as the kidnapping showed, anonymity is no longer an option. It is becoming harder and harder to stay in the shadows. Yet, for all that, there they are, in the late 1970s, one of the most remarkable phenomenons in the whole business world: the Hirsches, Borns, Louis-Dreyfuses, Andrés, Fribourgs, Cargills, and Mac-Millans, all survivors and all still in control. Not that founding families have disappeared completely from modern corporations. But in no other major industry in the world are *all* the leading companies private, family-owned, family-operated concerns right down to the last few issues of voting stock.

Pierre Louis-Dreyfus, who in semi-retirement still keeps a watchful eye on the progress of the family company, frets that it cannot last. "It's completely crazy—we haven't got the money to satisfy our appetites," he exclaims as he sits in a small, unpretentious office in the company's new glass headquarters on the avenue de la Grande Armée. But even as Pierre worries that the companies have outgrown the family owners, his own son Gerard is proving him wrong. In 1975, at the age of forty-four, Gerard became the fourth-generation Louis-Dreyfus with the title "Le Président."

That Gerard was there, at just the right moment, to pick up the mantle of responsibility testifies to the apparent ability of the Louis-Dreyfuses indefinitely to produce male heirs with the brains and the qualities to keep the line going. Gerard was particularly well suited to taking the helm in the "American era" of the grain trade. Back in the 1930s, his father, Pierre, had fallen in love with the daughter of an American industrialist and married her. She returned to America with Gerard during the German occupation of France and later the couple divorced. Gerard grew up as an American, went through the usual American phases of long hair and motorcycles, attended Duke University, attended law school, and got a job with the prestigious New York firm of Dewey, Ballantine. But underneath it all, Gerard was a Louis-Dreyfus. When the call came to step up to com-

mand of the Louis Dreyfus subsidiary in New York,* Gerard rose
to the occasion. Like Louis-Dreyfus père, Gerard was less than
inspired by the grain business. Both father and son felt that grain
was "here today, gone tomorrow." Where the father was interested in ships, the son invested in real estate. But when the
grain business boomed in 1972, Gerard saw that it was time to
give more attention to grain, and three years later he became
president of the firm worldwide. And there is no shortage of family successors if he wearies of the globe-hopping that goes with
this job. His younger cousin Robert, son of Pierre's cousin Jean,
and a graduate of the Harvard Business School, is already being
groomed.

In 1960, the MacMillans and Cargills suddenly found themselves without a qualified heir to take charge of their Minneapolis firm. Chairman of the Board John MacMillan had just died
and his ailing brother Cargill MacMillan (the man with the
name like a corporate merger) had stepped down as president.
The families were caught between generations. The most promising candidate to take over was Cargill MacMillan's son Whitney—but he was only 31 and not yet ready for command. John's
son W. Duncan was a year younger. So there was only one alternative: an interregnum. The families turned to the old-line Cargill professionals. H. T. Morrison was named chairman, and
Erwin Kelm, a taciturn Minnesotan who had spent his whole life
with Cargill, became president. In 1968, Kelm moved over to
chairman and Fred Seed, another nonfamily professional, replaced him in the presidency.

Meanwhile, Whitney and Duncan were being looked over.
Duncan was a reserved, scholarly young man, a graduate of
Brown University (John Peterson's old alma mater) and, it was
sometimes said, "brighter than Whitney." But Whitney was not
stupid, and he had an easygoing way that helped him get along

* The Leval-Stern-Kayaloff trust referred to in Chapter 4 had long since
been dissolved and the company had reverted to Louis-Dreyfus family control.

with people. Whitney worked as a merchant, oilseeds trader, and pinch hitter at various company jobs—and learned the names of hundreds of Cargill employes. In 1975, at about the same time that Gerard was taking over the presidency of Louis Dreyfus, the Cargill board of directors elected Whitney Mac-Millan president. It was a great relief for the families.

Not that there ever had been any doubt about who really controlled Cargill. "The families were very grateful to Erv Kelm and Fred Seed for steering the companies—while they were getting ready. But if there's any question in somebody's mind about who runs Cargill, that somebody won't be at Cargill for long," a company official said. The issue of "who runs Cargill" was settled early in the century during the struggle for control between the Cargill and MacMillan clans after founder Will Cargill died in 1909. Since then, Cargill has been a two-family hybrid, like the corn varieties it sells all over the world. But the MacMillan side is clearly dominant now. A majority of the stock is owned by the six surviving children of the brothers John and Cargill MacMillan.* Now Whitney runs the company while cousin Duncan handles the family money. In the terms of power within the family, that may make Duncan nearly as important as his cousin.

One advantage of private ownership—and perhaps one reason for the success in the grain families' perpetuating control—is the comparative easiness of moving money around. There are no public stockholders, no requirements to file detailed financial reports with federal regulatory agencies. In the case of the Mac-Millans, the money is handled through an operating company, Waycrosse, a name that apparently refers to the old LaCrosse connection. In the early 1960s, the Cargill and MacMillan families established another entity, the Salevia Foundation, in Switzerland. Several years later, Salevia took a 30 per cent interest in Cargill's Panamanian subsidiary, Tradax/Panama. Some of the

---

* There are twenty-three MacMillan grandchildren.

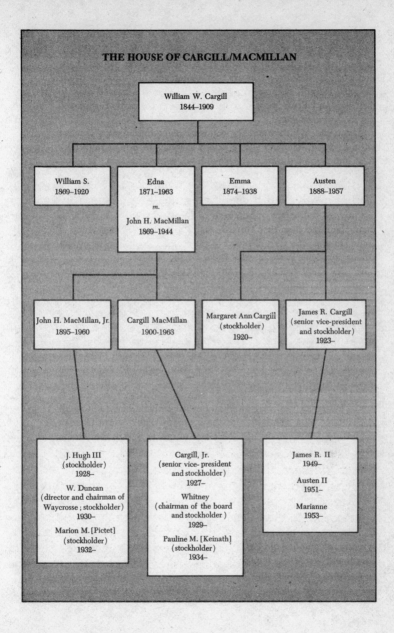

THE HOUSE OF CARGILL/MACMILLAN

William W. Cargill
1844–1909

William S.
1869–1920

Edna
1871–1963

m.

John H. MacMillan
1869–1944

Emma
1874–1938

Austen
1888–1957

John H. MacMillan, Jr.
1895–1960

Cargill MacMillan
1900-1963

Margaret Ann Cargill
(stockholder)
1920–

James R. Cargill
(senior vice-president
and stockholder)
1923–

J. Hugh III
(stockholder)
1928–

W. Duncan
(director and chairman of
Waycrosse ; stockholder)
1930–

Marion M. [Pictet]
(stockholder)
1932–

Cargill, Jr.
(senior vice- president
and stockholder)
1927–

Whitney
(chairman of the board
and stockholder)
1929–

Pauline M. [Keinath]
(stockholder)
1934–

James R. II
1949–

Austen II
1951–

Marianne
1953–

dividends accruing from Cargill's overseas operations were then channeled into the family foundation in Switzerland. There, they were sheltered from taxes until they were distributed to family members. In 1975, the beneficiaries of the Salevia Foundation were thirty-three members of the Cargill and MacMillan families. Another way of putting this is that some of the money Cargill makes from selling the grain of U.S. farmers abroad goes into a tax shelter in Switzerland that benefits less than three dozen people.

Just because they own the company does not mean that the MacMillans make all the decisions at Cargill. A finance committee determines where the company should put its money; major decisions are, of course, passed up to the board, where the Mac-Millans are represented by Whitney, Duncan, and Whitney's brother Cargill. But it is not the big things that the cousins usually disagree on—they can all agree that Cargill should go into the steel business (that it should spend $70 million building a new electric arc steel mill in Monroe, Michigan, for example)—but matters having to do with the family itself.

An article in *Town & Country* magazine in May 1976 lists the MacMillans as one of the seventy-four richest families in America—in the $400–$600 million bracket, along with such entrepreneurs as Stephen Bechtel, Sr., head of the international construction company. The MacMillans did not get rich throwing their money around. They are a Yale family (except for Duncan, who attended Brown), and they do give to the alma mater and, of course, to other causes. But they do not approve of ostentatious life-styles. One of the few luxuries permitted in the family is the Rolls-Royce belonging to Duncan's mother, Marion, who is still occupying a big house in the family compound. Sometimes the cousins fret that even this may be a luxury not quite suited to the frugal MacMillan image.

The MacMillans seem to bear out the general rule that merchants are not great mixers. They have long been considered standoffish by the gregarious, civic-minded citizens of Minneapolis. Most Minneapolitans don't know very much about Cargill or the families that run it. And they were surprised to read a few years ago that the "little old grain company in the woods" had annual sales equal to those of local companies Pillsbury and General Mills *combined*. Cargill people don't usually advertise their company's vast enterprises. While the Pillsburys, Heffelfingers, Crosbys, and Bells of Minneapolis flour milling were socializing and intermarrying, the MacMillans tended to keep to themselves. They were Scots in a community of transplanted Yankees and immigrant Germans and Scandinavians. The clans did not assimilate easily in the Midwest melting pot. The family has its headquarters in the woods of Wayzata, lives in its own compound near Lake Minnetonka, and is less active in boosting the community than the milling families. Whitney is more community-minded and outgoing than his forebears, but he and his cousin Duncan still concentrate their efforts on perpetuating the unity and prosperity of the family.

Their overall aloofness had as much to do with the structure of their business as with being Scottish. The Cargills did not have flour mills with the family name plastered all over them, making them a familiar institution in the community. They bought from farmers and sold to millers. Only recently did their company become industrial, with flour mills of its own and installations all over the world. But as it expanded into a national and then international company, its connection to the Minneapolis community became even more tenuous. The Pillsburys and the Heffelfingers of Peavey still are tied to the local resource—the wheat of the upper Midwest—just as the Weyerhauesers of Tacoma, Washington, stay close to their vast timber holdings in the state, and Texas oil men are rooted to their local natural gas and petroleum deposits. Not the MacMillans. They have gone global. There is no more reason for them to be in Minneapolis than for Kodak to be in Rochester.

Only rarely in the history of any of the grain families have individuals emerged as public-spirited, pillar-of-the-community types. In the 1930s, the Louis-Dreyfus family had been in the public limelight. Louis Louis-Dreyfus had been in politics and owned a newspaper. And what good had it done? It had made the family all too visible at a time when anti-Semitism was on the rise. Afterward, the family made it a rule to keep in the shadows. There had been a momentary shock in 1973, when Gerard's name showed up on President Nixon's "enemies list" because he had contributed money to Senator George McGovern's presidential campaign, and the White House in its wisdom targeted him for an audit by the Internal Revenue Service. But after the initial gasp of amazement, the Louis-Dreyfuses withdrew again into discreet privacy.

The *Town & Country* article listed Michel Fribourg in the same wealth bracket as the MacMillans. The man who probably knows more exact details of Fribourg's fortune than anyone else is his personal financial adviser, Sasha Maximov. (Reportedly the son of the last Russian tsarist ambassador in Constantinople, he is said to have been born in the Russian Embassy, but that may be just one more of the stories that make up the folklore of Continental.) It is softly acknowledged that Fribourg does his part for good causes. He is quietly active in French-American groups, and he contributes to foundations and scholarship funds. But you do not see his name popping up on the lists of prominent New York liberal Jewish philanthropists or activists. This is just not the Fribourg family way.

The Andrés are a little different. In a sense they *are* tied to a resource, if a whole country and its banking and tax laws may properly be considered a resource. The Andrés are fixtures of a sort—more settled than most of the wandering merchant families. But they, too, shun the spotlight. Conspicuous wealth is not for them. Georges André* spends a great deal of his free time in his chalet in Gstaad, which he reaches by a long, winding drive through the Alpine passes. The chalet is situated in a million-

---

* He has three sons, Henri, Pierre, and Eric, all ready and willing to take over.

aires' ghetto. Across the way is the home of the German publisher Axel Springer; down the street is the Palace Hotel, European winter headquarters of the international jet set. But André's own home is modest, a typical Swiss retreat with wood furniture and wood paneling. The only concession to luxury seems to be the large picture window, which looks out over the mountain passes that run down to the valleys far below. André dresses for the mountains in heavy woolen clothes, and the millionaire enjoys nothing more than driving off with his wife to eat a meal of brook trout and mountain mutton at a nearby village inn.

The Andrés are somewhat more aggressive about their community work than some of the other grain families. One reason is the family's deep involvement in missionary religion. The Andrés are members of the Plymouth Brethren, a strict sect of Calvinists that spreads its message to many parts of the world through missionary and charitable work. Jean, Georges André's brother, is the principal religious activist in the family. And so it is that religious faith, as well as grain trading, connects the multinationally minded Andrés to many parts of the world.

The tradition of strong family control in the grain business has always made good economic sense. A tremendous amount of money floats around in grain trading, and there is never enough time to put everything down on paper; so inevitably, those who operate these concerns want people they can trust—which has usually meant close family members with a vested interest or a share in the business. With outsiders, you never can tell. They might start using money to trade for their own account, or even make off with the funds. People with strong, extended families—Greeks, Jews, Scots, Yankees (and members of religious sects, such as the Andrés)—are naturally suited to the organizational requirements of the grain business.

In the earliest days of the grain trade, nepotism, far from being frowned upon, was considered smart business. Power struggles, such as they were, took place only within families—between rival cousins (such as the children of Cargill McMillan and John MacMillan, Jr.) or uncles and nephews, and even between fathers and sons.

At Continental after World War II, Vice-President Julius Mayer had several relatives working with him.* When Michel Fribourg married for the second time, following the death of his first wife, he brought in his new brother-in-law, Bernard Steinweg, and he became head of the grain department, a key position.

When outsiders have to be brought in because of a shortage of relatives, the grain companies go to the sons of well-known grain men, if at all possible. The notion of recruiting a company officer through an executive search service was unheard of until recently. For those who came in to the grain business by the old nepotistic route, promotion was assured; the system was as hidebound and traditional as that of any private club. When the playwright and actor John Houseman was apprenticed to a London grain company in the 1920s, family connections helped land the job: After the death of his father, who had been a well-known grain trader in Romania, old friends and associates took him and his mother under their wing and helped him to get a start. It was understood by everybody, including the clerks who had labored at the firm for years, that Houseman would move up the ladder quickly. Sure enough, after nine months, he was promoted to the wheat room—and to "a world of wealth and power that they could never hope to achieve."†

The kind of relationship the families (except perhaps for the MacMillans) like to have with their nonfamily employees was expressed by a Louis Dreyfus man: "I give Louis Dreyfus everything because Louis Dreyfus has given everything to me!" And

---

* Mayer later resigned from Continental and started his own brokerage company in Chicago—with his son-in-law as partner. Brother-in-law Harold Vogel went on to become vice-president of Continental.

† John Houseman, *Run-Through* (New York, 1972).

the companies are still laced through with the names of families whose members have worked for them for generations.

But these archaic traditions, which were believed to assure loyalty, make the grain business a profession for gentlemen, and screen out scoundrels and opportunists, can be sustained in the contemporary world only at a cost. When Born and Hirsch in Buenos Aires finally decided to bring in management consultants, the chosen British firm of Urwick Orr and Partners was appalled at Bunge y Born's centralized management structure. The two men did everything, under a carefully worked-out division of authority, and they personally screened candidates for each new vacant executive post. Not surprisingly, Urwick Orr recommended a drastic decentralization, and much of its advice was heeded. But inevitably, decentralization created new power centers. Walter Klein, president of the North American subsidiary, was given broad authority and slowly became one of the most powerful men in the entire worldwide company. "They don't go to the bathroom in Europe without Walter's knowing about it," said a New Yorker familiar with the internal politics of the company. Today, Klein's position has become virtually unassailable, a fact that annoys some of the company's younger traders.

Continental has had even more trouble than Bunge in overcoming the tendencies toward centrist family rule. Michel Fribourg makes all the major decisions. Managers who join the company expecting to move up, even to aspire to the presidency, are in for a shock. Fribourg's difficulty in sharing power has made Continental something of a "revolving door." He knows he has a weakness for meddling too much, for not trusting his top people (as the MacMillans trust theirs), and for being too idiosyncratic and unpredictable (if often brilliant). So a few years ago, he hired the consultants Booz, Allen to turn the company upside down and make recommendations on how it could be managed better. The Booz, Allen people did just that, and in the course of their survey even interviewed Fribourg himself (who stonewalled on most of their questions). Fribourg took some of the advice but for the most part went right on running the company himself.

Fribourg's way of showing an employee that he is less than pleased with a job is to roll up his shirtsleeves and start doing it himself for a few days. Fribourg's basic anxiety about surrendering too much authority to the managers has been evident in his frequent preference for putting two people in charge of one task. "Creative tension" has kept people from being too secure. In the 1960s, for example, supervision of Continental's American grain operations was divided between two executive vice-presidents, Loren Johnson for west of the Mississippi River and Harold Vogel for east of the river. (One year, trading wheat brilliantly, Johnson made millions for Continental. He quit in 1968, still on good terms with Fribourg but weary of the long hours and company politics.) "If you could make a quarter of a cent a bushel for *your* office's account and screw the Continental guy in Kansas City, more power to you," one old company man remembers. The system got results, but it made for haphazard growth and development.

In 1975, Fribourg moved the company headquarters from its old, cluttered office at 2 Broadway (former address of the Produce Exchange) to the spacious top three floors of a fifty-story office building in New York's midtown, at 277 Park Avenue. Fribourg was much closer to his own East Side home. But the new offices were structured as a sort of tiered metaphor for Continental's hierarchy of power. The traders were homesick. Fribourg and only a handful of close associates occupy the very top floor, a silent, isolated glass-wrapped tower, while the real activity of Continental takes place on the two floors below. The office layout tells Continental people what they already know: MF is above them. It was and is his company to do what he pleases with, another glittering possession in his personal fortune. And, as the saying goes, the "closer you get to the top, the closer you get to the guillotine."

The grain families can perhaps be pardoned for some of their reluctance to delegate authority. There have been enough unhappy experiences to make them suspicious. In the 1930s, for example, money was draining away from Continental's operation in Buenos Aires. The staff was bloated and living beyond their means. Schilthuis came down from New York, fired the chauffeurs, got rid of the limousines, and to pay some of the debts, sold Continental's grain elevator to Bunge. Things got back to normal. It was not until many years later that the loyalty question arose again in Continental, this time with far more serious consequences.

The conflict involved two strong-willed men: One was Michel Fribourg; the other was Marc Najar, an Egyptian who many say was the shrewdest speculator and trader in the whole history of the grain business.

Najar was born in Egypt, the son of a well-to-do businessman, and went to school in Switzerland until his father lost his money in a real-estate venture in Cairo and Marc had to quit school and go to work. He took a job in the Far East working for his uncle Leon Hakim, who was one of the first of Continental's many Egyptians. More and more of them came to work there during the 1930s, and Najar had no trouble joining the Continental organization in Asia under Hakim. Najar was said to have first shown his prowess as a speculator trading rubber in Saigon. Prices were as bouncy as the commodity itself, what with rumors of Japanese war plans that threatened the rubber plantations, and with the rapidly changing fortunes of American and European automobile manufacturers on which rubber's fate depended. (One story has it that Najar plunged in and lost—but recouped his losses and tripled his investment by the time all this became known back in Paris.)

Najar's movements after the Japanese takeover of Southeast Asia are unclear. The popular version is that he escaped from Singapore in a small boat just ahead of the Japanese. In any event, he did not surface again until near the end of the war, when he turned up in Buenos Aires with a new assignment from Continental to put the company on the map.

Najar was in luck. With the coming to power of President Juan Perón in 1946, Bunge and Louis Dreyfus had lost some of their advantages. Perón nationalized the grain trade, and grain began to be marketed through the governmental Institute for Promotion of Trade (IAPI). The profits from agricultural exports went into industrialization—and into the pockets of Perón's top bagmen, several of whom were putting away fortunes abroad. This was the way things were done, and all the commodity merchants in Buenos Aires played along with it one way or another. It was *de rigueur* to give favors to Perón's officials. (An American merchant recalls a shopping spree in New York City with Najar. At Tiffany, the Egyptian purchased a magnificent platinum cigarette case for about $20,000. "Mr. Perón's birthday present," said Najar matter-of-factly.)

Perón's agents in IAPI could release Argentine grain to any company they chose to, and for favored traders, the opportunities were considerable. The need for grain in Europe steadily pushed up prices in world markets from 1946 to 1948. It was a seller's market for Argentine grain, and merchants who obtained some of it usually needed to wait only a few weeks before selling it at higher prices. The black market also helped. Najar would take options from IAPI to sell thousands of tons of barley overseas. If the world prices advanced, as they usually did, Najar would exercise his option and sell the barley; if not, he would pay a 1 per cent penalty for canceling his option and use cheap, black-market pesos to pay the fine.*

Najar was a man of great charm and extravagant self-confidence. He spoke half a dozen languages and was the complete

---

* This account of how the merchants operated in Buenos Aires under Perón was related to me by the late Victor Romano, a relative and business associate of Najar's.

internationalist. In business, Najar was simply dazzling. He could compute figures in his head instantly. "Marc was always about two steps ahead of the rest of us," an American trader recalls of him. (To women he was ever attentive. Wives of business associates found perfume at their places when they came with their husbands to dine with Najar at the Jardin Luxembourg.)

It was clear to the people running Continental in New York City that they had an asset in the person of Marc Najar. The problem was that as Najar's successes multiplied, so did his appetite for bigger challenges. Najar had created two companies in Buenos Aires to serve the interests of Continental there: Continental de Granos and Contimar. Najar did not need much capital for these trading operations. Since the Argentine government had nationalized the grain trade, grain could be obtained from the authorities at dockside; it was not necessary to have extensive inland facilities.

As the years went by, Najar and his relatives discussed where they would go from there. (Najar, following the tradition of the grain trade, had by this time brought in his own Egyptian relatives to assist in South America.) In May 1951, he made a trip to New York City to see Fribourg, then still relatively young and inexperienced.

Whatever happened, Najar's connections with Continental ended then and there. In what manner and on whose terms was unclear then and has been ever since. Though Continental retained Continental de Granos, Najar took Contimar with him, and word spread through the company offices that Marc had "made off with South America."

The exit of the Egyptian caused a schism in the Continental ranks. Fribourg made clear that it was a question of loyalty: Fribourg or Najar. Even the Egyptians were split, and many of them stayed on with Fribourg.* Najar's departure intensified the

* Among the Egyptians who are still with Continental are Leon Hakim's son Victor Hakim in Mexico; the rice traders Raphael Totah and Salvador Amram; and Isaac (Zack) Pinto, in charge of shipping in Geneva.

paranoia that is pervasive in grain companies even in the best of times. Several senior officials came under suspicion of secretly continuing to communicate with Najar, even of tipping him off about Continental's tactical moves.

In the grain trade, outsiders watched to see what would happen next. The most immediate repercussion seemed to be that the incident steeled Fribourg's determination to master the company. From then on, it seemed to his associates, he was determined to run Continental himself and to rely much less on others.

As for Najar, he was where he wanted to be—independent and working on his own. Najar's exploits became part of the folklore of the grain trade, and he proved that he didn't need the Continental name behind him to perform acts of trading derring-do. He based himself in Paris, where he and his partners (most of them still Egyptian relatives) put together complex deals involving commodities and goods in three or four countries. These, called "switch deals" or "barter," helped countries that lacked foreign currency to finance imports. A Buenos Aires textile manufacturing company might need thread available only abroad but might not be able to obtain foreign currency to pay for it. Argentine banks could give importers "clearing units"—bookkeeping credits that enabled the holders to purchase goods up to a certain value—in, say, Switzerland. Swiss companies had the same arrangements with Argentina in reverse. In these bilateral barter arrangements, no currency changed hands; balance-of-trade accounts were kept on paper. The trouble was that Switzerland did not manufacture or sell cotton thread for export. The material was available only in Italy. This was where Najar the merchant would come in. Najar would get credit from a Paris bank to buy the required cotton thread in Italy for, say, $600,000. He would ship the material to Argentina and accept Argentine "clearing units" as payment. In such a transaction, Najar might get as much as $1 million in the paper units. The premium was because the paper was not negotiable. But it *could* be used to buy Argentine grain. When resold abroad, the grain purchased with the "clearing units" might bring $800,000—a profit of $200,000, or 33⅓ per cent on the initial outlay of borrowed money.

Najar liked gambling with "short" positions—selling commodities before he owned them. This got him and his associates briefly into trouble with the Argentine authorities. Najar had been in the habit of making short barley sales to Europe without owning grain, on the expectation that he could obtain Argentine, African, or North American barley at a cheaper price when it came time to deliver it. In 1953, some rival merchants in Buenos Aires began complaining that Najar was depressing the price of Argentine barley in world markets with his heavy short selling—in which he offered barley at below prevailing world prices. Najar was dining at Maxim's in Paris one evening when he received word of trouble in Argentina. The next day, Najar's brother-in-law, Jean-Pierre Lang-Willar, boarded a plane to Buenos Aires to see what was going on.

Subsequent events were positively surrealistic. Lang-Willar arrived in Buenos Aires on a plane carrying a load of film stars, after a journey during which much champagne had been consumed. No sooner had the bleary-eyed Lang-Willar stepped off the airplane than he was arrested and taken to a magistrate, where he was informed of charges against Contimar of "sabotaging the economy of Argentina." Lang-Willar was convinced that the basis of the charges was denunciations by competitors, though Continental apparently was not one of the accusers. The questionable barley contracts were sent for while Lang-Willar, recovering from the trip, was kept in relaxed custody at the Ministry of Justice. The contracts that arrived ten days later exonerated the company. The company sales documents did not specify that Argentine barley would be delivered against the commitments. Lang-Willar was released. It had been quite a lark, and it made a good story back at Maxim's.

Najar and his lieutenants were also engaged in other daring

schemes. They worked intricate arbitrages in cocoa, using discrepancies between cocoa futures in London and spot cocoa prices in Amsterdam to run up enormous profits. Najar was never far from his telephone at this time, even when he was vacationing in Spain. He would pick up the phone, contact the office in Paris, order his aides to sell 60,000 tons of salad oil, then hang up and go back to the beach.

Najar also became involved in the U.S. P.L. 480 program, which among other things financed exports of tens of millions of dollars of U.S. foodstuffs by Najar's American firm, Interoceanic Commodities. Najar even sent an Egyptian cousin to Washington to keep in touch with the embassies that were handling the P.L. 480 transactions. One year in the 1950s, Najar's company bought up most of the U.S. government's surplus linseed oil at bargain prices. Soon after that, the world market strengthened unexpectedly and Najar made a quick killing.

When Najar became interested in shipping he was at first characteristically successful. He fancied himself to be an instant expert, since he had made some profitable deals in which he had chartered tonnage on grain ships before the closure of the Suez Canal by British bombing in 1956. The shutting of the canal doubled the distance from Asia and the Middle East to Europe, kept ships at sea longer, reduced the tonnage available in ports, and ran up freight rates. Najar subleased the ships under his charter at higher rates and made huge profits. He formed his own shipping company, Grainfleet Steamship Company, with two Egyptian cousins for partners, and built several vessels. Was Marc Najar developing a grain company to rival that of his old employer, Michel Fribourg? It looked that way.

Not for long, though. As Najar pyramided his assets, ordered more ships, and chartered more tonnage, his relatives reminded him of his father—"a rich man who lost everything." Najar brushed aside the advice. But when the Suez Canal reopened, shipping rates tumbled and Najar was caught holding vast amounts of tonnage at prices way above world market rates. He had to settle with the owners of the ships he had chartered—and it cost him much, though not all, of his considerable fortune.

After that, Najar scaled down his operations. He sold Interoceanic Commodities in New York to an old friend, the American soybean and agribusiness magnate Dwayne Andreas, and began spending more time with his family at the magnificent estate he had purchased near Versailles. He took up gardening with a passion and learned to fly.

But the old speculative fever still afflicted him. In 1959, Najar's former associates in New York received calls from Paris. Where was Marc? Then came reports from New York bankers that Najar had been sighted in Buenos Aires, where he was rumored to be attempting an enormous wheat speculation. When Najar did indeed surface in the Argentine capital a few days later, he was all smiles. He had contracted to buy hundreds of thousands of tons of Argentine wheat—at prices quoted in current Argentine pesos. Several days later, the pesos had been devalued by 50 per cent, and wheat prices in pesos were increased accordingly. But Najar already had his deal at the old peso price, and he realized a windfall. Had old friends in the know in the Argentine government tipped him off? No one would ever know.

Najar returned to Paris and went back to gardening and flying. On a pleasant summer day in July 1960, he took his wife, Claudine, and two of their children to the airport at Toussus le Nobel and set out for England in his private plane. Soon after takeoff, the plane crashed near Mantes, killing all the passengers. The life of the last of the big-time speculators was over.

As for Fribourg, he could never forget Marc's defection in 1951. Twenty-five years later, when I interviewed him in New York, mention of Marc's name caused Fribourg to stiffen. "Overnight we found ourselves without any organization in Argentina," he said. "We had to start from scratch—there was nothing there whatsoever." Fribourg could not resist a dig at his old employee. "In two or three years we had again become the major exporter of Argentine grain. The service that Najar rendered to me was that I learned how he was doing business in Argentina. It was not compatible with my way of doing business."

Najar's defection from Continental stands as a vivid example of one of the hazards the families face. His action was a sign that the old days, when the grain-firm owners could expect undying loyalty, were on their way out.

The rise of Edward W. Cook posed a slightly different but equally worrisome problem. Cook was an intruder, an outsider who challenged the established companies on their terms.

Ned Cook also had a family line, but it was a short one by the genealogical norm of the grain business. Ned's father, Everett Cook, was a self-made man who had started as a five-dollar-a-week office boy in Memphis before World War I, gathered his modest savings, and decided to become a cotton merchant. He made his first excursion through the South in 1916, talking to farmers, offering them a swig from his bourbon bottle, and cutting samples from their bales. After he had been buying cotton for several days, he telephoned Memphis. Germany had begun its submarine warfare against North American shipping, cotton was down six cents a pound (cotton exports to Europe were seen as being in peril), and Everett Cook had lost everything he started out with.

Cook made the best of the situation. He joined the Army Air Force, won the Distinguished Service Cross for his exploits commanding a squadron in France, and rubbed shoulders with people like Eddie Rickenbacker before returning home to make a fresh start in cotton. This time, his luck was as good as it had been flying reconnaissance missions behind German lines, and his Memphis cotton business flourished and grew between the wars.

When World War II began and Everett Cook was called to Washington, he relished the opportunity for new challenges and adventures. He went to Peru, Argentina, Paraguay, Brazil, and Nicaragua to arrange for the United States to buy cotton for its wartime needs. And after that it was Arctic whaling expeditions, which Cook organized to bring back sperm oil for the Commodity Credit Corporation. His last wartime assignment was with General Carl Spaatz, commander of U.S. Air Forces in Europe. Meanwhile, at home, his Memphis cotton business, Cook and Company, kept growing. He toured Russia after the war and sold the Soviet trading organization Amtorg $7 million worth of cotton.

Ned Cook, Everett's gangly six-foot-three son, worshipped his father and longed to follow in his footsteps. Ned joined the Army Air Force in World War II, became a B-52 bomber pilot, was graduated from Yale in three years, and, naturally, went to work for his father in Memphis. By then, the family's original poverty had long since been obliterated. The Cooks were in the swirl of Memphis social life, and Ned Cook cut a fine figure playing polo. The Cooks had connections to money, to society, to government; they were doing well.

By the late 1950s, however, the American cotton business was suffering from the competition of synthetic fibers and foreign-grown cotton, and Ned Cook looked around for commodities with a better future. He found one in his own backyard: More and more cotton farms already were making the switch to soybeans, and it was logical for the cotton merchants to follow; Cook predicted that the region that once had supplied cotton fiber would soon be a source of vegetable protein for the whole world.

When Ned told his father that he wanted to go into the grain business, the older man was not enthusiastic. "Stick to things you know about," he told him. But in 1961, with the son nearly forty and the father in failing health, Ned Cook took the plunge.

His first deal turned out to be more difficult than he had expected. He experienced the power of "the club" of established insiders. Cook's man in Tokyo had sold 12,000 tons of soybeans and Cook thought he would have no trouble acquiring the beans and chartering a vessel to carry this cargo. Instead, it took days.

Established ship brokers did not want to help a newcomer for fear of offending the bigger companies. He finally found a young broker who was a neophyte like himself and got a vessel. But he ended up losing $14,000 and learned a lesson in the difficulties of long-distance grain trading.

Cook's temperament was not that of the typical merchant. Grain men tend to be wary, reserved poker players. Cook was folksy, easygoing, and very talkative. And his company men developed the same manner. Cook men looked different from the businesslike Cargill people, the suave Europeans at Continental, or the obscure Germans, Dutchmen, and Argentines who ran Bunge. Cook men wore loud clothes and open-necked shirts, drank bourbon, and went to barbecues. Unlike other merchants, they seemed to be having a good time. And Ned, with his big nose, twinkling blue eyes, and southern charm and informality, fit the mold. "You could put Ned in bib overalls and a straw hat and he'd be a barefoot sharecropper," said a close friend. That was how southern Ned Cook was.

Still, Cook was determined to press on with his new interest. He was one of the first to hurry to the Chateau Laurier in 1963, when Exportkhleb's Matveev was holding court; he wanted "in" on any American grain-selling consortium. When the consortium idea collapsed, he was the wiser for having rubbed shoulders with the big-time merchants in Ottawa.

Ned Cook took his biggest risk in 1967, sinking much of the family money into a $12-million grain elevator at Reserve, Louisiana, thirty miles upstream from New Orleans. Cook had decided that the time when a merchant could fly by the seat of his pants in the style of Marc Najar was past. He wanted his own facilities at the ports so he could accumulate grain from inland until vessels arrived. His judgment was good, but he paid a high price for acquiring the Mississippi River elevator: It forced him to go public. Cook was a $10-million company with a $12-million grain elevator, and the business badly needed capital and liquidity. After a series of complex transactions, he merged

his company with E. L. Bruce, a Memphis hardwood-floor–
manufacturing company with a net worth three times that of
Cook's firm and with publicly traded stock. Cook Industries, the
company formed from the merger, took over Bruce's listing on
the American Stock Exchange. It became the first big grain company with public stockholders. Cook and his sister retained 39
per cent of the stock, but Cook was now no different from Exxon
or Sears, Roebuck. Nosy public stockholders and government
agencies could pry into Cook's finances and business affairs.

For all the disadvantages of going public, Cook moved into
the grain business at exactly the right moment, and he soon hit
the jackpot with the Russians. To the Russian traders, Ned Cook
was invaluable, an outsider who was hungry for business and
would shave his bids accordingly and who, like Michel Fribourg,
was clearly the boss of his own company.

And Cook got along with the Russians. Cook was to tell a congressional committee after 1972 that a "good nose" was the best
attribute in the grain business. This drew laughter, for Cook
happened to have a very large nose, but there was a serious
point involved. Cook had proved that he had the attribute of a
grain merchant—the ability to sniff out customers and clients
who were serious in their intentions to buy or sell grain. As soon
as he learned that a Russian buying mission was in the United
States in July 1972, he jumped aboard his Lockheed Jetstar and
flew to New York City. Late the same afternoon he sold the
Russians 300,000 tons of hard winter wheat. To celebrate, he
brought out a bottle of his personal bourbon, Cook's Cotton
Special, 107 proof. The Russians liked it: Cook had broken into
the Russian market. A few weeks later, Cook lured them to
Memphis and sold them more grain. He gave them a boat ride
on the Mississippi River, entertained them at a cookout, and
played Perry Como records for them.

Cook's biggest coup that summer involved soybeans, not
wheat. One morning, Cook joined the Russians for breakfast at
Manhattan's Links Club, just off Park Avenue on East Sixty-

second Street. When the Russians sat down, Nikolai Belousov asked, "Is this room bugged?" At Belousov's request, they changed tables. Then Belousov leaned forward and whispered: "We want to buy soybeans." They did—1 million tons of them. Cook bought the beans immediately, before his big rivals caught on. No sooner was that done than the market began to move up, from $4.50 to a high of $13.00 a bushel. Cook kept buying cheap and selling at a higher price all the way up. That deal alone probably earned Cook $10 million. The company's pretax earnings rose from $4 million in 1972 to $40 million in 1973.

Cook's rising star was a challenge to the established order in the grain trade. He was the first new company to come on the scene for many years. The trend was toward fewer and larger companies, though there still were smaller firms that were successful dealing in particular commodities or limited areas of the world. Cook operated on a global scale. He hired professional traders and opened offices in Japan, South America, Europe. This was tough new competition for the others. Not only that, Cook always was a hard bidder who wanted volume and was willing to reduce his bids to the minimum to grab customers, which enabled him to take business away from Cargill and Continental. Importers certainly gave Cook's men a chance to underbid offers from the larger rivals, and Cook's men sometimes availed themselves of the opportunity. And Cook's low bids were useful to importers (such as the Russians). Cook may have forced Cargill and Continental to reduce their offers.

Cook annoyed the bigger companies for another reason. He was giving away secrets of the grain business—including the size of profits. It was the law. Cook disclosed this information in reports he was required to make to the SEC.

Ned did not care. He felt it "was the most exciting time to be in business in years." His bravado came through in blunt talk. "So, I lose money—tough! That's my right. What's wrong with that?" Or: "I see nothing wrong with taking risks; the worst thing that's happening is the overriding obsession with a riskless society. Safety! Security! To hell with all that! That's a hell of a way to run a country!"

It was, indeed, an exciting time in the grain business, and in October 1974 Cook unexpectedly learned just how true that was. Cook had been selling corn and wheat to the Russians. He had had discussions about this with Secretary of Agriculture Earl Butz, who conveyed a warning from the new Ford administration that supplies were tight and the government would look with disfavor on sales of more than 1 million tons of either of the commodities. Cook advised the USDA that he had sold the Russians slightly more than 2.2 million tons of corn. When the USDA did not react, he assumed he had the go-ahead.

On the night of October 4, however, Cook received a call from an angry secretary of the treasury, William Simon, telling him coldly to be in Washington the next day and advising him that the sale was being suspended. (Actually, the U.S. government did not have authority to suspend sales in such an informal manner. But if necessary, the administration could have promulgated more formal export controls. The power was there, and Cook knew it.) Cook and other grain trade representatives showed up in Washington the next day.* President Ford himself came and sternly advised the traders of the adverse consequences of such large, unexpected selling to the Soviet Union.

Butz was again the apparent culprit. As in 1972, he had been casual or vague about advising the companies precisely what the limits were. Now, to atone for his sins, he was sent out to tell the news to the press. The sales were suspended, but Butz said he hoped that the grain could eventually be shipped when the supply and price situation became clearer in the weeks ahead.

Cook was very exposed. He already had acquired most of the grain he would be delivering to the Russians, or had acquired futures contracts that would enable him to get it when he

---

* Continental's Bernard Steinweg was one of them; he had to explain his company's sale of 1.2 million tons of wheat to the Russians.

needed it. With the news of Washington's intervention, the grain markets collapsed. Cook now was holding all that grain—and now his contracts with the Russians to buy it were in question and prices were falling. If he had to sell out his grain holdings at the new, lower prices, Cook estimated, he would lose $25 million.

Cook was taken off the hook several weeks later. Simon, in Moscow to attempt to keep Soviet-American economic détente alive, reinstated the contracts.

But it had been a close call, a sobering experience with the realities of the business into which he had plunged with so much enthusiasm. When Senator Henry Jackson called Cook before his Senate Permanent Investigations Subcommittee in 1974, Jackson asked the Memphis merchant what would happen if the market continued to fall and the administration continued to suspend the sales. "I guess I will be out of a job, Senator," Cook responded.

It had been a difficult year. Cook had divorced and married again. His adored father had died, and Ned was now alone to fend for himself in a business that had been the preserve of the older merchants for a century and more. Ned Cook was a newcomer, an intruder, and some thought success had come too quickly for his own good. Everett Cook, after all, had told Ned to stay out of the grain business. And most people who had known Everett Cook in Memphis thought he was a wise man.

9

Catch-22

"It's illegal in Brazil—but this isn't Brazil!"
—GENEVA GRAIN BROKER

"The secret of success in the grain business is to sell
cheaper than you buy and still make money."
—GEORGES ANDRÉ

In Joseph Heller's *Catch-22*, Milo Minderbinder keeps the Air
Force messes supplied with fresh eggs. Milo buys the eggs in
Malta for 7 cents, sells them to the mess halls for 5—and still
makes a profit. Everybody has a share, and it isn't as hard as it
sounds. Milo first buys the eggs in Sicily for only a penny "at the
hen." He transfers them secretly to Malta, sells them for 4½
cents, buys them back for 7, and resells them to the Air Force for
5. When his friend Yossarian expresses puzzlement, he explains,
"I'm the people I buy them from."

Heller must have known something about commodity trading
when he drew this portrait of a war entrepreneur, because modern grain companies operate in a very similar fashion. Milo
functions in several different countries simultaneously; he makes
money on outlandish price fluctuations; and only *he* knows what
is going on since he is simultaneously buyer *and* seller. He is a
one-man international trading company—different from Cargill,
Louis Dreyfus, and Continental only in the scale of his activities.

Good information and mobility are what make Milo's dazzling operations profitable. And those also are the prerequisites for managing the global grain companies.

To their formidable physical assets the companies have added the intangible ones of speed, mobility, instant communications across time zones, and superior information. These are the qualities that make the multinational grain companies at one and the same time indispensable to almost every government in the world and yet rogue elephants in the global economy. The companies are efficient—more efficient than any nationally rooted government or company ever could be. They have a monopoly on privileged information about grain supplies and grain prices in dozens of countries, and so are crucially important to buyers and sellers alike. This is a service that certainly does have economic importance. The admirers of multinational companies, of which there are many, say that without such companies to straddle the world, cut corners, and take risks, farmers would get less for their grain and food would be costlier. But these same qualities also keep the companies a step ahead of governments, enabling them to transcend the taxation, the foreign-exchange regulations, and the controls that hamper smaller, national companies.

Tradax, Cargill's overseas subsidiary in Geneva, is a perfect expression of global capability, mobility—and anonymity. It keeps a low profile, Swiss-fashion. Tradax is housed inconspicuously in a six-story apartment building overlooking a small park in an outlying Geneva canton with which Cargill negotiated a "mutually satisfactory" arrangement way back in 1956. Behind this unimposing facade is the operations center from which Cargill covers the world. From here, Tradax men hurry off to Peking, Moscow, or Tehran to sell grain that other Tradax men have been acquiring in Australia, Argentina, or the United States. Tradax men spend weeks every year on airplanes. Its roster of merchants gives the company a cosmopolitan flavor typical of multinational companies these days. I last saw Tradax's senior vice-president for operations, Leonard Alderson, over a luncheon of brook trout washed down with Moselle wine at the Gentil Homme Restaurant, a few yards from the Lake of Geneva. He was just back from South America and a brief vacation in Marrakech, and a few months before that he had been in China. Alderson, as it happens, is an Englishman—one of those brisk, good-humored Englishmen in the tradition of the merchants who traveled everywhere and knew everything in the heyday of the Empire. Alderson thinks of settling down permanently in Switzerland someday. Tradax's Seattle-born chairman, Walter Gage, already has. He married a Swiss woman, took up the Alpine ice sport of curling, and became a Swiss citizen. Tradax's star salesman, Milan (Mike) Sladek, also switched nationalities, but in the opposite direction. Slovak-born, he became a naturalized Canadian.

Tradax buys and merchandises a little less than half the American grain that Cargill sells abroad each year. This makes it one of the world's largest grain companies in its own right. The Soviet Union usually buys American grain through Tradax, not Cargill, and Tradax also buys Russian grain when the Russians have grain to sell. Several years ago it bought 100,000 tons of Soviet barley, sold some to Hungary, and sold the rest to Italy; it has even handled the sale of Hungarian wheat to Russia. In 1976, Cargill told the Senate Subcommittee on Multinational Corporations that such transactions, in which it arranged trades between East European countries, were "not at all extraordinary."

Tradax was aided by advantageous connections to the Swiss financial community. When Tradax first arrived in Geneva, it was helped by Gustave Barbey, an attorney, who later became a director of the Tradax group. His brother, Raymond, was a partner in Lombard, Odier, one of the oldest of the Swiss banking houses. Their nephew, Thierry Barbey, another Lombard, Odier partner, later joined the Tradax board. The ties between Minneapolis and Geneva were further cemented when John H. Mac-

Millan, Jr.'s daughter Marion married Pierre Pictet, a member of the prestigious Pictet banking family.

Tradax is positioned to take advantage of a myriad of variables affecting the price of grain traded inside the Common Market—minute shifts in the exchange rates of marks, francs, and pounds, for example. As Alderson explained, Tradax has a world view: "In order to operate successfully in the Common Market you've got to be a world trader. If you're just domestic, you don't have the same tools as Tradax. The things that influence the market may not be known to a domestic company."

Most of the other big companies have found Switzerland as attractive as Cargill does. Socef and Zurfin in Zurich perform similar, if less important, functions for Louis Dreyfus and Bunge, respectively. (Socef was involved in some of Louis Dreyfus's first trades in the early 1960s with the Chinese Communist government.) Indeed, it may be said that Switzerland is the center of the world trade in "offshore," i.e., non-American, grain. When a small corn merchant from Kenya has some grain to merchandise, he gets on a plane to Geneva and talks to the people at Tradax or some other grain firm. And the officials of Exportkhleb talk on the telephone or send telex messages to Geneva almost every day. (When I inquired of a grain trader in Switzerland about his connections to the Russians, he grabbed a telephone and exclaimed, "Ask Viktor Pershin himself! I'll put you through to him at Exportkhleb—NOW!" He started to dial, then stopped suddenly. "Six p.m. Moscow time—Viktor's gone home.")

Not only grain men have found Switzerland an attractive place to do business, of course. Shipping companies, oil men, diamond traders (and smugglers of international art treasures), all have been attracted there. But how could it be that a grain company from heartland America would find such happiness in the faraway mountain country of Switzerland? When asked, grain company officials shuffle a bit, mention the bracing climate, the mountains, the lakes, the fact that a lot of Swiss speak English, the good airline connections, the pleasant restaurants, the history of economic and political stability and finally, when pressed still further, add almost as an afterthought, the "freedom from exchange controls and the limited corporate taxes."

Once Cargill had its Panama and Geneva subsidiaries in place, it could play as freely as other multinationals. When Cargill sells a cargo of corn to a Dutch animal-feed manufacturer, the grain is shipped down the Mississippi River, put aboard a vessel at Baton Rouge, and sent to Rotterdam. On paper, however, as tracked by the Internal Revenue Service, its route is more elaborate. Cargill will first sell the corn to Tradax International in Panama, which will "hire" Tradax/Geneva as its agent; Tradax/Geneva then might arrange the sale to a Dutch miller through *its* subsidiary, Tradax/Holland; any profits would be booked to Tradax/Panama, a tax-haven company, and Tradax/Geneva would earn only a "management fee" for brokering the deal between Tradax/Panama and Tradax/Holland. As Milo Minderbinder said, everybody is happy because everybody has a share—and Tradax *is* the people Tradax bought from.

Not surprisingly, the figures that Cargill chooses to make public about its taxes do not make the company look like a tax dodger. The company's effective worldwide tax rate of 37.1 per cent in the years 1970–76 resulted in payment of $423.9 million in U.S. federal and state taxes. Republican Senator Charles Percy of Illinois noted that there was nothing especially astonishing about the fact that Cargill also used offshore affiliates for tax reasons. As he pointed out, "scores and scores of companies" do. Percy, in fact, commended the men from Minneapolis: "As I have looked at your figures they do great testimony to the efficiency and the effectiveness of your company and also the good feeling that you have that you pay a good share of your taxes in supporting your government."

But, as material supplied later by Cargill showed, Tradax and its related companies were not doing so badly at the hands of U.S. tax collectors. Another Tradax company, Tradax Export, was established solely to sell American grain abroad. In 1974–75,

Tradax Export's sales were over $2 billion, but it paid only $3.3 million in U.S. taxes. Tradax Overseas (which became inactive in 1974) had sales of $896 million in 1973–74 and deferred *all* its taxes that year. The main Panama company, Tradax International, deferred U.S. taxes at the rate of 97.6 per cent in 1973, 71.8 per cent in 1974, and 86.1 per cent in 1975.

In the mid-1970s Cargill quietly demonstrated how a multinational company can make Switzerland work for it. In 1976 Congress tightened the tax code to make it more difficult for American companies to shelter income earned overseas, but it left a loophole. The tightened requirements applied only to subsidiaries in which the parent company owned more than 50 per cent interest. Cargill responded by setting up a new company to replace Tradax Export and Tradax Overseas and selling a half interest to Swiss Credit Bank—thereby removing the company from U.S. tax jurisdiction. Gustave and Thierry Barbey were asked to resign as directors. The tax lawyers felt that, given the Barbeys' long ties to the old Tradax company, the IRS might feel Cargill was not really forfeiting control, as required by the law. Whether Cargill did in fact relinquish control though the divestiture was something that was sure to baffle American tax collectors. After 1976 any IRS agents who showed up asking for records were likely to be advised politely that Tradax was exempt.

It was a major development in the interlocking geopolitics of the grain trade, but one that drew little attention at the time.

It is no wonder that when grain men talk about sunny vacation spots such as the Bahamas or Bermuda they are not thinking about suntans. These are mere addresses through which the grain trade's money moves. Louis Dreyfus uses a Panama subsidiary called Sesostrad. Bunge is owned by a holding company in the sunny island of Curaçao in the Dutch Antilles. (The beneficiaries of Bunge's tax-haven company are mainly the descendants of the Bunge and Born families.) Under a treaty between the Netherlands and the United States, dividends paid by U.S.

subsidiaries of Curaçao companies are subject to a tax of only 5 per cent—and Dutch authorities charge only 2.5 per cent on funds transferred to Curaçao. This is how Curaçao lawyers make money off the grain grown by the world's farmers.

Continental moved its European headquarters from Paris to Geneva in 1974—an emotional decision for Michel Fribourg, who kept postponing the move because of his strong ties to France. But when Continental did go, it went in style, setting up an "International Merchandising Center" in a large, modern office building and throwing a big reception at the Hotel Berg, to which almost everybody in the European grain trade (including prominent Soviet traders) was invited. The advantages of Geneva had finally proved decisive. Among these, a former Continental man noted, was "a tax rate of 8 per cent instead of 50 per cent." The move also greatly simplified the company's ability to maneuver in the commodity futures markets, for complicated reasons having to do with French rules on the movement of foreign exchange (dollars) out of France.

I visited Continental's new Geneva office not long after the grand opening. It was a time when many companies were taking stock of the dangerous new world of commodity trading, and all of them were trying to adjust to the enormous increases in the volumes of grain movements and to the wild markets that prevailed. The companies were discovering that they were not immune to expensive errors of judgment and timing. The new people at Continental's Geneva headquarters talked more like conservative Swiss bankers or insurance men than swinging grain traders out to make a speculative killing. "Risk management," not speculation, was the key to success in the modern grain trade, Continental vice-president James Good advised me, as we sat in a conference room adorned by a fifteen-foot-wide map of the world spread across one wall. (This was before Continental advised that it chose "not to participate in further interviews" with me.)

In their book about the multinational corporations, *Global*

Reach, Richard Barnet and Ronald Müller describe the men who operate these companies as "world managers" because they are the first men in history "to make a credible try at managing the world as an integrated unit." Sitting in Continental's offices in the twilight, talking with Good, I had a strong sense of the shrunken size of the planet. Through commodities such as grain or soybeans, it is possible to perceive the world as "an integrated unit" in which grain flows from deficit to surplus areas, with the "world manager" grain traders handling the transfer. The strategic importance of Geneva in managing the risks was evident as Good patiently proceeded to lead me through an example.

Suppose Continental signed a sales contract with Taiwan on a Tuesday in August to deliver 100,000 tons of soybeans in November, three months later. Continental, of course, would not need to acquire the beans until shortly before it shipped them. By then, though, the price of soybeans might have changed considerably. The price might have declined, in which case Continental's profit margin would increase; but it also might have risen above a level at which Continental could make a profit. In "risk management," the normal procedure would be to play it safe—to buy the equivalent of 100,000 tons of November-delivered beans in the U.S. commodity futures markets when they opened the next business day, and when the price of beans was still low enough to insure a profitable transaction. But the grain business is seldom so simple. Suppose, Good went on, that the Japanese trading house Mitsubishi also sold Taiwan 100,000 tons of beans on Tuesday. Mitsubishi could get the beans in Brazil or the United States, the two countries that supply soybeans in such quantities. If Mitsubishi decided to cover its contract in the United States, it might follow the same strategy as Continental. Then the two giants would meet each other in the commodity pits in Chicago the next day and begin bidding for soybeans as if they were priceless art treasures being auctioned at Sotheby's. This would be ruinous for both.

One solution would be for Continental to "cover" its Taiwan

sale in Europe on Tuesday, before the U.S. markets opened. Europe does not grow many soybeans, but its processing plants do produce products such as soybean meal. And oilseeds such as sunflower seed or rapeseed, which produce similar by-products, are grown in Poland, Yugoslavia, Russia, and other European countries. All these commodities respond to the same price pressures as do soybeans, the emperor of the oilseed world. Continental could cover its sale by acquiring any of these commodities. Eventually, Continental would still have to buy soybeans in the United States to make good on its commitment to Taiwan, but any losses presumably would be offset when Continental's Geneva office resold the European commodities it had acquired. As Good said, "Risk management is the name of the game."

Operating worldwide and offshore gives the huge multinationals opportunities that no other companies have. For one thing, the grain companies (the oil companies operate similarly in this regard) run their own private "commodity exchange," trading whole-ship cargoes of grain back and forth among themselves, sometimes for purposes of risk management (that is, they need the grain, or they have lost a sale they expected to make) or, in some cases for pure speculation.

Several years ago, this private, global market of the big dealers got out of hand and some of the companies got burned by a bunch of audacious Italian speculators. This insiders' market developed out of a need for alternative places to trade futures contracts other than the publicly regulated grain exchanges in Chicago, Minneapolis, and Kansas City. The major grain companies are probably the largest participants in those exchanges, but there are drawbacks. One is that the U.S. government sets limits on speculation. A grain company can buy an unlimited number of futures contracts if it has actual sales contracts to show that it will need the grain at some later date. But if it is just playing the market there are strict limits. Also, the lots traded are small in comparison with the needs of the companies—a wheat contract is 5000 bushels, about 150 tons. To fill even a medium-sized freighter, a company has to buy 100 contracts. In the public "pits," that volume of buying attracts attention.

So the companies began operating their own private "futures" market in whole-ship cargoes of 15,000–20,000 tons of grain. This insiders' market operated around the clock. Deals involving millions of dollars were often clinched in midnight, transatlantic telephone calls. The participants were the heaviest hitters in the grain trade: big companies, large millers, and (it was rumored) a government grain board or two. These big timers were not hampered by requirements to put up "margin money." The legitimacy of the deals and the sanctity of the pledges made were enforced only by the written contracts. It was assumed that, as always, the ancient ethics of the grain trade—"Your word is your bond"—would be observed.

In 1972, a small group of Italian commodity magnates became involved in this market, soon nicknamed the "Italian market." There had never been anything quite like it. The Italians were ready to take enormous speculative risks, buying and selling grain that they often had no intention of ever importing into Italy, on the gamble that they could resell it at a higher price. (At one point, most of the Canadian barley crop was said to have been in the hands of Italian speculators, who eventually resold most of it to Russia.) And in 1973 and 1974, the Milan grain exchange became the unlikely center for very large transactions involving commodities grown by American farmers.

Each Wednesday morning, Serafino Ferruzzi, a gray-haired, elegantly attired Ravenna corn-and-soybean importer and processor, strolled into the exchange—a sure signal that action would soon take place. Ferruzzi is the *padrone* of the Italian commodity business and one of the grain trade's most successful independent operators. His company does not rank with the majors, but it is richer and better established than newer traders such as Cook Industries. Some compare Ferruzzi with the late

Enrico Mattei, Italy's independent oil man who often challenged the majors of the petroleum industry. Ferruzzi, too, is a self-made man who boasts emotionally of starting in life "with these two hands." But a few years ago, Ferruzzi had sixteen grain elevators in Italy; his company imported 80 percent of Italy's barley and processed soybeans and had expanded abroad with thousands of acres of farmlands in Argentina and North Carolina, and a large grain elevator at the mouth of the Mississippi River.

Ferruzzi often met up with other Italian commodity men on his excursions to Milan: Romano Pagnan, a Paduan barley trader and cattle raiser; Enrico Miserocchi, from a Ravenna soybean-crushing house; the broker Elios Mazzotti; and members of the Carapelli family, which runs a Florence-based vegetable-oil business. The magnates would chat animatedly, then adjourn for lunch. Fortified with pasta and red wine, they would return in the afternoon to trade enormous quantities of foreign commodities.

The big grain companies liked having the Italians in this game. They "made the market." If a company trader wanted to pick up a cargo of corn for delivery in three months, he could grab the telephone and call a broker in Milan and it was done. Quietly. Quickly. Without upsetting—or informing—U.S. grain exchanges.

But in 1974, speculative fever gripped the grain trade as prices began to climb. Cargoes were changing hands twenty or thirty times before they actually were ready for delivery. Cargill might sell to Tradax, which might sell to a German merchant, who would sell to an Italian speculator, who could hand it off to another Italian, who would pass it on to Continental. Then, in early 1975, the bull market that had made it almost impossible to lose (the traders were always selling for more than they had paid as the market moved up) collapsed. Prices of soybeans and corn plunged, and the Italians were left holding contracts obligating them to take delivery of thousands of tons of the commodities at earlier, high prices.

Several of the Italians took their losses with dignity. Francesco Carapelli of Florence told Reuters in May that his company had mortgaged its property to meet its commitments to the big grain companies. The Reuters account conjured up an image of a Mediterranean tragedy, of children pulled out of private schools, of grim, silent dinners around the family table. But some other unnamed speculators (Ferruzzi was not among the losers) behaved in a less proud fashion. They refused to accept the commodities, canceling their contracts and claiming that the Americans had been shipping them "junk"—low-quality grain that they were not obliged to accept.

The atmosphere in the Milan grain exchange turned nasty. As an American government official recalls, "the Italians were saying the American exporters were SOBs—a lot of hot words were flying around." Cargill finally wrote off between $5 million and $10 million in bad debts as a result of contractual defaults.

One is inclined to ask, who cares? Cargill could afford to take such a loss. It was not exactly the innocent home-town dentist taking a plunge in the wicked commodity markets and losing his shirt. And eventually all the grain traded in the Italian market was sold, so farmers were not deprived of customers.

But in other respects the Italian episode was exceedingly important: It showed the multinationals' ability to conduct business out of sight of the public and beyond the scrutiny of governments that in theory know what happens to the grain grown under expensive, taxpayer-financed farm-support programs. The insiders' market made available to the companies an offshore market that was by its nature unregulated except by the law of contracts. It is naive to think that business activity of such magnitude does not have an effect on prices. When I asked Assistant Secretary of Agriculture Richard Bell in 1975 whether the Italian market affected U.S. farm prices, his answer was, "Of course it does." And Cargill, Continental, and Bunge affect public futures markets when they stay *out* of them as well as when they participate in them. One of the major justifications of the futures markets is "price discovery." The price quotations for grain are there, flashing across electronic boards and ticker tapes, for all the world to see. They are intended to provide a rough approximation of world grain prices, and can do so because the big companies *are* actively involved in them. But when the companies devise their own parallel futures market and invite some of the wildest speculators in the world to join in, it is at least questionable whether the public is getting the complete picture.

It is the companies' possession of global information which others do not have that defines their uniqueness and makes them at one and the same time so efficient and so ungovernable. For on any given day, a great deal of the information required to complete the picture of what is really happening in the global grain economy cannot be synthesized except by the multinationals.

It is easy enough to ascertain the spot price at which farmers sell their wheat to grain elevators in, say, Enid, Oklahoma. But it is next to impossible to learn the price at which Tradax that same day may have sold thousands of tons of U.S. wheat to Iran—or even whether such a sale occurred. Such is the privileged, proprietary information of the global firms, of the "world managers" of the grain trade, of a few big importers and government marketing boards. To this day, nobody except a handful of grain traders and Soviet grain officials knows the prices at which more than 40 million tons of American wheat, corn, barley, and soybeans were sold to the Russians between 1971 and 1977.

Not that the grain companies or Communist purchasing agents are the only ones who keep such information from the rest of the world. The Canadian Wheat Board (more on this institution in the next chapter) is as secretive as any grain company, as the unfortunate Clarence Palmby of Continental advised the Senate Permanent Investigations Subcommittee in 1973 when he gave his version of the Wheat Board's grain sales to Russia a year earlier:

The Soviet Union contracted with the Wheat Board to purchase 3.5 million tons of wheat from Canada, plus an additional 1.5 million tons to be shipped before the end of 1973. *The U.S. Department of Agriculture has no information as to the price the Soviet Union paid for the wheat.* (Italics added.)

The weekly *Milling and Baking News* of Kansas City publishes a column carrying news about recent grain transactions. The trouble is that nobody knows for sure how complete or how representative the listings are. Whether the sale is announced and whether the price is also reported depends on the foreign buyer and on the grain company involved. A typical column in early 1977 announced that Brazil had booked 20,000 tons of No. 2 hard wheat, 11.5 per cent protein, for $2.83¼ a bushel, through an American-based company. But the same issue had scant details about the sale of 484,672 tons of No. 2 western white wheat to Iran. *That* country's food-buying Foreign Transactions Corporation apparently wanted details kept secret. And *Milling and Baking News* respects the grain trade's code: It does not publish the identities of companies involved in these transactions.

Transactions affecting world grain supplies are often kept quiet for months, and even later, when the deals do become public, the actual prices are often known only to the global companies. In the spring of 1977, for example, there was widespread talk that Peking's agents had purchased 75,000 tons of Brazilian soybean oil from a private trader. This was a sizable enough transaction to affect the market in soybean oil, the basic ingredient in American margarine and mayonnaise. But nobody knew for sure if the sale had taken place, and I was told that "nobody *will* know until the ships come in." Needless to say, when the ships *do* come in, the companies' informants in Brazil will let them know. (The hapless dentist speculating in soybean oil might find out much later.)

The offshore operations of the companies make it next to impossible to tell who is selling what to whom. (Italian rice exporters in recent years have arranged their sales to Cuba through the Bermuda subsidiaries of multinational trading companies, a technique that makes it difficult to trace sales by a NATO member to a country against which the NATO leader the United States has imposed a trade embargo.) When commodities such as barley, rice, or durum (pasta) wheat are involved, international transactions become even murkier. There is not even a public futures market in those commodities to provide at least some clues to the worldwide prices.

Consider the question, "What is the price of wheat?"

At any moment, there are *hundreds* of prices for wheat all around the United States and throughout the world. The price of wheat depends on its grade and quality, its protein, its location, the availability of ships, railroad hopper cars, barges, and trucks to transport it, the need for it in Europe, and the ability of the buyers to obtain credit and financing. Predicting the price distortions caused by a myriad of variables is the meat and potatoes of grain trading. Here, a small country elevator may have an oversupply of wheat. The companies buy it at a discount. There, a heavy snowfall in Kansas may have interrupted the flow of wheat by truck to grain depots. That raises the premiums on wheat at those depots. An untimely freeze on the Mississippi River can interrupt barge traffic and increase the premiums on grain in New Orleans.* Transportation tie-ups, dock strikes, and bad weather change the value of wheat here and there. High-protein wheat from Minnesota may be selling at premiums while

---

* The Upper Mississippi usually freezes in the last five days of November and unfreezes between March 15 and April 1. Low water can be a problem in the summer.

white "biscuit" wheat from Washington state may be a drug on the market. And wheat prices will vary around the world. In late 1976, Argentina harvested a bumper crop. As storage depots became clogged, exporters moved it into world markets at as little as $104 a ton while wheat was selling in Galveston for $120 a ton.

These global variations are plotted at the front lines of the companies—at the "wheat desks," "corn desks," and "oat desks" in the trading rooms of the big firms. At that level, the grain trade is a business of tactics, strategy, bluff, and deception. This game, which the public never sees, has been described as having an intricacy equivalent to that of playing a hundred simultaneous chess games.

The men who work on these desks are avid newshounds. Away from their telex machines and tickers, grabbing a sandwich or a beer, they become nervous and edgy. There is hardly any event in the world that could not, potentially, affect grain prices. I know a trader who must be one of the few faithful listeners to the English-language service of Radio Moscow. He hopes that his patient loyalty to Radio Moscow someday will be repaid with a tip on the Soviet grain harvest. The companies all maintain their own steady traffic of information and reporting from agents and representatives around the world. (Cargill in Minneapolis receives more than 14,000 messages a day.) The daily reports may inform the desk men of "spot" prices in Rotterdam; the latest bids of the Japanese Food Agency; changes in currency and interest rates; adjustments of the CAP duties; the weather conditions in Siberia—and here and there a political nugget.

Thus prepared, the traders begin their daily routine. "We get the cheapest offer from some company and give their man a bid on the phone," a desk man explained. "We bid back and forth and maybe they give a little. I say, 'I'll call you back with a reply in five minutes'—and they don't want to be out of the market longer than that. Or maybe they'll say, 'We'll counter you in three.' Now maybe the guy on the other end just puts his finger in his mouth and sticks it in the air. Or maybe he'll call around to grain elevators in the interior to check on the price of spring wheat in the last three minutes of trading in Chicago. Or we'll sit on the telex line hook-up for an hour putting together a deal with all the elements."

The days of the great market corners in the Chicago Board of Trade are over—a casualty of better regulation and enforcement. But there are unreported corners every day in out-of-the-way places in the grain trade. In the summer of 1975, for example, some of the big companies found themselves caught in a squeeze as they attempted to obtain North American wheat with high protein to service millers in Europe. They found that several large cooperatives in the upper Midwest had "cornered the protein." They held most of the wheat the companies needed. The result was that the export firms paid premiums of as much as 90 cents a bushel above the price of wheat futures in Minneapolis. "For once we milked the big boys for all they were worth," a coop official chuckled.

Deception can be effective. One of the major companies once used it to fool a rival in the California rice trade. It secretly bought rice from a California miller but left instructions not to move the bagged rice to the port. The rice stayed in an inland warehouse. A rival firm, convinced that it controlled all the deliverable rice, submitted its bid to a foreign buyer, believing it was in a "seller's market." The secretive rival offered at a lower price and won the contract.

Mistakes can be expensive. A trader acquaintance of mine lost $100,000 in the morning and recovered it a few hours later, this way:

The New York agent of an Asian food buyer had called to get bids on 100,000 tons of corn. The young trader jotted down some numbers, did some quick multiplying, and gave an offer. The buyer accepted quickly—too quickly. The trader rechecked his figures and suddenly felt panicky. He had quoted the price for metric tons (2204.6 pounds) rather than for long tons (2240 pounds), as ordered. It meant the company would have to supply 35.4 pounds of free corn for every ton shipped. The miscalculation would cost the company $100,000.

In a state of some desperation, the trader asked the Asian customer to delay reporting the sale or booking the ocean vessels for a few hours. The young merchant knew that word of a large ocean-freight booking would spread through the grain trade in seconds. News of such freight bookings usually increases the price of grain. Traders in other companies pick up tips about freight bookings from their own shipping departments, who have heard them from brokers. So when vessels are booked, there is a strong risk that it will be found out and with it, details of a grain transaction as well. My acquaintance's customer helpfully agreed to hold off.

All through the morning, the price of corn slowly declined—a penny a bushel, two pennies, finally four. When corn was down four cents a bushel, the American merchant picked up the telephone and ordered the company's representative in Chicago to buy the equivalent of 100,000 tons of corn in futures contracts. The merchant had taken a calculated risk that corn would decline below the price at which he had sold the 100,000 tons. It did, and he made enough on this speculation to cover the money lost through his carelessness. Needless to say, this kind of maneuvering on a planetary scale is not for widows with annuities.

To be sure, a great deal of information is available on a more or less equal basis for everybody. Newspapers, commodity news tickers, and analysts all provide pieces that are needed to complete the jigsaw puzzle of the world food situation. When I visited Geneva not long ago, commodity men were poring over an interesting assortment of economic tea leaves, none of which were especially confidential. These included temperatures in wheat-growing areas of the Azerbaijan Soviet Socialist Republic; the impending Indian election (Mrs. Gandhi was importing more than the usual amount of vegetable oil, to please Indian voters); Mali's crop of groundnuts (an ingredient in European animal feeds); hearings in Washington on farm price supports; water levels in the Mississippi River's barge channel; the increase in the number of laying hens in Holland (perhaps foreshadowing a need for more corn and soybeans to feed Dutch chickens); and a French butter sale to Russia (which could reduce the Soviet Union's requirements for vegetable oil to make margarine).

Supply and demand are the ultimate factors in prices, and "fundamentalists" in the commodity business believe, with physics professors, that for every action there is a reaction. They saw quickly that a 1976 drought in Europe was a disaster for wheat farmers—*North American* ones. Corn and sugar beets suffered badly, but hardy wheat survived. The hot, dry weather produced European wheat with unusually high protein—the same quality that the United States and Canada usually sell to European millers to supplement the protein in the Continent's domestic wheats. On the other hand, a temporary shortage of fish oil in Colombia in 1975 was good news for the U.S. lard industry. Colombia had to purchase more American lard to cover its deficit of fat. High *sugar* prices in 1974 and 1975 hurt the American *flour* industry because bakers had to raise the price of sugar-rich cakes and pies, and consumers bought less flour in that form. Cause and effect in the commodity trade is almost unending. High prices for soybean meal naturally encourage processing plants to grind more soybeans. But that produces more soybean oil whether or not it is needed by domestic margarine and mayonnaise makers. If the prices of this U.S. vegetable oil fall far enough, the Philipppines, Indonesia, and Malaysia may have trouble selling coconut and palm oil to the United States, and the economies of those countries may suffer. If Indonesia's earnings decline far enough, Indonesia might have to curtail imports of American rice, which in turn would affect the farm economies of rice states California, Texas, Louisiana, and Arkansas.

The size of the American corn crop is so important to the merchants in Geneva and New York that every summer thundershower or 100-degree day can send commodity prices gyrating. Traders talk of "weather markets." In this situation, even the sex life of corn rivets the attention of the merchants. In the summer of 1976, Richard Donnelly began a column for the financial weekly *Barron's* as follows:

Throughout much of the Corn Belt this week, something overtly sexual will be going on; in these permissive times it is perhaps possible to tell *Barron's* readers about it, for the process (a vulgar one, like everything else in nature) is crucial to the development of the bumper corn crop that is promised. And a bumper corn crop means much—to be precise, cheaper feed grain costs that could keep down meat tabs next year.

Donnelly then went on to explain why his prurient interest was aroused by corn: The crop, he said, was at the critical stage of pollenization, which meant it was particularly susceptible to damage from strong winds and extreme heat. Donnelly explained:

Silking, tasseling. Then pollenization. The silk, which is the female element in all of this, appears first, then comes the tassel, which, hold on now, is male and *sheds its pollen on the silk!* Each silk, properly pollenized, will make a grain of corn, which in the normal developmental process, will become an ear of corn.

In addition to the media that provide this sort of sexy dope on commodities, numerous private services provide similar information with less sense of fun—and for a fee. The big grain companies themselves all use professional weather services that keep track of daily rainfall everywhere in the world. People interested in commodities listen to private crop forecasters as if they were soothsayers, and there is no shortage of such computer-worked predictions—many of which turn out to be extraordinarily accurate.

The USDA publishes more comprehensive data on crop conditions all over the world than any other government agency anywhere. That these reports are taken seriously was attested to in 1975 when Peru's newspapers denounced the American agricultural attaché in Lima as an "imperialist vampire" after he had forecast a large anchovy catch of 6 million tons. High-protein fish meal and oil extracted from ground-up anchovies are an important source of Peruvian foreign exchange, and the press was charging that the attaché had inflated his estimates so as to depress world prices and help American fish-meal importers. (Subsequently, the Peruvian Ministry of Fisheries made an identical estimate.)

The same year, the Brazilian cooperative Fecotrigo told its members that its four crop watchers based in the United States had concluded that U.S. government soybean-production estimates had been deliberately inflated to depress the price of Brazilian soybeans moving into world markets. Many Brazilian farmers took that as the signal to reduce their own production of soybeans and wait for a recurrence of the high 1974 prices. Instead, the American crop was excellent, just as the Department of Agriculture had predicted, and many Brazilian farmers received lower prices for fewer beans.*

As indicated earlier, commodity exchanges, when they function properly, do also provide valuable information about the grain economy.

A visitor approaching the trading floor first hears an incoherent din, like various dissonant choruses roaring the final notes of discordant pieces. On the floor of the exchange, the noise frac-

---

* Politics constantly distorts government agricultural reporting abroad. In 1974, fish processing plants in Chimbote, Peru, claimed they were getting fish-meal yields of 23 per cent—higher than the yields even for such advanced industries as Norway's. Government propagandists boasted that the high yields resulted from the nationalization of foreign owned commercial fishing interests. But later the Ministry of Fisheries discovered that measuring equipment had been tampered with to show artificially high yields.

tures into hundreds and hundreds of shouting voices. Men in the tiered, octagonal trading "pits" communicate by yells ("full out-cry") and hand gestures. Some of them seem about to launch murderous assaults—their bodies tilt forward, hands out-stretched and fingers flashing signs. Others, straining to hear over the din, beckon into the fray upward-turned palms. The traders address each other in a tense shorthand: "Bid forty for one November!" "Seventy for one!" "Sold!" It is said that the ac-tion moves so fast that traders "have to have the rules of thumb written on their eyeballs"—like bullfighters or jet pilots who have no time to think and must respond to danger automatically and instantly. Beginners practice their moves at home in front of a mirror, like karate neophytes in training. There are moments when the "longs" (the buyers) and "shorts" (the sellers) seem to reach a standoff in their combat—when the prices move a few cents this way, then back the other way. This is what the floor traders call "dancing between the raindrops."

Even in the most tranquil economic periods, futures trading is never dull. The largest exchange in the world, the Chicago Board of Trade, has always been a place where only the fittest, or luckiest, survive. But until the economic instability of recent years, the main speculative attraction still was securities trading on Wall Street. That changed after 1972. A seat on the Chicago Board of Trade, which had gone for $20,000 in 1960, cost more than $150,000 in 1976, exceeding the price of a seat on the New York Stock Exchange. Trading volumes at the Board of Trade and at the nation's nine other exchanges increased rapidly—not just in wheat, corn, and soybeans, but also in silver, platinum, lumber, plywood, pork bellies, livestock, and foreign currencies. In 1975, the Board of Trade opened a futures market in Govern-ment National Mortgage Association ("Ginnie Mae") certifi-cates, so traders could "hedge" against long-term changes in interest rates. The futures business was thriving as it never had before—on economic instability.

This was evident as I stood in the soybean pit next to a husky, twenty-seven-year-old trader wearing a Chicago Bears necktie, one day in August 1976.

A messenger ran up to him with a written order. A few seconds later, he shouted into the din, "Sell two hundred November at fifty." This was a very large transaction. He was offering to sell 200,000 bushels of soybeans for delivery in November at $6.50 a bushel. Some $1.3 million worth of soybeans was up for sale. Twenty seconds later, the trader had sold the entire lot; a grain company had bought 100,000 bushels and other floor traders purchased the remainder. I glanced at the electronic board at the line that indicated the direction of soybean prices in the various delivery months. The line read straight across: "UP . . . UP . . . UP . . . UP." One hour later, the price had advanced 10 cents a bushel, and the original 200,000 bushels of beans were worth $20,000 more than when they had been sold.

To anybody who cared to know, those few seconds provided useful clues to what was going on in the global food economy. The trader works for himself but he also handles transactions for a major grain company—that much is known to other floor traders, reporters, and others who watch the soybean pit. His activity suggested that the company probably had bought 200,000 tons of soybeans from farmers in the countryside that day. Now it was selling futures to "lock in" a price for those farmers' beans it planned to sell the following November. If prices declined between now and then, the company would be protected. Or his selling could have meant that the company was "bearish" on the future trend of soybean prices, anticipated a decline, and was just speculating. Or perhaps the company had bought soybeans futures expecting to make a sale that never materialized and now had no further need for the beans.

The fairness, morality, and economic value of this system of futures markets has been debated since the Board of Trade began in 1848. The markets would not have survived for 130 years, through numerous investigations, public outcries, journalistic exposés, and scandals if they were without redeeming qualities. As we shall see in the following chapter, wheat is not traded in open commodity exchanges in Canada; but there is no conclusive evidence that the Canadian system has served Canadian farmers and consumers better than the helter-skelter American system. The big grain companies are the most powerful factors in the grain futures markets, but although this system can be said to exist for their convenience, it is preferable to secret, privately negotiated forward contracting in which individual farmers would be at a considerably greater disadvantage in negotiating with huge multinationals. Whether it is preferable to a system built around a governmental grain monopoly (as in Canada) is another story.

The legitimacy of the futures markets depends on their functioning in ways that serve the public interest. The Board of Trade does not exist because it is "the hottest gambling game this side of Las Vegas," but because it reduces some of the risks of food processors and others who keep inventories of variably priced commodities and because it is a public information service about prices.

Officials of the Board of Trade insist that supply and demand are the ultimate determinants of the prices flickering across the electronic boards. When the question "Who sets grain prices?" comes up, representative grain companies and commodity exchanges always answer that supply and demand do.

Yet in a sense, the exchanges are less important than they seem. Because of their noise and drama, it is natural to assume that the exchanges are the main attraction of the global grain business. But watching the exchanges is a little like watching men wrestling under a blanket. It is evident that something is happening, and it is possible to make out the general outlines of the struggle, but the details are all covered up. The fact is that the places where grain is actually physically sold in huge quantities—Geneva, Winnipeg, Ottawa, Paris, London, and Moscow—are where prices are really made. What happens at the exchanges tells us about changes in the balance of supply and demand that usually already have occurred. The floor men have a more glamorous and exciting life than most, but it is the life of a mercenary sent into battle by generals who oversee the whole battlefield from some remote command post—from the wheat, corn, and soybean desks of Cargill, or from the map room of Continental far away in Switzerland.

Grain company executives say there are sound reasons for firms not to publicize their transactions. Cargill vice-president Barney Saunders told the House Agriculture Committee in 1972: "What commercial secrecy prevails in the grain export business is not an attempt to conceal facts from the public in which they have a legitimate interest, but rather to protect individual exporters from commercial disadvantage in a highly competitive, narrow margin business." (Cargill made $41 million after taxes that year.) From Cargill's point of view, this is understandable, but the trouble is that it sometimes leaves government policy-makers who need good information at a disadvantage. It is not enough for them to know that the Russians have poor crops. It is essential to know whether the Russians will cover their deficit with imports, use up their reserves, or tighten their belts. This, rather than Soviet crop conditions, is the strategic information that can affect the economic security of the United States. The companies always are in a better position to know this than the government.

In the United States government, the collection of timely information on major grain transactions is a recent development. As long as there were big surpluses, accurate data on the grain markets were not considered essential. The Census Bureau and the Agricultural Marketing Service at the USDA collected export statistics, but the information was not current. In June 1973, a full year after the "grain robbery," the Nixon administration finally did order the Commerce Department to start collecting information from the companies on their sales commitments for the following year. Commerce's figures consistently differed from statistics and estimates kept informally by

USDA, and some USDA officials claimed that the figures were inflated by the companies' foreign affiliates, which booked unusually large quantities of soybeans in expectation of government export controls. The companies insisted that all their sales reported to Commerce were "bona fide contracts."

When the Senate Subcommittee on Multinational Corporations asked Cargill in 1976 to provide information about its dealings with Tradax during the 1973 period when soybean supplies were under pressure,* it received a lengthy answer. In the first place, Cargill told the subcommittee, it was unable to provide information on Tradax's dealings in Brazilian soybean contracts (the other major foreign source) during that period because under Swiss law, "Tradax and its employees would be subject to criminal prosecution if they supplied this information to a U.S. government entity." As to the American parent company's soybean dealings with Tradax, Cargill indicated that it had indeed way oversold soybeans to Tradax Export up to June 13—when a panicky administration sought authority to embargo soybean exports.

On June 20, Cargill canceled the sale of 28 million bushels, but the Nixon administration still instituted an embargo on June 27. After these controls were lifted in September (the 1973 crop was turning out to be excellent), Cargill continued to cancel export contracts: 11 million bushels in September, 11 million more in October, and 7 million in November.

The embargo was extremely damaging to the United States' reputation as a reliable exporter of soybeans, and some have suggested that it was the embargo that prompted Japan to invest more heavily in the Brazilian soybean industry as an alternative source of the commodity. Given the chain of events, it is not hard to see why the subcommittee's suspicion fell on Cargill as a perpetrator of the soybean panic of 1973. But Cargill denies that

---

* Prices exceeded a record $10 a bushel and only 2 million tons were left over from the previous year's crop, a precarious balance.

it was responsible. It did sell forward and then cancel many of these sales, but it says this was justified by the actual supply situation.

What could not be disputed was the fact that the U.S. government still lacked, at that point, a clear idea of what went on its own grain markets. That August, Congress amended the Agriculture Act to establish a mandatory reporting system in the USDA. (Officials of the agency had *opposed* a mandatory reporting system during hearings on the measure!) This new system became operational in November. It required exporters of wheat, flour, feed grains, oilseeds (soybeans, cottonseed, rapeseed, and peanuts), and cotton to report all sales over 100,000 tons within twenty-four hours of their completion. This is the system that is in effect today.*

The system has certainly provided more information about American exports, but there is an uneasy feeling among a number of senior officials at the Department of Agriculture that it is anything but foolproof. There are gray areas—such as sales of American grain by the European subsidiaries of the multinationals. Also, reporting companies are permitted to leave the destination of grain "unknown" until it actually leaves port. As recently as November 1977, when the Russians came to the United States to purchase grain, senior USDA officials said they were unsure how much business was being transacted.

The companies, it is clear, are still the ultimate source of information about grain transactions and grain prices. The Minneapolis Grain Exchange is the world's largest single wheat market (Chicago dominates in corn and soybeans). The "closing price" in Minneapolis, flashed to grain elevators and farmers all over

---

* As noted in Chapter 1, the system was tightened temporarily in October 1974, to require exporters to obtain *prior approval* for any sale of more than 50,000 tons in a single twenty-four–hour period or of more than 100,000 in a week; but this was abandoned in March 1975. On August 11, 1975, it was again temporarily imposed for sales to the Soviet Union but later discontinued again, this time in October.

the Midwest, is the basis for buying and selling of actual grain that takes place between the time the exchange closes in the early afternoon and the next morning when it reopens. The closing price, which is the final price offered and bid, is determined by a committee. The members of the committee recently included eight grain companies, including Cargill, Louis Dreyfus, Bunge, and Archer-Daniels Midland (the last a huge soybean-processing company). In characterizing this system, Senate staff member Richard Gilmore of the Senate Subcommittee on Multinational Companies called it a "circular arrangement" that was "all tied in—dependent on the companies as far as price determination is concerned."*

Governments, including the U.S. government, are even more reliant on the private companies for information about grain transactions taking place outside the United States. Here Washington has no legal authority for collecting information and it falls back on legwork, contacts, and "good will."

In 1976, Assistant Secretary of Agriculture Richard Bell made an unusually frank admission of the government's dependence on the companies' information. It came in connection with his support for a tax break for Cargill, Continental, Cook, and other American-based companies. A tax amendment before the Senate Finance Committee would have excluded from American taxes the profits that American-based multinationals earned in their offshore trading. Congressional analysts concluded that the exclusion would reduce government tax revenues by $17 million in

---

* Gilmore brought out information that the European Common Market "eurocracy" relies on company price reports to fix its CAP import duties, which are based on the price of grain arriving at the huge grain port of Rotterdam and other major harbors. The companies report to the Royal Netherlands Grain Trade Subcommittee, which reports to the Dutch Product Board, which reports to the Common Market's grain division. The secretary of the Netherlands Grain Trade Subcommittee refused to provide Gilmore with the names and functions of its informants. Gilmore asserted at the 1976 hearings that grain companies were represented on the Product Board. Cargill denied this, but it did not provide a list of the Product Board's members.

fiscal 1977. But Bell argued for the tax break. "There's a U.S. public interest in supporting the companies," he said. "They're the ones who keep us posted as to what's going on all over the world. Their system is ahead of our system." The amendment was defeated and the companies' tax liability remained ambiguous—but not for lack of support from the Department of Agriculture.

It is difficult, if not impossible, to ascertain whether or not the USDA's present system for keeping track of what is going on in the grain markets is thorough and accurate. The few documents available on the past performance are not encouraging. In a memorandum written in 1967, the American agricultural attaché in Hamburg, Allan Trick, said that government representatives in contact with grain companies there had trouble getting information on wheat transactions in Europe. He said it was "probable we learn of less than 75 percent of this business," and went on to say that "in the case of rice prices and sales, we constantly feel that one or two of our sources are trying to what we call 'whipsaw' us, and so it is a constant problem of checking and rechecking information given us." One would like to believe that the grain companies are more forthcoming today than they were when Trick was trying to scrounge information from them.

Given the information monopoly enjoyed by a handful of big grain companies, it is understandable that the firms find ways to circumvent the regulations that governments establish to regulate the commodity trade. Such regulations become less obstacles than new variables on which to speculate. Louis Dreyfus created an entire division to grapple with the elaborate financial rules of the Common Market and—quite frankly, according to a Louis Dreyfus man—to find legal loopholes. (There have been occasions when Common Market meat traders have shipped truckloads of meat back and forth across European borders on endless journeys to collect the "equalization payments" on the various currencies.)

The multinationals also speculate on the floating CAP duties of the Common Market. These "levies" are set according to the difference between the internal, protected grain price in Europe and the price of grain arriving from abroad on ships. The more the price of grain outside Europe sinks below the CAP internal price, the larger the levy the Europeans charge on incoming grain. But there are times when world prices are changing too fast for the European bureaucrats to adjust their levy. By using a complicated arbitrage between the CAP levy and the Chicago futures price and playing the time difference between Europe and the United States, the companies can sometimes offer foreign wheat, corn, and flour at discounts to European millers and sneak more foreign grain into the Continent.* This may be good for the United States but it is not what European authorities intended.

This technique used to be employed in reverse in the United States. The multinationals would speculate on the American export subsidies (the compensations the government paid exporters when they sold costlier U.S. wheat into depressed world markets). This practice stopped, of course, when the subsidy program was abandoned in September 1972. The comptroller general of the United States said in a report that some of the exporters could have earned windfall profits speculating on changes in the subsidy before it was abandoned. Certainly for the companies that were selling the Russians grain, it did not take much analytical brilliance to deduce that tomorrow's subsidy would be higher than today's, and so on through the summer. In July 1976, Cargill, Continental, and Bunge in fact conceded that they had profiteered on these compensations in 1972. When government investigators looked into their subsidy transactions from that summer, the companies agreed to return $1.6 million of the federal payments.

---

* The CAP levy is adjusted to price changes in Chicago—but nearly a day later. In the interim exporters book the levy at the old price—before it is adjusted. Sometimes even the merchants get confused trying to do this.

10   Pyramid of Power

"Whoever controls food exports controls the world."
—JACQUES CHONCHOL, CHILE'S FORMER MINISTER OF AGRICULTURE

Almost from the day in May 1973 that Continental Grain Company opened the first modern flour mill in the West African country of Zaire, the New York multinational had troubles.

Two out of the twelve concrete silos used to store wheat for the mill collapsed two months later, interrupting the milling operations.

Shortly thereafter, Continental representatives learned that their flour was running into local competition. An uncle of President Mobutu had received licenses to import European wheat flour and distribute it to Zairean bakeries.

New difficulties developed with a decline in international copper prices, on which the Zairean economy depended. As dollars in the central bank's reserves dwindled through 1974, Zaire fell behind in its payments to Continental's mill for the American wheat the grain company was using. The American wheat cost dollars, but the company's efforts to obtain the foreign exchange from the central bank went nowhere. It seemed that the giant grain company would just have to take its place in the long line of Zaire's creditors, which included many other banks and companies that had failed to anticipate the country's financial troubles. (Citibank was not even getting replies to its urgent cables to Kinshasa.)

But in a rapid sequence of events in late 1976, Continental demonstrated forcefully that it could, if necessary, wield unique power over governments and people that depended on its wheat. Its patience exhausted, the grain company took simple and direct action. It held back its monthly wheat shipment to its Zaire facility, and the mill at Matadi, on the Congo River downstream from Kinshasa, reduced its daily output of flour. As John Williams, the American agricultural attaché in Kinshasa, explained Continental's action in a December 3 letter to the Department of Agriculture: "They diverted a shipload of wheat destined for Zaire to help the Government of Zaire realize just how important wheat is to their urban population."

The realization was not long in coming. "The lines and hoarding that occurred at various bakeries were almost spontaneous. The mill did not shut off the flow of flour to bakers—they just merely slowed it down to put pressure on," Williams wrote home.

Zairean officials hastily convened with representatives of Continental and agreed to all the company's demands. It promised that the Central Bank would pay cash for all subsequent wheat shipments; that Zaire would start repaying its old debt at the rate of $1 million a month; that only American hard wheat would be imported, except in some special circumstances; that Continental would have exclusive rights to mill flour in Zaire; and that the company would have the right to approve or disapprove all requests by others to import flour into Zaire. In other words, the company became Zaire's sole importer of wheat and sole manufacturer of flour, and it received authority to control imports of any competing flour almost as if it were a government agency.

It has long been recognized that oil for energy and capital to buy technology are necessary for a country's development. As the Zaire episode showed, a third resource recently has become necessary: adequate amounts of imported grain.

In the early 1960s, there still were many countries where bread was not widely eaten. The "desert plant" did not thrive in tropical conditions. In 1962, the wheat deficit of developing countries was only 13 million tons. But by the time of Zaire's difficulties this had increased to 31 million tons. And by then, the surpluses in North America had dwindled away and wheat prices were at record levels. Bread had become a popular food in countries where people had sustained themselves for centuries on rice, maize, beans, and cassava.

Grain was part of the network of global interdependency. Land in some of the poorest countries in the world was being used to raise agricultural products for export—bananas, pineapple, sugar, palm oil, coffee, cocoa, and rubber—and the income used to pay for the importation of staple cereal grains. In this situation, the prices that commodities such as copper or rubber brought in international markets could have an effect on domestic nutrition. The relationship was succinctly described by Great Plains Wheat, a company that promotes American wheat exports abroad. It noted that in West Africa the "expansion potential" for wheat imports is "subject to the extremely volatile shifts common to countries that are highly dependent on exports of coffee, cocoa, peanuts, palm kernels, rubber, copper, iron and petroleum. . . . Since the prices of these commodities fluctuate, foreign exchange earnings are erratic and have a direct effect on the quantity of wheat imported."

What this was saying was that countries such as Zaire stood in double jeopardy. A recession that brought about a slackening demand for copper pipe for new home construction in North America could affect Zaire's ability to pay for food. And so could a round of Soviet grain purchases that pushed up wheat prices in the United States.

The other consequence of this pattern was the enhanced importance it gave to multinational companies. The fact that grain now flowed among nations as easily as oil and capital put the grain houses in the same pivotal position as petroleum companies and banks. Their power lay not in the fact that they produced the resource, but that they distributed it and processed it into flour for humans and feedstuffs for poultry and livestock.

Zaire was no isolated example of dependence on the grain companies, extreme as its plight did become in 1974 and thereafter. Many other countries also found that multinational grain companies were suddenly extremely important to their food and agricultural systems. It is worth examining Zaire in somewhat more detail only as a sort of "worst case" study of the roots of this dependency and how they grew.

Zaire's dependence on foreign wheat developed gradually. Bread was virtually unknown as a food there until European colonists arrived in the nineteenth century. Much later, some wheat was planted in the Kivu area, adjacent to Burundi and Ruanda, but the main food crops were white maize (corn) and manioc. Europeans continued to import small amounts of flour for their needs. After Zaire became independent from Belgium in 1960,° the United States shipped some flour through the P.L. 480 program. The population of Kinshasa swelled, and the government paid cash for imported flour. Fortunately, foreign flour and wheat were cheap, and governments made credit available. It was cheaper and considerably easier to import flour to feed the rural-urban migrants than to increase agricultural production and improve the rural transportation and distribution systems. A network of bakeries appeared in cities and towns, and a whole new system of food distribution was constructed around imported flour. As this happened, a slow but steady change took place in the diet of the Zairean urban population.

Bread was not the only food. Technicians from China arrived

° As the Democratic Republic of the Congo. It was renamed Zaire in 1971.

to help improve rice production. White maize grew widely, even turning up in empty city lots. (Maize was heavily cultivated in the Shaba province, where it served the high caloric needs of hard-laboring miners in the European concessions that in early 1978 were attacked by invaders from Angola.) And manioc root, boiled or dried in the sun, was still the staple food for the tribes and villages, as it had been for centuries. The large, leafy plant, with roots penetrating several feet below ground, grew almost everywhere. It was eaten at breakfast as *chikwanga*, a starchy preparation that sometimes was accompanied by fish or meat, and as *fufu*, a floury white paste, at other times of day.

By the time Continental arrived on the scene in 1967, with a proposal for a modern flour mill near Kinshasa, bread was displacing the more traditional Congolese foods in the capital. In the early morning hours, smoke rose from fires of makeshift stoves as native women baked their bread dough at the curbs of broad, chestnut-lined streets. Agricultural attaché Williams, an enthusiast of "market development," was to note in a report to Washington that bread was "winning against chikwanga at breakfast." Bread, he added, had the advantage of its "psychological connotations": It had been "the staple diet of the colonial masters and was adopted by the elite. Because of the effect of imitation, bread consumption identifies with progress and modernity for the masses."

There were practical and economic reasons, too, for bread's popularity. The supply of flour usually was more dependable than the manioc that was carted or trucked from the surrounding countryside. Bread kept well, it was relatively inexpensive, and it tasted better than manioc. Washed down with tea or Coca-Cola, bread was ideal for the lunch boxes of workers without access to canteens. The high status of bread was suggested by the fact that it was eaten by Mobutu's elite corps of bodyguards (along with such delicacies, unavailable to most other Zaireans, as tinned sardines from South Africa).

The bread that was available, even in limited supply, provided a margin of security against famine—against a worsening of the malnutrition that was evident in the bloated stomachs of children and in the spindly legs of the beggars who crouched on the steps of the American Embassy in downtown Kinshasa. In a sense, the bread supply was as much of a pacifier of the urban population of Zaire as the bodyguards who patrolled Mobutu's palace grounds.

But there were costs. A distribution system grew up in Zaire around imported food: first, the European flour, later the American wheat. With the installation of Continental's mill at Matadi, the system was made permanent.

It could hardly have been a great incentive to Zaire's farmers to have so much food from abroad pouring into the major cash market. But not until the sharp increase in wheat prices in 1973 and 1974 and the drop in copper revenues in 1974 did the Office of National Cereals begin taking steps to increase production of native corn. Then it doubled the price at which the government procured grain from farmers. But it was too late. Corn output did not show any great improvement.

Continental advised the American Embassy in 1975 of its difficulties getting paid for the wheat. The situation merited "concern," according to cables. That is, the diplomats worried about what would happen to United States–Zaire relations if the New York company cut off the wheat. Anxiety grew when in June Ambassador Deane Hinton was expelled on Mobutu's orders, after Mobutu charged a group of Zairean junior officers with plotting to overthrow him and blamed the Americans for complicity in the alleged conspiracy.

As it turned out, Continental's men understood the politics of wheat considerably better than the diplomats at the embassy. The decision to go ahead with the wheat cutoff more than a year later had no perceptible effect on diplomatic relations, for Mobutu's government was in no position to quibble with Continental: Zaire had to have its wheat. Once the government accepted this reality and capitulated to Continental's terms, American wheat began flowing to Zaire again. Imports of U.S. wheat increased rapidly. By 1977, they reached 140,000 tons, triple the amount imported three years earlier. Great Plains Wheat predicted that Zaire's wheat imports would reach 210,000 tons by 1982, making it the largest U.S. wheat customer in West Africa after Nigeria.

From Zaire's point of view, this was definitely a mixed blessing. The imported grain preempted foreign exchange that might otherwise have gone to economic development—or to agricultural projects. Purchases of technology had to be postponed and work at existing plants slowed down. (When Goodyear's tire plant outside Kinshasa could no longer obtain currency to import raw materials, it did not close the plant; but it did slow down production and its stocks of tires were depleted. Soon there was an active black market in tires, and after a while many buses and trucks ground to a halt.) It is not fair to blame Continental Grain for the economic and nutritional problems of Zaire. If Continental had not built a mill in Matadi, Zaire still would have needed to buy foreign flour, and there was some advantage in having the processing of the raw material—wheat—take place in Zaire. But the episode illustrated the centrality of the grain multinationals.

To understand fully this power of the major grain companies all over the world, it is essential to examine the structure of the grain business in the United States, the largest single reservoir of surplus grain anywhere. At first glance the American grain market seems a diverse and intricate system in which it is difficult to discern any clear pattern of corporate domination. The agricultural map of the United States is a complex patchwork of many crops, all moving to markets through a network of small, rural grain elevators, many of them owned by local businessmen or farm cooperatives.

As spring turns into summer, the harvest wheels north, from

the Texas panhandle in May to the Dakotas and southern Manitoba and Saskatchewan in September. The American farm country is a mosaic of corn, soybeans, barley (for malting), sunflower seeds (for cooking oil), flaxseed (for paint). Each crop can be further broken down into components that go into different products and therefore move through different chains in the market. For example, some corn goes into plants that produce starch or corn sweeteners, and some is destined for the whiskey stills of Cincinnati. Wheat also has its specialized markets: The "bread" wheats of Kansas and Oklahoma are likely to go to the Kansas City flour mills, while the durum wheats that grow in the Dakotas go to mills that make flour for macaroni and other pastas in Buffalo. The soft-kerneled wheats from Ohio and Indiana are ideal for cookies, which determines their route to markets. With the advent of huge poultry industries in the southeastern states, corn and soybeans that once stayed in the Midwest to feed hogs are now hauled by freight trains in great volumes to Georgia and Arkansas. Vast quantities of these crops also move on the Santa Fe Railroad and other major grain carriers to the cattle feedlots of the Southwest.

As this suggests, the domestic grain market in the United States is a pluralistic institution, with millers, feed producers, feedlots, brewers, and many others all competing for parts of the harvest. Yet it is the international grain companies that still dominate it.

In the United States, Cargill, Continental, and Bunge have all moved aggressively into domestic grain "refining" with their investments in flour-milling, soybean-crushing plants, and ultramodern facilities for manufacturing feed ingredients or corn sweeteners. So, even before the grain moves abroad, the companies, in their role as manufacturers, claim their share.

But it is after the myriad domestic requirements for grain have been satisfied that the big grain companies really make their economic power felt. The bulk of most United States crops ultimately go abroad, through the facilities and logistical networks of the big firms. In the last twenty-five years, for example, the Mississippi River has become the world's single greatest grain artery. Very little wheat moves on the river; most of the acre-sized fleets of barges that float down it to the depots at New Orleans are filled with corn and soybeans—crops that grow in abundance in the fertile bottomlands along the river and its great tributaries, the Illinois and Ohio rivers. It is said that anything growing within twenty-five miles of these waterways "belongs to the river." The dozens of barge terminals up and down the river draw off the crops from the adjoining counties. In St. Louis, grain-company agents track the barges, buying more grain or trading it to cover commitments to vessels arriving to load grain at the export terminals downstream.

Ultimately, most of this river of grain—some 50 million tons a year—belongs to the international grain trade. Cargill, Continental, and Bunge have facilities up and down the river systems; the grain moving downstream ends up in ten huge export terminals belonging to Cargill, Continental, Bunge, Mitsui, and other giants, located in the estuary between Baton Rouge and the Gulf of Mexico. Cargill is the colossus of this grain gateway; a quarter of the entire grain-loading capacity of the New Orleans area is controlled by the Minneapolis firm. More than one hundred vessels a week load up at these downstream depots. The majors also control a substantial amount of the port storage of Puget Sound, Washington; Portland, Oregon; Buffalo, New York; Houston and Galveston, Texas; and Pascagoula, Mississippi (the location of Louis Dreyfus's Gulf terminal).

When Myron Just, North Dakota's commissioner of agriculture, testified in 1976 before the Senate Subcommittee on Multinational Corporations, he described the logistical power of the big grain companies graphically:

The pyramid of power, as I see it, is thirty thousand North Dakota farmers selling through about five hundred grain elevators in North

Dakota, farmer-owned but discreetly Minneapolis-run in my estimation, into one grain exchange, which in turn sells mostly to six large exporters. So, you know, the grain moves in that direction, and the marketing power and marketing information really concentrates as it moves on up. You could say that we really have two and a half million farmers that feed into this thing and that the power really becomes concentrated at the top.

. The USDA had reported a year earlier, in 1975, that "U.S. grain exporting is dominated by five grain companies that account for about 85 per cent of the total volume." The agency noted that "these exporters have tremendous economic power, being highly diversified and having worldwide operations." In 1974 Cargill's share of the American grain exports was 42 per cent for barley, 32 per cent for oats, 29 per cent for wheat, 22 per cent for sorghum, 18 per cent for soybeans, and 16 per cent for corn. On average, Cargill and Continental each handle about a quarter of total U.S. grain exports.

The reason for this domination is the companies' investments in transportation, grain loading, storage, and processing. The companies' big investments in storage facilities at the ports of Houston and Galveston give them a powerful position in buying the wheat moving by train out of the rural wheat belt in Texas and Oklahoma. The big companies are the gatekeepers on this grain's only route to world markets.

On the Mississippi River Cargill is a force in transportation. It owns its own fleet of barges, and its subsidiary, Cargo Carriers, owns tow boats that handle its own grain barges and those of its less well equipped competitors. (Cargill's annual bill for transportation runs around $400 million.)

The companies' emphasis on transportation was evident in a letter that Continental's transportation director, R. J. Helm, wrote to an executive of the Milwaukee Railroad in March 1974. It was a "major objective of Continental quite frankly to gain control of the transportation and logistics of the grain flow from the country to its export elevators," Helm wrote. He added that by the summer of that year, Continental would have the largest private fleet of grain hopper cars in the country—"more than many railroads." He concluded: "We are also investing large sums in train loading stations to originate grain and control transportation." By then, Continental already operated nineteen grain "shuttles" of its own between Midwest rural depots and export terminals in Superior, Milwaukee, Chicago, and Norfolk. (Small grain companies complain that the railroads favor the majors in allocating railroad cars that are needed to ship commodities.)

Similar logistical control exists worldwide. Cargill, for instance, has an estimated 7 million tons of storage space around the world. Corn and soybeans from the American depots of Cargill and Continental move on company-leased or company-owned ocean vessels to company facilities in Ghent, Amsterdam, and Rotterdam in Europe.

Cargill's investments in processing have been concentrated not in flour milling but in the "protein sector." We saw in Chapter 7 how Cargill's reach has extended to the poultry-, corn-, egg-, and broiler-processing "systems" of the Philippines, Taiwan, and South Korea. Its positioning in the world's soybean "system" is even more impressive. It has established an almost perfect intercontinental "straddle" in soybeans that permits it maximum flexibility in processing and trading the commodity. The only countries with an exportable surplus of soybeans are the United States and Brazil. The largest market for soybeans and soybean products is Europe. Cargill is represented with plants in all three places. It is one of the largest soybean crushers in the United States; it has four plants in Europe and a new, modern plant at Ponta Grossa, Brazil, near the fastest-growing source of surplus soybeans in the world. This gives Cargill maximum maneuverability to export either raw soybeans for processing in Europe, or meal and vegetable oil processed close to the point of origin in the United States or Brazil. Few other refiners of raw materials find themselves in such an enviable position.

Thus it is that even abroad, the majors' share of the grain trade is impressive. In 1974 the Big Five handled 90 per cent of the Common Market's trade in wheat and corn, 90 per cent of Canada's barley exports, 80 per cent of Argentina's wheat exports, and 90 per cent of Australia's grain sorghum exports. This global capability is the essence of the economic power of all multinational enterprises, not just of the multinationals of grain. It is true that in the 1960s and 1970s OPEC and other organizations representing producers of natural resources took steps to strengthen their bargaining power with global companies. Legislatures enacted stricter laws on foreign investments, forced foreign firms to give up some of their equity in local ventures, and in many cases nationalized sectors of the economy responsible for basic resources. This pattern had been long established in grain. Canada and Australia have had public wheat boards to sell grain, and other nations have set up public agencies with responsibility for acquiring grain in international markets. Yet all governments still continue to rely heavily on multinational grain companies to organize the distribution systems, process the grain into usable commodities, and provide financing for vast movements of grain around the world.

The majors do, of course, have their competitors, although the field narrows all the time. The ability to stay in the grain business against such economic power has usually depended on special circumstances—specialization either in one particular commodity or in one fairly narrow market.

A few determined independents, such as Italy's Serafino Ferruzzi and the Hamburg grain man Alfred C. Toepfer, do challenge the majors here and there. Toepfer, still vigorous at eighty-four, is one of the most successful of them. Toepfer is in agribusiness, shipping, and banking and owns inland grain elevators in the United States. The Toepfer holding company has a substantial minority interest in a Hamburg bank (Bankhaus

Hesse Neuman), and in German terms he is a big businessman. Toepfer, in 1974, handled 16.7 million tons of commodities and its sales reached nearly $3 billion, but this was thanks to his specialization in the European importing market. He has managed to corner fairly well the expanding North American grain trade with East Germany. ("We can't crack it!" exclaimed one official of a bigger company.) As for Ferruzzi, he has interests in American farmland, owns a port elevator at the mouth of the Mississippi River, and is involved, as we have seen, in all kinds of commodity trading in Italy.

The competitors of the big five grain companies include soybean exporters Archer-Daniels Midland and Central Soya in the United States, The Andersons Co. (which handles half the wheat exported from Toledo); the Japanese trading companies Mitsui, Mitsubishi, Marubeui, Citoh, Sumitomo, Nisho-Iwai, Tomen, Kanematsu Gosho, Nichimen, Yuasas, and Ataka; Ferruzzi and Pagnan in Italy; Compagnie Grainier, G&P Levy, and Cam in France; Peabody in the United Kingdom; Intercorn in Belgium; Schouten and Granaria in the Netherlands; Toepfer, Cremer, and Kampfmeyer in West Germany; Transafrica in Spain; Cobec and Fecotrigo in Brazil; Nidera, Aca, and Faca in Argentina; Krohn, Cremer, and Toepfer in Thailand; and United Grain Growers, Xcan, Agro, Richardson, and Northern Sales in Canada.

But this list belies the economic power of the majors. Even in Germany, strong, locally based companies have not been able to prevent the multinationals from penetrating and obtaining an ever larger share of the market. From 1965 to 1967, Toepfer and two other larger German companies, Becher and Kampfmeyer, formed a compact to keep Cargill out. Cargill, through its European subsidiary Tradax, was starting to sell wheat, corn, and other commodities direct to mills and feed processors. The German importers boycotted Cargill and went to other suppliers of grain. But the boycott did not work. The Germans often found that the Americans had the best bargains to offer, and they surrendered unconditionally. "They decided it was better to buy than fight," said Cargill vice-president Clifford Roberts with a wink.

Cooperatives representing farmers have had trouble competing with the majors in the export trade for similar reasons. The cooperatives are committed to sell the grain of their farmer-members. They cannot offer overseas customers grain from, say, Argentina and Australia when it is available at a discount in those countries. But the multinational grain companies can and do, and time and again this enables them to grab business away from cooperatives. The cooperatives serve a useful purpose for commercial grain companies a good deal of the time—storing grain until the exporters have found a customer for it. The USDA estimates that the American farm cooperatives sell 70 per cent of their export-bound grain not to foreign customers but to the major commercial companies. The French farm cooperatives have had similar difficulties in grain exporting. The French wheat and grain coops are well-financed and well-organized and they enjoy the support of the French government, which still depends heavily on the rural and farm votes. But when the coops try to go it alone in world markets they find Cargill and Continental there ahead of them. Recently, one of the coops has finally begun to do better. It is the French Union of Cereals. Its fortunes changed after it moved into offices adjacent to the Louis Dreyfus Company in Paris. The French Union of Cereals had the political clout and it had the wheat. But Louis Dreyfus had the customers and the expertise. The Union formed a partnership with Louis Dreyfus. It was an odd marriage of convenience, since coops were established, in part, to gain independence from the big interests such as grain houses and railroads. The only hope for real independence may be for cooperatives in several countries to form their own multinational cooperative to give them the same advantages as the private companies have. In 1979 five U.S. and European cooperatives announced they were forming a consortium to market grain worldwide. West Germany's Toepfer agreed in principle to sell a 50 per cent interest to the consortium.

The world's farmers need the commercial companies not only to sell their grain but also, in many cases, to sell *them* the seeds from which to grow it. This is a relatively new development. Merchants have always spread seeds—merchants brought Russian wheat seed to Canada a century ago. But there was a time when farmers grew most of their own wheat, barley, oat, and corn seed. They held it over from the previous year's crop, stored it, replanted it, and let nature take its course. The crops were pollenized in open fields. Today, however, farmers are buying more and more of their seed from commercial companies. And while there are advantages—the seed gives much higher yields, is resistant to drought and less vulnerable to certain kinds of insects and diseases—there are drawbacks. Depending on an outside commercial source is risky, and plant geneticists worry that the standardization of crops through central distribution of seed and through the "genetic engineering" that produces the new varieties is not only breeding out undesirable qualities and weaknesses but also breeding in certain new vulnerabilities. Wheat that is short ("dwarf") and therefore less likely to be blown over by wind ("lodged") may require more fertilizer or may be more prone to infection from some plant diseases than the ancestors from which it was bred. Hardy, wild varieties of plants are being lost and with them some of the natural vigor of crops; the agriculture map resembles less and less a patchwork of different varieties with disparate disease immunities than a monotonous spread of a few varieties that could be subject to massive losses if infected by various diseases.

It has been only in the last thirty years that private companies have become so extraordinarily important in seed distribution. This commercialization of the seed industry was the result of the development of hybrid corn and "miracle" wheat. Today, the companies (Cargill is prominent in seed research and commer-

cial distribution) are close to developing commercially accept-able hybrid wheat—perhaps no more than a year or two away.*
With this development, they will become the source of this kind of seed, just as they are at present the source of virtually all the world's hybrid corn seed.

Genetic improvements were, of course, responsible for the rapid expansion of the food supply after World War II. Research on hybrid corn had been done in the United States in the 1920s and 1930s, but not until after the war did farmers begin con-verting to hybrids in a big way. Meanwhile, research on high-yielding wheat had been under way since 1943 at a center in Mexico financed by the Rockefeller Foundation. By the 1960s, "miracle" wheats developed under the supervision of Nobel Prize–winner Norman Borlaug began to spread around the world.

Governments and nonprofit organizations and foundations provided the initial financing for this early corn and wheat re-search, and they continue to provide much of it today. But in the case of corn, international companies have taken over research and commercial distribution, for the most part leaving govern-ments to encourage and observe the work. Hybrid corn is sweeping the world. Virtually all the corn planted in the United States, as well as most of it in Argentina, Brazil, South Africa, and France, comes from hybrid seed, and most of that seed is supplied by a handful of companies that dominate the business.†
A few years ago, when corn prices reached record highs and countries all over the world tried to expand the acreage planted to grain crops, profits in the hybrid-corn seed business were un-precedented; average profits increased 20 per cent a year from 1972 to 1975. Because of their profit picture, the seed companies

* Wheat hybrids have been produced, but the yields are not significantly higher than those of conventional wheats.

† Two companies, Pioneer Hy Bred International and Dekalb, supply about 55 per cent of the hybrid market; six others—Cargill, Funk, Ferry Morse, Trojan, ACCO, and Northrup King—dominate the rest.

became the target of takeovers by huge pharmaceutical companies, which found them compatible because of their heavy emphasis on research. Ciba-Geigy and Pfizer are two drug firms that have recently acquire seed companies.

From a commercial standpoint, the key fact about hybrid seeds is that farmers have to buy new supplies of them every year. They do not reproduce themselves. This is what makes the investments in research worthwhile. Hybrids are obtained by crossing "parent" plants possessing distinctive traits to get a vigorous hybrid. It is the control of the male and female parent lines that gives any particular firm a monopoly and control over the hybrid seeds it develops. These parent lines are developed separately by company researchers and plant geneticists who know how to isolate and reproduce certain desirable traits. Most of the breeding of the parent lines is done on special plots in the southern United States and Mexico. It takes at least four generations to produce a desired genetic variety, and seeds sometimes are moved back and forth between the United States and Mexico to take advantage of two growing seasons. Wheat is a self-pollinating crop which can perpetuate itself generation after generation. But corn has male and female elements that breed with other plants. In a regular corn field, the wind carries the pollen from the male tassels to many different female silks. In the controlled hybridization process, the silks of the female parent line and the tassels of the male parent line are covered, to guarantee the desired cross-fertilization and the production of the hybrid.

Hybrid seeds yield 20–30 per cent more corn per acre than seeds from corn pollinated naturally in open fields. But as already indicated, there is a drawback—or, from the companies' viewpoint, an advantage: The ears of corn from hybrids will not produce seeds that duplicate the same good results; hybrids do not pass on their vigor to the next generation. This biological fact of life has made a few companies the sole source of "hybrid power" for many of the nations.

In the absence of hybrids, the gains in wheat development have come from laborious plant breeding that is supposed to (and does) give the process of natural selection a helping hand. The foremost source of the "miracle" wheat produced in this way is the International Maize and Wheat Improvement Center at El Batan, Mexico. The center grew out of the Rockefeller Foundation–financed work of the 1940s whose purpose was to develop wheat strains suitable for tropical countries, which tended also to be countries with food deficits. Through painstaking selection of wheat plants with desired qualities in the fields, Dr. Borlaug obtained higher-yielding plants that were also resistant to drought, insects, and disease. "Lodging" was a serious problem in the tropics because of high wind and slashing rains. Borlaug and his team at El Batan found a solution in crossing the Mexican wheats with certain strains of Japanese "dwarfs" with short, tough stems.

A type called Norin-10 from the island of Honshu was tough enough to survive Japanese typhoons, and it proved to be the cross that made possible the "Green Revolution" in wheat. From 1960 on, the Mexican research station released a long list of wheats—Nainair 60 (for 1960), Pitic 62, Penjamo 62, Sonora 64, Lerma Rojo 64, Inia 66, Siete Cerros 66, Super X 67, Yecora 70, and Cajeme 71—that with proper amounts of fertilizer and irrigation could thrive within twenty degrees of the Equator.

The Green Revolution, although it never entirely fulfilled its early promise, evoked tremendous interest and excitement around the world. Governments and farmers viewed it with great hope, and ready markets for the new seeds sprang up in many countries—India, Pakistan, Iran, Algeria, Morocco, Tunisia, Iraq, Saudi Arabia, Turkey, Kenya, and Egypt.

In the early stages, private companies were much less involved in these developments than they were in the development of hybrid corn. Once a farmer had obtained his "miracle" wheat seed, he could save part of his crop, replant it, and produce a second "miracle" crop the following year. In Mexico, reproduction of the special wheat seeds was originally handled by a government agency, the National Promotion Agency for Seeds. But as the demand for Mexican seed increased, several cooperatives and at least one private company began producing certified seed.* Mexican banks financed some of the development, but Cargill and Continental began making "forward" arrangements with farmers and cooperatives for seeds. The wheat-seed business was highly risky and speculative. There were many different varieties of the seed, and the demand for particular kinds from government ministries in dozens of countries was difficult to predict. The Mexican government controlled production not only through the seed agency but also by adjusting the support price of various other crops in ways that made it either more or less attractive to plant wheat for seed instead of some other crop. Worldwide demand for wheat seed varied, depending on the outlook for grain prices. Mexican seed exports fluctuated by as much as 30 per cent from harvest to harvest—from lows of 10,000 to highs of 30,000 tons. In addition, wheat seed, unlike regular wheat, was perishable. If it was stored too long, its ability to germinate was reduced.

To encourage farmers to take the risks of planting enough wheat seed, Cargill and Continental began in the 1970s to guarantee them the difference between their extra costs for raising wheat as seed and the price they could get at market for ordinary wheat. That way, if there was no market for the wheat seed, it could be sold to make flour and Cargill covered the extra expenses. Sometimes Cargill offered to share the risk with the farmers—in which case farmers who grew wheat seed would share part of the profits if Cargill found a market for it abroad. In this way, the private companies often had a "call" on a sub-

---

* To be certified, the wheat had to be grown under special conditions: Other crops could not have been grown in the ground recently and the wheat had to be a specified distance away from other crops. Producing "miracle" wheat for seed, therefore, cost more than producing an ordinary crop of wheat.

stantial amount of the miracle wheat from Mexico, still the world's leading supplier of the high-yielding seeds.

It was a risky, hazardous business. On one occasion, Cargill sold several thousand tons of wheat seed, thinking it had a firm contract with a Mexican seed supplier. But, according to Cargill, the supplier reneged and Cargill was left embarrassingly "short." In the fall of 1977, several independent grain men in Europe found themselves in a similar position: They had sold several thousand tons of seed to buyers in Algeria and Portugal, but when they tried to acquire the seed in Mexico, they found that Cargill and Continental had a "corner." What happened after that is difficult to ascertain. One version is that the seed prices (which run two or three times higher than regular wheat prices) began to fall, and the European merchants were able to acquire the seed from the companies. Cargill itself was cryptic when I requested information. When I asked Cargill for more details, Bill Pearce wrote:

We were involved in the Mexican seed business last year. It was extremely competitive, in short supply. There were substantial risks and those who weren't successful, no doubt, suffered losses. Those of us who compete in these businesses recognize the risks and learn to live with that experience. Beyond this, we are not prepared to discuss the experience because, although there was nothing illegal or improper in our activities, a full account of the events involved could be embarrassing to people with whom we must continue to do business.

Bill Pearce's reply leaves some questions unanswered, but there is no doubt at all about the companies' strategic importance in the seed distribution system.

This is not something the companies like to advertise. They reject, and vehemently, the whole notion that they are powerful because of their central role in the international economy. They describe themselves as "middlemen," neutral, to a fault, in the allocation of foodstuffs all over the planet. As they see it, the determinants of food and seed distribution are the laws of supply and demand, and the ability of customers to pay. Traders speak of their nonpolitical, arm's-length relationship with governments, and they lament, privately, that government regulations or government laws on foreign investment more and more limit their freedom. Tradax's senior vice-president for operations, Leonard Alderson, was emphatic when he told me: "Whether or not food goes to poor countries is not something we make decisions about. . . . I don't think we make a country buy grain if it otherwise wouldn't. We aren't creating a need in these countries' minds."

Yet, in a sense, Alderson is describing exactly why multinational companies *are* so strategic, and so indispensable. It is *because* they are "neutral," because they can claim not to represent national governments, because they are devoid of a political ideology that they can go everywhere and do everything.

This was clear in 1972 when Russia bought large quantities of Western grain. The Russians went to the companies, not to the U.S. government. The companies provided the services that the Russians needed: secrecy and access to grain from all over the world. But the companies' most important service was to be buffer between the Soviet and American governments. If the Russians had gone to the USDA and proposed buying such an enormous quantity of American grain, there immediately would have been political problems. The administration would have had to deal with a public that still was not accustomed to providing food to Communist countries on such a scale. There would have been demands for "linkage"—for comparable Soviet concessions in other areas. (As we shall see in the next chapter, this was precisely what happened in 1975 when a somewhat wiser U.S. government responded to Soviet secret buying that year.) With the companies, it was a matter of price and availability of wheat.

In oil, multinationals perform similar functions. It is expedient for Arab oil producers and their customers to deal through oil companies rather than directly with each other. In 1973, the companies dutifully allocated oil according to the terms of the Arab oil embargo. At the same time, they were also useful to consumer countries because they could juggle supply lines in such a way that oil kept coming through from other sources even though the letter of the embargo was being observed. Everybody made his political point, but economies did not grind to a halt. Today, Japan prefers buying oil from Exxon to contracting for its long-term supplies with a Saudi Arabian government that might try to use this leverage to extract diplomatic concessions. For their part, the oil sheikhs find it politically advantageous to let the companies manage their embargoes and to enforce their price increases. The companies take the blame for higher gasoline prices abroad and can be offered up as scapegoats at home when radical elements complain that Arab policy is still too soft on the West.

Illustrative of this point is the obscure but interesting example of how Rhodesia managed to export huge amounts of white maize all during the period when trade supposedly was embargoed by the United Nation's 1968 "Resolution 253." Oil not only kept flowing *into* Rhodesia but white maize kept flowing out, along with chrome, sugar, tobacco. This would not have been possible without the knowledge and assistance of private companies.

From 1968 to 1975, an estimated 1.6 million tons of white maize worth at least $200 million was exported from Rhodesia. U.N. officials believe that substantial amounts of it ended up in Japan and Belgium and that the grain got there with the help of Swiss or Swiss-based companies. These exports provided foreign exchange for the economy of the white-ruled country, did their part to keep Rhodesia economically "afloat," and circumvented the political aims of the U.N. embargo.

To backtrack momentarily, white maize is an important human food all over southern Africa, and it is also used in industrial countries to make starch. South Africa was the major international supplier of white maize for this purpose until the mid-1960s, but white maize apparently did not become an export crop in Rhodesia until a few years later. This odd development is evident only through a careful study of world trade statistics. Beginning in 1968, trade analysts at the United Nations noted a sharp increase in Rhodesian maize production. Until then, the country had raised between 800,000 and 850,000 tons annually—about enough to meet its own domestic requirements. By 1972, Rhodesia, by its own statistics, produced nearly double that—1.5 million tons.

The U.N. Sanctions Committee, which was charged with enforcing the embargo, soon learned of several more curious developments. There was also a sharp increase in neighboring Mozambique's maize exports—but this did not coincide with any apparent increase in Mozambique's own maize *harvest*. These exports continued at a strong rate until the country achieved independence from Portugal and became a sovereign nation in 1976, whereupon its maize exports dropped sharply.

The Sanctions Committee also detected an increase in South Africa's maize exports. South Africa itself did not report any such increase, but countries trading with South Africa regularly reported receiving more maize than South Africa said it had sold.

The implication, of course, was that Mozambique, until independence, and then South Africa were conduits for Rhodesian maize.

As the Sanctions Committee studied these curious figures (along with equally strange statistics from southern Africa for exports of chrome, tobacco, sugar, and other commodities produced in Rhodesia), specific complaints about violations of the Rhodesian embargo began to reach it. Between 1969 and 1977, the Sanctions Committee received fourteen such complaints and investigated them all. In most cases the governments implicated in shipping or receiving the "white gold," as maize was called, either refused to respond to United Nations' inquiries or denied knowledge of Rhodesian imports. Making a charge of embargo-busting stick seemed to be very difficult. Two complaints in 1971 concerned shipments of maize of Rhodesian origin to Venezuela in the Greek vessels *Armonia* and *Alexandros* (the latter owned by "Panamanian interests"). It took Venezuela five years to answer the numerous inquiries of the Sanctions Committee, and when it did, it denied receiving any Rhodesian maize in 1971. Christoforos Tsakoumakis, captain of the *Armonia*, was acquitted by a magistrate's court in Greece of knowingly carrying Rhodesian maize to Venezuela: The grain had been identified as Mozambiquean on the loading certificate.

As the Sanctions Committee probed more deeply into the complaints, suspicion fell on Swiss companies. Switzerland is not a member of the United Nations and Swiss nationals could not, therefore, be directly enjoined from breaking the embargo. Nevertheless, the Sanctions Committee repeatedly requested that the Swiss government examine the complaints and take action voluntarily to prevent any Swiss-based companies from aiding the Rhodesians. These requests were always rejected. Swiss authorities noted that the alleged violations took place outside Swiss territory and jurisdiction and did not violate Swiss laws.

As I traveled through Europe in 1976 and 1977, I kept hearing from grain traders about the lucrative Rhodesian maize traffic. The subject would come up in odd ways. Traders resented the fact that companies other than their own had been chosen to handle this business. One trader described his fruitless efforts to persuade the Rhodesian government to shift the business to his firm. "We like the arrangements we have," he was told.

When I saw the amiable Georges André, I asked him if he knew anything about these arrangements. His firm was known to handle South Africa's maize sales to Venezuela. André ships about 160,000 tons of it a year, and other companies claim to have difficulty breaking into this business. But on the matter of

Rhodesian maize André denied any specific knowledge. His people and several others had handled shipments of maize from Mozambique and South Africa, but he did not own the maize when it left the ports. Rather, he said, the firm had bought the grain from South African companies on the high seas after it had left port. In some other cases, he added, André found customers for the maize through its global network of agents and sold it as a commissioned broker for the South African companies. "André was selling for South Africa," he told me. "How they obtained it, I don't know. The South Africans chartered the ships. It was going out with South African and Mozambique certificates. It's *possible* it had been exchanged against Rhodesian. Our buyers accepted it."

Rhodesia's circumvention of the U.N. embargo and sudden "shocks" such as the Russian "grain robbery" raise the same fundamental question: Who is in control of the global grain economy? The short answer is, "Nobody." As an official of the Organization for Economic Development said, "The impression that governments are running the system is false—neither the governments nor anybody else knows what's going on."

The "impression that governments are running the system" has been enhanced by the fact that almost every nation in the world has some kind of agency, authority, or marketing board to supervise or manage the exportation and importation of grain. It is a given that grain is simply too basic to be left to grain merchants entirely. Australia and Canada have wheat boards; Russia has Exportkhleb, Poland has Rolimpex, Iran has ETKA, and Japan has its Food Agency. The big exception is the United States, and from time to time, there are demands that we too stop relying entirely on the commercial companies and create a government monopoly to sell American grain.

After the Russian purchases in 1972, there was some congressional interest in this idea. The feeling was that only the U.S.

government was strong enough to deal with the Russian buying monopoly on terms that would get the best deal for farmers and would protect consumers from food inflation. James Weaver, an Oregon Democrat (and the only ex–commodity broker in Congress), introduced a bill to have the Commodity Credit Corporation take over the marketing of American grain. "We have a world of monopoly buyers and monopoly sellers and a few grain companies. The free market is a fraud and a delusion," said Weaver. In his view, an American grain board would help the United States become an "agricultural OPEC"—a power denied to it by the present fragmented system in which individual companies sell American grain to the highest bidder. Wheat farmers could get $10 a bushel if the government were doing the selling for them, Weaver argued. But there was little enthusiasm on Capitol Hill for his idea. American ideology is tilted against government cartels and monopolies, and liberals worry that the Executive Branch might misuse a grain board—blackmail enemies and threaten to deny grain to countries opposing U.S. policy.

No country has come up with an effective alternative to relying on the multinationals that trade and process grain—and all the other basic commodities and raw materials, for that matter. It has already been seen how even the Russians call on them; and it was recently reported that Cuban troops were guarding Gulf Oil's installations in Angola!

The ability of governments to control and to derive maximum value from their own resources has become one of the most urgent problems for countries in the 1970s. Government intervention in agriculture in the 1930s was mainly a response to political and social developments such as the poverty of farmers. Today, the concern over resources is geopolitical and macro-economic. Price and access to supplies are critical concerns to countries that purchase food or other commodities, just as getting top value is crucial to countries with resources to sell.

The success of the Middle East oil cartel has made the developing countries more acutely aware of their bargaining power in dealing with giant multinational enterprises and with consuming nations. This is evident in the heightened tension between companies and governments. Governments are seeking long-term agreements with their customers to stabilize prices of their basic commodities. In tin, timber, bananas—and, of course, oil—there are moves by governments to see to it that not just the multinationals profit from the basic resources. New techniques of taxation, export quotas, and local equity participation are in vogue.

But in grain the problem of controlling multinational companies is different in that only two countries classed as "developng" are major sources of grain and soybeans—Argentina and Brazil. The rest—the United States, Canada, France, South Africa, and Australia—are in the "advanced" category of nations.

And among this select mixed bag of big grain suppliers—the world's sellers in what more and more is a seller's market—ideas on controlling the grain resource, and the grain multinational, vary widely.

Certainly there *are* strong arguments in favor of the companies. They *are* efficient, and they *do* provide international services and take risks that nobody else does. They are progressive in their transcending of nationalism, their view of the planet as a single entity, and they even bridge the world's adversarial ideological blocs. The companies, say their admirers, are the most efficient organizations ever devised for transferring resources and wealth among countries. When the state takes over, a whole new set of problems comes to mind—inefficiency, bureaucracy, and managers who are subservient to political pressures.

However, in the absence of effective supervision or governmental guidance for the transnational firms—in the absence, in fact, of much hard data on their activities—national interests can get lost in the shuffle. Huge corporations cannot and do not make decisions on the basis of what is in the best interests of the countries where they are represented. This is not to say the companies always act *against* these best interests.* It is just that the companies have a different set of interests from those of individual nations. And because of their immense wealth and their global operations, they can do things that harm a country without any special costs to them. The diversion of wheat away from Zaire does not have much effect on Continental's internal balances, but the repercussions in Zaire are cataclysmic.

Argentina, for example, had been an unsupervised playground for the private companies in the 1920s and 1930s, but when Perón came to power he quickly nationalized the grain trade and created IAPI, which controlled exports with a strong hand and diverted the profits to industrialization (and to the bank accounts of Perón's henchmen). This was an unpleasant period for the established companies such as Bunge and Louis Dreyfus, although the likes of Marc Najar could parlay the situation into big profits. However, it ended in 1959 after Perón was ousted and the companies took over again. When Perón returned more than a decade later, back went the grain trade under state control. This was in 1973. A National Grain Board assumed authority over internal and external marketing of wheat, corn, and grain sorghum.

During this period, the companies kept up a barrage of criticism against the government intervention, blaming it for most of the accumulating misfortunes of agriculture. And indeed, Argentina, which had been the world's leading grain-exporting nation in the 1930s, became a minor factor alongside the United States and Canada in the 1950s and 1960s. By the 1970s, it produced scarcely enough barley for its own uses and it was har-

---

* An interesting example of how the interests of a government and a multinational company can converge is to be seen in Ghana. Officials of Firestone Tire say they are urging the government to push for agricultural self-sufficiency. Food imports are draining so much of the country's foreign exchange that Firestone has been unable to get foreign exchange to import rayon and nylon fabric for its tires.

vesting only a few million tons more grain of all kinds than in the 1930s. Shortly after Perón's death, however, the government again changed course. In 1976, the military government of President Rafael Videla dismantled the old government controls and reinstituted a free market. Videla eliminated state monopolies in grain and meat, returned the international exports to private companies, increased farm price supports to raise production, and encouraged more foreign investment in agriculture. This was a policy that could almost have been written by the grain multinationals, although, in fairness, it has also contributed to a recovery of Argentine grain production and agricultural prosperity.

In neighboring Brazil, the conditions for their investments have been even better. The firms have been deeply involved in the Brazilian "soybean miracle." The soybean boom that began in the late 1960s in Brazil was comparable to an oil strike in the petroleum business. Within several years, this new resource literally sprouted all over southern Brazil, largely on the strength of a sure demand for vegetable protein for animal feeding in Europe and Japan.

Parts of Brazil began to look like the world headquarters of multinational corporatism. Companies such as Bunge's subsidiary Sanbra, Cargill, Continental, Cook Industries, Anderson-Clayton, and Louis Dreyfus built multimillion-dollar processing plants and organized soybean "corridors" to the Brazilian ports. A report on the soybean boom commissioned by the French Government Center for External Trade noted that "this very strong penetration of foreign capital has the advantage of opening the sector towards the outside. In addition the sheer size of these firms allows for large-scale investment. From our discussions with executives of these companies we may affirm that they are entirely capable of increasing their production by 15 to 20 per cent for the next five to ten years." (It should be noted that Japanese companies were very heavy investors, as they are in all countries with resources that the Japanese need.)

However, soybean expansion increased at the expense of production of corn, which is a human food in Brazil while soybeans are not. Land devoted to growing black beans (*feijao*) also was reduced and there was a 275 per cent increase in the price of beans and then rationing in Rio de Janeiro in 1973. Brazil, of course, needs soybean exports to pay for oil imports, and the world needs Brazilian soybeans. But under the present policy, it does appear that multinational companies are having as much to do with setting the national food and agricultural policy of Brazil as the government.

The Brazilian government has controlled the grain trade with a fairly light and discreet hand, using such techniques as exempting profits earned in exports from corporate income taxes (to promote exports), and then removing this fiscal incentive, or others, when it wishes to reduce the outflow.

The control of the multinationals, or lack of it, became an issue in 1974. Farmers got about $130 a ton for their soybeans that year while the world market price reached $400 a ton. The result was large profits for the export companies. Cooperatives (which still handled 60 per cent of the transactions with farmers) objected to the role of the international companies in the export of beans and bean products. Brazil's semiprivate trading company Cobec,* which had been helping the Brazilian government work soybeans-for-oil deals with Middle Eastern and West African countries, complained especially bitterly.

In 1975, the activities of the multinationals came under scrutiny again. A Committee of Investigation of the Multinationals was formed to look into their political, economic, and commercial power. The committee concluded that foreign investment laws gave Brazil sufficient control over the companies. But the activities of the multinationals came up again: A year later an unofficial report by some of Brazil's independent millers charged

---

* In which the Bank of Brazil, several Brazilian commercial banks, and U.S., European, and Japanese banks and trading companies are stockholders.

that Bunge monopolized the country's wheat trade and used its influence to promote wheat imports at the expense of government support for domestic agriculture and Brazilian self-sufficiency. The political issue of economic concentration and control was clearly still very much alive in Brazil.

As marketing boards go, the Canadian Wheat Board is the most powerful and prestigious in the world. It has an awesome reputation, and its gray stone headquarters in Winnipeg underscores its power and apparent impregnability. Although it is run on behalf of farmers and is supposed to account for its actions to its farmer members from the prairie provinces of Alberta, Saskatchewan, and Manitoba, it is often as secretive and aloof as a grain company. It never tells what price it receives when it negotiates with the Russians or Chinese or other foreign governments that want to purchase Canadian wheat. The board justifies this in terms of its sacred mission: protecting the interest of prairie wheat farmers. Grain traders in Winnipeg grumble privately about the Wheat Board's power, and charge that it is too slow and bureaucratic to take advantage of the fast-moving world markets, but they never do so in public for fear their unflattering comments will bring down the wrath of the board upon them.

The current Wheat Board was established by an act of Parliament in 1935 to market prairie grain. It was something that Canadian wheat farmers had wanted for a long time, and they finally got it after the Depression had loosed powerful currents of prairie socialism across Canada. American farmers got the agricultural programs of the New Deal; Canadians got the Wheat Board. The Board was a monopoly that pegged prices, regulated the amount of grain moving into local grain elevators from farms, and sold Canadian grain abroad. The system is controlled through the mandatory inspection of grain, the regulation of transportation costs, and various internal subsidies.

Long after the Wheat Board was established, the private grain trade kept trying to discredit it. It was said that the board was a "socialist plot," with its compulsory prices and regulations on farmers and grain companies alike that destroyed initiative and threatened the free enterprise system. Speakers from the Grain Exchange in Winnipeg crisscrossed the prairies in the late 1940s and early 1950s, trying to influence farmers against it. But farmers were not persuaded. The Wheat Board survived.

Today, there are big differences in the mood and pace of life on the two sides of the Canadian-American prairie border. When I dropped in on the North Dakota town of Rolla in late 1975, farmers still had a lot of unsold grain from the recent harvest in their bins, and they were gambling all the time. Several in-town elevators buy grain in Rolla, but they offer almost identical prices. These change rapidly, even crazily, in response to fluctuations in Chicago, and wheat growers poke their heads in all day long to stay informed. Wheat prices changed as much as 30 cents a bushel in an hour or two. It was agricultural roulette, but the farmers who were still in business in North Dakota plainly liked the excitement. None of those I talked with wanted a grain board.

Just a few miles away in Canada, the mood and tempo could not have been more different. In Manitoba, farm buildings looked a little older, and abandoned wooden elevators looked like dilapidated relics from the 1940s. Fence posts and wooden telephone poles marched down the highway; here and there a quail burst from the roadside cover and flew off into the surprisingly hilly countryside, colored in the prairie twilight with soft mauves, yellows, and greens. The Canadian farmers who gathered in the office of their in-town elevators to gossip and klatsch were relaxed. They seemed in much less of a hurry than people just across the border, and they could not have cared less about prices. The farmers all received the same $2.04½ cents a bushel for their wheat. Later, they would receive a premium depending on how well the Wheat Board did selling the wheat all over the world. That was the Wheat Board's problem, not theirs. At least in the parts of the Canadian prairies I visited, the Wheat Board was popular—a seemingly permanent institution that is working well.

On close examination, though, the Canadian Wheat Board does not look quite so all-powerful. It does have offices in London; it negotiates with Russia, China, and other large customers, including British millers and big importers in Europe such as Serafino Ferruzzi. But when the Wheat Board finds itself running into the problems of marketing an unsold bumper crop, it often turns to the grain companies after all. It sells them the wheat and lets them take risks, find the markets and—in some cases—earn the windfalls. When crops are big, private companies sometimes sell as much as 30 per cent of Canada's wheat crop.

The Wheat Board's maneuvers in the summer of 1976 showed that Canada's is, thus, a mixed private-public system. Canadian farmers brought in a bumper harvest of 20 million tons of wheat that year. As the Wheat Board's huge grain depots in Lake Superior became clogged with grain, concern mounted in Winnipeg. By late August, the first cool breezes were wafting down from the Arctic, a reminder that the Canadian grain ports would not be ice-free too much longer.*

When the Wheat Board's chief strategist, G. N. Vogel (a former Bunge man), returned from vacation, he took a look at the situation and calculated that the board could find customers for no more than 12 or 13 million tons of the 17 million tons that Canada needed to market abroad. He studied the grain markets. Prices were firm in Chicago, but Vogel decided they would not hold much longer, with large American and Canadian crops now moving off the farms. He called in representatives of several private companies and made them an offer they couldn't refuse. He offered to sell them wheat—4 million tons of it—at a substantial discount from the price at which it was selling in the United

---

* The Welland Canal between Lake Erie and Lake Ontario, the gateway to the St. Lawrence River, closes anywhere from December 10 to December 20.

States. American spring-planted wheat comparable to Canada's wheat was selling in Minneapolis for $148 a ton; the board offered it at $135 a ton. This gave the companies a chance for a highly profitable arbitrage. They could sell wheat futures in Minneapolis for something close to the $148 figure and obtain the actual grain in Canada for considerably less than that. It would be up to them to find their own cash customers.

The first people to sense that something was going on behind the scenes in Winnipeg were Minnesota wheat farmers, for the "spot" grain market collapsed abruptly in the Midwest as international companies ceased buying American wheat and made arrangements to sell Canadian wheat from across the border. In the absence of any international rules, the Canadians could do as they pleased. They had been the victims of numerous "dirty tricks" by the USDA over the years, and they had no intention of tipping off the officials in Washington to what they were up to. Soon, however, the USDA began receiving hints. In September, several weeks after the Canadian sell-off, the department received reports that an unidentified international grain company was offering Canadian wheat to Indonesia at a substantial discount from the American price.

When the USDA tried to find out what was happening, its requests for information were coldly turned away by Wheat Board officials. Cables went out from the department protesting to the Canadian government that price-cutting could lead "to unnecessary weakening of the general level of world wheat prices." But when the American agricultural attaché in Ottawa tried to find out what the Wheat Board's price was, he was told bluntly, "We're not telling you that. Stop interfering with our business."

Meanwhile, Cargill, Continental, Louis Dreyfus, and other firms were moving the Canadian wheat aggressively into markets in Europe, South America and the Caribbean. Assistant Secretary of Agriculture Richard Bell was told, in fact, that Louis Dreyfus had sold some of the Canadian wheat to *American* millers in Buffalo! Bell was furious. Here he was trying to unload a bumper American wheat crop abroad, with farm prices beginning to fall and with a presidential election not more than two months away, and the Canadians were selling *their* wheat to American millers. Or rather, Bell was told, Louis Dreyfus was. The Americans protested to the Canadians, but were told curtly that there were "no limits on the destination of Canadian wheat." By this time, the Wheat Board officials must have been having a good laugh at the expense of the people at USDA. Apparently, no Canadian wheat actually got through. Maybe the Lakes iced over. But it had been a major coup for the Canadians in the ongoing grain wars with the agricultural superpower to the south. And it had come at a good time, politically, for the Wheat Board.

If the Wheat Board's critics have their way, private companies will have an even more active share in the Canadian grain trade. There have been complaints that Canada missed out on some of the grain price increases of 1973 and 1974, and that the Wheat Board has lost some of Canada's share of world markets to the United States. Livestock farmers in eastern Canada feel that the board's authority over feed grains (such as barley) keep domestic feed prices artificially high and that consumers pay higher meat prices as a result. And critics of the board also maintain (though seldom for attribution) that the commissioners too often are political appointees rather than skilled businessmen.

So, several years ago, the federal government in Ottawa began trying to streamline the country's grain-marketing system. The federal minister in charge of the Wheat Board proposed abandoning, for efficiency's sake, hundreds of miles of railroad spurs reaching prairie wheat outposts. And, more significantly, in 1973 the Wheat Board lost absolute control over the marketing of barley, Canada's main feed grain. Farmers had an option of selling to the Board, or to the private grain trade.

Cargill moved deep inland in Canada in 1974, buying 195 elevators of the National Grain Company (an old Peavey subsidiary). Canada's Foreign Investment Review Agency, which had been put in charge of Canada's resources, quickly approved the takeover by the world's leading multinational grain company. This prompted Stuart Thiesson of Canada's National Farmers Union to warn, "Potentially, the companies are powerful enough to control the pricing and marketing of *all* Canadian grain. This takes on global importance in terms of world food supplies. And in Canada, the implications for farmers are very serious."

This was the very time when the managers of international companies of all kinds were bemoaning the trend toward more restrictive government policies on foreign investment. It was not a trend that seemed to be cramping the style of the grain multinationals, least of all in the homeland of prairie socialism.

11

The Food Weapon

"Dig tunnels deep, store grain everywhere,
and never seek hegemony."
——MAO TSE-TUNG

In an early October dawn of 1975, a solitary figure clad in a sweatshirt and tennis shorts jogged along the banks of the Moscow River. KGB security agents on bicycles pedaled after him at a discreet distance. The man seemed a frail figure, silhouetted as he was from time to time against Moscow's immense office buildings. But for the rulers of the Soviet Union, the lonely runner represented a new and unfamiliar kind of threat. The jogger was Under Secretary of State Charles Robinson, a physical-fitness buff whose running helped to relieve the considerable tension associated with his mission to Moscow. For "Chuck" Robinson was there to present the Soviet government with a most unappealing proposal: Unless the Soviet Union agreed to ship the United States 10 million tons of oil a year at a substantial discount from the price charged by the OPEC cartel, the Kremlin might not get the grain it urgently needed to make up for a disastrous harvest.

In Washington, this bold initiative was the idea of Robinson's boss, Secretary of State Henry Kissinger. And it had the support of President Ford. To these men, Russian oil was an important potential energy source not subject to OPEC embargoes or price increases. If the Soviet Union wanted American food as badly as Ford and Kissinger suspected it did, a discount would be a small price to pay. This was the message that the trim, bantam-sized man running along the Moscow River brought to the rulers of Russia.

The Soviet difficulties had emerged slowly during the spring and summer of 1975. Month after month, reports from the collective and state farms told of a deteriorating situation in the grain fields. The winter wheat had not fared too badly. Deputy U.S. agricultural attaché Panasuk had correctly reported to Washington in May that conditions for a good Russian harvest existed—but his report had been based only on his inspection of the winter wheat. The spring-planted grains from the Volga River basin eastward had been devastated by drought. Now, the whole Ninth Five-Year Plan, with its promise of improved diets, was jeopardized. Enormous amounts of foreign grain would be needed if the country was to hold to this plan.

The first phase of the Soviet strategy to cover its growing deficit with imported grain had gone smoothly. The Russians were much more subtle and secretive than in 1972, when they had sent Belousov and Co. from Exportkhleb to travel all over the United States buying grain. The buying spree had caught the Americans napping, but it was not likely that the Americans would fall for the same trick twice. That had been an audacious Cossack raid. In 1975, the tactics were those of a night infiltration. Viktor Pershin, the new chief of Exportkhleb, stayed in Moscow and directed his grain ploy from that well-protected location. Soviet shipping agents based in Geneva had secretly contacted Jean Lerbret, the Paris shipping broker, through whom they "covered" their chartering of grain vessels through the Glenas front. Then, Pershin had begun quietly negotiating with traders in the European subsidiaries of the American companies. That done, the Soviet Union was able to buy almost 10 million tons of grain and charter the ships to carry them before the Ford administration had any clear idea of what was going on.

But by the early autumn, very little of that grain had been delivered. The Ford administration was preventing the companies from selling the Russians the additional quantities they wanted, and the tactical advantage the Russians had gained by their early machinations had been lost.

Worse than this, the "peace" that had been worked out with the American labor unions in 1971 to permit the continuation of the Soviet-American grain trade had abruptly broken down. Not only were additional grain purchases questionable, but the maritime unions had renewed their threat to boycott the loading of the grain already committed. Unless there were more jobs for American seamen and safeguards that the sales to Russia would not cause food inflation, the maritime bosses had declared, Russia would have to do without its grain.

The unexpected "hold" on grain movements to Russia created a new situation, one in which the United States rather than the Soviet Union seemed to have the upper hand. The conditions finally existed for the United States to get something back for its grain besides money. It was this that had brought Robinson to Moscow to apply a new kind of leverage on the adversary: the leverage of American "grain power."

American food, to be sure, had played a part in American foreign policy for most of the century. "Food Will Win the War" was a slogan in World War I, when American farmers increased food production and American consumers ate less bread to free more food for their hard-pressed allies. Herbert Hoover, who took charge of wartime and postwar relief as U.S. Food Administrator, contended that without the food, "The allies would have collapsed from deprivation of food by the German submarine warfare [and] . . . a score of nations would have been destroyed by the flames of anarchy or communism."[*]

[*] Herbert Hoover, *An American Epic*, Vol. II (Chicago: Henry Regnery, 1960), p. 2.

After the Armistice, the Allied powers applied their control over food shipments to Germany in a particularly cruel way, again for political reasons. The terms of the Armistice indicated that food would be allowed into Germany. But the Allies continued their wartime blockade pending a final peace agreement and the surrender of the German merchant fleet. The American government objected but (at first) accepted the Allies' refusal to let in American food. Then came widespread reports of starvation in Germany: The population, it was said, was 20 per cent underweight. Beginning in 1919, President Wilson and Hoover lobbied for the lifting of the blockade. "Bolshevism is steadily advancing westward," Wilson warned. "It is poisoning Germany. It cannot be stopped by force, but it can be stopped by food." Hoover's concern was not only starvation in Europe, but also a huge buildup of unsold pork in the United States, and he lobbied with Prime Minister Lloyd George and senior European officials to let some food go through. Finally, on March 14, 1919, the Allies agreed to let in 300,000 tons of cereals and 70,000 tons of fats a month (most of it from North America). In Hoover's view, political damage had already been done by the delays. "The Germans were for many long years unceasing in their denunciation of the continued blockade, and the effect was to poison the minds of their people and to sow the dragon's teeth of war."

In December 1921, Congress appropriated $20 million to finance corn shipments to the "distressed and starving people of Russia." One reason was to help buttress American grain prices, then undergoing a postwar slump. But another aim was to support still active "anti-Bolshevist" elements in Russia, and to embarrass the Bolshevik government. And when World War II began, there were once again calls to farmers and consumers to respond patriotically. "Food is a defensive weapon; without food Britain cannot stand between the United States and the aggressors," one official at the Department of Agriculture said.

America's postwar food relief always had a political component. Subsidized U.S. food supported Marshal Tito's drive for independence from Soviet influence after Yugoslavia refused to join the Cominform in 1948. And the lion's share of P.L. 480 food aid went to foreign countries in which the United States had a political, economic, or military interest. Military clients such as Pakistan, South Korea, Israel, and Turkey all received substantial amounts of this food assistance. So did Yugoslavia and Poland, the two most independent Communist countries in Eastern Europe. Brazil and Indonesia, the sources of enormous reserves of raw materials, were also beneficiaries of subsidized American wheat, rice, and cotton. A State Department official justified the cotton and rice shipments to Indonesia succinctly: "They have the oil, we have the food." And the P.L. 480 leverage could also be used in reverse. When Egypt went to war against Israel in 1967, P.L. 480 stopped.

Food's function in diplomacy was extended and broadened under President Nixon and President Ford, and the food-aid programs were politicized as never before. In 1972 and 1973, 70 per cent of all the P.L. 480 dollars purchased food for the war economies of South Vietnam and Cambodia. In the final stages of that war, Food for Peace was cynically nicknamed Food for War by critics in Congress who maintained that the assistance was only helping to prolong suffering and postpone the inevitable. Elsewhere, the granting or withholding of food aid was used alternately as carrot and stick in nations whose economies and populations had become dependent on imported food. The food-buying credits of P.L. 480 went to South Korea in 1971 in return for that government's secret promise to reduce textile exports to the United States; to Portugal the same year in return for the continuation of American base rights in the Azores; and to Bangladesh in 1974 only after that country agreed to halt its exports of jute to Cuba.

Chile provides the best example of a country where the American food tap was turned off and on again in response to political developments. Subsidized food shipments to Chile were stopped after the Marxist Salvador Allende was elected president in 1970,* and it was one of the first forms of aid to resume after he was overthrown on September 11, 1973. This was part of the covert tactics of "destabilization" adopted by the Nixon administration against Allende.

Chile had imported large volumes of wheat before Allende became president—between 380,000 and 600,000 tons a year—covering a quarter to a third of the country's requirements. Most came from Australia, Argentina, or Uruguay, but as much as 200,000 tons was shipped from the United States. When the American government credit for food buying stopped, imports of U.S. wheat dropped to the tiny amount of 8,000 tons in 1971–72.

There is no doubt that trouble in the food and agricultural sectors helped to bring about Allende's eventual downfall. But these difficulties certainly were not exclusively the result of his administration's mismanagement. New and untried governments dedicated to reform and experiment usually make mistakes at the beginning, but Allende's problems were compounded by external pressures beyond his control. As the government followed through on its promises to redistribute wealth and guarantee milk to Chileans every day, demand for food products increased faster than food production. Chilean wheat production actually *increased* by 5 per cent in the 1970–71 crop year, but wheat imports were nonetheless essential. By 1972, the Nixon administration not only had stopped P.L. 480 and other U.S. assistance, but also had succeeded in blocking some loans from international organizations. So, the Chilean government dipped into its limited foreign exchange reserves to pay for 700,000 tons of imported wheat—this at a time when world grain prices were undergoing their steepest in-

* Except for one $3.2-million credit in 1971.

creases since World War II. (Wheat had tripled in price between mid-1972 and late 1973—partly because of the purchases
by Russia, the country that, ironically, Allende now looked to for
support.)

By the summer of 1973, Chile's food sector was in desperate
straits. Agricultural production had declined* and food consumption had increased. There were breadlines, and meat products were in unusually short supply owing to shortages of feed
grain. The government made arrangements with the Australian
Wheat Board to import 250,000–500,000 tons of wheat after
January 1974—presumably in hopes of obtaining credits from
some source by that time. To help tide the country over, it
counted on 100,000 tons of Soviet-financed wheat from Bulgaria,
East Germany, and Australia. But as the global shortages worsened, the difficulties of trying to get by without American
wheat became more and more acute. In August, agents of the
government grain board went to the United States and arranged
to buy American grain with the aid of financing from France and
Mexico. Cook and André's American associate, Garnac, filled
orders for 300,000 tons.

When Chilean military leaders launched their coup against
Allende on the morning of September 11, 1973, about 100,000
tons of wheat financed or shipped by socialist countries was en
route to Valparaiso. The U.S. Department of Agriculture reported that the shipments were diverted. The wheat never
reached Chile, though where it did end up is uncertain. Probably the Cubans received some of it.

Grain, in any case, was a crucial priority for the new military
rulers who had overthrown Allende's elected government, and
on September 26, the government ordered 120,000 tons of
American wheat from Continental, Bunge, Dreyfus, and Garnac.
Since the regime had no money to pay for it, the purchases were

* Bad weather and a truck drivers' strike, partly financed by the CIA, hindered distribution of seed and fertilizer in 1972 and 1973.

conditioned on approval of a $24-million American government line of credit.

In Washington, there were two major problems in this Chilean request for aid. One was that American grain was becoming increasingly scarce and high-priced in the United States itself. New food-buying credits for other nations had been frozen for several months. The other difficulty was Chile's questionable credit-worthiness. It had $450 million in foreign debts, and the "destabilized" Chilean economy was on the rocks. But on October 4, the National Advisory Council on International Monetary and Financial Policies, acting on a "strong recommendation" from the State Department, granted the credit line. The NAC justified the loan under a provision of the law allowing such financial aid "for overriding foreign policy considerations." The loading of U.S. wheat for Chile began at the Gulf of Mexico that very weekend.

On November 13, NAC authorized a second line of credit— $28 million for corn purchases. The justification, which could just as easily have applied during the Allende period, was that Chile "is faced with a critical supply situation for protein products such as beef, pork and poultry." In 1974, Chile was put back on the list of countries eligible for the special "soft" loans of P.L. 480. The next year the United States shipped about 600,000 tons of wheat to Chile—about five times the volume immediately before Allende came to power. Chile's dependence on American wheat continued long after the new regime had seized power. The country joined Iran and Southeast Asia as a "grain protectorate" of the United States.

A year later, Kissinger directed that the food-aid "carrot" be similarly used in the Middle East. In September 1974, the United States pledged 100,000 tons of wheat aid to Egypt. It was an extremely significant step—the first such assistance since relations between the two countries had been ruptured in the Six-Day War of 1967. Kissinger said this assistance was the ultimate in "humanitarian" aid, in that it might prevent war. As this suggested, the food deliveries were conditional upon Egypt's readiness to cooperate and participate in the peace plan Kissinger was then drafting.

The food incentive was a powerful one indeed. As Egyptians' memories of their glorious military deeds in the 1973 war faded, President Anwar Sadat was left to deal with the mundane realities of everyday life. His country was rapidly sinking into an economic quagmire. Cairo was one of the world's most overcrowded cities. Squatters camped in cemeteries on the urban outskirts, and camels, busses, and humans vied for space on the downtown streets. Basic food staples were heavily subsidized, and the food imports required by Egypt were a drain on its dwindling foreign-currency reserves. Food, in short, was essential to President Sadat's political survival. It was against this background that Kissinger directed that the flow of American food aid, halted for seven years, be resumed.*

The United States thus obtained political and economic benefits from the food it dispensed to Egypt, Chile, and other countries through the P.L. 480 aid program. But these were nations at the periphery of American diplomacy, and the subsidized food shipments were like any other foreign aid: an effective weapon in foreign policy only because the nations receiving it were weak, poor, or lacking in the foreign exchange needed to pay for food in world markets.

As long as other countries were doing the United States a favor by relieving it of food surpluses, the opportunities for extracting political concessions in return for food were limited to P.L. 480 clients. To policy-makers conditioned for years to the perennial surplus, the notion of withholding food from *rich* allies or adversaries in order to obtain political advantages seemed nonsensical.

What modified this thinking in Washington, at least in some

---

* By 1978, Egypt was the largest recipient of P.L. 480 assistance. It received more than 1 million tons of subsidized wheat a year.

quarters, were the developments in 1972 and 1973 that suddenly focused attention on basic resources. These years shook fundamental economic assumptions. With the Russian "grain robbery" and the Arab oil embargo, and price increases of both commodities, the old world of cheap oil and food gave way to unprecedented global inflation and shortages. America, which had seemed so economically invulnerable, was revealed as just one more client of the oil kingdoms of the Middle East. Russia had to buy immense amounts of grain to carry out its economic plans. The superpowers looked wobbly. And less powerful countries—European nations and Japan, for example—were even more dependent on outside sources of raw materials and food. Politicians accustomed to viewing the world in terms of the ideological struggle of the previous two decades began paying attention to the posted price of oil in the Persian Gulf, the spot price of Rhodesian chrome, and the corn "basis" at the Gulf of Mexico.

The OPEC oil embargo took the United States by surprise and forced not only the United States but every country in the world to reexamine its international relations at the most basic level. From this perspective, nothing was more important than raw materials, resources, basic goods, and food. Kissinger, a statesman in the century of ideology, was also a historian unusually well acquainted with the economic drives that had shaped diplomacy in the eighteenth and nineteenth centuries. While financial details—exchange rates, devaluations, and balances of payments—bored him, he quickly mastered the politics of global resources, which he saw as coming down to a question of who has what, who wants it, and how much are they prepared to pay in diplomatic as well as economic terms to get it. The United States depended on foreign countries for oil, bauxite, rubber, copper, chrome, molybdenum, and many other commodities and materials. But interdependence worked two ways. Many of the countries that had an abundance of these resources also relied on the United States for food, and for the technology and capital required to grow food or to extract minerals. This was true even for oil exporters. Nigeria, Iran, Indonesia, and Venezuela all sold oil to the West, and each country received substantial amounts of American food.

Formal arrangements to reduce the instability caused by the dependency of some countries on the resources or food of others fit naturally into Kissinger's diplomatic schema. His whole diplomacy strove for a stable world, a world of "balanced" politics dominated by the superpowers. As he saw it, food deficits were potentially destabilizing and therefore not usually in the long-run interests of the United States (except in special cases such as Chile under Allende). Kissinger became a strong advocate for agricultural foreign-aid programs that increased farm production overseas. He also became the leading proponent, beginning in 1974, of commodity agreements between importers and exporters. He favored pacts that gave importers access to markets at reasonable prices and gave exporters assured customers. This ran counter to the traditional American preference for "free trade" and was closer to the preferences of European governments for trade agreements linked to political and economic cooperation. But it was Kissinger's view that grain was a national resource that was simply too important to be left to the devices of the marketplace or to the dealings of grain traders.

In August 1974, the connection between grain and national power was clearly drawn in a study by the Central Intelligence Agency—"Potential Implications of Trends in World Population, Food Production and Climate." The CIA analysts concluded that the world's increasing dependence on American grain surpluses "portends an increase in U.S. power and influence, especially vis-à-vis the poor, food-deficit countries." North American grain-growing areas, being less vulnerable than most to unpredictable weather, would be an even more crucial food source. If the climate took a turn for the worse, as some climatologists predicted it would, "the United States might regain the primacy in world affairs it held in the immediate post–World

War II era." Unlike most of the agency's studies, this ominous piece of futurology was released to the public. It could hardly have eased the alarm that was already then spreading through world grain markets.*

The statistics of the global grain trade are less well known, but in some ways even more startling than the ones showing how dependent most of the world is on the oil of the Middle East. In the case of wheat, corn, and soybeans, the exportable surpluses are located in just a few countries: soybean surpluses in the United States and Brazil; corn surpluses in the United States, Argentina, South Africa, and Thailand; wheat surpluses in the United States, Canada, France, Argentina, and Australia. The United States dominates the rice trade, and in barley the leaders are the United States, Canada, Argentina, and Britain.

For many countries, the United States is not only the main supplier but also a main source of the *overall* grain supply. In wheat, the United States provided 2.8 million tons of Brazil's total 5.8 million tons consumed in 1975; 221,000 of Ecuador's 246,000 tons; 510,000 of Venezuela's 651,000 tons; 1.6 million of South Korea's 1.7 million tons; 487,000 of the Philippines' 525,000 tons; and 370,000 of Israel's 655,000 tons. In corn, for which there are fewer suppliers, America is even more essential. The nation provided 5.5 million of Japan's total 7.6 million tons; and 1.8 of 1.84 million tons of the corn of *East Germany*.

Food dependency on the United States is an undeniable reality. But could this be converted into political power or diplomatic leverage? This was not clear in 1975. To take one hypothetical case, Panama was a country that got virtually all its

---

* That same fall Kissinger ordered his State Department staff to make its own study of the implications of "food power." The State Department has repeatedly refused to release any part of the study, citing "national security." It says the study describes the vulnerabilities of certain countries to food embargoes and, therefore, the release of their names could harm U.S. relations with them. Perhaps the State Department under Cyrus Vance is reluctant to release a document whose findings might prove useful in the future.

wheat from the United States, and it was easy to imagine a situation—a threat to the Panama Canal, for instance—where an embargo might seem appropriate. But if American wheat were suddenly unavailable in Panama, Panamanians might get enough from a sympathetic government in Mexico to survive—or they might eat more root crops or grow corn and wheat (not easy in the tropics) in place of sugar cane.

In the aftermath of the oil embargo against the United States, the possibility of a counterembargo of grain against the Arabs was discussed at the Treasury and State departments—and rejected. So was a modified embargo that would have imposed an export tax on OPEC-bound grain. Neither idea stood up to careful analysis. Most major oil-producing countries, such as Saudi Arabia, were sparsely populated and could easily fulfill their small grain requirements elsewhere. Iran, potentially more vulnerable because of its large population, was of course an important market—half a billion dollars a year—for American farm commodities. The farm lobby in Congress had no desire to see this market abandoned on behalf of gasoline users in big cities. "We freeze, they starve," was a threatening phrase heard in Washington, but the realities of politics and economics caused the talk of counterembargoes to fade away.

American trade embargoes in the past had, in fact, proved dismally ineffective. Trade blockades of China, Cuba, North Korea, and North Vietnam did not bring those nations' governments to their knees. One of the main victims of the American economic boycott of Cuba turned out to be Gulf Coast rice farmers, who lost one of their best markets. The ineffectiveness of the embargoes was preordained by the fact that Canada continued to sell China, Russia, and Cuba wheat all through the times when the U.S. government had closed these markets to American farmers.

The areas of the world that plainly would be most vulnerable to an American food embargo for political reasons—Europe and Japan—were hardly likely candidates for such an exercise of

American international clout. There was, however, one country that not only had begun to rely on enormous quantities of imported grain—quantities so large that only America could satisfy the needs—but also was a political adversary from whom concessions would be useful. This, of course, was the Soviet Union.

Long before the Glenas cover had been lifted in July 1975, Ford administration officials had been discussing the possibilities of exploiting this situation. Robinson's information that the Russians were selling lots of gold in Switzerland had been added to another clue of possible Russian farm trouble: The Russians unexpectedly sent word that they would like to participate in talks in London on a new international wheat agreement. Under the grain reserve plan then under discussion, signers of an agreement would have first access to an international pool of grain. Earlier, the Russians were uninterested. Now it suddenly seemed that the Russians wanted to be among those with access to the pool.

The talks about the grain situation, authorized by Kissinger and organized by Robinson, took place in the office of presidential adviser L. William Seidman in the Executive Office Building—a suite with a view of the front portal of the White House itself. The discussion centered on avoiding another Russian "grain robbery."

Robinson believed that the United States should benefit from the grain trade with Russia in a way commensurate with its position as the market of last resort for the Russians: Farmers should be well paid, American shipping companies should receive a fair share of the business, and ways for obtaining other, indirect benefits from the Soviet dependency should be examined. Robinson had come to the State Department only a few months before from the Marcona Mining Company. He was a practical man, with a background in management and the "hard" science of engineering, and he approached this new job as a doer, a catalyst, a creative businessman among diplomats. In his view, if America's enormous grain resources gave it leverage, this leverage should be used. To this extent, he was a believer in "grain power."

Joining the talks were Labor Secretary John Dunlop; Director James Lynn of the Office of Management and Budget; and Alan Greenspan and Paul MacAvoy of the Council of Economic Advisers. These participants had one thing in common. All of them were suspicious of the secretary of agriculture. Dunlop, formerly head of President Nixon's Cost of Living Council, felt that Earl Butz cared more about his big-farm constituents than about the welfare of American food consumers. Lynn was convinced that Butz had mishandled the 1972 sales to Russia and given the Russians an unnecessary bargain. MacAvoy was suspicious of the crop estimates, statistics, and economic information issued by Butz's department. Butz was absent from the meetings in Seidman's office. He was not invited.

Butz's desire to maximize grain exports to cash-paying customers had already put him in conflict with others in the administration who were evidently more concerned about inflation than he was. As we have seen, in October 1974, officials at the Treasury Department and at the Special Trade Representative's office at the White House countermanded two large private grain sales to Russia without waiting for Butz to return to Washington for the decision. And the State Department had also won a number of skirmishes. The USDA had opposed extending P.L. 480 food-buying credits to Portugal and to Chile in 1973 because it feared that these shipments would raise prices of food to regular foreign customers, but the State Department had prevailed and the credits had been approved. And in November 1974, Kissinger upstaged Butz at the World Food Conference in Rome, appearing as keynote speaker and delivering a major address on international agricultural policy.

Privately, Butz chafed at the "striped pants boys" at the State Department who were trying to take over his agricultural prerogatives. And in the bureaucratic warfare within the State Department, Butz had some effective forces of his own. He came to

Washington with a ready-made constituency: the rich, influential, and perennially underestimated agricultural Establishment of large commercial farmers, grain companies, food processors, millers, and retail chain stores. In 1975, agriculture and food were a $200-billion slice of the nation's economic pie. Food was a huge industry. Commercial interests, not farmers, dominated the lobbying that went on around farm bills.* And Butz catered to this group. People living in cities thought the 1972 grain sales to Russia and the high food prices that came afterward were a fiasco. But the developments were not perceived that way by farmers, fertilizer companies, seed dealers, and farm machinery companies, which prospered as never before. Earl Butz traveled the Midwest speaker's circuit, telling farmers they had never had it so good and advising them to plant "fence post to fence post."

In the spring of 1975, Butz and his aides had taken secret precautions against the inflation fighters and "grain power" enthusiasts who were plotting elsewhere in the government. Senior USDA officials were frequently in touch with the grain companies; when Assistant Secretary Richard Bell learned from these contacts that the Russians were interested in buying grain from the United States, he told the companies that there should be no objection to their selling 10 million tons—a risky assertion in light of the furor that had arisen over previous big deals. But Bell's assurances seemed good politics. Farm prices were beginning to slip, and on May 1 President Ford had demonstrated his commitment to "whip inflation now" by vetoing an emergency

---

* In addition to sugar-beet raisers and cane growers, those lining up to lobby for or against sugar-price-support legislation included sugar users such as Coca-Cola and Pillsbury; corporate sugar growers such as U.S. Sugar Corp., with thousands of acres of plantations in Florida; and companies such as Cargill and A. E. Staley, which operate plants that make liquid sweeteners from corn. In fairness, it must be said that Butz, philosophically a free marketeer, disliked special farm-support legislation. He spoke of the "vicious little lobbies" that developed around sugar, peanuts, rice, and tobacco.

farm bill that would have increased price supports for grain. Bell did not, however, convey his advisory to the grain firms to the Economic Policy Board. As he was to say later, "All they could say was no." It was Butz's policy to push exports and boost farm prices. Bell was doing his job.

The Soviet buying that ensued in July came, therefore, as no particular surprise to the Department of Agriculture. At the Economic Policy Board, however, there was astonishment at the size and speed of the sales. John Dunlop was furious and his anger was not abated by assurances from Bell that the United States could easily sell 14 million tons in the foreign market without affecting domestic food prices. To the Council of Economic Advisers' MacAvoy, Bell's assumptions seemed to ignore all the lessons of the previous three years; he was so skeptical that he commissioned two private consultants* to prepare their own estimates of the likely effect of the sales on world grain supplies and grain prices.

The sales not only raised new concerns about inflation, but also deprived the Robinson group and the "grain power" enthusiasts of any opportunity to act. The grain was contracted for and committed. The government's machinery for estimating Soviet grain requirements and for regulating the flow of grain out of the United States had malfunctioned.

Even then, the requirement that companies obtain prior approval of large grain export sales—abandoned in March—was not reinstated. On July 24, the administration finally asked the exporters to "voluntarily" hold off on any *new* sales. It was not until August 11, when reports on the American corn crop gave an indecisive verdict about its probable size, that the administration finally placed a "moratorium" on further contracts with the Russians. And by then, of course, 10 million tons already had been committed. The horse had left the barn.

* John A. Schnittker Associates of Washington, D.C., and Connell Rice and Sugar of Westfield, N.J.

It was the unions that came to the rescue. President George Meany of the AFL–CIO was a steady critic of détente with the Soviet Union—"the one-way street," as he called it. He was at his best when lambasting Russians. There was nothing artificial in this; it came as naturally to him as lighting up one of his thick cigars. Of the July sales, he grumbled: "Why should we help these people out? Why should we compensate for their failure to provide food for their own people, at a time when they're spending a tremendous proportion of their national income on armaments, on trying to achieve military superiority?"

There were practical as well as philosophical reasons for Meany's unhappiness with the July deal. The United States and Russia had agreed in 1972 that American vessels would carry one-third of Soviet-bound American grain. But Meany believed that the Russians had been cheating; the American shipping quota had not been fulfilled, and the American merchant marine was hurting. On July 31, the International Longshoremen's Association issued an ultimatum, which was supported by the executive council of the AFL–CIO: Unless the government provided guarantees that the sales to Russia would not increase food prices, U.S. longshoremen would not load the grain. On August 11, longshoremen walked off the job while loading a Russian-bound vessel in Houston, only to be ordered back to work the next day. One week later, the *Hellas in Eternity*—the Greek vessel whose charter to Glenas had first tipped off the brokers at the Baltic Exchange to the impending grain deals—loaded a cargo of wheat for Russia without incident and steamed out into the Gulf of Mexico. But Meany and the longshoremen still reserved the right to boycott the Russian-bound ships. In doing so, they shifted the balance of power in Ford's divided administration to the advocates of "grain power."

Robinson and Kissinger had discussed the possibility of trading American grain for Soviet oil even before the *fait accompli* of the July sales. They reasoned that such an exchange would be in Russia's interest as well as the United States'. The Soviet government was always short of foreign exchange; if it was to continue to buy foreign wheat, corn, and soybeans, it would need money to finance the transactions. In 1975, the price of 10 million tons of oil was about equal to the price of 6 million tons of wheat. Robinson suggested that the United States might also sell the Russians offshore drilling technology. The Soviets, it was thought, could finance the equipment by selling the incremental oil production resulting from it to the United States.

Indeed, the Soviet Union already was the world's largest petroleum producer. The 9.8 million barrels that it pumped daily from its wells exceeded the production of either the United States or Saudi Arabia. The Russians *had* a surplus. They exported about 2.6 million barrels a day. Most of this went to Eastern Europe, but 880,000 barrels a day went to Western Europe. None of it, however, went to the United States, a fact which made the United States almost wholly dependent on oil from members of the OPEC cartel.

From the beginning, Kissinger expressed interest in the "psychological impact" of a grain-for-oil strategy. The United States would gain a source of oil outside OPEC. Not only that, Kissinger believed that the Soviet Union could be persuaded to give a *discount* from the Arab price, if it needed American grain as badly as it seemed.

In 1972, surplus U.S. grain had been just one American asset to induce the Russians to partake in a dialogue. But in 1975 the situation was very different. American grain surpluses had dwindled, and wheat, corn, and soybeans sold at premium prices. More than that, the international situation and the domestic scene had changed significantly. The American military withdrawal from Southeast Asia was over, so that Soviet cooperation in that area was no longer necessary. The initial euphoria over détente, created by Nixonian "summitry" and a flurry of new Soviet-American agreements, also had passed. The Nixon administration had the strategic arms limitation agreement it wanted and a second agreement, SALT II, appeared headed for prolonged negotiations. With the honeymoon over, the relationship between the powers was settling back into a more conventional mode.

Domestic attitudes toward détente had hardened by the summer of 1975. Nixon-Kissinger policies on strategic arms, trade, and grain were criticized by hawks for failing to demand adequate reciprocity. It was Congress that had written in requirements for emigration rights for Soviet Jews as a condition for lowering U.S. tariffs on imported Soviet products. (Russia rejected these conditions.) And Gerald Ford, already bracing for a challenge to his nomination in 1976 from Ronald Reagan, was moving toward a more conservative position across the bargaining table from the Russians.

Perhaps more significant, Kissinger's attention was now on the Middle East. Through the whole summer of 1975, he was engrossed in Middle Eastern problems. As he embarked on a crucial round of shuttle diplomacy in late August, the possibility of making final agreement on grain shipments contingent upon Soviet good behavior in that volatile area undoubtedly crossed his mind. Grain was an asset that could and should be used to advance American diplomatic interests. As he told a Cabinet meeting that summer, it was "unthinkable for the United States to take this [grain] counter off the board and say it belongs to Cook Industries."

The idea of using the grain "counter" to obtain cheap Soviet oil continued to germinate at the State Department all through the summer, as the public clamor over the grain sales mounted. Kissinger and Robinson discussed a discount of as much as 10 per cent—$1.00 a barrel—on the price of oil landed in the United States. This was a discount that bore little relationship to the realities of world oil markets. Gulf Oil at that time was earning margins of no more than 10 cents a barrel on the Soviet oil it delivered to Italy. When Kissinger broached the idea of the discount to Treasury Secretary William Simon, Simon agreed to give it a try, but privately, he was to say later, the idea struck him as "ludicrous." The Treasury secretary was a believer in free trade; what Kissinger had in mind was extortion. The United States wanted the market price for grain, yet it was asking below-market prices on oil that the Soviet Union already could sell in Western Europe. Simon, a former New York City bond salesman with little knowledge of diplomacy, thought the diplomatic genius at the State Department had gone slightly mad.

Still, the grain-for-oil idea had developed enough by the time President Ford went to Helsinki on July 31 for the summit conference on European security so that he had a written reminder in his briefing papers to raise the possibility of an oil-for-grain swap with Leonid Brezhnev. He did, and the Soviet leader expressed interest, but apparently Ford did not mention anything about a discount for Soviet oil. On the return trip, American diplomats in Ford's entourage took out pencils and paper and began scribbling calculations on oil and grain prices.

Back in Washington, Robinson assigned Ambassador Deane Hinton to look into a possible barter deal. Hinton was wandering around the State Department corridors without a job at the time and wondering about his future. He had just been expelled from Zaire and was uncertain of how Kissinger had reacted to Mobutu's charges of American involvement in plots to overthrow him. The assignment gave him his answer. It was a welcome signal that he was still in the secretary's good graces, and he threw himself into the task.*

Right away, it was clear to Hinton that there were problems. Oil companies importing Soviet oil that was being sold at a discount would earn windfall profits. That could be avoided by having the federal government buy the Soviet oil for its strategic petroleum reserve. But other problems remained. The Russians

---

* Hinton is probably the State Department's leading expert on food issues. He later became U.S. representative to the Common Market in Brussels.

already had a logical, nearby outlet for oil surpluses—Europe. And the plan for enticing the Russians with the promise of off-shore oil-drilling technology had to be scrapped: Congress would never permit the United States to provide the Russians with such high-grade know-how.

It was Labor Secretary Dunlop who had the most difficult task of all that August, however. Ford gave him the job of keeping the grain moving while finding some way to mollify the unions and to help Kissinger get some diplomatic benefits from the situation. Despite the "hold" on new contracts with the Russians, grain prices continued to rise all through August. But in early September, the hold finally began to have the desired effect. Prices began to slide down again. Now, the administration had to contend with irate farmers. President William Kuhfuss of the American Farm Bureau called on Dunlop to express displeasure. Gruff and forbidding as Dunlop, a Harvard economics professor turned Labor Secretary, could sometimes be, he couldn't shake Kuhfuss off. "Do you mean to tell me that in our total relationship with the Soviet Union we can't use grain because your interests are involved?" he asked Kuhfuss impatiently. "The interests of the *country* are involved here."

It was clear to Dunlop that, at the very least, something finally had to be done to normalize the erratic Soviet buying. Meany wanted a long-term agreement regulating the size of grain purchases and the procedures for them, a scheme that fit well with the strategy Kissinger, Robinson, and Hinton were developing. Such an agreement—along with improvements in the shipping arrangements—was what Dunlop promised to the unions in return for keeping the grain moving.

On September 9, Dunlop guided Meany and other labor leaders into the Oval Office at the White House for a meeting with President Ford. It was a political set piece. Presidential adviser Seidman read a prepared question: If the United States attempted to negotiate a permanent agreement that would establish ceilings and a regular procedure for future Soviet grain transactions, would the longshoremen load the ships? Silence. Dunlop nudged longshoremen President Teddy Gleason. "Yeah," said Gleason.

Butz was not invited to the meeting or to the press conference that followed. Then, the very next day, Butz suffered another humiliation. State Department officials had learned that while new American grain sales to Russia were blocked, the big grain companies were continuing to sell grain to Russia's close ally, Poland. In effect, this was a leak in the embargo, for Russia supplied the Poles with several millions tons of wheat a year and every bushel the Poles could buy in the United States was that much less they would need from the Russians.

Kissinger, Robinson, and Dunlop urged Ford to put Poland under the embargo, and the President agreed. Butz, who was present for this meeting in the Oval Office, was sputtering with anger by the time the President left the room. He had gone along with the hold on further sales to the Russians but now the embargo was being extended. The anti-Butz faction, he felt, was ganging up on him and undermining the grain exports that had been the basis of his agricultural policy ever since the 1972 "grain robbery." "You're treating me like a country cousin," he hissed at Robinson. "I'm on the team, and I expect to be treated as a member." Still, it was Kissinger's counsellor, Helmut Sonnenfeldt, not Butz, who telephoned the Polish Embassy later that day and suggested that Warsaw be "requested" to cease buying grain in the United States until further notice.

On September 11, Robinson arrived in Moscow to open talks on a long-term grain agreement. At that point, nothing had been made public about the Kissinger-backed oil initiative. Robinson stayed until September 16. On his return home for consultations, he said that he already had reached agreement "in principle" on a commercial grain agreement.

In the United States, the unrest in farm country over the delays in approving additional sales was growing, and so was Butz's annoyance. When Polish Minister of Agriculture Kazimierz Barcikowski visited Washington on September 22, Butz stunned him by describing the Polish embargo as a "sad occurrence" and admitting that he personally had resisted it.

However, Kissinger was more adamant than ever about getting Russian oil at a discount. A meeting of OPEC oil ministers on September 27 only strengthened his determination. The oil states increased petroleum prices by 10 per cent, raising the market price of a barrel of oil from $10.46 to $11.51. The increase would add $10 billion in the next year to the world's oil bill, of which $2 billion would be from the United States. By this time, the Kissinger initiative had considerable support among Ford's political advisers. As they saw it, the longer the embargo stayed on, the more essential it became for the United States to come away with some positive Russian concessions. None was more politically appealing than the prospect of cut-rate Soviet oil.

On September 29, Robinson arrived back in Moscow with an expanded delegation for a second round of talks. But right away, he and his aides began to have misgivings. Plenary meetings took place almost daily, and detailed work began on a grain accord. The Russians wanted a promise that they could buy a minimum amount of corn and wheat from the United States each year; the Americans wanted a ceiling above which the U.S. government had to give approval. This presented no serious problem, and the two sides moved quickly to work out the technicalities. The Soviet Union already had made one concession, agreeing to increase the grain rate for American vessels on the Black Sea run to $16.00 a ton. But on oil they were unbending.

The daily scenario became familiar. Robinson would meet with Foreign Trade Minister Nikolai Patolichev and advise him that there would be no more U.S. grain without oil. Patolichev would reply that his countrymen would "starve to death" before they succumbed to any such political pressure. Occasionally the Russian picked up the phone, dialed, and spoke hastily. "That was Brezhnev," he would say after hanging up. "He says no." He became almost commiserative with his American negotiating partner. "Mr. Robinson, you can have your grain agreement and ride back to Washington on a white horse—but that horse is getting dirtier every day!"

Robinson, activist businessman turned diplomat, felt frustrated and thwarted. He borrowed a pair of tennis shorts from Ambassador Walter Stoessel and set out in the early morning hours on his five-mile running jaunts along the Moscow River. The jogging eased some of his tension, and Patolichev was impressed. "The KGB is having trouble keeping up with you," he joked.

Joseph Bell of the Federal Energy Administration had joined the delegation because his expertise about oil was needed, but in Moscow he became the most underworked man in the American delegation. At the Hotel Peking, he helped Hinton with his work on the grain agreement and found time to see *Don Quixote* at the Bolshoi Ballet. But he had only one brief, inconclusive meeting with Deputy Foreign Trade Minister Mikhail Kuzmin, a stocky balding veteran official who had collected three Orders of Lenin in his long career. Kuzmin had not earned these honors by beating around the bush. "Do you insist on a discount?" he asked Bell bluntly.

Bell felt that the word "discount" was slightly harsh. The Americans had left open the possibility that the substantial price reduction they wanted could be disguised by Russia's paying the cost of cleaning the holds of tankers or increasing shipping rates. "We are looking for a mutually advantageous deal," he replied with deliberate evasion.

"Will you pay the market price?" Kuzmin pressed him.

"That is a complicated thing, the market price," Bell said.

At the end of each day, Robinson cabled the State Department. And as the days wore on and Russian intractability on oil continued, these cables became blunter. The messages conveyed the delegation's belief that there was no way the grain and oil accords could be linked. A discount on the landed price of oil was unacceptable to the Russians, no matter how it was disguised. If Russian oil arrived in the United States, it would be clear to the OPEC countries that the Soviet Union was making it economically possible for the oil companies to move it. "Your white horse is getting dirtier," Patolichev told Robinson.

But Ford was by now politically committed more than ever to the barter plan. His domestic advisers, then planning his election-campaign strategy, clung to the hope for it. On October 10, he finally announced at a press conference that the United States was seeking a "potential oil deal with some favorable aspects." He began to boast about American negotiating prowess: "We are trying to be good hard-nosed Yankee traders. And when we end up with an agreement I can assure you that the U.S. will do as well in the areas where we want help as they will." The next day, Yankee trader Robinson, in Moscow, read this on the news wires and groaned.

Kissinger continued to take a hard line despite the pessimistic messages channeled back from Robinson each evening to his antechambers, where Counsellor Sonnenfeldt and Assistant Secretary of State for Economic Affairs Thomas Enders would examine them and bring them to Kissinger for a command decision. "I want to be a little tougher than Chuck," Kissinger would say.

The Russians, it seemed to Robinson, were not bluffing. It was evident that their hand was strengthening. For one thing, the old-boy network of Soviet and Western grain merchants was busily sweeping the world for every available particle of surplus grain. The Americans had regained control over U.S. exports, but they could not control what the multinational grain houses did elsewhere. Powerful as the U.S. government was, it had little power to control what Cargill, Continental, or Cook did in Europe, Australia, or Argentina. The companies all felt free to sell the Russians grain from those sources. The Ford administration had not imposed a moratorium for any stated *political* purposes: Ostensibly, the reason was concern over the adequacy of grain supplies in the United States and the fear of a new round of food inflation. So all through August and September the companies had kept scrounging up grain for Russia. (In August, the Russians bought 1.5 million tons of wheat from the Common Market and soon followed this up with another 750,000 tons before turning to Canada for 50,000 tons of oats.) Even as Robinson and Patolichev continued their discussions in Moscow into October, Cook, Toepfer, Tradax, Louis Dreyfus, and some other unidentified companies continued to sell grain to Exportkhleb. From Romania came 400,000 tons of wheat, from Brazil 400,000 tons of corn and some soybeans, from Argentina more than 1 million tons of corn, and from Sweden, wheat. Several members of the American delegation were invited to the office of Viktor Pershin, head of Exportkhleb. There on the wall hung a souvenir: a Cargill advertisement.

The mood in the American delegation was as bleak as Moscow, a city that, in October, already had one foot planted in winter. Muscovites donned their woollen coats, hats, and kerchiefs against the first cool winds blowing down from the Arctic. In the outdoor marketplaces, the open-air food stalls that had displayed fresh tomatoes, melons, and cucumbers all summer began to offer more ordinary staples—potatoes, turnips, and sauerkraut put up in wooden barrels. Across the vast expanses of the Soviet Union, one cycle of planting and harvesting was ending and another was beginning. Mounds of sugarbeets lay in the open fields. In the Ukraine, the north Caucasus, and the "black earth" regions of central Russia, the collective farms began sowing the dark, tilled soil with the wheat crop for the following year. The summer grain harvest was over, but a new crop already was going into the ground.

At the Ministry of Foreign Trade, Patolichev seemed to grow more confident each day. The Russians, so secretive about their grain buying earlier in the summer, now advertised each new transaction to the Americans. Patolichev called a meeting of all the members of the two negotiating teams, and began a long soliloquy. He spoke of the great Soviet-American wartime alliance. He pleaded with the Americans to understand the importance of mutual trust in the new era of détente. He was passionate, subdued, eloquent, tedious. Negotiations were impossible when one side believed it had its "boot on our necks." Had the Americans come to talk politics? If so, they should ask for a meeting with Foreign Minister Andrei Gromyko. Patolichev talked for an hour, which stretched to two, then five.* Viktor Pershin of Export-khleb looked across the table at Agriculture's Dick Bell and smiled.

The message was clear: The Soviet Union had suffered an agricultural disaster, but it would endure with or without the American grain. Russia had had experience of famine and foreign siege. If the Americans believed that the Soviet Union would trade its political principles—its support for the OPEC cartel—for a few cargoes of grain, they should read history. The Americans staggered out of the meeting and repaired to a hearty Russian lunch, hosted by a jolly Patolichev.

Did Patolichev mean business? Or was this one final bluff, using the oldest trick in the Russian book? To Robinson, it seemed plain that hope was gone.

The technical details of a grain agreement had been worked out in forty-eight hours of intense negotiations between Hinton and the Russian trade officials. It authorized the Russians to purchase 6–8 million tons of wheat and corn a year—and more if the U.S. government determined that American grain supplies were plentiful enough. The pact did not, however, commit the Soviet Union to supply the United States with regular informa-

---

* Several of the Americans had not had an opportunity to go to the bathroom after swallowing several cups of coffee at breakfast and they passed the final hours of the Patolichev soliloquy in acute discomfort. But they did not excuse themselves. They had their instructions from Robinson the jogger: "Do not show weakness."

tion about the status of Soviet crops or its grain-buying intentions, and it did not require the Soviet Union to participate in any new international grain-reserve scheme.

That done, the Americans went home, except for Robinson, who departed for Paris to attend a mid-October meeting of the Organization for Economic Cooperation and Development. From Paris, the weary Robinson called the State Department and gave his impressions to Sonnenfeldt. Within a few hours, Robinson received a message that stunned him: Kissinger ordered him back to Moscow to make one last try at concessions on oil.

By this time, the mood across the American farm states was menacing. Senators, congressmen, and the whole range of corporate interests in agriculture were pressing the Republican administration to wind up the talks, come home, and get the grain moving again while the Russians were still in a buying mood. But if Kissinger and his associates at the State Department accurately perceived the political damage that the moratorium was doing to Ford in the President's home constituency of the Midwest, they did not appear to show it.

Robinson returned, as ordered, but the best Patolichev would do was help the Americans save face. He accepted from Robinson a letter that spelled out an "understanding" that the two governments would "commence negotiation promptly to conclude an agreement concerning the purchase and shipment of Soviet oil." The future agreement would, the letter stated, enable the United States to buy annually 10 million metric tons of crude oil and petroleum products. About 70 per cent was to be crude oil, with the remainder to be diesel oil or other petroleum products. The letter said that "prices for crude oil and petroleum products will be mutually agreed upon at a level which will assure the interests of both the Government of the United States and the Government of the U.S.S.R." Nothing was said about any discounts.

As it happened, further lengthy discussions between the

United States and the Soviet Union on oil purchases took place in 1976 (with the price concession issue now buried). But the talks were unfruitful and, in that election year, the oil initiative simply faded away.

The grain agreement was announced October 20, 1975. (The President had lifted the Polish embargo ten days earlier. Officials of the Polish Embassy in Washington had been traveling around the Midwest telling Polish-American organizations that the Ford administration was planning to starve their relatives back in the old country that winter.) It was the first step toward stabilizing the disruptive grain trade between the two countries; and it did achieve a positive result. But it was a limited result, with high political costs.

Perhaps, as some of his advisers now believe, Kissinger never seriously expected the Russians to capitulate and give the Americans the "visible" discount on oil. Some of them speculate that he merely wanted to engage them in drawn-out negotiations to keep them distracted and off-balance during his Middle East diplomacy. On September 4, Kissinger's efforts had resulted in the signing by Egypt and Israel of the United States–mediated interim accord on Sinai. But time was needed to make sure that the agreement was not upset by unforeseen circumstances. None other than Butz was to say that the embargo "contributed to the Russians' sitting on the sidelines while the Egyptian-Israeli agreement was being negotiated."

Ultimately, however, Ford paid a political price for overestimating the chances for a grain-for-oil *quid pro quo*. The concessions he had hinted at in his October 10 press conference were not forthcoming. Instead, Ford had to deal with resentment in the farm states at his interference with grain exports. Some farmers, blaming the embargo for the decline in grain prices, filed suit against Robinson and the federal government for damages resulting from the restraints.

As for Earl Butz, he continued to smart over the humiliations he had experienced the previous summer and to plot his revenge. He was particularly annoyed at the administration's organization of food policy making, in which he was only one of many officials with "input." At the October press conference announcing the grain agreement, Butz had been asked whether published reports of his loss of influence were correct. "I still set the hours that people come to work at the Department of Agriculture," said Butz with one of his quick, hard smiles. Behind the scenes, Butz worked through the fall and winter with his friend Rogers C. B. Morton, Republican chairman (and soon to be a director of the Pillsbury milling company), to get Kissinger dumped from his role in international agricultural policy making. And in May 1976, Ford took a big step to placate supporters in the farm belt, where Butz was still popular. Fighting for his political survival in the Illinois primary against Reagan, the President announced that he was putting Butz in charge of all domestic and international agricultural policy. To Kissinger and Robinson (both men were out of the country at the time), the move had the look of a palace putsch.

As the November election drew near, Ford continued to worry about the Midwest. In late October, he raised wheat price supports. This gesture seemed touched with desperation and may have come too late to make much difference. A few days before the election, a sign posted at a grain elevator near Enid, Oklahoma, declared defiantly: "Remember the Embargo!"

Ford's greatest concession to the Midwest had been his choice of a running mate—a Midwesterner and "farmer's friend," but a man with little appeal and many liabilities in other regions: Senator Robert Dole of Kansas. Dole campaigned vigorously in farm states, and as it turned out, Ford swept the region. But the price had been high. Bill Seidman said the grain sale moratorium "incited Ford's strongest supporters to great and continued opposition" and may have cost Gerald Ford his presidency. The selection of Dole shored up Ford's own strongest constituency but precluded a running mate with appeal to voters in the big East Coast states that the President lost.

The briefly fashionable notion that American grain supremacy might be usable for diplomatic purposes was one of the casualties of the summer of 1975. Of this notion, Senator Hubert Humphrey said: "I think it is time for us to think of what we are going to say to the Russians—we will be nice to you and accept your oil at five per cent less, when all the world needs oil? It's just stupid."

As for President Ford, he made his position clear to the American Farm Bureau in January 1976. The President ruled out any "political" grain embargo against Russia as a response to Moscow's involvement in the Angolan civil war. "There is not the slightest doubt that if we tried to use grain for leverage, the Soviets could get along without American grain and ignore our views." The President, of course, spoke from experience.

12   The Diplomatic Crop

"Lobbying is built into the American system. Teachers
and labor unions do it. Why shouldn't foreign countries?"
—SOUTH KOREAN RICE BROKER TONGSUN PARK

"Henry Kissinger is our best rice salesman."
—AN ARKANSAS RICE GROWER

Americans throw rice at brides, process it into certain kinds of
beer, and consume mushy quantities of it in soups. But most
Americans are not great rice eaters. Every year, 14,000 rice
farmers grow much more than the country requires.

Therein lie the roots of a story that, starting in 1976, colored
American diplomacy and politics, disrupted relations between
the United States and a close Asian ally, introduced the public to
a cast of shadowy grain merchants and secret foreign agents, and
sent many congressmen scurrying for cover. This was "Koreagate," the Oriental puzzle in which commissions from rice sales
to South Korea ended up in the pockets, or campaign funds, of
American politicians.

Political Washington and the commercial grain business—the
first so showy and public, the second so elusive and private. One
would have to think hard to imagine two more different worlds.
But it is not surprising that Washington was first infiltrated and

finally outlandishly seduced by a man who was part of the second world—by the rice broker Tongsun Park.

That commodities relate to foreign relations and politics is a truth that does not often occur to most people in the nation's capital. To be sure, Washington is changing. It is not the pleasant, provincial, "southern" city it once was. Its society is in transition. Invitations to dinner parties given by Georgetown hostesses are no longer a sure badge of membership in the Establishment. And the Establishment itself is becoming difficult to define. It now includes investigative reporters along with high-powered lawyers, and as the city slowly grows into a world capital, it has attracted its own Bohemians, ethnic minorities, dissident groups, and foreigners seeking political asylum. Dowagers who once exercised absolute social power in the city now gaze from their chauffeur-driven Lincolns at the dozens of new sidewalk cafés along Connecticut Avenue and probably wish they were young again and wearing jeans.

Washington is more cosmopolitan, more complicated, more sophisticated, more cynical, more informed than it was only recently. But about some very important things it is still appallingly ignorant. One of these things is grain.

For years grain and the grain trade have been part of a complex web that connects the United States to half a dozen Asian countries that are strategically important to American interests. Within this web, rice has a very special place. Japan and Okinawa received American rice for years after World War II. Cambodia and South Vietnam only stopped receiving it when their military governments fell, and South Korea and Indonesia now receive large quantities of it. Rice is an issue with Japan and Thailand from time to time, not because they buy it from America but because both countries want to sell more of their own to some of the same markets as America's.

Foreign and domestic political interests overlap in rice. Almost since the end of the Pacific war, congressmen from rice-growing states, officials at the State Department, and Asian rulers have had a common interest in U.S. rice exports. The shipments helped out the rice growers, provided a "carrot" for the State Department to offer in Asia, and propped up Asian economies. Asian leaders found it both economically and politically expedient to import rice from across the Pacific rather than reform their own agricultural systems. American rice was a means for curbing food price inflation—and, indirectly, safeguarding political stability. U.S. rice sales came to serve the double purpose of helping American farmers and friendly governments.

Yet there are very few people in Washington who appreciate the importance of rice. Commodities are not a fashionable subject, compared with such other topics as the abuses of the CIA and the FBI, spies, dissidents, the Pentagon's budget, and the activities of the White House staff. The city's obsession with government and political power is narcissistic; it shuts out curiosity about other forces that shape the life of America. The people who make the laws invariably find themselves uninformed compared with the determined people who are trying to *shape* them: the lobbyists for business and banking. The workings of whole important sections of the American economy are little understood in Washington. This ignorance about something as central as grain was at the root of Koreagate.

In Asia, of course, rice has always been the staff of life—the world's second-largest cereal grain crop, after wheat, and the main food of the 2.5 billion people who live between Pakistan and Japan. Rice is basic to life, culture, and religion. Family life revolves around the planting and harvesting of rice, and the "collectiveness" of rice farming, with its requirements for family cooperation and division of labor, is embedded in the mores and social thinking of Asians. In the view of the Brazilian economist Josue de Castro, "the doctrines of Confucius would not have penetrated and taken such deep roots in the soul of the Chinese people if his precepts of love for one's family and worship of one's ancestors had not coincided with the people's economic interest. The need for hands to grow food . . . has built a whole social structure favorable to a high birth rate." Elsewhere, rice has been tribute and rent in the feudal societies of Asia from time immemorial.

The awesome power of rice over the lives of Asians is most dramatically and vividly conveyed in the great Indian filmmaker Satyajit Ray's *Distant Thunder,* which depicts the starvation and social disruption caused by the devastating Bengal famine of 1943. On one level, *Distant Thunder* is a powerful drama about human responses to a desperate situation: A beautiful young woman submits to the sexual advances of a hideously burned man—in return for rice. A choice for survival over dignity. On another level, Ray makes an important demographic point: The village is isolated, helpless, totally dependent on its own rice.

Since 1943, the isolation of Asian villages has been lessened by new roads and improved communications, but this sometimes has increased rather than decreased the need for imported rice in Asia. Massive famine is now less likely, but more rice is needed in the crowded cities to which the rural people have migrated. The modern rice trade serves the requirements of these urban areas. The quantities involved are small: an average 6 million tons a year in a global grain trade that reached 150 million tons in the 1970s. But the trade is critical. The demand for rice is constant. Shortages are intolerable. And even small shortfalls cause panic and hoarding. In 1973, the world rice crop declined by only 5 per cent (14 million tons) but rice prices rose by 300 per cent (from $200 to more than $600 a ton).

In Brazil—the largest rice-growing country outside Asia—authorities use the international rice trade to protect against domestic speculation. When supplies run low before each new harvest, the government purchases foreign rice—20,000–40,000 tons of it—and threatens to dump it on local markets. The rice is usually resold before it ever reaches Brazil, but the threat of imported rice is usually enough to dampen prices and discourage speculation and hoarding.

Nowhere in the world is there a huge surplus of rice comparable to the surpluses of wheat in the Great Plains or the Argentine Pampas. Rice is grown and consumed in the countries with the densest populations in the world and most of it stays home. Among them, the Asian rice-producing countries of Japan, Thailand, Burma, and Pakistan have only 4 million tons of rice at most left over to sell abroad each year. This is why a nation of steak- and wheat-eaters has become the leading merchant of rice to the world.

Rice emerged only gradually as a significant American crop. English colonists planted rice along the Carolina coast in pre-Revolutionary days and used the proceeds to build regal mansions. But rice cultivation dwindled in the Carolinas and Georgia after the irrigation systems fell into disrepair with the end of slavery, and today the "rice mansions" of Charleston, Savannah, and their environs are all that remain to remind Carolinians of rice's first foothold on the North American continent. Near the end of the century, however, rice found a new home in the inland valleys of California where wheat growing was being phased out.

At about the same time, farmers also began planting it in the coastal plains of Texas and Louisiana. The Gulf Coast, with its rich delta soil and ample fresh water for irrigation, was ideal. Farmers cleared the land and used modern steam pumps to send water through earthen irrigation channels. The rice industry got a helping hand in World War II, with the high price supports to encourage production at the outset of the war. Later, as cotton's glory faded, rice acreage increased still further.

The contrast between modern American and Asiatic rice farming is the contrast between two cultures, two stages of economic developments, two eras in time. In Asia, the planting, cultivating, and harvesting of rice is back-breaking labor.

Women, children, and water buffalo provide most of the muscle. Peasants knee deep in muddy water plant each seedling individually on plots of a hectare or two. But in America, the rice business is a high-technology, capital-intensive enterprise. Tractors level the paddies and dig the irrigation ditches; airplanes seed the fields and spray them with fertilizer and chemical pesticides; water levels are controlled by elaborate irrigation and drainage systems; self-propelled combines harvest the crop when it is ready. The only jobs that machines do not perform are repairing and maintaining the levees that hold the water on the crop land. Farming operations as large as 600 acres are common.

This kind of costly farming is possible because the government made rice a very profitable commodity to grow. It began supporting the price in 1941 at 85 per cent of "parity"—an artificially established fair return for the crop. After the war, the support price was increased to 90 per cent of parity, the equivalent of $4.00 or $5.00 for a 100-pound bag, even as the yields increased. By this time, American rice fields yielded three times as much per acre as ordinary Asian fields. Near harvest, a rice field in Louisiana was as thick and green as an overgrown bluegrass lawn. The cost of the price support system was evident in the checks that the government mailed to some big rice-millers in the 1950s—nearly half a million dollars in some cases.

In 1955, Congress passed allotment.and quota legislation that had the effect of closing the door to new rice farmers. From then until 1976, when the government rice program was overhauled, rice was grown by this closed club of farmers, or by farmers who leased allotments or bought farms covered by the allotments.

It is not hard to figure out the reason for the privileged position of the rice business in American agriculture. It is only necessary to examine the roster of powerful congressional committee chairmen—the "southern barons"—who ran Congress in the 1950s and 1960s. The barons were friends of rice. There was Wilbur Mills of Arkansas, chairman of the House Ways and

Means Committee; J. William Fulbright of the same state, chairman of the Senate Foreign Relations Committee; W. R. Poage of Texas, chairman of the House Agriculture Committee; Otto Passman of Louisiana, chairman of the Foreign Operations (foreign aid) Subcommittee of the House Appropriations Committee; Allen Ellender of Louisiana, chairman of the Senate Appropriations Committee; and Russell Long of the same state, chairman of the Senate Finance Committee. It was said that Wilbur Mills never wrote a tax bill without getting something for rice. Rice was a small crop, but the people who raised it and milled it showed that they were as good at cultivating political support as at cultivating rice.

The result of farm programs in this period was a surplus of almost everything. There was too much cotton, peanuts, tobacco, soybean oil, and wheat, not just rice. And each of these commodities had its friends and backers on Capitol Hill. The links ran every which way. Dwayne Andreas, chairman of the rapidly growing soybean- and corn-processing company Archer-Daniels Midland (ADM), was a close friend of Senator Humphrey. Money from the agricultural sector moved easily into U.S. politics.°

° Andreas's name surfaced in connection with Watergate. Investigators learned that $100,000 received by Nixon and his secretary, Rosemary Woods, at the White House in 1971 was given by Andreas. Andreas told investigators that this was an early contribution to Nixon's 1972 campaign. Andreas made another secret contribution to Nixon's campaign, this in the form of cash given to Nixon's Midwest fundraiser Kenneth Dahlberg. This money, in the form of a cashier's check made out to Dahlberg and then deposited in the bank account of one of the Watergate burglars, provided investigators in 1972 with the first concrete connection between the Watergate burglars and Nixon's campaign committee. In 1978, Andreas's gift of $72,000 in stock to an educational trust fund for the children of David Gartner, a former Humphrey aide who was appointed to the Commodity Futures Trade Commission, caused a controversy in Washington. President Carter urged Gartner to resign, but Gartner refused.

The "cram it down their throats" policy adopted by the government in the 1960s flowed from the need to dispose of all sorts of surplus commodities abroad, including rice. But the rice lobby faced special problems. The prospects for developing huge new markets were less promising than for the other grains: Two-thirds of the world's population already ate rice, and while this population was growing, it did not have money to pay the commercial costs of buying rice in the United States. Those rice-eaters who *could* pay for imported food—the middle class and the civil service, in particular—showed an interest in eating less rice and more bread or grain-fed poultry or beef. Then, too, a ton of rice cost about twice as much as a ton of wheat. Wheat could be exported through the grain pipeline as it came off the farm, but rice had to be given a light milling to shell off the hulls, clean, and bag it. Local acceptance also was another problem. People had developed a taste for special varieties of rice over centuries. American rice often tasted different—and not so good.

There were commercial outlets for some of the rice at home. The Anheuser-Busch and Coors companies used broken rice in their brewing process; Kellogg's bought the medium-grain and long-grain rice from the Gulf states for breakfast food; and a few large milling companies, such as Uncle Ben's Blue Ribbon, Comet, and Riviana, bought the long-grain rice of the Gulf states for the parboiled, minute rice and packaged markets. California's shorter-grain rice was sold in Puerto Rico and distributed to American cities with large populations of Spanish or Oriental rice-eating minorities which preferred the gummier, shorter-grained kind. But even after all this rice was sold at home and farmers had held back quantities for seed, two-thirds of the crop was still left over. And only about half of that could be sold to cash customers abroad.

As usual, the government in Washington had an interest in disposing of this surplus. The less rice there was in the United

States, the less rice the U.S. government would have to buy at the support price. So, once again, the old standbys, P.L. 480 and export subsidies, were used to push the crop abroad.

The rice dumping sometimes caused frictions with Burma and Thailand, the two largest Asian exporters. In a column they wrote in 1956, Joseph and Stewart Alsop called attention to the aggressive maneuvers of the U.S. rice trade in Asia and warned of political repercussions. Because of U.S. exports to Japan, "Burma has been forced to make a deal with the communist bloc, to exchange Burmese rice for machinery. If Southeast Asia finally goes communist, it will be due in part to American agricultural policy," so wrote the Alsops.

But Congress approved. Its policy until as late as 1967 was to forbid U.S. foreign technical or economic assistance for purposes of increasing rice production. Aid to Pakistani and Burmese rice farmers was denied for this reason.

Developments in the 1960s were not helpful to the commercial rice merchants. President Kennedy's decision in 1962 to embargo trade with Cuba cost the Louisiana and Arkansas rice industry one of its best markets. And at the same time, rice output was increasing in Asia. By 1966, Japan (which had once been the largest U.S. commercial rice market) was self-sufficient in rice. Japanese government subsidies to its rice farmers made the lavish American subsidies look like wartime austerity measures, and as more Japanese switched to bread, less imported rice was needed. By 1971, Japan had 7 million tons of unsold rice of its own—enough to cover world trade for an entire year.

These developments embroiled the Congress in the details of the international rice trade. California congressmen were drawn into the fight to prevent Japan from taking over the Okinawa rice market between 1968 and 1972. Okinawa was not a particularly large buyer of California rice, but the 50,000–70,000 tons it purchased each year brought some $14 million a year into the state's rice economy. When word of Japan's attempt to break into the market reached Congress in 1968, the United States still held an important trump card: It ran Okinawa. Under terms of the Japanese surrender in 1945, overall authority was vested in a U.S. High Commissioner. And although the Pacific war had been over for twenty-three years, the Californians were determined to preserve the Okinawa stronghold for their state's rice.

When, in November 1968, a California rice miller named Curtis Rocca wrote to Representative Robert Leggett of his concern that Okinawan rice importers would turn to Japan, he suggested to the Democratic congressman that he might "impress upon the military that the High Commissioner convey his interest in maintaining the flow of rice from the U.S. to Okinawa." This was done. Leggett sought the help of several fellow Californians, including House Whip John McFall, and the Californians wrote a letter to President Johnson that paraphrased most of the concerns first voiced by Curtis Rocca.

What then happened is not known, but the following month, Rocca wrote to McFall with the good news that the Okinawa importers had contracted once again to purchase all their rice from California. Still, there must have been continued concern, for in 1970 Leggett filed a memorandum as follows: "The continuing military presence of the United States in Okinawa, constituting at least 50 per cent of their G.N.P., should give the United States continuing bargaining power."

Two years later, Okinawa reverted to Japan, and U.S. "bargaining power" was lost. Despite repeated interventions by Leggett and McFall on behalf of Rocca and the California rice industry, the Okinawan importers began buying their rice from Japan.

Even with that kind of congressional backing over the years, the surpluses of unsold rice built up in California and in the Gulf Coast. Fortunately, there always was one sure and steady outlet: diplomacy, and the P.L. 480 program. Rice was always available to the State Department, to be used as a reward for diplomatic cooperation and as assistance to the economies of "friendly" countries. When American rice farmers congregated in towns in

Arkansas and Louisiana, the talk often as not turned to foreign policy. The farmers conceded that "we're growing this stuff for the State Department," and that "some of it goes to dictators." It was certainly a new and different sort of chapter in the ancient saga of rice.

The connection between rice and diplomacy was demonstrated plainly in 1971, when President Nixon dispatched his ambassador-at-large, David Kennedy, to Seoul, to try to do something about the Korean textile exports that were hurting the southern textile industry and indirectly undermining Nixon's strategy to win southern states in the 1972 presidential election. Kennedy's solution was to offer the South Koreans P.L. 480 loans to buy food—mainly rice—in return for their "voluntary" restraint on (i.e., reduction of) textile exports to the United States. Kennedy promised that Korea's losses from reduced earnings from textile exports would be offset by an increase of $175 million in P.L. 480 loans and $100 million in other kinds of loans. This was an offer the Seoul government couldn't refuse. This agreement was kept secret and was not reported to Congress until three years later, when it came to light only as a result of an investigation by the General Accounting Office.

War in Southeast Asia, which had been disrupting agriculture and food distribution in one of Asia's most important rice bowls for years, also soaked up American rice surpluses. Rice aid to South Vietnam had begun in 1965 and built rapidly, as President Johnson expanded the American war effort and backed it up with large-scale U.S. military and economic assistance. In 1967, more than half a million tons of subsidized rice went to the South Vietnamese government. This food was not automatically distributed free to ordinary Vietnamese, though some of it was. Most of it was purchased by the Vietnamese government with long-term, low-interest dollar credits and resold to local merchants or distributed to army commanders. The government used some of the piasters earned from the sale of the food on the local economy to procure material, clothing, and services for the army, and for "internal security."* These infusions of American rice proved extremely helpful in easing the effect of the war on the Vietnamese economy. The rice kept Saigon markets supplied, slowed the rate of inflation, and generated revenues for the defense budget.

Prior to Cambodia's entry into the war in Indochina, Cambodians not only were self-sufficient but also exported about 50,000 tons of rice a year. But with the overthrow of Prince Sihanouk and the establishment of a pro-American regime in Phnom Penh in 1970, serious food difficulties began. The Khmer Rouge insurgents controlled the country, leaving the city in the hands of the Cambodian government and without a reliable supply of rice.

In this situation, the United States took over responsibility for filling much of the government's rice requirements with direct shipments convoyed up the Mekong.† The Cambodian government sold the rice to private agents and merchants through its export-import monopoly, paid the U.S. government in local riels, and then borrowed back the riels to pay soldiers, policemen, and civil servants. In this case, Washington did not even maintain the fiction that this rice was on "loan." It was, plainly and simply, a welfare program.

By 1974, the whole P.L. 480 program had become geared to assisting the food economies of Vietnam and Cambodia, two countries whose total population was 24 million people. More than a million tons of U.S. rice poured into the war zone in 1973 and 1974—approximately 10 per cent of the entire American

* Congress halted this practice as of July 1, 1974.

† Elizabeth Becker, correspondent of *The Washington Post* in Phnom Penh, reported that merchants were able to buy incoming American rice (hauled in by freighters that made the dangerous journey up the Mekong River) for 155–165 riels—a heavily subsidized price. The rice sold in markets was then marked up steeply. Cambodian military officers received rice quotas for their troops and Becker wrote that it was a "general assumption that generals and Chinese merchants built their villas in France with proceeds from the aid program."

rice crop. Of the $567.6 million worth of all commodities shipped in fiscal 1974 under Title I of P.L. 480 (the dollar credit section of the food aid program), just under $400 million worth was sent to the two nations.* In late 1972, shipments to other countries with considerably greater needs for subsidized rice were curtailed because of the massive flow of rice to Indochina. A Department of Agriculture memorandum to Secretary Butz in November of that year noted that "a major food grain problem exists this year in Indonesia," but added that "our ability to supply quantities is limited because of urgent requirements in Indochina and [because of] budget restraints."

The rice aid to Indochina served as backdoor economic assistance at a time when Congress was closing off the military and economic aid spigots. Given the power of the congressional rice lobby, Kissinger knew that rice aid would be the last assistance to be voted down. But eventually the distortions in the food aid program became too glaring even for the farm bloc. Congress finally ordered limits—but not before the war in Indochina had provided an important outlet for the American rice surplus for almost a decade.

Shifting social, economic, and demographic patterns in Asian countries had made the rice supply a critical political issue in Asian capitals as well as in Washington.

Indonesia's failure to produce enough rice was the single most important reason for its economic difficulties. It had timber, oil, natural rubber, and minerals and was exporting all of these commodities, yet Indonesia was constantly in debt because it was obliged to import enormous quantities of food. No Indonesian government was willing to take a chance on food shortages. Runaway food inflation had been one cause of President Su-

---

* As noted in Chapter 5, only the agricultural commodities go abroad. The money stays at home. The dollars "loaned" for buying food are transferred from the U.S. Treasury to an American bank. The exporter collects this money upon submission of documents certifying the commodities have been loaded.

karno's downfall in 1966. Drought, such as the one that hit Java in the summer of 1972, reduced output, disrupted food procurement, and automatically caused a state of emergency. The government did not hesitate to use oil revenues to pay for drastically increased rice imports. It advised parliament in late 1972 that there was a need for 1.5 million tons of rice costing several hundred million dollars. Indonesia survived—with the help of 200,000 tons of subsidized U.S. rice and additional amounts from Thailand, Japan, Pakistan, and Hong Kong.

In South Korea, U.S. rice imports were central to the country's ambitious plans for economic development. At first glance, South Korea did not seem to be a promising bonanza market for the American rice industry. It is a country where the cold grayness of the rugged terrain is frequently relieved by signs of a thriving rice culture: dark, emerald rice paddies beneath terraced mountains. But the appearance of a bountiful rice crop is deceiving. Only a fifth of the country's land is arable, erosion and flooding are constant problems because so much land has been stripped of trees for firewood, rainfall is spotty, and there is a shortage of underground water for irrigation.

During the 1930s, Korea exported rice to Japan—but only at the cost of many Koreans' going hungry. These were called "starvation exports" because some Koreans lived on wild grass in the weeks before the harvest so that export requirements could be met. Despite the difficult problems faced by agriculture after the Korean war, rice yields were high, exceeding those in Japan and Thailand. Korea received some P.L. 480 food and imported some rice, but not large amounts. In 1965, the country produced 3.5 million tons of rice and an equal quantity of barley, wheat, potatoes, peas, and beans. Its rice imports in that year were only 180,000 tons.

After that, however, Korea's rice-based food system changed radically, as the government began to emulate the "Japanese model" of economic development. This called for investment in light industry under controlled conditions. Above all, inflation had to be avoided, for it would force up wages and decrease the competitiveness of Korean products in world markets—the key to the success of the "Japanese model." If Korea was to sell products in the United States, subsidized American rice, wheat, and other grains would be needed.

The movement of 3.5 million rural people to urban areas between 1961 and 1971 caused strains on South Korea's food supply. Fortunately, the domestic rice market was well developed: One-third to one-half of the rice grown by Korean farmers was bought by local merchants and moved into commercial channels; the government procured some more from farmers to feed the armed forces; and the rest was consumed where it was grown. But as the government put its capital and energies into industrialization, agriculture was neglected. Astonishingly, at a time when more food was urgently needed to supply the markets in the expanding cities and towns, rice production remained unchanged, and so did total food output.

The answer was, of course, to import more food. In 1970, a year of unusually heavy spending on imports, South Korea imported a million tons of rice—nearly a quarter of all the rice consumed. By then, South Korea was importing about a third of its *total* food grain requirements (compared with a fifth a decade earlier). Wheat imports—by no means all of them subsidized by P.L. 480—had grown even faster than rice imports, reaching 1.4 million tons in 1971.

None of these difficulties was unusual for a country that was attempting to emulate the "Japanese model." Japan and Taiwan, both of which had made the transition from rural to industrial countries, were even more dependent on food imports than South Korea. In 1971, the two countries imported 62 and 41 per cent respectively of their *total* grain supply (most of it from the United States). The South Korean situation did, however, cause a policy debate in the U.S. government. Some officials at the Agency for International Development felt that Korean agriculture was being neglected at considerable risk.

Another concern of more enlightened officials was that the massive P.L. 480 rice deliveries to Asia could depress world markets and adversely affect the economies of countries such as Thailand. P.L. 480 rice is special—brown, unpolished rice with up to 20 per cent broken kernels—not usually in commercial demand. But P.L. 480 rice does substitute for commercial imports. "The U.S. has fouled up world rice markets—everybody knows that, it's not even debated," a U.N. official said.

There was general agreement in both Washington and Seoul that South Korean agriculture had fallen behind, and that one reason was the massive food surpluses readily available in the United States.* However, AID's arguments for restraint on exports were overruled by other Washington agencies and by Congress, which had a vested interest in maximizing grain shipments. South Korea's food imports did not diminish in the 1970s, though farm prices were increased. The country imported $700 million in American food in 1974. This was a fact that greatly pleased Agriculture Secretary Butz, who extolled "the dynamite market in Korea for U.S. agricultural exports."

Through all these developments, remarkably little was known in Washington about the whole skein of *commercial* transactions by which the rice moved to Asia. It was clear that vast sums of money were involved. But less was known about who handled the contracts and earned the commissions, what companies profited, and who actually received the American food across the Pacific. The transactions were arranged through the private channels of the grain trade, the long list of merchants, brokers, shipping agents, millers, and insurance companies that are involved in large grain movements.

But grain merchants and foreign policy-makers live separate lives. Only in the P.L. 480 program do the government and the

* Paul Kuznets wrote in his book *Economic Growth and Structure in the Republic of Korea* (New Haven, 1977) that the heavy imports had a "depressing effect" on domestic food production.

grain trade intersect. This convergence occurs in an obscure corner of USDA headquarters, on one of the many long corridors of the agency's vast building at Fourteenth Street and Independence Avenue, from which, for years, the P.L. 480 program has been supervised. It is a classic Washington story: a $1-billion-a-year program looked after by bureaucrats whom nobody has ever heard of. There *are* people in Washington who know about the nitty-gritty side of the grain trade—about shipping schedules, prices in Rotterdam, and the difference between c.i.f. and f.o.b.*—but they are not the people who go to Georgetown parties. The people who head up the P.L. 480 division tend to live in the suburbs, play golf on weekends, and check out of the office at 4:30 to make the carpool. This is the life-style of a G.S. 16.

Yet even these people, the government's only true grain experts, had trouble knowing what was happening in rice.

Perhaps the international diamond trade is more specialized and closed than the rice trade, but even that is not certain. Rice is not a business in which the people involved are accustomed to making waves. There are no more than two or three dozen people in the world who have an ability to trade rice globally. Raphael Totah of Continental is probably the grand master. He is one of the company's wizardly Egyptians, reputedly a relative of Marc Najar (last of the big-time speculators) and of Leon Hakim, who joined Continental back in the 1920s when it was still run by Jules Fribourg. Then there are others who go only by their first names—"Boris," "Jean-Pierre," "Sal," to mention several. (I never was able to track them down or find out the last names.) In Thailand, a few Chinese traders and millers, nicknamed the Six Tigers (actually there are seven of them), dominate the rice business. Who knows what deals have been cut, what relationships

---

* Cost, insurance, and freight, and free-on-board. c.i.f. contracts oblige the exporter to deliver the grain to its destination. F.o.b. contracts leave it up to the foreign importer to handle his own transportation. He takes possession as soon as the grain is loaded onto a vessel.

have been established around the steamy Gulf of Siam by these merchant-entrepreneurs to ensure their continued monopoly? Whatever they have done, when importers in Hong Kong, Indonesia, and the Philippines want Thai rice, they do not go to Totah, the grand master. They go to the Six Tigers.

Trading rice makes trading wheat or corn look like the two-dollar window at the racetrack. If it is difficult to know the price of wheat, it is next to impossible to know the price of rice. Thai authorities post a rice price, f.o.b. Bangkok, but everyone in the rice business knows this is only the roughest kind of guide. There are more than *eight thousand* varieties of rice, and though not all of them, by any means, move in world trade, enough of them do to make the price f.o.b. Bangkok only a general indicator. Rice is a mysterious commodity. Wheat and corn are proletarian crops; although there are many variations in quality, type, and utility, there are still only a small number of grades and classes. But rice is a feudal society with a hierarchy that ranges from the lowly serfs—the P.L. 480 brown rice with 20 per cent broken kernels—to the lordly basmati rice of South Asia with its long grain and its light, fluffy qualities when cooked. Some rices become a gruelly mess in hot water—but that makes eating them with chopsticks much easier. Some rice tastes bland; other rice is as sweet and flaky as freshly ground coconut.

Rice merchants have to know the preferences of many people. They have to know that Puerto Ricans (in New York as well as in San Juan) prefer short-grained California rice, which is gummy after cooking, to the premium, long-grain "table rice" from Louisiana that non-Latin Americans and Europeans like. On the other hand, Cubans like long-grain rice, which before the trade embargo they got from the Gulf Coast and now obtain from Italy, Central America, and sometimes from China.

And the merchants have to maneuver through a labyrinth of government regulations (import duties, export subsidies) and sudden government policy changes, not to mention "dirty tricks." There is a widespread feeling that rice merchants in Europe get tipped off early to changes in the European Common Market's export subsidy for Italian rice so that the Italian rice can be offered abroad at a discount.° "The price will drop twenty per cent overnight because of the ignorant action of bureaucrats in Brussels!" a broker lamented.

Even Cargill, which naturally enough is in the rice business, can get caught short, as it did recently when it sold some American rice to a commercial customer abroad. Cargill didn't own the rice, and when the time came to obtain and deliver it, the price was way over what Cargill thought it would have to pay to make good on its sales contract. It was the U.S. government that had thrown Cargill off. For whatever reason, it had allocated an unusually large amount of rice to the P.L. 480 program, and as foreign governments began obtaining this subsidized rice, domestic prices in America had risen rapidly. Cargill was, indeed, caught short. And when the world's most efficient grain company misjudges, it is certain that the rice business is a rough one.

The majors do not dominate in rice as thoroughly as they do in other basic commodities, for reasons that have to do with the structure of the rice industry. Grain companies buy wheat, corn, or soybeans direct from farmers, and they also process these commodities. But the companies have not yet invested in rice mills, and these hold the key to control of the rice pipeline. Rice coming off farms looks pretty much like wheat. But unlike wheat, rice needs some light, intermediate processing to remove the hull and clean the kernel. Also, most American rice is still shipped bagged, for the convenience of customers (as California wheat was in the last century). Because of this basic fact, independent rice millers scattered through Texas, Louisiana, Arkansas, and California are crucial in the distribution chain.

° Bureaucrats in Brussels adjust these export subsidies for European grain just as the USDA adjusted the export compensation payments on wheat from 1949 to 1972.

Many of them are strong middlemen in their own right, who buy rice from farmers and make their own arrangements with trading companies (including the grain companies). And because the supply of surplus rice available for export always is limited, these miller-intermediaries exercise considerable leverage. Yet the millers still need customers, and some, though not all, still depend on trading companies to complete the last stage of the pipeline.

About ten years ago, the rivalry for domination of the American rice export business narrowed to two companies. It became a David and Goliath struggle between Continental and Connell Rice and Sugar, a smallish firm (by grain-trade standards) based in the unlikely setting of suburban Westfield, New Jersey. It was an odd, detached location for a company involved in such a worldly pursuit, the business of rice trading. Grover Connell, a soft-spoken man, had a father who came north from Texas and founded the business in 1912. Connell the son was a tenacious specialist, a pure trader who did not have processing plants, mills, or grain elevators, but instead invested in computers and hired the most expert merchants he could find. His company's computer model for predicting crops and food supply and demand was consulted by government agencies.

By 1968, Continental and Connell so dominated the P.L. 480 rice trade that the Department of Agriculture asked Attorney General Ramsey Clark to investigate whether there were antitrust problems. In 1966, it noted, there were twenty-one exporters (many of whom were the smaller millers mentioned above) but by 1967 only seven participated in the P.L. 480 rice sales; Continental and Connell supplied 80 percent of the rice. The following year, the department also forwarded a complaint from the AID mission director in Saigon stating that Connell may have received "preferential treatment from officials of the Government of South Vietnam" in subsidized rice transactions. (The investigations into both matters did not, however, uncover any wrongdoing.)

In actual fact, there was little love lost between Continental and Connell. A 1967 rice transaction illustrated the depth of the rivalry. South Korea had agreed to buy 80,000 tons of West Coast rice from Connell. Then, while Connell was still ironing out the contractual details, the Koreans unexpectedly switched the order to Continental. Continental then had the contract— but no rice. When Totah tried to obtain the rice he owed Korea, he learned that Connell owned all the exportable supplies. Connell had a "corner" on available rice. Rice prices were rising rapidly, and Continental finally went to Connell. It bought at high, prevailing prices, and took a heavy loss.

Soon after this, with the two companies locked in their struggle, Tongsun Park entered the picture.

Tongsun Park once described himself as a typical American success story. But if so, it was not one in the Horatio Alger mode. Park was born in 1935, in Pyongyang (later the capital of North Korea), the son of a wealthy distributor of the products of Gulf Oil. He came to the United States as a teenager to attend high school under the guardianship of a Korean diplomat who was a friend of the family. Later he enrolled in Georgetown University, where he ran a laundry service for students in his spare time. Apparently, he missed serving in the armed forces during the conflict in his country that took the lives of 33,269 Americans. After he was graduated from Georgetown's School of Foreign Service he put his days as a laundry entrepreneur behind him and went into more lucrative businesses. He and his brother inherited their father's Gulf Oil outlets in Korea, and they built up other concerns dealing in imports, quarrying, building products, and oil transport.

The deal that was to get Tongsun Park and many others into trouble was arranged in 1968 and it involved rice. That August—the stormy month in world history when the Soviet Union invaded Czechoslovakia and riots disrupted the Democratic National Convention in Chicago—Park and a Democratic congressman from California named Richard Hanna paid a visit to Kim Hyung Wook in Seoul.

Kim was a feared man in South Korea. He directed the Korean Central Intelligence Agency, which then was suppressing all domestic opposition to the regime of President Park Chung Hee. Park would not tolerate Communist infiltrators or even democratic critics disturbing his plan for economic modernization along the lines of the "Japanese model." His agents in South Korea and abroad could be ruthlessly efficient. In 1967, they kidnapped twenty-two South Koreans living in West Germany and spirited them back to a prison in Seoul to face "espionage" charges. (It was asserted that they had been working with North Koreans living in East Germany.) Two of them, a physicist and a professor, were condemned to death but the sentences were commuted after strong West German protests.

This was the man to whom Tongsun Park and Congressman Hanna turned for help in 1968. It was the time of the California rice industry's first difficulties with the Okinawa rice importers, and Hanna had come over to try to persuade South Korea to buy more California rice.

It is not entirely clear how Hanna had become acquainted with Tongsun Park, but the two men quite obviously had a common interest. Hanna was pushing California rice, and Park wanted to be the commissioned broker—but of a very special kind. While Park listened inscrutably, Hanna strongly recommended to Kim that Park be appointed as the rice agent.

Why, exactly, South Korea might have needed more help and good will in the American Congress is hard to figure out. It was said in Washington that South Korea was a model of good Asian-American relations and the best example of the advantages accruing from close ties with America. But apparently the Hanna-Park proposal found a friendly reception, for the South Korean government consummated a large P.L. 480 rice purchase while Hanna was still there, and soon after that Park was named agent for OSROK, the South Korean government's rice-buying office in New York City.

At about the same time in 1968, Park began showing up at various grain companies boasting of his unusually good connections to the Korean government and of his ability to arrange business in the American-Korean rice trade. One place Park went to was Continental, but Totah and his people were wary of the man with the perfectly combed jet black hair and porcelain face who spoke English like an American. People making claims of that kind were the bane of the grain merchants. Every capital in the world (except, until then, Washington) had half a dozen fixers and middlemen who claimed to have a cousin in the local grain agency who could do wonders for business. Some really could deliver, but their value sometimes disappeared quickly when governments changed (as they did frequently in so many countries) while others were fakes and confidence men who were taking the companies for a ride. Continental said no thanks to Park.

Park had better luck in California, where Hanna provided the entrée. The congressman introduced the Korean to the mayor of San Francisco, Joseph Alioto, who in addition to his mayoral duties was executive director of the Rice Growers' Association of California, the state's largest cooperative of rice farmers. Hanna told Alioto that Park had connections in Korea that would assure a steady market for California rice. Alioto was puzzled about this and, he was to say later, he rejected the idea. RGA had been doing well in the Korean market with its own brokerage arrangements, but when an RGA representative went to Seoul after the inconclusive meeting in Alioto's office, he was treated coolly. Korean authorities made clear that RGA had problems—problems that could easily be overcome by naming Tongsun Park sales agent. Soon after that, RGA fired its broker and hired Park, and RGA then made a South Korean sale of 400,000 tons of rice.

Meanwhile, Grover Connell began to have problems with *his* rice transactions with South Korea. In 1969 he had sent his own representative to Seoul to discuss Korea's seeming lack of interest in doing business with him, but this effort had no appreciable result, and the New Jersey firm received only a very small share of the total business with South Korea.

The following year saw the company's fortunes improve considerably, however. A Supreme Court decision involving the operations of farmer-owned cooperatives had the effect of forcing RGA to stop selling rice directly to South Korea, and RGA instead began exporting through Connell. RGA already had used Connell to distribute its short-grained California rice in the Latino community of New York City, so employing Connell was a natural step. Soon after that, Connell hired one of Tongsun Park's companies, Korean Development Fund, as its agent in South Korea, and the company's problems there quickly evaporated.

Park's commissions by then were beginning to roll in. He received $200,000 for the 400,000-ton RGA sale in 1969, and thereafter upped his commission from 50 cents to 95 cents a ton. The private companies he was dealing with were hardly in a position to complain about this, and it is unlikely that they did. Records show that Connell paid Park at least $202,000 in 1970.

Even so, Park needed more money. To cover his expenses, he had $100,000 in cash transferred from his Seoul bank account to a KCIA agent friend at the United Nations, via diplomatic pouch. At least some of this money went to support a life-style that was lavish by Washington standards. His friend Hanna genially called him "the Asian Great Gatsby." As money came in, Park gave up his rented house in Georgetown and moved to a $300,000 brick mansion off Massachusetts Avenue, the Main Street of official Washington. This was a home made for entertaining. And because it was surrounded by dignified-looking embassies with shiny limousines parked out front, it gave the Korean a new panache. Soon he purchased a second and even more expensive home on a Northwest Washington estate. He filled these houses with treasures: rosewood Korean chests from the seventeenth and eighteenth centuries embellished with silver and brass; rare Korean ceramics and jade from the collection of King Farouk of Egypt. Park also collected contemporary playthings: a $32,000 cable stereo system, a Lincoln limousine, a Jaguar, a Mercedes, and a Rolls-Royce. He entertained prominent personalities from the old-guard Washington political establishment. New Dealer Thomas Corcoran was soon batting out melodies on Tongsun's piano while Anna Chennault, the Chinese-born widow of the Flying Tigers' commander, listened appreciatively.

Park seldom discussed business with these wealthy guests and none of them seemed interested, except in the vaguest way, in how he was acquiring his riches in a city that has never thought of itself as a commercial hub. But Park would also appear in the far less glamorous ambience of the bureaucrats in the P.L. 480 division of USDA to inquire about upcoming P.L. 480 rice allocations. In this setting, the G.S. 16s treated him with considerably less awe and reverence than the Washington Establishment. The officials knew Park was a middleman, for his name began to appear on P.L. 480 documents as sales agent in rice transactions. When Park's name came up over lunch, it always brought smiles and raised eyebrows.

If there was mystery about where the money was coming from, there was even more about where it was going. But Park assured his friends in the KCIA that there was method behind his party-giving. He assured them that he was influencing politicians in Washington, as Hanna had promised in the original conversation in Seoul with KCIA chief Kim. When Park founded the George Town Club—a private lunch and dinner club in an exclusive quarter of Washington, where guests ate off fine pewter plates and drank from pewter goblets—he gave the KCIA a description that read as if it had been written by an applicant for a federal grant. His establishment would:

(a) introduce Korea and influence people through some club members who are prominent in political, economic, journalistic and scholastic fields.

(b) offer round-table conferences, special receptions for constituents, and other meetings for Senators and Congressmen. In this way we can achieve our goals ... we will sponsor fund-raising cocktail parties free of charge so as to help in raising funds for Senators and Congressmen.

(c) We will undertake necessary information gathering activities utilizing the club members and their acquaintances by sponsoring the above-mentioned meetings.

To an outsider, the idea that a little-known Korean of mysterious financial means could so blatantly and purposefully go about "influencing people who are prominent in political, economic, journalistic and scholastic fields" might seem preposterous. But in the context of the times, it was not all that strange. Korea and America had become intertwined—politically, financially, and corporately. Nixon and Kissinger had embraced the Park regime despite its domestic repression: South Korea was "needed" while America was "winding down the war" in Indochina. American multinational companies (such as Cargill) were moving into Korea and being encouraged by the federal government to do so, and there was a "fifty-first state" quality to the country's economy.

But there was another side to this, the side that obviously worried the Park regime. This was the mounting opposition in Congress and in the American press to the political values of many U.S. foreign allies. Liberals were disenchanted with the dictators that American policy had been propping up all over the world. In the shambles of American policy in Southwest Asia, "client" governments seemed to exercise as much leverage on American policy-makers as the other way around. This, in fact, was precisely what Park's KCIA-sanctioned operation in Washington was attempting to do. What had been discussed between Park, Hanna, and Kim at their 1968 meeting were transactions that resulted in the ultimate corruption of American foreign policy—its *self*-corruption. The mechanics were that American legislators would work for economic (and military) aid to South Korea—a policy that helped perpetuate South Korea's Establishment in power—and the commissions generated as a by-product of this assistance would be used to influence the congressmen on behalf of still more aid.

From what can be ascertained, Park first began to justify his role as a "secret agent" in Washington by getting involved in what is referred to in the jargon of the capital as "invitational diplomacy"—the specialized art of getting influential legislators to make trips abroad where they can be flattered, entertained, and lobbied on behalf of the country's needs.

In 1969, Park and Hanna helped to plan a Korean trip for Speaker of the House Carl Albert. Park was waiting in Seoul when Albert showed up. He also was in on the early planning of a trip the following year that was to have fateful consequences. It was this trip that acquainted Park with the Louisiana rice industry and its backers in Congress. These included one of the most powerful of all the congressional "barons," Representative Otto Passman.

It is generally acknowledged that Passman was a strange bird, even by the broad standards of congressional eccentricity. He was a workaholic who went to his office even on Sundays and seldom if ever was seen at a Washington cocktail party. He walked around the corridors in his stocking feet, summoned government officials to 8:00 A.M. hearings, gave lectures in his singsong voice to anyone who would listen about his deep personal commitment to the service of the "American people." Passman appeared to have very few personal interests. He collected Swiss watches and liked traveling abroad, but other than that he seemed to be a "no frills" congressman. His great and overriding passion was cutting money from the foreign aid budget.

Passman's power came from his chairmanship of the House

Appropriations Subcommittee that oversaw the foreign aid budget. He treated this as a personal crusade against waste. "Son," he once told a representative of the Agency for International Development, "I don't smoke and I don't drink. My only pleasure in life is kicking the shit out of the foreign aid program of the United States of America."

Passman's approach was to bore in on the details of the various spending programs. Why were West German condom manufacturers getting the bulk of the contracts in U.S.-government-financed population-control programs? he would ask. Weren't American condoms good enough? And wasn't it a fact that children in developing countries were just blowing them up for balloons anyway? AID witnesses who experienced such a barrage from Passman at one of his hearings would retreat in a state of shock.

Not until 1970 did Passman develop a deep interest in rice. Actually, Passman was not a rice congressman; his district was in the northern part of the state, while most Louisiana rice grew in the south. What really drew Passman into rice was the Louisiana democratic primary of 1971.

Passman's favored candidate and protégé was fellow representative Edwin Edwards. Edwards could not have been more different. He was suave, debonair, a lady-killer and high-liver who enjoyed flying off to Las Vegas for a weekend. Edwards was a politician in the classic Louisiana mold, a man who seemed cut out to succeed in the twisting bayous of Louisiana's politics, heavy as they were with the scent of intrigue. And Edwards *was* a rice congressman. His home town of Crowley advertised itself as the "rice capital of America." The main hotel was The Rice. The culture of Crowley and the surrounding area revolved around Cajun music, crawfish, and rice. Rice was the main cash crop and Crowley had several rice mills. Gordon Dore, who runs one of the largest rice mills in the state at the Crowley railroad tracks, was an Edwards supporter and political fund-raiser.

In the early summer of 1970, as the rice fields turned lush

around Crowley, the perennial problem developed: a surplus. Thousands of tons of the previous year's crop still crammed storage bins. And as Edwards launched his campaign to take over the governor's mansion in Baton Rouge, he was determined to upstage his opponent with a rice coup. For help he turned to Otto Passman and Tongsun Park. As chairman of the subcommittee overseeing the foreign aid budget, Passsman could be helpful in "persuading" countries that received large amounts of American economic aid to purchase some of the surplus. And he also brought in Park, whom Edwards knew from his socializing in Washington. Edwards knew enough of Park by then to be sure that he was also interested in promoting rice sales to Korea. And his colleague Passman virtually controlled the flow of foreign aid dollars to Korea.

Given this *Realpolitik* of rice, the gallivanting young congressman and the crusty old Capitol Hill baron really were not such an odd couple after all when they arrived in Seoul that fall to seek help in electing Edwards governor of Louisiana. The incongruous threesome was completed by the ubiquitous Tongsun Park, who was waiting for them with Korean hospitality when they arrived.

The main problem was that Japan already had sold South Korea 400,000 tons of rice. Yet Passman did not see this as an obstacle, nor did the powerful subcommittee chairman have any trouble getting an appointment with President Park Chung Hee. If Korea canceled the Japanese contract and purchased American rice, Passman assured the president, American loans to cover the rice purchases would be forthcoming. Passman also reminded Park Chung Hee of his own strong support for military aid to Korea.

Back in Washington, Passman discussed the rice deal with President Nixon. He stressed how important this was, and he reminded Nixon, as he had reminded Park, that he was a strong supporter of U.S. military aid—including aid to South Vietnam.

Soon after that the U.S. government issued credits* for Korea to buy nearly $80 million worth of rice.

Congressman Edwards was to say later that the rice sale was "the greatest coup of my political career." American rice prices, which had been stagnating at around $4.60 for a 100-pound bag in early 1971 began to rise in May and June as the Korea-bound rice moved out of the Gulf of Mexico and California. It is no surprise that Edwards credited the rice sale with helping him win a victory over his opponent in the December 18 gubernatorial primary.

The rice sale generated sizable commissions for Tongsun Park, and, judging from evidence pieced together later, it was about at this point that Park began to direct some of this money back to American politicians. Sometime before Edwards's narrow victory, Park flew down to New Orleans, went straight to Edwards's campaign headquarters in the Monte Leone Hotel in the French Quarter, and caught up with the candidate. Edwards was to say later that Park offered him a "substantial" contribution, but the debonair candidate had plenty of money already and he says he refused. But Park persisted and later pressed a gift on Edwards's wife Elaine: $10,000 in cash.

Certainly this was not a great deal of money, given the amount that was coming in. In fact, it was Park's greediness at this time that almost did him in as the primary rice broker in the American-Korean rice traffic. Park had continued to pop into the USDA from time to time and his name showed up on papers filed with the government as Connell's agent. The bureaucrats did not like Park, that much was clear. On one occasion, they had the Justice Department check him out for possible income tax evasion, but it seemed to Justice that his taxes were in order.

---

* Some of the credits for buying rice were in the form of P.L. 480. But Korea also received $31 million in funds from the foreign aid program, which Passman supervised.

Nevertheless the officials were still uneasy. They did not feel they had tight control over the P.L. 480 traffic with Korea. The Korean rice-buying office in New York, when it was in the market for rice, often negotiated with the private exporters. There was no open, public bidding. The prices that the New York procurement office was paying to Connell and other export companies *looked* reasonable, but given the secrecy of the rice trade, it was difficult to ascertain whether the companies were receiving the world market price or something more than that. Inflated prices could have suggested that the premiums, or part of them, were being kicked back to Korean officials. And the dollars involved were coming out of the federal treasury.

In March 1972, the South Koreans' New York office sent all exporters a letter notifying them that henceforth Tongsun Park would be the sole intermediary in *all* P.L. 480 rice transactions for South Korea. (The letter was all the more curious for having been sent from Virginia!) Grover Connell was mystified by this. He had understood that Park was *his* agent. He sent the letter on to the USDA. It provided exactly the justification some officials had been looking for to ban Park from the program altogether. The letter strongly suggested that Park was working for the Korean government in some way—otherwise the government agency in New York would not have tapped him as sole intermediary.

The Department of Agriculture notified the Korean government that Park was no longer authorized to be a sales agent. Astonishingly, however, the New York office's secretive buying practices went on pretty much as before. The closed-door negotiations with exporters went right on. And because the rice commissions were financing an influence-buying operation that had been approved at the highest level of the Korean government, the Koreans privately insisted that Park still be cut in one way or another.

In May 1972, a month after the USDA ruling, Connell hired a new sales agent, an old, established Korean textile company by the name of Daihan Nongsan, and began making payments to Daihan Nongsan's bank accounts in Washington and Bermuda. Over the next three years, Connell paid more than $600,000 into these accounts, as commission on P.L. 480 rice sales to South Korea. However, it was not anybody from Daihan Nongsan who opened the accounts or withdrew the commissions. It was Tongsun Park.

By this time, Park had already spread a considerable amount of money around town. In addition to the $10,000 present to Elaine Edwards (her husband defeated his Republican opponent easily and took over the governor's mansion in Baton Rouge in 1972), Park had also given a good deal of money to his admirer, Representative Hanna. From time to time, people living on staid old Embassy Row saw a Brink's truck roll up in front of Park's mansion. The neighbors figured that the young Korean's business was going well—whatever the business was.

Park was busy writing checks to the election campaign funds of people he knew. He wrote checks of $300 to $1000 in 1970 to the campaigns of Philip McMartin, Morris Udall, William Ayers, Thomas Kleppe, Frank Thompson, Ross Adair, Lawrence Hogan, Melvin Price, Thomas Foley, Eligio de la Garza, Peter Frelinghuysen, Spark Matsunaga, William Broomfield, Stuart Symington, and Harry Byrd. He gave a $3000 check to the D.C. Citizens for Montoya in 1972. The same year he gave $1000 in cash to House Whip John McFall, who had been actively promoting rice sales. In 1974, he handed Representative John Brademas an envelope containing $2950 in cash.

Park, in this period, had become such a famous host in Washington that, reading the social news in *The Washington Post,* one almost had to believe that Tongsun Park had been born in black tie and dinner jacket. An "Asian Perle Mesta," someone called him, paraphrasing Representative Hanna. A few of his newer guests mistook him for the Korean ambassador. For all the status that attached to him, however, Park did not do much lobbying on behalf of Korea. Most people who knew him thought he seemed bored with political issues. He did not approach his political friends and ask them to vote in certain ways on issues vitally affecting Korea. There was only one favor that he did ask of a number of his congressional acquaintances. This was to write President Park Chung Hee that he, Tongsun Park, was doing a fine job for Korea in Washington.

In the summer of 1972, Park himself brought the draft of such a letter to various congressmen. The letter was several times retyped on House stationary and sent to Seoul. None of the letters sent to President Park were more glowing in praise of Tongsun Park than the one signed by Passman. "Complete honesty prompts me to say that Tongsun Park performed magnificently in the consummation of the rice sale.° Through his diligent efforts he has acquired many new and lasting friends for Korea."

The friends of lobbyist Tongsun Park in Congress, it is clear, were a lobby for Tongsun Park in Seoul.

Passman's eager endorsement of Park, it seemed on the surface, grew out of a desire to help rice farmers from his home state. But it is clear from documents that became available later that Passman's effort went less to helping rice farmers than to assisting Grover Connell's trading firm in New Jersey, whose commissions on rice sales to Korea were being collected by Park.

Passman knew Connell. He spoke of him as a "friend" and characterized him in a letter as "one of the oustanding businessmen in America." And while Passman was a powerful member of the House of Representatives he frequently did favors for Connell. In 1973, Passman went to Indonesia and pleaded with authorities there to allow Connell to revise a rice-sale contract that the New Jersey company had with the government in Jakarta. For a man who frequently spoke of his devotion to the American rice farmer, his pitch was curious. Passman asked the authorities to accept 82,000 tons of *non-American* rice in substi-

---

° A reference to a 340,000-ton transaction that year.

tution for the American rice committed under the contract. (This was at a time when American rice prices, due partly to massive P.L. 480 rice allocations to Southeast Asia, were at record high levels.) And in 1974, Passman wrote to Taiwan's minister of economic affairs to ask him to approve export quotas enabling Connell to sell Taiwanese mushrooms, pineapples, and asparagus to Switzerland and Canada. (The quotas were approved.) Again, in 1975, Passman, at Connell's request, was writing to the American ambassador in Paris asking him to help obtain the minutes of a meeting of authorities in French-controlled Réunion Island at which delays in American rice shipments had been discussed. Or, in 1975, Passman spoke out publicly in favor of Connell's position in a dispute with Continental over the award of a P.L. 480 contract for rice deliveries to Bangladesh.

That a powerful congressman should take such an interest in the fine details of a grain company's operations even when his constituency was not normally involved seemed more than strange. And, in fact, investigative reporters and federal agents had been collecting scraps of information about Park and his political connections as early as 1972. But the trail seemed to lead nowhere, and the high-level politicians who showed up at Park's parties seemed uninterested in the credentials of their wealthy host. (In 1973 and again in 1974 Park threw gala birthday parties for House Speaker Tip O'Neill. Vice-President Ford showed up at at least one of Park's parties, and in 1974 Park gave a big send-off for William Saxbe, the former senator then on his way to become U.S. ambassador in India. According to the society reports, a good time was had by all.)

Park's most effective cover was, in fact, Washington's ignorance of, and lack of curiosity about, the seamier side of the country's commercial relationships all over the world. This is what kept people from probing more deeply into the shadowy side of Park's life in Washington while they were accepting his gifts and hospitality.

It was more or less by accident that Park's cover was finally blown.

In 1975, while preparing a series of articles on the P.L. 480 program for *The Washington Post,* Don Oberdorfer and I stumbled on Park's rice connection. Oberdorfer, in Seoul, kept hearing about a middleman called Tongsun Park who paid for the hotel accommodations of American rice merchants and congressmen when they visited South Korea. Soon after our articles appeared, I received a call from a man who said he had more information about Park and who invited me to meet him in a bar off Connecticut Avenue in downtown Washington. At the appointed place, the man hinted that he worked for the CIA. Did I know that Park was the conduit for millions of dollars of Korean money pouring into U.S. politics, he asked? I did not. He handed me a document, and as I squinted at it through the darkness, barely able to make it out, I saw that it was a report from the U.S. Customs Service about an incident in Anchorage, Alaska, in which Park had been detained briefly for failing to declare a watch. In the course of a routine search, officials found a piece of paper in Park's possession listing the names of congressmen. Figures—apparently amounts of money—had been scrawled after the names and the writer of the report said that the list must have been a sensitive one because Park at one point attempted to swallow it.

I told my editor, Harry Rosenfeld, of this curious encounter, and he assigned the investigative reporter Ronald Kessler to look into it. Another *Post* writer, Maxine Cheshire, who had been digging into Park's social connections, was also intrigued by the rice link. A bridge between Washington high life and the murky grain trade could finally be made out like the first outlines of a photograph coming clear in a developing solution.

I came across Park's trail a few months later in 1975, in Louisiana. Clyde Vidrine, a tall, pistol-toting Louisianan who had handled Edwards's cash and later quit in a disagreement with him, claimed to have handled a cash gift from Park to Edwards in 1971. When I asked Edwards about his connection to Park, he denied accepting any cash. But he did say Park had offered him a substantial contribution.

In late 1976 Cheshire and two other *Post* reporters, Scott Armstrong and Charles Babcock, drawing on their netwcrk of sources in the police, intelligence, and code-breaking agencies of the government, finally put together a comprehensive story outlining Park's use of rice commissions to pay congressmen, and quoting sources as saying the U.S. government had electronically monitored a 1970 meeting in the "Blue House" (the presidential palace in Seoul) at which the Korean leaders had approved of Park's lobbying activities.

At that point, the party was over for Tongsun Park and his friends. These journalistic disclosures shook Congress and forced it to take the unusual step of investigating itself. The House Committee on Standards of Official Conduct—a sleepy institution that usually devotes itself to protecting House members from outside prying—began an inquiry. The committee hired Leon Jaworski, the retired Watergate special prosecutor, to investigate Korean bribery.

A Justice Department investigation, which had begun even before the story broke in the newspapers, also began to turn up new leads. It was no Watergate, but it was the most exhaustive investigation into the ethics of congressmen for many years. Park himself hurriedly left the country and was incommunicado in Seoul, where he redecorated his stone-and-wood villa in mixed Korean-American style, with some of its rooms cluttered with Western furniture and Oriental rugs, and others kept in the spare Asian style, with pillows on a heated floor. To friends who still saw him, Park insisted he had done nothing wrong and had been done in by enemies who envied his wealth and success.

A grand jury in Washington came to a different conclusion. In mid-1977, it indicted Park for conspiring to corrupt congressmen. Park's friend Congressman Hanna was indicted on forty felony counts involving bribery, conspiracy, mail fraud, and failure to register as a foreign agent. Hanna pleaded guilty to a single count of conspiring to defraud the United States, after plea-bargaining with Justice Department lawyers. All told, the documents said, Park had paid Hanna $156,640 directly or through his companies between 1969 and 1975, when Hanna quit Congress and went into export-import.

In January 1978, the South Korean government finally permitted Justice Department investigators to question Park and administer a lie-detector test to him in Seoul. This questioning produced admissions from Park that he had channeled hundreds of thousands of dollars into American politics—but he continued to deny that he had done anything wrong.

Park's testimony in Seoul clinched the government's case against still another suspect, Otto Passman, who had been dealt an unexpected defeat in the Louisiana congressional primary in 1976. An indictment handed down in April 1978 against the one-time foe of waste in the foreign aid program was perhaps the most stunning document of all. The grand jury charged that Passman had received more than $175,000 in cash and some valuable watches from Park in return for using his office as a congressman to influence U.S. government agencies to increase loans they were making to purchase U.S. rice. The grand jury said that Park's cash payments to Passman ranged from $10,000 to $50,000, and the indictment proffered some tantalizing tidbits of intrigue.

In May, the same grand jury indicted Connell. The indictment charged that Connell knew Daihan Nongsan's bank accounts in Washington and Bermuda were fronts for Park and that the company continued to use Park as an agent long after the USDA had banned him as an authorized intermediary in rice transactions with Korea. Connell chose as his attorney the now former mayor of San Francisco Joseph Alioto—the same Californian whom Park and Hanna had approached in 1968 about hiring Park to expedite rice trading with Korea, and who had been skeptical then about Park's connections. Alioto called the indictment "an outrageous miscarriage of justice" engineered by a Department of Justice that had "gone berserk." The denouement was a major defeat for the Justice Department. Passman was acquitted by a hometown jury in Monroe, Louisiana—a venue that his critics said made a mockery of efforts to obtain an unbiased verdict. To add to the carnival atmosphere, Tongsun Park, under a grant of immunity, appeared as prosecution witness and gave testimony that was at odds with government allegations. Charges against Connell were subsequently dropped.

Sentiment against the domestic policies of President Park's regime was already running high in Congress when Koreagate was exposed. The South Korean government's rejection of some requests that it provide witnesses to the investigation only worsened matters. In June 1978, the House approved by a 273–125 vote an amendment prohibiting further financial assistance to Korea under the P.L. 480 program. Majority Leader Jim Wright said the reason was the refusal of the Korean government to cooperate with House requests to question former South Korean ambassador Kim Dong Jo. "In defense of the honor of this institution we have no other recourse," he said.

In the end, Park was as mysterious as ever. Had his motives really been to influence Congress in ways that benefited his country? The bulk of the evidence did not suggest that. His activities may have persuaded a few congressmen to be more pro-Korean, but there is no evidence that he ever achieved any great lobbying coups—except the ones that benefited him personally. The pattern of his activities suggested that his main interest, other than parties, was to perpetuate his own grip on the Korean-American rice trade that was making him a rich man. Park was, aside from everything else, a social climber and self-promoter who found it extraordinarily easy to charm and dazzle powerful people. But the lessons of Koreagate went beyond warnings to beware of rich, mysterious foreigners. Koreagate was a symptom of decay in the empire.

In the period of hope and optimism that followed World War

II, the United States had set out to rebuild devastated countries and to promote their economic development. There was, of course, a strain of self-interest involved in strengthening countries against Communist penetration and creating new markets. But there was also genuine conviction behind the idealistic hopes expressed by American leaders for equality, democracy, material well-being, and freedom from hunger. It was no accident that Tongsun Park came on the scene and flourished when he did. For by the 1970s, many regimes that the American government supported around the world were run by and for political and business establishments that were indifferent, at best, to the ideals expressed earlier. This was the situation not only in South Korea but in the Philippines, Indonesia, Nicaragua, Brazil, and other countries too numerous to mention. For his part, Tongsun Park was an agent not so much of South Korea as of "Korea, Inc.," the interlocking business/political coalition that runs the country and benefits the most from the economic development that depends on heavy rice imports.

In this sense, Park's payments to politicians expressed the ultimate contempt for American ideals. Park showed that, as far as he was concerned, the United States was "America, Inc." Foreign policy was just one more business deal with a cost of doing business attached to it. It was all part of the corporatization of American diplomacy. And unfortunately, his assumptions were shown to be all too true.

Koreagate was revealing also for what it told about the global grain trade. The "rice connection" benefited rich American farmers, the grain trade, congressmen, and the regime of President Park Chung Hee. But that is not exceptional. The grain trade had become a link in the interlocking directorate of the American empire. Grain is not always effective as a political "stick," as Henry Kissinger found out in his attempt to get cheap oil from the Russians. But in a subtler way it is far more effective. Grain has truly become a political currency.

The main hall of the New York Produce Exchange a hundred years ago.

Buying and selling at the Produce Exchange in the 1870s.

The Baltic Exchange in London today.

Opposite, above: A typical grain elevator of the American interior.

Opposite, below: The Farmers Union 12-million-bushel terminal grain elevator at Superior, Wisconsin.

The fire following the explosion in Continental's terminal grain facility north of New Orleans, December 1977, in which thirty-six people died.

Corn from a grain cooperative being loaded for export at Charleston, South Carolina.

A shipment of Chinese rice (bagged) being unloaded off leiters in Jambi, Indonesia, 1978.

The Least Forgiving Business 13

"The grain business is the least forgiving."
—CARGILL EXECUTIVE

On the evening of Friday, May 20, 1977, Ned Cook, president of Cook Industries, was starting a journey from Memphis to New York City aboard his company's Lockheed Jetstar. On the plane Cook settled back and began to examine the financial statement that the company's vice-president for finance, Joseph McLeary, had handed to him before takeoff.

It was with a special sense of relief that Ned Cook felt the plane climb up into the warm southern sky on that particular weekend, for the work he had once so heartily enjoyed seemed recently to have turned into an endless series of crises and emergencies.

The last few days had been particularly trying. The previous Friday, his daughter had had to have an eye operation. Then, just as some Russian grain men were arriving in town, his father-in-law had died unexpectedly. He had had the Russians over for dinner and then hurried off to the funeral the next day. The trip to New York would provide a temporary escape from the heavy cares of Memphis. Cook Industries was at that moment tangled in the legal and financial aftermath of a sordid waterfront scandal involving grain loading. And Cook knew there was much talk going around Memphis that the old merchant firm his father had built was in legal difficulties now that he was in charge. In addition, the company's once-good fortunes in the commodity markets had evaporated. At the end of March, Cook Industries already had been $27 million in the red from its operations in the first nine months of the financial year. Cook knew well that there would be more losses in the final quarter.

As Cook began to examine closely the financial report on his lap, he stared at the pages in disbelief. These were not just heavy losses that he was looking at, but the trace marks of a financial disaster. Ned Cook's fortune had not just dwindled in the last two months; it had all but disappeared. The bottom line that Cook read at the end of the statement was that Cook Industries, Inc., was heading for losses of $60 million *in the final quarter alone.* In New York two and a half hours later, Cook ordered the pilot to prepare to return to Memphis early the next morning. There would be no weekend in New York after all. For five years, the tall, ebullient Ned Cook had been the maverick of the grain trade—the former cotton merchant who had reached the pinnacle of the grain business with bold tactics and self-confidence. It had been an audacious performance. But now it was clear that Ned Cook's gambling days were over.

Such a reversal of fortune would have seemed highly implausible if not impossible only two years earlier, when money was pouring into the treasuries of all the big companies. At that time, prosperity was evident from the financial report of the only grain company that regularly released such statements, the publicly owned Cook Industries. Cook's profits and growth were the talk of the grain trade. The name Cook Industries had spread around the world. Company agents sold grain in Valparaiso and Tehran, and job applicants lined up for interviews.

The boss of Cook Industries was jaunty as a rooster—a damn-the-consequences capitalist who liked to throw his feet up on his desk and startle visitors with blunt statements. "If I make a bad decision and Cook Industries were to go broke, well, tough!

That's my business." With that, Ned Cook would chuckle. This was bold talk for a neophyte in the perilous business of grain. But this was in 1975, when all the companies felt prosperous and secure.

Cook's older, established rivals were no less confident than Cook. The privately owned Big Five, in fact, seemed to have the best of all worlds. They were making a lot of money and accounting to nobody. The public's interest in them had faded again after the 1972 "grain robbery." Senator Henry Jackson's Permanent Subcommittee on Investigations had harried them for a few months, looking for evidence that the companies had acted illegally, and some unpleasant publicity had followed from these probes. An official of the Department of Agriculture had told Jackson's subcommittee that Continental and André's associate Garnac had filed "misleading" reports on their futures trading in the summer of 1972; Continental had responded that any reporting inaccuracies were due to "clerical errors," and in Garnac's case the bookkeepers had apparently lost track of the company's trades in the hectic dealings. But the companies' private ownership gave them a certain immunity from more searching investigation, and they had slid back into the shadows.

Then, in the middle of the second wave of heavy Soviet buying, in the summer of 1975, the companies were thrust rudely into the limelight, but this time the publicity had nothing to do with the Russians. The Montoneros' humiliation of Bunge in Buenos Aires in June had been bad enough. But even as the Hirsch and Born families were regrouping after this trauma, the company learned that a federal grand jury in New Orleans, on July 21, had indicted it and thirteen of its present and former employees, on criminal charges of "systematically" stealing grain and soybeans as these commodities passed through the huge Bunge depot on the lower Mississippi River in Louisiana. This time there was no hiding-place for the merchants.

New Orleans is to grain what Bahrein is to oil. If one sips cocktails at dusk in one of the rooftop lounges of the French

Quarter's elegant hotels and looks out over the harbor, there is almost no moment when grain ships are not in sight, slipping out to some far-off point in the world with a load of corn or soybeans. New Orleans sits at the neck of a vast funnel of grain. Corn and soybeans primarily, but also some wheat, converge on it from all over the Midwest, by barge, truck, and rail.

In the global chess game of grain, it is essential to be positioned at the mouth of the Mississippi, and all of the dominant merchant houses are. Not surprisingly, considering the strategic location, the majors own or lease most of the space in eight huge steel and cement grain-silo complexes that are spaced out along the lower 160 miles of the river. Continental, Cargill, Cook, Bunge, and Italian soybean magnate Serafino Ferruzzi's Mississippi River Grain Elevator Company owned or leased five of the eight in 1975. Louis Dreyfus had an arrangement to use Continental's installation, and Garnac (André's associate in New York) had a partnership with Archer-Daniels Midland to lease space in a public grain-loading facility.

This riverfront world of grain loading is far removed from the pleasant old-fashioned world of the French Quarter of New Orleans. Driving out to the depots takes a motorist through wistful Delta country: roads elevated above bayous where country folks go after crawfish underneath the thick overhanging moss and branches of swamp trees. The flat Louisiana rice land—the heartland of the "diplomatic crop" that landed Representative Passman in such difficulties—is farther west. And out of this strange, misty Louisiana bayou land the enormous windowless grain silos rise awesomely, each set back behind the earthen levy but reaching over it to freighters and barges with quarter-mile–long belts, enclosed in spindly-looking housing, through which grain can hurtle at the rate of a thousand tons an hour into the holds of ocean-going freighters.

The lower Mississippi has always been a place where petty thievery thrived. "River rats"—small-time pirates in boats—helped themselves to grain from open barges, sometimes with the connivance of well-bribed barge captains. And thieves in trucks loaded up the grain that spilled around the sides of eleva- tors. But as the volumes and value of grain pouring down the Mississippi River barge, truck, and rail corridor increased, more sophisticated forms of larceny were devised.

Measuring and loading grain is an inexact science even in the modern grain trade. The fact is, it is not easy to "weigh" 20,000 tons of grain, a typical cargo today. The draught of the ship gives an indication—that is the reason for the numbers on the hull—but the draught can vary depending on the saltiness of the water, which changes constantly with the ebb and flow of tides in the Gulf of Mexico. So the elevators use powerful scales for weighing grain in bulk before it goes on board.

From the outside, a modern grain elevator looks like a simple enough concrete structure, but inside it is a labyrinth of pipes, ducts, ventilators, belts, and shovel lifts, all controlled from a command room complete with console and flashing, colored buttons. From there it is possible to "blend" grain from different silos so that the foreign customer gets no more than the mini- mum quality ordered—no more, but no less either, of permitted broken kernels, pieces of weeds, insects, bits of straw, wild gar- lic, and wild onions. Once the grain is blended, it rockets out along the belts that run as far as a quarter of a mile to reach a waiting ship. A fine, choking dust fills the air, clogs the lungs, and covers clothing, reminding a visitor that a century after Cadwallader Washburn's A Mill exploded in Minneapolis with a thunderclap, the problem of grain dust has yet to be solved. Grain elevators are still volatile, explosive places—mines above ground. The grain trade really *is* a dirty business.

The dirt, the heat, the isolation along the lonely Mississippi River, the sheer size and complexity of the facilities—all of this seems to invite abuses in the loading of grain. And at the time of the Bunge indictment, the system for preventing such abuses was a mockery. The law governing grain quality was the 1923 Grain Standards Act, which Congress had passed in response to an earlier scandal.* The act did not require federal inspection of grain being exported, only federal *licensing* of private inspectors (and federal review if the private inspectors were too hard in their grading, something that was seldom a problem). Under this system, seven of the eight depots on the lower Mississippi contracted with private franchised businessmen and paid them according to the volume of grain they cleared for export! If ever there was a sweetheart arrangement this was it, and naturally enough, it led to abuse. (Bunge even loaned a local businessman between $10,000 and $15,000 so he could form a company whose sole business would be to inspect Bunge's grain, Senator Dick Clark of Iowa revealed on one visit to New Orleans.)

The lack of a uniform federal system meant that the Department of Agriculture's undermanned grain inspection division delegated the responsibility for grain grading to no less than 111 autonomous inspection agencies at 183 inspection points inland and at the ports.

Over the years the department had had many warnings that something was terribly amiss in the Louisiana elevators. On February 25, 1969, the grain division's John Browning wrote his superiors that European customers believed American grain inspection "was subject to bribery or fraudulent issuance of certificates." And in 1973, Stephanides, the U.S. agricultural attaché who put up such a game fight against Russian sunflower oil in Iran, complained about the quality of American corn, barley, wheat, rice, and vegetable oil arriving in the Persian Gulf. "We trust our greedy exporting companies too much," he wrote in April of that year. "We spend millions and expect our agricultural attachés and marketing agencies to promote our commodities—but have no control concerning quality and grading

* Problems with grain quality are as old as the grain trade. Dirt and filth in the wheat arriving in London from India in the 1880s infuriated many of the British millers, but the London Corn Trade Association held out against a reform of the purity standards because several big millers had invested in their own cleaning equipment and wanted to exploit this advantage!

regulations." These warnings and many others reached a Department of Agriculture that was conditioned by years of close cooperation with the grain companies to ignore them. The department's grain division depended on the companies for information about developments in world agricultural trade. The companies, after all, had been the department's agents in moving the nation's burdensome grain surpluses abroad in the 1950s and 1960s. There was little stomach at USDA for a campaign against waterfront corruption that could lead right up to friends in the companies.

The sweetheart relationship existed not only between the companies and the businessmen inspecting them, but also with the Department of Agriculture itself. When the inspection scandal broke, Bradley Skeels, a former regional director of the grain division, asserted that "approval to pass lower quality grain for export could be obtained by the grain trade with telephone calls to the right Washington personnel." In August 1972, the grain inspection division finally asked the office of investigation to probe "eight apparent violations" by Cook Industries of the 1923 Grain Standards Act. That request reached the office of investigation *ten months later.* How it had been derouted is unclear, but in any case nothing happened.

It was the Federal Bureau of Investigation, not the Department of Agriculture, that developed the first incriminating evidence against the grain companies. The episode that gave the FBI its break was like the opening sequence of some tawdry daytime television detective serial. The date was March 14, 1974; the place was the American vessel *Achilles,* anchored in the lower Mississippi River; the subject was bribery. A marine surveyor who had come aboard the ship overheard a strange conversation between the captain and a steamship agent. The two men were debating how much money they should pay the federally licensed inspectors who were coming aboard to certify that the vessel's holds were in a sanitary condition to receive grain. It seemed from the conversation that several inspectors had been bidding to certify the ship, one demanding $5000 and another offering to do it for only $2500. The eavesdropping marine surveyor told the Federal Maritime Commission about this conversation and the FMC told the FBI.

As Assistant U.S. Attorney Cornelius Heusel brought witness after witness before the New Orleans grand jury, evidence of the companies' misconduct grew. All kinds of activities came to light that showed how company employees schemed to misgrade or diminish the quantities of grain destined for foreign countries. Adnac (a partnership of Archer-Daniels Midland and Garnac), Continental, and Ferruzzi's Mississippi River Grain Elevator Company were indicted in 1975, pleaded no contest, and paid heavy fines. By the end of the year, the grand jury had issued a total of thirty-one indictments, covering 265 federal criminal violations against forty-eight individuals; thirty-eight had been convicted, and the rest were awaiting trial.* ("Johnny" Rametta, Ferruzzi's local manager, hastily returned to Italy just before being indicted.)

These indictments painted a sordid picture of the everyday activities of grain companies at the grass-roots level. While wealthy merchants and traders in well-tailored suits entertained foreign customers at expense-account restaurants in Geneva, Paris, and New York, employees of the companies down on the Mississippi River were rigging scales and tampering with inspection samples so they could ship these same customers "junk," or less grain than they had ordered.

Intricate accounting methods covered up the skimming. In several cases, the companies accounted for the extra grain they accumulated by entering fictitious deliveries by phantom barges. But employees sometimes turned these schemes against the companies: At one elevator they underloaded ships, put the grain "saved" this way onto barges, and sold it upstream to a

---

* Cargill emerged "clean." Louis Dreyfus also was unscathed. Its elevator at the Gulf was at Pascagoula, Mississippi.

small grain company that specialized in fencing stolen commodities.

Witnesses told of federally licensed grain inspectors watching while elevator superintendents "cleaned" samples of corn—removed the weevils and broken kernels—and then handed the "samples" over to the inspector for analysis and "grading." The investigators were told how scales could be put on "hold" before a weight was recorded, the controls switched to "manual," and the grain dropped from a hopper directly onto the moving conveyor belt. In this way, excess accumulations of grain could be shipped to a company's overseas subsidiary without ever being weighed and recorded.

In one instance, a ship was certified as having been loaded with No. 2 grade wheat even though no such wheat was in the silo. Managers had to send to another company for a can of wheat of the certified grade so it could be retained as the "sample" for the misloaded vessel.

Grain is always a difficult, unpredictable cargo. A ship with corn in apparently good condition can arrive in Odessa with a cargo, putrified by the acids oozing from thousands of tiny cracks in the corn kernels. Wheat containing invisible weevil eggs can erupt with a mass of crawling insects on an ocean voyage.

Different ports use different kinds of equipment to detect the cheating. Unloading grain at the ultramodern GEM terminal outside Rotterdam is one thing. A forty-thousand-ton tanker can discharge its cargo in a little more than a day: "Vacuvators" suck grain from the holds as fast as it has been put in. But in ports in Africa and Asia, the system is slow, primitive. Grain may be unloaded offshore or even taken out pound by pound. American rice arriving in Cambodia at the peak of the war in Southeast Asia was unloaded by dozens of men and women, dressed in sarongs, their heads wrapped in towels against the heat of the day. The work went on all day, and not very efficiently. Mothers would break to nurse babies or cook meals under shady trees.

Rice from punctured sacks was slipped into the folds of sarongs and pants pockets, and later, when the work was done, the laborers would dump the paltry amounts of pilfered rice into pots. With such primitive systems, it is difficult to tell if there has been cheating, and if so, who is responsible. The whole system invited the oldest trick in the book—the grocer's thumb on the scales—on a grander dimension.

Cook Industries was drawn into the loading scandal late, but when the company finally was indicted in March 1976, the evidence against it was damning and detailed. The only good thing about it, from Ned Cook's standpoint, was that one of the principal accused no longer worked for him. Phillip McCaull, who was with Cook for a few years in the late 1960s and early 1970s, epitomized the new breed of grain merchants who thrived on the bull markets of the 1970s. McCaull was contemptuous of the old guard—the Europeans with their polish and their nepotistic ties to the family owners who still controlled so much of Continental, Garnac, and Louis Dreyfus. He was impatient, demanding, aggressive. Some older veterans criticized McCaull as a hip-shooter who did not ask enough questions before putting company money on the line in the markets, but McCaull had the credentials to go with his bold style: He was a former Cargill man who had attended "Cargill University," the Minneapolis company's training program. McCaull soon gained Ned Cook's confidence and became his senior commodity adviser.

As spelled out in court documents, the incident that was to get both Cook Industries and McCaull into serious difficulties with the criminal justice system occurred in the summer of 1970, in an appropriately conspiratorial setting, a Memphis public park on a bluff overlooking the Mississippi River. Present were McCaull, Vice-President Michael Ragen and Melvin Hibbits, manager of the company's new downstream elevator at Reserve, Louisiana. (This was the very facility that Cook had gone public to acquire.)

When it began to rain, the three men huddled under a tree

and Hibbits was given his instructions. Vessels bound for modern ports such as Rotterdam and Hamburg were to be loaded to within one-eighth of 1 percent of the amount of the loading manifest. Those bound for India and Pakistan—countries lacking modern grain-handling and loading facilities—were to be cheated by as much as 1.5 per cent. (A few months later the underloading of the vessels to the poor, least-favored nations was ordered set at 3 per cent.) Since grain does not grow in elevators, company accountants entered deliveries by fictitious barges to account for the excess grain in Cook's facility.

After a personal disagreement in March 1972, McCaull left Ned Cook and was hired by Gerard Louis-Dreyfus, who was looking for prize talent to strengthen the Paris firm's American grain-trading operations. But the cheating scheme continued at Cook after McCaull's departure, and when Hibbits went on vacation in the summer he left written instructions on how to underload vessels that would be taking on grain during his absence. The *Golden Gate*, scheduled to leave with a cargo of wheat for Bangladesh on August 9, was to be underloaded by 3 per cent (saving 1000 tons, worth about $148,000). On the other hand, only 1 per cent of the corn was to be skimmed from the Japan-bound *Troll Forest*.

On May 6, 1976, Cook Industries was indicted in the conspiracy. The company paid a fine of $370,000 after entering a plea of no contest. On August 17, McCaull, Hibbits, Ragen, and a man named Jack Coleman, a local elevator operator for Cook, were also indicted for conspiracy, and in November all four pleaded guilty before U.S. Judge Edward Boyle in New Orleans. But Gerard Louis-Dreyfus stood by the convicted conspirator he had hired four years earlier. He told Judge Boyle that McCaull was the most capable grain man in the United States. Judge Boyle was unmoved. Before sentencing him to three months in federal prison and fining him $500, he told McCaull: "Of all the cases that have been before the court here, yours is the only one that involved such a highly placed executive. The higher up the ladder you get, the higher responsibility one has to see that the law is obeyed. I believe you could have steered another course."

McCaull served three months at the light-security Allenwood Federal Penitentiary in western Pennsylvania. The other defendants received suspended prison sentences. Then McCaull went back to his job, president of the Louis Dreyfus subsidiary in the United States.

Ned Cook's personal role in the corruption scheme at Cook Industries was a matter of speculation in the grain trade. Ned Cook *was* Cook Industries. But neither the federal prosecutors in New Orleans nor any former Cook executives ever accused Ned Cook, and Cook himself said he first learned of the skimming from newspaper articles. Only then, he claimed, was he told of the meeting under the tree and "felt like someone had kicked me in the stomach." Thereupon, he ordered a Memphis law firm to conduct an independent investigation. This outside inquiry was supposed to clear the air. Instead, it clouded it and raised fresh suspicions. Lawyers for Cook succeeded in suppressing the law firm's report on the grounds that it contained material that would be useful to claimants then attempting to collect damages resulting from cheating. But suppression only caused new speculation as to whether the company had even more to hide.

Ned Cook's friends were convinced he was guilty mainly of naïveté. The Cooks were wise to the ways of the cotton business, but grain was a very different trade. Cotton had always been peculiarly southern in its customs and codes. It was run by southerners—by people like the Cooks, who sent their children to Yale, joined country clubs, wore Brooks Brothers suits, but were still "southern boys" at heart. When the Cooks were in cotton, they knew the farmers and the rival merchants up and down the river, and these people knew the Cooks. They all met down on Front Street. All the cotton merchants prided themselves on being southern gentlemen and men of their word; the merchants and the farmers were all part of the southern cotton economy. Memphis was proud of its good citizens the Cooks when the government called on Everett Cook to come to Washington in World War II, and his son Ned went off to fly bombing missions in Europe.

But by the 1970s, the old cotton warehouses along Front Street in Memphis were closed, and corn and soybeans had eclipsed cotton. Ned Cook found himself in a new business that was itself being transformed. Everything moved faster—money, contracts, and the commodity itself. Grain merchantry was brutally competitive—nothing at all like the leisurely, paternal old cotton trade. The doors of the grain business were opened to aggressive young traders and managers unburdened by any loyalty to the family owners and unconnected to old traditions and codes.

The scandals and the publicity gave Cook his first taste of what a tough, unforgiving business it was that he had entered so enthusiastically a few years before. And he was far more exposed than any of his older, more experienced rivals. Continental, Bunge, and Garnac could withdraw behind their curtain of privacy to lick their wounds, but not Cook. He had to go on filing detailed financial reports to the Securities and Exchange Commission, answering the questions of public stockholders, and undergoing the whole ritual of corporate confession required by stringent new ethical standards established in Washington in the wake of Lockheed, ITT, and other corporate payoff scandals.

The 1972 Russian sales, which for a while had seemed forgotten, kept coming back to harass even the most private of the merchants, for rumors that the companies had profiteered in the transactions would not die.

In December 1976, the Interstate Commerce Commission held hearings in Chicago to determine why some small grain elevators inland had been unable to obtain covered hopper cars and grain boxcars to move their commodities during a freight car shortage in 1973. The grain transportation system had been overtaxed when the unusually heavy grain exports to Russia began to move toward the ports. Small elevators had been unable to obtain railroad cars, and they had fallen behind on their deliveries to the export companies. Continental agreed to provide railroad cars to haul the grain—but in return for discounts of 7.5 per cent or more on the commodities shipped from the rural warehouses.

The hearings showed what a close working relationship existed between certain railroad companies and the grain firms. Illinois Central Gulf Railroad, for example, allocated large numbers of cars to Continental's grain trains shuttling between the ports and inland collection points. In effect, Illinois Central Gulf delegated to Continental the responsibility for allocating railcars during the shortage. At issue was whether the railroad or grain company used its control of boxcars to circumvent the ICC's transportation rates for grain traffic. In July 1977, the ICC commissioners issued an ambiguous decision that was mildly critical of the allocation practices of Illinois Central Gulf. The ICC took no stand on the discounting practices, but the case was one of those reminders of the growing power of the companies.

In most other sectors of the economy, higher transportation costs in this period were passed on to consumers and customers. In grain, the costs were passed back to farmers and small elevator managers, who paid for a transportation shortage that was not of their making.

These disclosures were not unique to the grain business. A great deal was coming to light about the ethics and morality, or lack thereof, of all the huge multinational companies that had come to exercise such sway over the production, processing, and distribution of raw materials. Companies whose names were synonymous with American business—ITT, Gulf, Lockheed— were found to have been involved in conduct that seemed more appropriate to the crime underworld than to old, established companies. This included bribing high government officials abroad to obtain contracts; maintaining secret accounts or setting up dummy companies for the purpose of concealing this activity; making payments to politicians or political movements; conspiring to fix prices; and keeping separate accounts to evade taxation.

The business conduct that began to come to light in the 1970s was pervasive, rather than a matter of isolated incidents. Executives of American multinational companies admitted freely that they paid off people abroad because it was necessary to do business. They maintained that if American companies did not do it, European firms would.

Several factors appeared to be contributing to the abandonment of traditional American values of honesty and ethical conduct. (Many businessmen no longer even *claimed* that these were desirable.) One was the rapid concentration of economic power over resources, technology, and distribution in the hands of fewer and fewer giant corporations, which lacked any meaningful checks on accountability. And the managers of companies that were growing more powerful failed to develop a sense of ethical accountability. This, at least, was the gist of one theory about the evidence of widespread corruption. Another theory was that as growth of markets in industrial economies slowed down and the companies began doing more new business in developing countries, they simply adopted the business practices of their hosts—countries in which business was done through connections, bribery, and "baksheesh," rather than by offering superior products and service. Some of this go-along business morality was evident in Koreagate; and by the time John J. McCloy revealed Gulf Oil's worldwide kickback arrangements, it was well known that corrupt payments were common in the international commodity business.

Bribes, kickbacks, "back contracts," overpricing, and other schemes were routine. Almost every nation in the world exports or imports agricultural commodities, and it is not unusual for tens of millions of dollars to be involved in a single export or import contract. Although many of the transactions are arranged at open, public tenders, more are negotiated privately between government trade officials and grain company agents. Given the variability of world prices of commodities on any single day, deliberate underpricing or overpricing for the purpose of concealing hidden payments is difficult to detect. (See Chapter 9.)

In conducting my own research for this book, I was given detailed descriptions of several kickback arrangements that, I was told, were fairly typical. One case involved the sale of rice to Iran by a New York dealer. The Iranian government buyer agreed to purchase the rice at a price slightly higher than those prevailing in world markets, on condition that the difference went into his Swiss bank account. After the rice merchant received the Iranian government payment, he transferred part of it to his wife, who in turn transferred it to the designated account of the Iranian in Switzerland. In effect, this particular official had simply stolen money from his own government with the help of the rice seller.

Another kickback scheme involved the sale of Romanian urea fertilizer to the United States in 1974. Urea comes from natural gas flared off in oil fields. It is an important source of foreign exchange for Romania—and urea fertilizer is important to American agriculture. In 1974, supplies were limited, and traders could take advantage of the scarcity to earn windfalls. In the episode described to me, a Romanian government official selling 10,000 tons of Romanian urea to an American importer deliberately *underpriced* it. In return he demanded that the American importer pay him a $2.50-per-ton "commission," and the Communist official designated a Swiss banker to receive the $25,000 payment. Soon after the transaction was completed, the Swiss banker flew to New York City and collected the money on behalf of his Romanian client.

In March 1977, Cargill reported to the Internal Revenue Service that it had disbursed $5 million in "unusual payments" in the United States and thirty-eight other countries. None of the payments involved "illegal" political contributions, the company asserted, but it was later reported and not denied by Cargill that it had only recently ended the practice of keeping two sets of books in Spain to reduce some Spanish tax liabilities.

Cargill subsequently provided a summary of its report to the *Minneapolis Star*. But once again it was Cook that had to go farther than any of the privately owned companies in baring its corporate secrets. In April 1977, Cook filed with the Securities and Exchange Commission an extensive report, prepared by a New York law firm at the request of Cook's board of directors, that disclosed a number of "sensitive payments" made by the company between 1971 and 1976. There was no indication in the report that Cook had made any domestic or foreign political contributions; but there *was* "evidence that some independent commission agents with whom the company did business may have made questionable payments to government officials or employees of private customers in eight foreign countries. . . . Certain present and former officers and directors of the company, in varying degree, knew that such payments might have been made and condoned the practice." The most dramatic episode occurred in 1973 when in some unidentified country a Cook agent, in his zeal, committed the company to selling commodities at a price lower than it was actually prepared to do. When the agent told the government in question that Cook could not sell the commodities at this low price, he was told to come up with the money to "correct" Cook's bid—or else. Cook forked up $252,000 because, as Ned Cook later said, "his life was endangered"—and then fired the agent.

Cook payments were also made to speed up the collection of money owed it by foreign governments because of their delays in unloading grain ordered from Cook. The report also said there had been occasions when foreign importers overpriced their offers to Cook. Cook cooperated, got the business, and in return paid the difference into some local official's bank account in some other country. (Ned Cook said later this was money paid to an Egyptian lawyer as legal fees for collecting this money.)

Another $720,000 went to the owners of a couple of foreign companies who had been promising they could get the local government food-buying agency to do business with Ned Cook's firm.

Then there was a mysterious item about $497,509 in some unreported account that "may have enabled the recipients to avoid local tax laws." What happened, Ned Cook told me, was that the Mexican subsidiary of Cook Industries had some employees who preferred to receive some of their salaries and bonuses in Panama, instead of Mexico. So a company called Sefitex, owned by Cook's Mexico City boss, disbursed this money to the accounts those people set up in Panama. "It didn't go for bribes," Cook assured me. The only bribery he recalled was $1850 to a Mexican trade union official.

Finally $195,000 went to a Cook agent in still another unnamed foreign country, and this agent passed the cash on to local importers so that, back in the United States, Cook could postpone his shipment to the importers. The delay was "profitable to the [Cook] company"—meaning, presumably, that prices of the commodity to be shipped were falling and Cook was able to cover his delivery commitment at a lower price. (Ned Cook identified the country as Korea.)

By the standards of the grain business, these were tiny sums, but for the lucky recipients they were not. Here was an American company doling out money to some foreigners in amounts that must have put their annual compensation well above many of Cook's own top executives. One has a vision here of villas sprouting up in Swiss resort towns, inhabited by Romanians, Iranians, Koreans, Mexicans, and Filipinos—all owing their life of leisure to nothing more than one lucrative encounter in the bowels of some seedy bureaucracy with the local agent of some multinational company.

In fairness to Cook and Cargilll, it should be said that a great deal of downright extortion is practiced by officials of foreign countries, many of whom use the money ("dash" in Africa, "baksheesh" everywhere else) to supplement inadequate salaries. "What goes on in the Mediterranean basin you wouldn't believe!" Cook told me. Cook also made the point that the U.S. government is the only one in the world that forbids payments made in the course of getting business. French and German tax officials, he said, permit write-offs of such business-generating payments as long as they are made to foreigners and not to Frenchmen or Germans. For all that, these payments often result in the diversion of money from treasuries of developing countries and to bureaucrats in those countries. Western countries need to cooperate to put an end to these foreign extortion rings.

Nevertheless, Cook himself must have been disgusted as he read the report prepared for the SEC. This was not the way his father had done business. And even though Ned Cook knew he was operating in a very harsh world, all these payments to government officials to get business hardly fit his own raw-boned "free market" philosophy. Ned Cook knew that, and he ordered every one of his foreign agents to swear in writing that no money he received from Cook Industries would ever be used for illegal payments again.

The problem of illegal payments and corruption abroad was, however, only the beginning of the trouble that Cook and his rivals now began to experience.

The wildly fluctuating markets that began in 1972 created a whole new set of hazards. The big companies were much better situated than anyone else to predict the fluctuations and to profit from them. But even they were sometimes adversely affected. Contractual defaults are rare in the grain trade, but when commodity prices abruptly declined in early 1975, and Turkey's government wheat-importing agency canceled the wheat import contracts it had concluded earlier at higher prices with Continental, Bunge, and Cargill, Continental lost an estimated $35 million.*

Michel Fribourg was appalled. Savagely competitive as the grain trade always had been, the old "your word is your bond" rule was still assumed to apply. But there was no solidarity among the companies. While Continental went into an arbitration court in London seeking a judgment against the Turks, several of its competitors (including Cook and Alfred Toepfer, the independent German grain magnate from Hamburg) continued to do business with them. Cook explained later that, for his part, he had no guilt feelings, in light of the refusal of his rivals to show solidarity with him in a similar situation in 1973. This was at the time of the U.S. export embargo on soybeans. Cook, complying with the embargo, reduced shipments to Algeria, Libya, and Syria—which promptly retaliated by breaking a contract to sell Cook Algerian barley. When Cook went to Cargill and Continental suggesting a boycott of those Arab countries, Cook recalls being told: "Look after your business and we'll look after ours."

Opportunities for big profits, which the companies had looked forward to in the doldrums of the 1950s and 1960s, certainly were present. But the enormous volumes and the volatility also created unprecedented risks, as Michel Fribourg learned once again from an even greater fright in the summer of 1975. For while Henry Kissinger and Chuck Robinson were down in

---

* Continental sustained its losses as a result of a foreign exchange transaction of a kind that is fairly commonplace in the grain trade. The Turks promised to pay in Swiss francs. So the company immediately made a forward contract to cash the francs in for dollars at the time it expected to receive the Swiss money from Turkey. Continental's experts were right in thinking the rate would be less favorable for switching the francs into dollars later on. But since Continental never received the Swiss francs, the company had to go into the exchange markets to obtain the Swiss money, which then was available only at a stiff premium.

Washington figuring out how to get cheap oil from the Russians, Fribourg was figuring out how to ship all the grain he had promised the Russians without losing a pile of money.

When Continental's Francis Turion wound up his sale to the Russians of 4.5 million tons of corn and 1.1 million tons of barley, he could congratulate himself on having made a deal that, if it was not bigger than Continental's transactions in 1972, probably involved more money. It did not take a genius to calculate that Continental had committed something in excess of $600 million worth of grain at prevailing prices—though, of course, nobody except a few people in Continental had the slightest idea what the exact price was.

But there was no triumphant announcement. Rather, there was only a terse confirmation of the sale from New York, and then silence. The fact of the matter was that something finally had gone wrong in Continental's phenomenal, eleven-year business relationship with Exportkhleb.

In Chicago, the corn markets had erupted in bedlam at the first rumors of the secret chartering of tramp freighters by Glenas. On July 1, corn to be delivered in December traded at $2.36 a bushel. All through July and well into August the price relentlessly moved up; by August 20, corn futures reached $3.20 a bushel. This increase of 84 cents a bushel since the bull market began in early July amounted to $33.60 a ton—and meant that the 4.5 million tons of corn that Continental had contracted to sell the Russians was worth $151 million more than on July 1. If Continental had actually purchased the corn that it had committed to the Soviet Union before the price increase, this would have presented no problem. The trouble was that the company had not done that. It was "short."

Turion was not worried about this. The Frenchman had courage—though, of course it was not his money that had been committed, but his friend Michel Fribourg's. Turion was a world traveler who had a pretty good idea at any given moment of what the year's crops were like, whether a country would be buying grain or economizing. He was an old-school grain trader who trusted to his instincts. Not surprisingly, the new American methods of "risk management" did not appeal to him. People at Continental in New York who would try to second-guess him about grain price movements soon found out that Francis Turion had a "back channel" direct to Fribourg.

Turion was not alarmed by the company's extremely "short" position. His information and intuition told him that corn supplies would be adequate and that prices would drop down again once the initial panic over Russia subsided. It was true that when Turion left Moscow in July it was too early to know the size of the world's largest single crop—the American corn crop—but he still was unworried. Also, Turion left Moscow with the impression that the contracts contained an escape clause that permitted some renegotiating if prices began to get away from the New York company before it could fill its Russian order.

Fribourg was, as usual, summering in Europe. The Americans working at Continental through the hot New York summer were uneasy. And as the days went by, unease gave way to alarm. For the cables that had begun to arrive from Exportkhleb in Moscow concerning the recent grain deal said nothing about any escape clause. The Russians wanted their corn and barley—and at prices that now were well below the prices flashing across the board at the Chicago pits.

The Russians wanted their corn. The discrepancy in price was no trivial matter. It involved contracts for more than half a billion dollars' worth of American grain. With this controversy brewing in New York, the situation became so worrisome that Fribourg interrupted his August vacation at his mountain retreat at Crans sur Sierre in Switzerland and called a meeting at the company's Paris office. Turion came up from his holiday villa at Saint-Tropez, and others in the high command arrived from other distant places. Fribourg's associates always said that "MF" was a "man who could die inwardly but never show it." In Paris, he seemed icier, more in charge than ever. By this time Turion had obtained copies of the contracts in question, and they seemed to support his memory of the escape clause, so the Continental men decided to exercise the renegotiation provisions. They would use up some of the good will built up with the Russians. Turion and Fribourg hurried off to Moscow soon after that.

What Fribourg arranged with Viktor Pershin in Moscow is one of those well-kept secrets of the grain trade—like the origins of Glenas. Once again, the big events were hidden; the people involved refused to talk. From what can be learned from special sources, the Continental officials did renegotiate the delivery dates and, possibly, the price of some of the grain owed to the Russians. Continental had done many favors for the Russians over the years, beginning with the 1963–64 wheat business, and perhaps now the Russians agreed to reciprocate.*

In any case, the big Continental organization continued even then to react only sluggishly to developments affecting the corn markets. On August 1 Secretary of Agriculture Butz announced on behalf of the Ford administration that the moratorium on any new grain business with the Russians was to continue indefinitely. Kissinger, Dunlop, and Robinson had had their way. But Continental's strategists must have thought either that the embargo would be briefer than it eventually was or that the Russians later would buy more grain than they eventually did. For Continental bought substantial quantities of corn to cover its "short" position at peak prices—just as the prices began to slide down again. It now looked as if Turion's view of the grain markets had been right all along.

The episode was a sobering one for Michel Fribourg and his

* U.S. Agricultural attaché Roger Kneads caught sight of Michel Fribourg leaving the Ministry of Foreign Trade in August, but the company otherwise did not communicate its difficulties to the U.S. government. Continental refused to discuss any details of the summer of 1975 with me. A spokesman did confirm that the company fared badly on its corn sale, however.

company. The situation probably had never jeopardized the immense Fribourg fortune; Continental's survival as a company had never been at risk. But there had been sleepless nights and nervous days. Michel Fribourg was tired of living so dangerously. When in October 1975, two months after the crisis, Viktor Pershin sent word to Continental's office in Geneva that he would like to buy another 2.5 million tons of corn, Fribourg was ready for some peace and quiet. The glory days of grand slams in the Russian trade were over. The head of Continental declined to bid for the Russian business.

Within a year, Fribourg was ordering a shake-up in his Geneva office—and many people in the company said it had to do with lax financial management and the near fiasco of 1975. Many of Continental's Geneva people quit or were reassigned to branch offices elsewhere; Turion went into business on his own in Geneva, and Carlos Oris de Roa, a young Argentine, was appointed head of the Geneva center. De Roa, who had run Continental's soybean and milling facilities in Europe, was a business manager, not a trader, and his appointment signified a new, more cautious era. (Francis Turion died in 1978.)

Continental was not the only company to experience trading troubles. Most of the companies now insisted that the Soviet Union share more of the risks. Louis Dreyfus, for its part, set up a system of compensating balance sheets with the Russians. In effect it worked for the Russians on a fixed commission; losses in any given transaction would have to be recovered in profits on subsequent transactions—and in this way the firm kept its trading record with Exportkhleb in the black.

Louis Dreyfus had been having enough trouble keeping up its books in the tumult of trading. An irritated company vice-president, John Finlayson, wrote in 1975 to a branch office to complain about misplaced purchase contracts: "The market loss on corn and beans from this, I guess, is perhaps $750,000—and we understand this same circumstance is true in wheat, which can be even more. Why do we hear only at the end of February that the audit completed in November was incomplete and the figures we got were wrong? The total losses on this, if the wheat error is big, are going to be *very* significant. . . ."

All the dark mystery and confusion of the markets in this hectic period was captured in the daily chaos on the several thousand feet of floor space at the Board of Trade in Chicago. It had become even better theater than usual, when the post-1972 conditions had raised the stakes for all involved.

All the companies could and did speculate in the futures markets. In theory, there were legal limits—3 million bushels (75–80 thousand tons) "long" or "short" at any one time for wheat, corn or soybeans. "Speculation" was what it was called when a company bought or sold the 5000-bushel futures contracts for purposes other than protecting its inventories against price changes. But since the companies always had enormous inventories all over the world, plus actual commitments to buy or sell real grain over the next months, it was practically impossible to ascertain whether a company was "hedging" or actually playing the markets.

It was easy enough to speculate. And this could be done by *not* going into the markets at all. If a grain company anticipated that prices would rise after it bought farmers' grain, it might decide not to sell this grain in the futures market but instead to hold it against the hope that the grain would appreciate in value. Since the company was not using the facilities of the regulated commodity exchanges in this case, there was no limit to how much of this kind of speculation could be done.

Until 1975, supervision of the American commodities markets was entrusted to the weak and understaffed Commodity Exchange Authority, housed in the Department of Agriculture. Its "authority" was limited by statute and by the USDA's philosophical inclination against interference in grain markets. In

1974, Congress finally legislated a new, independent government agency to police the exchanges. The Commodity Futures Trading Commission began work in April of the following year with a staff of twenty-nine investigators and forty attorneys. Its chairman, William Bagley, was fond of reminding people that the CFTC had fewer "policemen" than the Rockville, Maryland, Police Department—and this to monitor the commodity exchanges* that are among the world's most complex economic institutions.

Half a century ago, Edward Jerome Dies had written in his book *The Wheat Pit*, "It is almost as easy to corner the stars in the sky as to corner the wheat market of today." But powerful speculators could and did disrupt and distort the markets. In 1976 a group of buyers and sellers had attempted to manipulate the price of Maine potatoes traded at the New York Mercantile Exchange. And the price variations in other exchanges were sometimes puzzling. Prices of frozen pork bellies (from which bacon is cut) bounced up and down like a yo-yo on a string in the summer of 1976, moving from 60 cents a pound to 72 cents and back down to 57 cents in a few weeks—and all without any apparent change in the supply of frozen pork bellies required by Americans for their sandwiches and breakfasts.

Cook Industries had a reputation as the boldest speculator among the big companies. The commodities brokers in Chicago reasoned that the Memphis company had not earned a fortune between 1972 and 1975 by hedging all its inventories and earning profits of a fraction of a penny a bushel. The tradition went

---

* These exchanges deal in futures contracts and options on just about everything. Potatoes, platinum, plywood, foreign currency, eggs, and pork bellies (bacon). They are, in addition to the Chicago Board of Trade, the Mercantile Exchange, and Mid-America Commodities Exchange (also in Chicago); the Mercantile Exchange, Coffee & Sugar Exchange, Cocoa Exchange, Cotton Exchange, and Commodity Exchange (all in New York); the Kansas City Board of Trade, and the Minneapolis Grain Exchange.

back to the free-wheeling McCaull days. The company's financial statement spoke for itself. Clever speculation had made Ned Cook rich. But in late 1976 trouble apparently started in the soybean pit at the Chicago Board of Trade.

In the past decade soybean markets have been unusually volatile. The global demand for vegetable protein increases year after year as consumption of meat and poultry increases. (Japan now also depends on the United States as a primary source of soy for feeding humans.) American soy exports rose steadily from 6.1 million tons in 1965 to almost 12 million tons in 1972. This demand, and a decline in the anchovy catch off Peru in 1971 and 1972, caused tight supplies of protein all over the world. Dramatic price fluctuations continued in subsequent years. In 1976, the bushel cost of soybeans traded in the Chicago futures pits advanced from $5.00 in April to $7.77 in July, before plunging to just over $6.00 a few weeks later. Each year trading follows a suspenseful course: In the spring, as the supply of American soybeans from the previous year's harvest dwindles, prices rise; then, at the end of August, they drop again as the new crop is harvested. The major soybean trading companies are in a position to exploit this volatility, and indeed at times the companies' protective actions indirectly influence the markets and distort the prices.

Ned Cook always had been fascinated by soybeans, the new glamor crop that thrived in his regional backyard. Soybeans were replacing cotton on many farms of Arkansas, right across the muddy Mississippi River from Memphis. The special volatility and unpredictability of the soybean pit appealed to Cook; and he had made his first fortune by going "long," buying soybeans and soybean futures as fast as he could in late 1972. Afterward he said that "the real glamor of the grain business is in beans."

Cook had high regard for the staff of young men he hired after the departure of Phil McCaull in 1972. They were known in the commodity trade as "Cook's whiz kids." Former Assistant Secretary of Agriculture Carroll Brunthaver headed the research department, and the daily trading was masterminded by a gifted former Oklahoma farm boy by the name of Willard Sparks. In the spring of 1977, Sparks was thirty-eight years old; he received a salary of $500,000 a year; and he had the title of senior vice-president. A quick-witted and cool man with a strong grasp of the technical problems of commodity trading, Sparks was a living example of the sort of person he had once said the grain trade needed: "go-getters and self-starters, people who involve themselves and make things happen." The one characteristic that is important in a trader, he had gone on to say, was the ability to make a decision without throwing in qualifying recommendations. "We need people who cannot be pushed around and who defend [their] point of view."

Sometime late in 1976, Cook Industries made a fateful decision. After careful analysis, Cook's research department decided that the country would have an abundant stock of soybeans by the time the 1977 crop was harvested the following September and October. The company would go "short" in the coming year.

Almost from the start, the strategy went wrong. Cook's men expected that the price would start declining by the end of the year. They stayed "short"—meaning that they sold some soybeans that they did not own, anticipating that beans would be getting cheaper. Instead, there was a late-harvest drought and strong foreign demand; prices rose somewhat, so Cook had to buy higher-priced beans to cover the future sales commitments as they came due. All the time, Cook was also buying actual beans from farmers and selling them abroad—but not always at a profit.

For the first quarter of its 1976–77 fiscal year ending August 31, 1977, Cook reported a loss of $13.5 million. A company statement blamed "inability to hedge certain large commodity transactions" because of "rapid and wide fluctuations in the futures markets." The company lost only $700,000 in the next quarter, but in the third quarter ending February 28, the company again lost heavily, to the tune of $13 million.

The Cook executives had other problems to deal with besides the situation in the soybean pit. Primary among these was the litigation that had resulted from the grain-loading scandal and the lingering questions it had left about the honesty of Cook Industries. The Indian government had filed a $35-million suit against Cook, alleging that it had been robbed in the underloading scheme, and the United States government had gone to court to recover $23 million from Cook in connection with underweight or misgraded P.L. 480 grain shipments.

The claims against Cook seemed inflated. For all the bad publicity, many government and private audits had failed to turn up excess grain accumulations of anything like the magnitude that might have been expected in a corrupt arrangement that had lasted for five years. Cook believed that the suits eventually would be settled for only pennies on the dollar. But the litigation distracted the management's attention at a time when the company was moving into much more serious financial trouble. By the time the company entered its final quarter of operations, stockholders were beginning to tie up the company switchboard, attempting to find out what had gone wrong. As the pressure mounted to recoup the company's losses, there was new trouble.

This time, the culprit was the weather. At Cook headquarters in Memphis, former college football quarterback William Gore figured that he could start moving bargeloads of Iowa, Illinois, and Missouri corn down the Mississippi River to New Orleans by late February. But the winter of 1977 was one of the coldest, driest winters in the United States in years. The upper Mississippi River stayed frozen solid long after the date of the usual April thaw, and when the ice finally broke, the water levels were too low for the barges to get through. The big grain companies scrambled for railroad cars to move corn to the ports. Downstream, where Midwest corn supplies were being choked off, prices rose steeply. Now Cook was "short." He had no alternative but to pay premiums for the corn he needed to load on the ships waiting at the Gulf ports.

All through February 1977, Sparks kept sending instructions to Cook's representatives in the pits: "Sell soybeans." Sparks was living by his own credo as a grain trader—showing he could not be pushed around. But as Cook's representatives in Chicago screamed across the bedlam of the pit, other voices answered, "Sold!" Somebody was disagreeing with Ned Cook's assessment of the market in soybeans. Cook was selling soybeans for delivery in May and July; the company's judgment was still that the price would soon start sliding down. But instead, soybean prices moved upward relentlessly under strong buying pressure from unidentified speculators who were going "long" against Cook's "short" position.

The identity of the powerful buyer or buyers puzzled Cook's analysts in Memphis. They theorized that the Brazilian government was probably the main bull in the soybean market. Brazil had a vested interest in buying futures in the American markets to inflate the price of a commodity that was important to Brazil's economy. Chicago set the price for the world. As the Brazilian harvest neared completion in the Southern Hemisphere's fall, hundreds of millions of dollars, as well as the financial well-being of Brazilian soybean farmers, were at stake in the price.

Probably the Brazilians were trying to muscle the Chicago market, but as later became clear, they were not the only ones. Somebody else was betting against Ned Cook, somebody whose name would have spelled extreme danger to Sparks and his people if they had heard it early enough: Hunt. Hunt of Texas, of oil, of fortunes so extravagant as to make the likes of Ned Cook seem like poor southern farm folk. The late H. L. Hunt had been one of the fabled oil tycoons of Texas's frontier era. And when he had died a few years ago, he not only left an enormous fortune and a bunch of sons to fight and quarrel over it, but also passed on his buccaneering spirit to Bunker and Herbert, two of the sons. Bunker Hunt liked oil; he went his own independent way and could thumb his nose at the major oil companies. He made his own deal in 1973 with Libyan ruler Col. Muammar el-Qaddafi when the majors of oil were trying to hold to a hard line against the desert nationalist, then bent on nationalizing the concessions.

After Libya, Bunker Hunt began looking for new worlds to conquer. He appeared to be homespun and folksy, but underneath were the hard, cold instincts of a born commodity speculator. Bunker turned to silver. He felt comfortable with silver. It came out of the ground, like oil, and it was almost as basic to the economies of the Western world as petroleum. When automobiles, gasoline, clothing, and food increased in price, so did silver. Owning silver was almost as good a hedge against inflation as owning oil.

Hunt was no ordinary commodity trader. While most traders in the futures markets cancel out their contracts and take their profits or losses, Hunt actually took delivery of the silver. He stored hoards of bullion in warehouses and then tried to gain control of a company that operated the nation's largest silver mine. The next year, Hunt moved just as purposefully into sugar futures, and invested $33 million in Great Western United, which controls the largest sugar-beet-processing firm in the country.

In late 1976, Hunt moved again, this time into the protein sector of American agriculture. Agriculture had captured his fancy. The world was in the midst of basic diet changes that had created a tremendous need for high-protein animal feeds. Hunt wanted to be part of the protein expansion. And he started buying soybean futures. Since there was the 3-million-bushel limit on speculation to worry about, Bunker brought in his brother Herbert and five members of their families, and together they all began secretly accumulating the maximum allowable—21 million bushels in all. This was approximately a third of the total beans that forecasters thought would be left over when new soybeans from the 1977 crop became available. This was not a corner, but it was getting near to one.

Cook Industries, on the other hand, had kept selling soybean futures, and by April 1977, the firm was "short" by about as many bushels as the Hunts were "long." And it began to look as if the price was not going to drop as Sparks had predicted. It was inexplicable to Sparks, the computer-minded man. Cook had done its homework. The soybeans were out there, he was sure, in sufficient quantity. Yet the market in Chicago kept going up. The company now felt itself squeezed from all sides. Brazil had imposed stiff export taxes on soybeans in March in order to hold Brazilian beans off world markets and keep the bullish pressure on prices (proving that even with the private grain trade functioning freely in Brazil, the government had developed adequate means for controlling it).

It was probably in mid-April that Cook and his people learned that they were going up against the Hunts in the soybean pit. How this intelligence was obtained can only be guessed at. Ned Cook had old and close ties to Texas money. One of his directors was John Murchison, a Yale roommate and member of a wealthy Dallas family. Another director was none other than J. Stuart Hunt, a distant cousin of Bunker's and Herbert's. Bunker did not usually share business confidences with his cousin, but he did, apparently, issue a veiled warning to Stuart one day when the two of them met and compared notes on commodity markets. Stuart mentioned that he was "short" on soybeans—and so, in fact, was Cook Industries. Bunker simply advised his cousin that Ned Cook was wrong about soybeans.

Within a few days of that conversation an executive of Cook telephoned CFTC commissioner Robert Martin in Washington to express concern about certain "manipulative positions" in the soybean market. Later the Hunts' attorneys and several newspapers were to raise questions about this call: Martin had been an officer of Cook Industries in Chicago before joining the new regulatory agency in 1975. But there is no question that the complaint was serious, regardless of its source. Martin passed it on to CFTC chairman Bagley. On April 21, Bagley inquired at the Board of Trade in Chicago about possible manipulation in the May and July soybean futures. The next day, a Saturday, the board's business conduct committee met. Nothing apparently came of that meeting, but word of it must have leaked out, because on the following Monday soybean prices suddenly collapsed. Rumors of the Hunts' enormous position began to circulate on the trading floor. There were reports of impending CFTC action that could require the Hunts to divest their enormous holdings, flooding the markets with soybeans and depressing prices. In four days, the bushel price of soybeans dropped $1.21, or more than 10 per cent. Down in Memphis, Cook and his men held their breaths.

On April 28, Bagley announced at a press conference that the Hunts held some 23 million bushels of beans, and the CFTC would go into federal court in Chicago to force the families to reduce their holdings down to the limit for a single person or company. The Hunts were working "in concert" to evade the speculative limit of 3 million bushels, he said.

This was all unprecedented. For a government official to announce what a speculator in the sacrosanct markets was doing was a completely new departure from the system of confidentiality that had always prevailed at the exchanges, those bastions of the free-market system that were supposed to be such faithful detectors of the global tremors of supply and demand.

Yet the announcement did not have the effect Cook hoped for. There was no rush to get out of soybeans, which would have broken the price rise. On the contrary, the fact that it was now known that the powerful and seemingly invincible Hunts had bet on the "long" side only seemed to confirm hunches that prices would go still higher. Moreover, the Hunts refused to give up their soybean contracts, and the stage was set for a long court battle. By early May, prices had rebounded.

All through May, Sparks and his associates maneuvered desperately to improve Cook's position. Word leaked out of the trading room that the company was on the wrong side of the market, but as Ned Cook strode around the headquarters, he rallied his executives. "We're gonna pull this out," he told them. Sparks moved Cook out of soybeans and into soybean meal, then into soybean oil, and back into soybeans. The trading became so hectic that the company lost track of the "bottom line"—of Cook's ultimate liability.

On Saturday, May 21, the day after Cook finally received a full accounting from McLeary on the losses that the company was facing, Sparks still believed that Cook Industries was right. He was convinced soybeans were overpriced. Most of Cook's losses were still only on paper. They would not become real until the company liquidated its futures contracts by buying beans at a higher price to meet the commitments. The July contract did not come due until July 20, but that, unfortunately for Ned Cook, could have been a century away.

In commodity trading, it is easy to get into the game. Margin requirements are small—10 per cent is typical. A trader buying or selling a 5000-bushel soybean futures contract at $8.00 a bushel ($40,000) puts up only $4,000. But the speculator must deposit the full amount of his losses with the exchange if the market moves against him. A speculator who sells a 5000-bushel soybean futures contract at $8.00 suffers paper losses of $10,000 ($2.00 a bushel) if the price reaches $10.00 a bushel. Cook had sold millions of bushels and the paper losses were enormous. As they increased, the Board of Trade increased the margin requirements for Cook, adding to the squeeze. Cook's credit lines at some fifty banks were in the hundreds of millions of dollars, but by the end of May the company had reached its borrowing limit.

Cook already had sold off some assets to raise capital that year. (The E. L. Bruce hardwood flooring company, the major acquisition in Cook's 1969 expansion program, went in February. Cook's just-completed new grain elevator at Galveston followed in April.) Now Cook called his lawyers after his fateful weekend trip to New York City. They advised him to suspend trading. Cook knew what that meant. He and a couple of his men went through the dreary business of calling Cook's fifty-odd banks. Cook knew that they would not extend additional credit. He had no alternative but to close out his holdings in Chicago, take his losses, and pay his creditors.

On June 1, Cook Industries issued a news release that had the look of having been written by the company's lawyers. It announced that Cook had asked the American Stock Exchange to halt trading in its stock; that the losses in the final quarter of the company's financial year were "likely to be in excess of $60 million"; that Sparks and another highly paid vice-president, Christopher Parrott, had resigned; and that the company was meeting with its major bank lenders to achieve an "orderly repayment of debts." The release stated further that Cook "intends over a period of time to reduce the scope and volume of its grain merchandising operation ... [and] intends, from time to time, to dispose of certain grain merchandising facilities not required at the reduced level of operations."

In the middle of all this, there was a comic-opera touch. A Russian delegation showed up, and, as if to show loyalty and solidarity with Ned Cook in his darkest hour, purchased several hundred thousand tons of wheat.

The dismantling of the holdings that Cook had acquired in better days proceeded rapidly. Within a year, the company that Ned Cook had built into one of the highest-flying grain companies in the world had all but disappeared. Hundreds of employees drifted away. Sparks—still insisting that his view of the soybean markets had been essentially correct—formed his own consultancy. Cook was silent about Sparks' role. And Sparks also never said a word against his old boss.

For a while, it looked as if the collapse of Cook Industries would be the signal for Pillsbury—which had stuck mostly to the milling business Charles Pillsbury had begun in the Midwest in the nineteenth century—to come into the international grain business. Pillsbury sniffed at the Cook elevator installations but talks were broken off.

Instead, the final outcome was to have very broad geopolitical implications for the grain trade. The final buyer was not an American firm but Mitsui, the giant Japanese trading company which, overall, made the international grain companies look like village shopkeepers in comparison with its multibillion-dollar global interests in many businesses. For years, the Japanese had sought an "upstream" foothold in the United States, the country on which their entire food supply depended. But they had been denied it because of the continued control of the port facilities by the European and American majors. The Japanese trading houses were therefore usually compelled to buy from the American-controlled companies. But now Cook transferred his company's lease on a Portland, Oregon, elevator to Marubeui and then sold seven inland elevators in Iowa, Illinois, and Missouri, as well as the scandal-ridden port facility at Reserve, Louisiana, to Mitsui. Cook never hesitated for a moment. When the time came to close the deal, he called half a dozen interested potential buyers, told them what the price would be, and said that the first to bring in a contract would have the elevators. The men from Mitsui arrived within twenty-four hours. And with that the Japanese were positioned at the great gateway of American grain.

This development, along with the fact that Cargill had given the Swiss Credit Bank a 50-percent interest in one of its flagship subsidiaries (Tradax Export) for "tax reasons" in 1974, began to make it look as if the United States was surrendering much of its control over America's unparalleled grain resources. It was a curious consequence of the new era in which American grain's importance had so immeasurably increased.

Ned Cook, in Memphis, stayed on to face the wrath of Cook Industries stockholders. Even with the sale of its assets, the company kept experiencing losses, most of them from residual grain sale commitments that the company still had. With its operations cut way back in the grain markets, the company was like a cripple. It had lost its mobility and maneuverability. Getting out of the grain business was at least as difficult as getting in.

Whenever he could, Ned Cook escaped to a retreat in Switzerland. He seemed remarkably unfazed by all his problems but the jauntiness was gone. "Agatha Christie could have written the damnedest book about this business," he said, shaking his head.

In the aftermath of all these troubles in the grain industry, the federal government did intensify its supervision. Congress ordered the creation of a new agency, the Federal Grain Inspection Service, to take charge of inspecting grain for export.

The government's attempt to get some control over the nation's commodity exchanges met with less success. The Commodity Futures Trading Commission litigation against the Hunts resulted in not much more than a gentle judicial slap on the wrist. U.S. District Court Judge Frank McGarr found that the Hunts had indeed acted "in concert" to pile up a huge holding of soybean futures, far above the speculative limits, but there were no charges of manipulation and he refused to order the Hunts to give up their profits or liquidate any excess holdings that they might still have. It was a hollow victory at best for the government. *The Wall Street Journal* quoted sources saying the family was "about $100 million" ahead at one point.

Just what an unforgiving business grain really is was demonstrated in a sudden, thundering moment of horror across the river from New Orleans in mid-morning of December 22, 1977. The laborers and warehousemen who work at Continental's terminal at Weswego were taking a break. It was just before Christmas, and the pace was a little slower than usual; the men sat in the cafeteria, talking about vacation plans. The Continental management had handed out Christmas gifts: hams. Suddenly there was a deafening roar and tons of concrete crashed through the roof of the cafeteria killing everyone present. The tops of the 130-foot silos had blown off like a chain of ignited Roman candles, hurtling a thick mushroom cloud of black smoke skyward. A Norwegian vessel being loaded with grain weighed anchor and pushed off into the stream, for even though it was a quarter mile from the silos, flying debris pelted it. Secondary explosions ripped through the structure.

Two days after Christmas another devastating explosion crumpled the one-year-old, $26-million grain elevator complex at Galveston that Cook had sold only months earlier to the cooperative Farmers Export Company. Store windows a mile from the elevator in downtown Galveston were shattered. The diesel engine of a train unloading grain at the time was blown off the tracks and into a forty-foot–deep tunnel.

It was almost as if some terrible, swift punishment was being visited upon the merchants of grain. The final casualty toll at the Continental silos was thirty-six dead. Six months later fires were still burning at the scene of the Continental disaster. Firemen were afraid to bulldoze the ruins for fear of weakening the levy and letting the whole Mississippi river cover the flood plain.

Rescue workers picking their way through the mangled metal, charred concrete, and smoldering grain had recovered twenty-five bodies by nightfall after the explosion. "It's like a holocaust," muttered the Rev. Anthony Serio, administering the last rites over the unrecognizable bodies of the disaster victims.

Michel Fribourg, reached at Continental headquarters in New York, was stunned. He declared it to be the worst disaster in the history of the company. The grain trade was indeed an unforgiving business.

Blood Brother to the Earthquake 14

"Nobody is qualified to become a statesman who is
entirely ignorant of the problem of wheat."
—SOCRATES

"We think of ourselves as people who feed the world."
—CONTINENTAL OFFICIAL

Two front-page *New York Times* articles several days apart in
May 1977 illustrate one of the most extraordinary paradoxes of
the second half of the twentieth century. The first story quoted
"food experts" as saying that the period of grain shortages, scarcity, and high food prices appeared to have ended for the time
being. There were record stocks of wheat on hand. "When harvests begin this summer," the *Times* reported, "the world will
have a two-month supply of grain—about 172 million tons."
Several days later, the *Times* printed another article headlined
THOUSANDS IN HAITI FACING STARVATION IN SEVERE DROUGHT.
"Desperation is evident in this bleak, drought-stricken country
where many are always hungry," said the article, and anybody
who knew anything about malnutrition knew what this meant.
The longer the drought and food shortages continued, the
greater the likelihood that vulnerable groups—old people and
children—would die of starvation-related infections, or would

suffer brain damage and impaired chances of leading a useful life.

Still another report, this one from British journalist Simon Winchester, described a four-year-old girl's death from starvation in a small village in Honduras. "A nurse placed a piece of muslin over her face to keep the flies away for the last few minutes—the child's breath scarcely fluttered the cotton and she was dead within half an hour," he wrote. Winchester described how a drought had wiped out most of the country's paltry corn crop. Doctors in Honduras estimated that 60,000 children needed immediate hospitalization because of the spread of diseases related to inadequate nutrition.* Dr Carlos Medina, head of the nutrition department of the mother-and-child hospital in Tegucigalpa, said that the primary need was for "money from outside—to improve agriculture, to make better roads, to allow for building grain silos and buying trucks, to educate the rural people in better ways of feeding their children, to allow Honduras to buy grain—no matter how costly—on the international markets."

Haiti and Honduras are within 800 miles of the United States. People are not starving in those nearby countries because the world is running out of food. They are starving because they are poor—poor and beyond the reach of the vast commercial system that produces food and transfers it from one country to another.

The U.S. Department of Agriculture said in a report issued in 1974 that if the estimated 460 million malnourished people in the world each received only 500 additional calories a day, their hunger would be alleviated. Cereal grains could provide these calories. An extra .15 kilograms per person a day of either wheat, rice, corn, sorghum, or millet would give this additional allotment of 500 calories. This, in turn, would require 21.9 million tons of cereals a year.

This amount of food is well within the ability of the world's

---

* Less than the minimum requirement of 2200 calories a day.

farmers to provide. It is a tiny fraction of the 172-million-ton, two-month supply mentioned in the *Times*'s article. The 21.9 million tons is equivalent to only 2 per cent of average annual world cereal production in the last decade. But unfortunately, world hunger has not turned out to be as simple a problem as it was once perceived to be.

Hunger persists in countries that have received vast amounts of American food aid (such as India); in countries where enormous amounts of capital and technology have been put into farming (such as Brazil); in countries that import large amounts of food (such as Indonesia). It is clear that the long-term solution to endemic hunger will not be for Americans to organize relief shipments to Port-au-Prince, or for Americans to eat less steak and bread to "save" grain; or for the United States to increase its food exports. None of these things have had a substantial effect on hunger in the past and are not likely to do so in the future.

It would be wrong to suggest that the unprecedented growth of the America-centered postwar grain trade is without its benefits. It often has helped hungry people avoid starvation, and it has helped economies to modernize and progress during times of international change, development, and recovery from war. American food has been a source drawn upon by almost every country in the world. The world would be quite unrecognizable today without American grain surpluses—and quite likely a less happy and hospitable place than it now is.

But fundamental questions have not been resolved in the global food economy. Foremost among those are the questions of how to reform the system to make it more responsive to the needs of the poor, the malnourished, and the vast majority of underprivileged peasants.

Hunger was not intended to be a prominent topic of this book. Hungry people do not "make the markets" in Chicago; they do not have much effect on futures prices, the Rotterdam spot market, or the European agricultural import duties. The reverse of this is that nobody who has money to pay for food is starving.

Even in Haiti, which qualifies as one of the world's "hungry nations," many people have enough to eat. "Baby Doc" Duvalier, the country's hereditary despot, is not starving; neither are his bodyguards, nor the bureaucrats and shopkeepers of Port-au-Prince. It is *poor* people who are starving in Haiti.

It is tempting to blame the grain traders for this sorry situation. The playwright Bertolt Brecht once did. "Famines do not occur," he said. "They are organized by the grain trade." Given the pervasiveness of malnutrition, the money that a handful of merchant families make in the food trade does seem an affront to common notions of economic justice. But to blame the merchants for conditions that have promoted enormous food imports and continuing malnutrition is to miss the economic and political point, which is that commercial markets, not famines, interest the merchants. The companies thrive upon and in fact encourage a system that excludes the hungry. But other than the fact that they deal in foodstuffs and agricultural commodities, the companies are not really different from other great multinational enterprises—from the banks, oil companies, electric companies, and aluminum firms. They are businesses, not welfare organizations. The companies are at the heart of one of the world's central systems—but it is a financial and commercial system, not one that began with any premise of easing human misery. If people who are now too poor to buy food had money, the merchants would not hesitate to sell food to them. At the present time, it is money, not food that is badly distributed across the planet.

Since multinational grain companies, like other multinationals, respond to the laws of balance sheets and profit and loss statements, it does not make sense to expect them to correct either the system or themselves. Business often does things that are socially progressive, productive, and in the best interest of developing countries, but business does not do those things out of a social conscience, but because they are profitable. It is up to others, particularly those with political power, to make the necessary modifications.

Once it is clear that poverty rather than inadequate food production and the population explosion is at the root of the problem of world hunger, it is necessary to confront a second economic reality. This is that the United States, as well as the companies, has benefited from the growth of a commercial system in which other countries have become more and more dependent on imported food without any fundamental improvement in world nutrition. From the early 1950s onward, it was the objective of U.S. policy to increase *commercial* food exports. With the benefit of greater historical perspective it is possible to see that what once passed as American generosity in the distribution of food was primarily a response to the domestic political problem of the food surplus. Starting in the early 1960s, trade replaced aid as the driving imperative behind the American-centered grain trade. Once the surplus was gone, U.S. food aid became a small factor in the country's grain exports. In the first year of this decade's food shortages—1973—we exported $863 million in food under government-subsidized programs. But we sold twenty times that amount ($16.8 billion) to cash-paying customers. Most of the food went to feed livestock and poultry in industrial countries. Now as the Carter administration attempts to deal with the "stagflation" undermining the U.S. economy, agriculture is again seen as an ace in the hole, and efforts are being intensified to expand grain exports. Corn and soybeans have become the great, global defenders of the dollar and of American economic hegemony, and agriculture still stands as the one unshaken pillar of the empire.

The other side of this, of course, is that to a good many countries food imports have become as economically burdensome as oil imports. They are taking money away from more productive economic development and indirectly contributing to the problems of Western economies by draining the resources and economic vigor of nations that are potentially the growth markets for Western technology and products, and therefore an asset in reviving U.S. industry and providing more jobs for Americans.

Food is produced, food is distributed, food is consumed. This has always been so. For most of history, most food has been consumed close to where it was produced and only fairly small volumes moved into the commercial distribution system. But in the last thirty years there has been an enormous bulge in this sector. Before World War II, Africa, Asia, and Latin America were net *exporters* of food. Then countries such as India, Chile, and the Soviet Union, traditionally grain exporters, became importers of massive quantities. When wheat was selling for $50–75 a ton, as it was for most of the 1960s, the imports were manageable, but as volumes and prices increased, the situation changed, to the detriment of food-deficit nations. The food import bill of developing countries increased by $6 billion between 1973 and 1974, compared with an only slightly greater increase of $10 billion in imported oil costs.

This was money that went to Continental, Cargill, and ultimately to the United States, instead of into local economic development, or local agriculture, and the pattern is now established. Foreign exchange that might go to improving agricultural production is instead pre-empted by food imports. Or, as often happens, whatever foreign exchange is left over is invested in agriculture that produces *export* crops rather than food for the people: sugar, coffee, cocoa, palm oil, rubber, or jute, instead of rice, cassava, or maize. And so the vicious circle continues.

Colombia is a good example of what is happening in dozens of other countries. The UN's Food and Agriculture Organization says that this Latin American country has the capability to be a *major exporter* of food. But first, the bad news. As an article in the March 25, 1977, issue of *Latin American Week* noted, Colombia "must live with the present." The article continued:

It is now barely capable of feeding itself, and its population is growing by leaps and bounds. There are almost 26 million Colombians, making the country the second most populous in South America, and the annual population growth rate is 3.2 per cent. Last week, President Alfonso Lopez Michelsen was forced to announce that foodstuffs, as well as some manufactured goods, would have to be imported in order to combat growing shortages and prevent speculators' "making hay while the sun shines." In a statement made when signing a collective agreement giving 12,000 dockworkers a new wage hike, he said: "We have to import many items to make up deficiencies because nothing is more dangerous than a captive market in which demand exceeds supply and where equilibrium is sought by pushing up prices." The president warned the country was running up against an "unprecedented economic emergency." The emergency Lopez Michelsen spoke of is largely the result of the fierce and prolonged drought that has scourged almost all of the country. Not only has farm output suffered—no figures on the precise losses due to the drought have yet been published—but electricity production has also fallen as the water for hydroelectric dams has declined. This has had a marked effect on the country's industrial centers, which have had to put up with blackouts and brownouts for months. In the president's view the country's bad climatic luck is being exploited by speculators of one kind and another. When announcing that more articles would be imported to make supply come into line with demand, he had harsh words for the industrial concerns which manage to show healthy profit sheets while the real wages of workers across the nation have declined. The government has been grappling with a tidal wave of strikes and industrial unrest in recent weeks.

Note that economics and politics, not hunger and starvation, are the reasons given for the imports.

Today, food imports determine the balance between stability and a "tidal wave of strikes" or other civil disorder. This helps to explain the steady growth of grain imports of developing countries—from 32.9 million tons in 1965 to almost 50 million tons in 1976.

The food crisis is like the oil crisis in that the figures on production, reserves, and demand can be juggled to suit any theory about the future. There are those who say that doomsday is just around the corner, that the world already has reached the outer limits of its capacity to feed itself. Others, such as Lester Brown, director of the Worldwatch Institute, are only slightly less worried. Brown sees the problem as an arithmetical one—of growing numbers of people and diminishing amounts of natural resources. Still another group believes that reactionary or feudal political and social structures are at the root of the food problem. The one certainty that all agree on is that if present trends continue, strains will develop, and rich and poor countries alike will be affected.

A "World Food and Nutrition Study" undertaken for the National Research Council in Washington in 1977 concluded that by the year 2000, *industrial* countries will require an additional amount of grain equal to what the United States now produces annually. The population of developing countries, meanwhile, is expected to grow by nearly 1 billion to 2.9 billion in 1990; by the turn of the century, this population will require food equal to one and a half times America's present yearly production.

It is likely that this amount of additional food can be produced. Since the 1974 food emergency, world grain production has expanded rapidly enough to meet the demand for grain in world markets. There have been excellent grain harvests in India throughout this period, and grain traders talk about India again becoming a grain-exporting country. Bangladesh, the international "basket case" in 1974, has recovered sufficiently from war, drought, tidal wave, and flood so that in 1977 it was able to repay a Soviet wheat loan of several years earlier by purchasing American wheat and earmarking it for Russia. In the United States, policies of planned scarcity have again been adopted to curb the growth of American stockpiles of unsold grain. In August 1977, Secretary of Agriculture Bob Bergland announced that wheat farmers would not be eligible for price supports in 1978 unless they could show that they had fallowed 20 per cent of their total wheat land. Officials were hoping to cut wheat acreage by 11 million acres. In February 1978, Bergland took additional steps, this time to try to curb corn production, and made a further plan to reduce feed-grain in acreage. Once again, a sense of complacency settled over Washington.

All this suggests what virtually all serious agricultural economists believe: The world is not running out of food and is not likely to in our lifetimes. The question is one of price, just as it is in oil. As the strains continue, it is a certainty that prices will rise.

The World Bank estimates that wheat prices in current dollars will go from a 1976 value of $124 a ton to $325 a ton by 1985 and rice from $254 a ton to $680 a ton. Corn and soybean prices will rise at a comparable rate. There is a strong likelihood that not only the Soviet Union but also China will be commercial grain buyers. Some 600 million Chinese now living close to a local food supply in rural communes cannot be left there indefinitely. No country in the world has yet been able to industrialize without at least some temporary increase in food imports, necessitated by the decline in the agricultural labor force and population shifts. China has been spending heavily for modern chemical fertilizer plants. This is a sign that China is planning to make changes in its agricultural economy, but much larger food imports may be necessary during the adjustment period.

More food can be produced, but the price of the food could put some countries out of the market. Either those nations take steps now to enact policies that will make them more self-sufficient, or they will face lower nutritional levels, wrecked economic plans, and worsening political unrest.

Most of the OPEC countries and wealthier developing countries such as South Korea, Taiwan, and Brazil can afford to cover their food deficits with imports; with somewhat more difficulty so can another group of countries including Argentina, Thailand, and Pakistan; but countries at the bottom end of the economic scale, such as Haiti and Honduras, will be squeezed out of the markets.

Poland, an industrial country which is not in this last category, is nonetheless an example of a country that is at the edge of disaster. Poland once exported wheat, barley, and oats to western Europe, but today it is one of the world's largest importers of grain. It is one of the givens of current international affairs that Poland is never more than a cargo of wheat away from violence and bloodshed in the streets. Its agriculture is a shambles—a system of inefficient state farms mixed with private farming on plots too small, too underequipped, and too deprived of government support to produce more food. But it is a political question how Poland will come out of this mess. Collectivization of agriculture, tried earlier and abandoned, is no longer a realistic option, for the situation is too precarious for experimentation on that scale to be attempted. But it is also ideologically unacceptable to the Polish communists to allow Western patterns of land ownership and government support. The Polish leaders are therefore stymied.

The United States was not spared the effects of the strong inflationary pressures on the global food supply. The higher prices of steak in American supermarkets in 1978 can be traced back to the sudden increase in the price of corn in 1973, and the costs this added to fattening the beef from which tender, marbled steaks are cut. In fact, the global trend toward higher grain prices is making America into a "hamburger society" instead of the nation of steak eaters it once was.

Inflation is only the most direct and obvious effect of higher grain prices in the United States. Higher grain prices also drove up the price of farmland all over the Corn Belt (Illinois corn land that sold for $500 an acre in 1972 sold for $1200 in 1978), and these higher land prices attracted banks, insurance companies, and foreign investors. Even before 1972–73, the nation had been losing 2000 family farmers a week. With each passing season it is more and more difficult for young families to buy the land they need to be farmers.

The higher grain prices also encouraged sloppy farming practices and wasteful agricultural use of water and fuel. History had already taught some harsh lessons about the effect of high grain prices on soil: the grasslands that were farmed when grain prices were at record levels in the 1917–20 period had turned to dust in 1934 and 1936, when wind blew away the loose, drought-dried topsoil. When wheat prices increased in 1973, nearly 20 million acres of at best marginal land were planted to wheat or feed grains in dry areas of western Texas, Oklahoma, Colorado, western Kansas, Nebraska, and the Dakotas. Farming is economical in these marginal lands only when grain prices are high enough to pay for expensive irrigation equipment. But now, underground water tables in parts of the old Dust Bowl country of Oklahoma and western Kansas have been falling, and they are not being recharged by normal rainfall. There has been a heavy loss of topsoil. In grain farming, there is no free lunch. The nation is already paying a price for the shifts in the global grain economy.

The fact that many countries now seem resigned to dependence on very large amounts of imported food may not be a bad thing *per se*. England was so all through the last half of the nineteenth century without diminishing the power and influence of its empire. Greece and Rome imported food in their prime. Saudi Arabia and the Soviet Union can easily afford to import large amounts of grain, and the economies of Japan and Taiwan continue to run at high gear despite their heavy food dependency. This is not to say that these nations would not be better off were they agriculturally self-sufficient. Greece and Rome fell; England's empire dissolved because of economic decay at the center; and the Russian imports have caused it to lose prestige and to reallocate resources. Nations are not stronger for being food importers. But these countries at least make, or made, rational use of the food they imported.

It is, however, shocking that in another, unfortunately lengthy, list of nations, food imports have become a means for perpetuating outmoded policies, for continuing feudal social structures, and for maintaining the power and privileges of small ruling business and political groups.

The burden of food imports on the economies of developing countries is clear enough from the statistics but there is nothing like visiting these countries to experience the causes and the costs of this phenomenon. In the fall of 1978, I traveled extensively through Asia and Africa. I half feared before the journey that the conclusions I had reached from the remote vantage point of Washington would seem less valid inside the Third World. Instead, the trip provided stunning confirmation of what I had perceived from afar.

In all the countries I visited—Liberia, Morocco, Ghana, the Philippines and Indonesia—the level of food imports had reached crisis proportions. Food was draining nearly as much money from national treasuries as petroleum. A sign outside the Liberian Ministry of Agriculture in Monrovia encapsulated all of this governmental concern. It stuck in my mind long after I had left Liberia: WARNING! IT'S NO JOKE. NO MORE RICE IMPORTS AFTER 1980.

The remarkable thing is that all these nations have enormous, unrealized agricultural potential. These are not stark, "hungry nations," but countries rich in resources. Liberia, for example, is a lush, underpopulated, verdant land. The extremely heavy seasonal rainfall in the coastal lowlands makes farming difficult, to be sure. The water tends to leach away fertilizer and nutrients and even rot the roots of crops such as wheat and maize. But the conditions are adequate for paddy rice, as proved by the success of test plots operated by the Taiwanese and more recently by mainland Chinese. Still, rice imports continue to increase and rice sells in the marketplaces of Monrovia for 25 cents for a small cup, a huge markup over the world price.

As Liberian government officials now concede with chagrin, agriculture has been badly neglected. Investment has gone to iron mining and minerals. Small farmers have not grown more paddy rice because the work is extremely hard, there have been few people to show them how, and the incentives offered by the government have not made it worthwhile. Illiteracy and ignorance of farming methods may be widespread among the tribesmen of the bush. But rural Liberians are neither "lazy" nor "stupid." In fact, they are quite smart economists. Rural Liberians can live satisfactorily, if not well, on fish, cassava, beans, upland rice, and bananas. A farm-to-market system is lacking and only recently has the government raised rice prices. It will take more incentives than that to persuade Liberian villagers to give up their easygoing life for the hard work of farming. And so the hundreds of people who have come to Monrovia from the bush for jobs building the sprawling new headquarters of the Organization of African Unity will continue to be fed on rice from the Gulf Coast of the United States.

The situation in Morocco is, in some ways, even more dispiriting. Moroccans are used to living on bread and tea sweetened with sugar. Wheat and sugarcane have always grown easily in that country. It was not so many years ago that Morocco exported wheat to France and Spain—such were the rich grain harvests yielded up by the fertile soil of the Maghreb. Now all this has been turned around. Morocco is spending *nearly half a billion dollars a year* to import wheat from North America and sugar from other parts of the world. This is about what Morocco earns by exporting phosphates from its deposits, the world's richest.

The equation is basic: Unless Morocco can produce more food, it will squander the benefits of its phosphate wealth. There is no reason why Morocco *cannot* grow more food. All that is

lacking is a policy that supports agriculture with capital investment and price incentives. Belatedly, the government of King
Hassan II has recognized this, but it is possible that this realization has not come in time for Morocco to avert political consequences of the previous policies. In mid-1978, an austerity
program was announced. The importation of "nonessentials"
was curtailed to conserve foreign exchange, which was needed
to pay for food, oil, and other basic equipment (and military
supplies for Morocco's Sahara Desert war against the Polisario
liberation movement). Most affected by this decree were members of Morocco's new urban class—the sons and daughters of
shepherds and camel herders—young Moroccans who poured
into Casablanca in the last decade, bought cars, and came to expect a steadily rising standard of living. It is no exaggeration to
say that the political malaise among this group of people is
traceable to the neglect of agriculture, which has had such a
negative effect on the balance of payments.

The reasons for the disarray in the food economies of the
countries I visited can be explained only partially by the neglect
of agriculture as a national priority. To that must be added factors which are more human and cultural than political. The most
glaring of these is corruption. In this regard, the realities of political power and political decision-making in the Third World
look very different close up than they do from the distant perspective of Europe or the United States. In Washington, one develops theories about a world neatly divided into rich nations
and poor nations. One assumes that if only the developed countries would provide more aid and more trade concessions to the
Third World, "development" would take place. Unfortunately,
some of the worst exploitation of Third World populations today
is perpetrated by the business and political rulers of Third
World nations. In the Philippines, Indonesia, Iran, Zaire, and
Ghana, hundreds of millions of dollars—perhaps even billions of
dollars—that might have gone into agricultural development
have been stolen by the tribal clans, families, and political rulers

in command of those governments. Governmental theft is one of the great unreported crimes of modern times, and Third World corruption is one of those unmentionables that does not appear in the studies and reports of the World Bank or the Food and Agriculture Organization of the United Nations. But it is a pervasive reality that is a major obstacle to development.

When I arrived in Ghana in September 1978, the economy was in a disastrous predicament. Factories which make such essential goods as truck tires and flashlight batteries had shut down temporarily because the central bank had no foreign exchange available for importing necessary raw materials. Ghana could no longer pay its bills and there was a flourishing black market in practically all essential goods, including food. (Food, in fact, was so scarce that one American Peace Corps volunteer was spending most of his time looking for food for the other volunteers.) Foreigners living in Ghana were making trips abroad to load up on food, detergents and other basics required for everyday life.

But Ghana is not a poor country. It is rich in minerals and maize and it is one of the world's leading producers of cocoa. Cocoa prices were at record levels in 1977 and 1978—yet Ghana's cocoa production declined in those years and a substantial amount of the cocoa found its way into neighboring Togo, where cocoa farmers received a higher price for their crop!

In September 1978, the government of President Acheampong had just been deposed by another army faction. And by then it was permissible for diplomats and high government officials to speak candidly about the reasons for the nation's problems. A great deal of money had simply been stolen from the economy during the corruption that ravaged the country in the last four years of the Acheampong regime. Officials of the central bank had refused at times to make letters of credit available to importers except in return for kickbacks of as much as 10 per cent. In other words, some of the dollars that should have been available to importers went instead to the private accounts of Ghana bankers. The government also issued import licenses in return for kickbacks. As often as not this meant that those receiving the favors of import licenses were bringing in not essential raw materials and machinery but nonessential goods (such as women's shoes with platform heels) that could be sold at huge markups on the black market. One of the mysteries that economists were investigating was where the $800 million that the country supposedly had earned from cocoa exports during the previous year actually had gone. Certainly, it had not gone to agricultural development. Four years earlier, Ghana's farmers had begun to increase their rice crop. But then, as corruption took hold, importers were unable to get licenses for tractors and spare parts. Much of the rice harvest spoiled in the fields in 1974. Thereafter, Ghana's farmers planted less rice.

This shows that corruption and mismanagement are often at the heart of the problem. Policies—not population growth—are the obstacles. The unfortunate truth is that many of the world's most food-dependent nations are also those with the lowest nutritional standards and the most archaic agricultural structures.

In Pakistan in 1974, 60 per cent of farmers received only 3 per cent of the bank credits; in the Philippines, the 27 per cent of farmers with the largest farms got 98 per cent of the credit; in Brazil 3 per cent of the farmers got 34 per cent of the credit. At the same time, their governments have held down farm prices in order to decrease the subsidies they pay on food distributed to urban consumers, civil servants, and soldiers.

Indonesia is a country where other curious paradoxes are glaringly evident. Vast amounts of foreign capital are at present being poured into the development of rubber plantations and tropical hardwood forests. Oddly, as U.S.-based multinational timber companies—"multipulps," as they have been nick-named—develop the forests of Kalimantan (formerly southern Borneo), peasants in the Javanese rice-growing valleys have stripped their hills of firewood and left them exposed to devastating soil erosion. To make up for the loss of rice production, the Indonesian government imports up to a million tons of rice from the United States, Thailand, and Japan.

The list of countries in which the best land, the access to commercial credit, and the best services go either to large commercial farmers, government cooperatives, or plantations involved in the agricultural export trade (rather than production of wheat, beans, cassava, corn, or other human foods) is too long to recite here. Whether the country is Indonesia or Bolivia, similar sights can be seen: peasant hovels hugging the side of a barren hill while fertile valleys are given over to export crops.

Indonesia, the Philippines, Brazil and Pakistan, four of the nations mentioned above, have several things in common. They all import sizable quantities of American food; their own production of food lags; there is a very uneven distribution of wealth; and they are run by either a small group of military officers, or (in the Philippines) a family clique with business interests of their own. Three of them, Brazil, Indonesia, and the Philippines, are notably hospitable to foreign investment in agriculture and forestry—timber, rubber, pineapples, sugar, and soybeans.

In all of these countries (and of course in others, such as South Korea under the regime of President Park Chung Hee), American agricultural imports are an underpinning not only of the food system but of the power base of the regime. The interlocking interests of the regime, the grain trade, the locally based multinationals, and the American farm bloc are not difficult to untangle. Agricultural imports are, to begin with, a means of maintaining the status quo. The availability of the imports makes it possible to postpone radical domestic reform, land redistribution, and the redirection of credit to different sectors of the society. The sale of the imported food on the local economy (the government does not give the food away) generates money that can be used to pay the civil servants, police forces, and soldiers who make up the regime's base of political support. And the imported food helps to hold down inflation, which is a primary cause of unrest in the middle class (students, merchants, businessmen).

As this suggests, food imports play a much more complex role than just feeding hungry people. The imports shore up a coalition of interests that include local political groups, U.S. farm lobbies, agribusiness, the grain trade and other multinational companies, and banks; where U.S. bases or strategic outposts are involved, it extends to the Pentagon as well.

It is significant, but hardly surprising, that the new international emphasis on financing projects that serve "basic human needs" (especially by supporting indigenous small farmers and agriculture)* is unpopular among many of the Third World's technocrats, industrialists, and Western-trained managers and bankers. Some of them have told World Bank officials that they suspect that the "basic human needs" financing is a cynical ploy to avoid supporting new technical and manufacturing industries (such as textiles and aluminum), which could compete with plants already operating in rich countries. But another reason for their opposition is that the "human needs" approach, departing as it does from the old system that excluded the poorest people from the benefits of foreign aid, threatens the status quo.

It is not easy to be optimistic that foreign rulers will change their policies or their priorities in ways that will begin to attack the multitude of causes of endemic hunger and inadequate food production. The overthrow of the Allende regime in Chile, which, whatever its weaknesses, was publicly committed to many of the steps in land reform and wealth redistribution that experts at the World Bank and the United Nations have begun to espouse, leaves little doubt about the difficulties facing reform-

---

* For the fiscal year ending June 30, 1978, the World Bank and its affiliate the International Development Association loaned $3.3 billion for agricultural and rural development, compared with $956 million in fiscal 1974. Estimates were that World Bank projects would produce an additional 13 million tons of cereal grains by the late 1980s.

ers. But the very cost of maintaining a system so dependent on imports has forced at least some governments to reassess their priorities. This could turn out to be the best thing that has happened yet to the world's hungry.

Cuba, the model for so many Latin American Marxists and for the American Left, is no agricultural paragon. Cuba imports virtually all of its wheat, a substantial amount of its rice, not to mention all of its oil, and is able to pay for all this only because the Soviet Union in 1978 buys sugar from it at three times the world price. Yet the benefits of food imports are spread fairly in Cuba, where there is little or no hunger or malnutrition. In Mexico and Brazil, however, countries with about the same average availability of food per person, there are serious nutritional deficiencies. Income is the crux. As many as 30 million Brazilians earn too little money to buy enough food. And in Mexico it has been reported that 30 per cent of the population consumes only about 6 per cent of the nation's food supply, while the richest 15 per cent consumes nearly half of it. (In Mexico, corn is the most important item in the diet of two-thirds of the population; yet production of wheat has grown much faster than corn production.)

China has taken a different route. Even the admirers of the country's extraordinary accomplishments know that these were achieved through harsh and sometimes repressive methods. But there is no doubt that in the process, China, the world's most populous country, made itself independent of foreign food. (China's fairly small grain imports in recent years apparently were for reasons of logistical convenience. It was easier to import grain for the large eastern cities than to transport it across China.) Nobody goes hungry in China, a nation that imports less grain than some countries with one-tenth its population. In that sense, China has made a larger contribution to fighting global food inflation than any single country in the world.

On the American side, the Carter administration has taken a strong position in favor of agricultural development programs in foreign aid. And there is deeper understanding of the complex relationships between poverty, hunger, development, and trade. Of this, the National Research Council wrote in 1977:

The major immediate cause of hunger is poverty. Hunger and malnutrition cannot be addressed solely by food programs. The processes of social and economic development must be considered, including programs concerned with access to resources, distribution of income, control of parasitic diseases, extension of health services, provision of safe water supplies and literacy and general education. *In most countries, social, economic and political measures not directly related to food are necessary to reduce malnutrition and improve health.* (Italics added.)

Even if every country in the world were to adopt sensible food and agricultural policies tomorrow, however, commercial food imports will continue to grow for a long time. Self-sufficiency in grain is as distant a goal for most countries as self-sufficiency in oil. Most countries will never attain it completely and, for rational economic reasons, many others will not attempt to. The big-volume, big-money grain trade is with us to stay for many years. Given this reality, it is obvious that stable world grain prices are in everyone's long-range interest. Grain prices that go out of control, as they did in 1973 and 1974, contribute mightily to global inflation and undermine the best efforts to reach economic objectives. Grain prices that decline too far, as they did after World War I, and as they did in the 1950s and 1960s, discourage nations from investing in food production and can be as harmful as high prices in the long run.

Astonishingly, almost nothing has been accomplished in international negotiations since 1972 to provide more security against such "boom and bust" cycles. There is no rational system in place for stabilizing grain prices. Complacency is fast returning. There is no international plan for reserve stocks of grain, no pricing mechanism, not even a binding procedure for consultation among countries.

In the summer of 1978, world grain stocks were still a sizable 175 million tons. The unsold surplus grain in the United States amounted to 33 million tons of wheat and 43 million tons of feed grains, the largest amount since 1963. As ample as that seemed, the world had learned in 1972 and 1973 that grain could disappear quickly. (In 1972, world grain stocks dropped by 40 million tons; America's stocks of 23 million tons of wheat dwindled to a paltry 6 million. The cupboard was nearly bare.) Almost everyone knowledgeable about this subject agrees that some kind of international system of grain reserves is essential to prevent a recurrence of the near calamity of 1972–74. The effect of a similar burst of inflation would be much more severe today than it was in 1972. Just such a system of food reserves was advocated by delegates to the United Nations World Food Conference in 1974. The Carter administration favors it; so do development experts.

The fact that there is so much grain available in 1978 is reassuring; but it is not a safeguard against the kind of planetary panic and hoarding that took place earlier in the decade. Countries panicked then because the stocks of grain were not under any governmental control. No grain was held back, but instead, it moved into the private grain trade for sale to the highest bidder. Today, there is nothing to prevent this from occurring again.

In October 1977, delegates of seventy-three countries met at Geneva and completed an international agreement aimed at stabilizing sugar prices in world markets. The plan was to take effect at the end of 1978. There were to be export quotas and buffer stocks of sugar. The plan would also stabilize sugar prices between 11 and 21 cents a pound (compared with the then prevailing price of around 7 cents a pound).

For forty-five years, governments have been trying to work out a comparable arrangement in wheat. But the first wheat "agreement," in 1933, in which the principal wheat-exporting countries had pledged to reduce their domestic output, was not successful. It had been the dream of Henry Wallace, secretary of agriculture in the New Deal, to have an "ever normal granary," not just to provide reserves during scarcity but to even out fluctuations in price. His idea did not take hold in the political, economic, and agricultural confusion of the 1930s.

When representatives of twelve major exporters and importers of wheat* met at the International Wheat Council in London in June 1978 to try once again, they failed to make progress on a price stabilization plan. It began to seem as if they would be at it for another forty-five years. Most governments still considered grain too important to surrender sovereignty over it.

The Carter administration sent its representatives to London with a proposal for a 30-million–ton world wheat reserve, and it had already taken one constructive step in this regard: It had created a "farmer reserve," which encouraged grain growers to store grain on their own farms for up to thirty-six months when prices were low. (The government was to pay the farmers for storing it for the last twenty-four months, or until prices moved up above specified minimums.) But even under this system, all the grain could drain away if prices went high enough to entice farmers to sell. Carter's representatives in London said that the United States would be willing to maintain half of the proposed 30-million–ton world reserve. The idea was that stocks would accumulate when prices were low and would be released when prices began to exceed certain specified ceilings. Carter's men viewed this as a rather minimal insurance policy. They estimated that it would cost $750 million a year to store the grain, keep it in good condition, and pay the interest charges on loans, pending its sale. This was a small price to pay, they said, for an insurance policy against another round of ruinous food inflation on top of the global inflation already evident.

After their critical meetings in June, the U.S. officials returned

---

* The United States, Canada, the Common Market, Argentina, Australia, Japan, Kenya, Egypt, India, Brazil, Finland, and the Soviet Union.

to Washington discouraged. The representatives in London had bickered about technical details and financial questions. Who would pay the cost of maintaining the stocks? Where would they be stored? How expensive would wheat have to get before stocks were released to the private grain trade? Early in 1979 the importers and exporters convened in London for one final try. This time, the major objections came from the representatives of developing countries, which thought the international floor price should be lower than what Canada and the United States wanted. They also resisted paying more of the costs of storing the reserve. The talks collapsed, perhaps for good.

And so, an opportunity passed.

This leaves us without any insurance policy—without any guarantee of a stable agricultural order.

The United States and Canada can still battle each other behind the scenes for wheat markets. When Secretary of Agriculture Bergland was asked in 1977 what was to prevent the Canadian Wheat Board from cutting prices to grab markets away from American wheat farmers, as happened in 1976, he replied, "Nothing." That is still so.

The Russians can and do go on negotiating secretly with the grain companies for massive quantities of wheat. The only American government "handle" on this trade is the clause in the Soviet-American grain agreement of 1975 requiring the Russians to get permission to buy volumes of more than 8 million tons.

As for the grain companies, they operate as secretly (and nearly as freely) as always, despite the difficulties they sometimes experience maneuvering in the volatile markets. They have suffered only some small losses of sovereignty. The introduction of a new Federal Grain Inspection Service to certify all exported grain in 1977 meant that the companies could no longer hire their own grain inspectors; they protested that American grain exports would suffer, but this did not happen. The Commodity Futures Trading Commission is getting somewhat tougher on manipulations in the futures markets (as the agency's entry into the Cook-Hunt affair showed), and there is the requirement that the companies report their largest sales to the government. But the basic grain trade is untouched.

After the food-price inflation of 1973 and 1974, Cargill and Continental both moved to modify their policies. Their major concern was that the government might take some really radical step, such as creating a government grain board that would take over exports, make deals with countries abroad, and fix the price of wheat as if it were OPEC posting the price of oil. The companies that had invested billions in inland facilities to lower grain-handling costs and to compete for markets opposed such a grain board. But they had little reason for concern. There was no real sentiment in Washington for such a board. The specter of a government monopoly controlling the grain, and possibly doling it out according to political or diplomatic considerations, appealed to liberals almost as little as it did to conservatives—though both of them thought that the time would eventually come when the government would have to step in.

The companies began to take what seemed the "responsible" position in favor of some kind of worldwide grain reserve system, preferably under private control.° It may have been more than fear of still stronger governmental controls over the grain trade that prompted them. For the companies were shaky from the volatility and instability that toppled Cook and cost Michel Fribourg some sleepless nights. And there was the embarrassment of the loading scandals and the gruesome elevator disasters to remind them of their vulnerability.

° Michel Fribourg said in a speech in London in May 1977 that he favored such a reserve, but he strongly opposed any international pricing mechanism to control wheat prices: "High world prices are a means by which consumption is rationed and low world prices are a means by which consumption is stimulated, and it is self-defeating for governments to try and alter these consequences artificially through rules and regulations." It was an unusually candid avowal of the philosophy that guides the grain men.

Yet the companies still were rogue elephants in the international economy, as large, central, and almost unaccountable as ever, so it hardly seemed likely that they and their ruling families were nearing the end of their extraordinary saga. And what a saga it had been!

In October 1977, shortly before he announced that he was selling out of the grain business, Ned Cook showed up for one last gala reception at the Soviet Embassy in Washington. The host was Soviet Ambassador Anatoly Dobrynin and the guests were Viktor Pershin of Exportkhleb, senior officials of the Ministry of Foreign Trade, and select Western grain men.

There was tall, thin Walter Klein, president of Bunge in New York, looking none the worse for the battering the company had taken in the grain-loading scandal. Phil McCaull showed up, chipper and unfazed by the three months he had spent at federal prison earlier in the year. Trailing along with Cook was Patrick Mayhew, dapper and exuberant as he had been on the day in 1963 when the Russians gave him a tip about their plans to shift policy and buy grain abroad.

But the real survivors were the families themselves. As he glanced around the room, Ned Cook, underneath his usual easy joviality, must have wondered how he could ever have belonged to an assemblage of such strange and antique lineage. There was Michel Fribourg, graying, immaculate, cool, as polished and composed an an archbishop. Ned Cook's rise and fall had spanned no more than a brief moment in the history of the House of Fribourg, with its ancient roots in Napoleonic Europe. Helping himself at the buffet was short, burly Gerard Louis-Dreyfus, looking slightly rumpled in his gray pinstripe suit. Dreyfus! A name that had been on the lips of Russian peasants a whole century ago.

Cook stayed, made conversation, and then excused himself from this gathering of men among whom he had always been considered an outsider. The families carried on. But the strains on them and their oligopolies were increasing. The size of their organizations, their sudden, unwelcome exposure to public scrutiny, and the new volatility of the markets as the world entered a period of scarce basic resources must tax their ingenuity and make their ultimate survival at least questionable. If the experts are right, the companies will have to be more forthright and governments finally will have to pool their courage and their wisdom to tame the grain tiger—beginning with reforms needed in their own societies. But until then, the merchants of grain are still the ringmasters.

Afterword

When this book was first published in the summer of 1979, a defiant new bumper sticker had begun to appear on the back of farm pickup trucks: "Cheaper Crude or No More Food." The farmers' message was that the United States should force the Organization of Petroleum Exporting Countries to hold down oil prices by denying grain to the oil cartel. Members of the militant American Agricultural Movement suggested they would settle for merely raising grain prices in step with any oil price increases ordained by the cartel. It would be a fair exchange: " a bushel of grain for a barrel of oil."

This notion that grain should be used as a diplomatic or economic tool was not one that appealed to many policymakers in Washington. Most people at the State and Agriculture Departments dismissed the militant farmers as rural xenophobes. They argued that it would be both impractical and immoral for the United States to deny grain to another country for political reasons, and they cited the 1975 episode, described in Chapter 11 of this book, in which former Secretary of State Kissinger tried and failed to withhold U.S. grain from the Russians in return for a promise of cheap Soviet oil.

Yet despite all these reservations, the food "weapon" had suddenly become a major part of American diplomacy by early 1980. President Carter had announced his decision to withhold

17 million tons of American grain from the Russians in retaliation for the invasion of Afghanistan. U.S. longshoremen had refused, in November of 1979, to load grain on ships bound for Iran, pending the release of the hostages held at the American Embassy in Tehran. As banks froze Iranian government assets—assets needed to pay for grain purchases—America's food trade with Iran came to a complete halt.

This policy reversal was, clearly, the result of unusual circumstances. In the Soviet case the President had turned to a measure that, in light of Kremlin aggression, was better than the extreme alternatives. It was better to withhold grain than to do nothing or to resort to a resumption of the arms race. The action of the longshoremen in the Iranian case was an indignant reaction to a very emotional situation; it was a patriotic gesture made in a moment when almost no other response seemed possible because of the safety of the hostages themselves. In both cases there was a recognition that grain is an element of national security in the broadest sense, and that it will remain so in the world being transformed by the politics of the 1980s. Perhaps the Soviet Union could get along without American grain in the early months of the embargo, but in the long run the Soviet people were bound to feel the effects. The Soviet Union had turned to the United States for grain in 1963—had turned to its chief global political adversary—because only America could supply grain in the volumes required. This was true in the 1970s as well, when consumerism was in bloom in the Soviet Union, and détente and trade became a means for fulfilling the hopes of ordinary people for better and less costly food and housing. Therefore, economic uncertainty and perhaps increased political instability in Eastern Europe was sure to be the result of the American action.

Yet it is necessary for policymakers to look beyond the militant slogans and beyond the debate over the merits of food as a weapon. The events of late 1979 and early 1980 have underlined the importance of getting policymakers to face up to the need for a real grain policy for the United States in the coming decade. Such a policy, unfortunately, does not exist now.

There are strong arguments, for example, for the creation of a public authority that would establish the price of grain exported to countries abroad. There are even good arguments that can be made in favor of a grain-exporting nations' cartel—an "OPEC" of grain—but the justification does not rest on the need to punish other countries. It rests on the recognition that most other countries now play by different economic rules from the United States, that American (and Canadian) taxpayers have been subsidizing North American grain exports to overseas customers, and that there have been tremendous costs and penalties, as well as the more obvious benefits, associated with the grain-export boom that began in the early 1970s. It has become urgent for policymakers to consider whether, in the 1980s, America can leave it to the grain companies and a "free market" to allocate and price the nation's grain surplus.

Americans have always believed in free trade. After World War II the United States built economic bridges that spanned the world. Free trade was the ideology that guided the nation's international economic policy. The United States led the way in establishing a world economic order in which raw materials, capital, and technology could flow freely across borders. America gained access to raw materials and markets, and other countries received U.S. capital and technology. In the 1970s, however, this system that had worked so well began to break down. It became apparent that most other nations were not following the "free trade" model established by the United States. OPEC was only the starkest example of price fixing and economic manipulation by governments. Many other governments took steps to gain firm control over basic resources. This frequently meant dictating economic and financial rules that served national interests but restricted free trade. A whole array of government measures—export subsidies, tax concessions, and rebates—determined the flow of trade as much as the free market. In business abroad a willingness to pay bribes to local officials and "agents" was often more of a factor than the kind of competition economics majors read about in their course materials, and in the Communist countries huge state trading monopolies played Western companies off against one another to gain advantages.

In the new economic order the world grain market stands out as a major exception. This is because the dominant exporter, the United States, does not attempt to control the trade or fix the prices of agricultural commodities going abroad.

There are, in fact, striking parallels between the present grain market and the world oil market of the late 1960s, before the OPEC cartel reached maturity. That was a time when oil prices were relatively low, when the major oil exporters were disunited, and when a handful of multinational companies organized the marketing, refining, and distribution of the oil surplus. This is a rough approximation of the situation prevailing a decade later in the world grain economy. Dominating the system that markets the American surplus are a handful of companies that resemble the oil giants in their control of communications, processing plants, depots, transportation and financial facilities.

This is, to be sure, an extraordinarily complex system that benefits from the flexibility provided by private companies. The U.S. grain-producing regions are a mosaic of thousands of farms producing crops ranging from wheat to grass seed, connected to world markets by elaborate transport systems. For the U.S. government to attempt to run this system would be deeply disruptive. Yet for the government to allow private traders a completely free hand in allocating and pricing American grain all over the world raises equally serious problems.

Starting with its farm programs during the New Deal, the government accepted full responsibility for agricultural planning. After World War II the government was also involved in agricultural trade—not through a heavy-handed takeover of the system but through extremely sophisticated programs that included Public Law 480, "market development," and wheat export subsidies; government and the private sector were in a partnership that was highly successful from the standpoint of American self-interest. It was only in the 1970s that the government's role in agricultural trade diminished. Higher farm prices and strong demand for U.S. commodities enabled the government to stand aside and let private companies sell U.S. food on world markets with relatively little interference. The 1970s were good years for American agriculture and for the businesses and grain companies that support it, but a strong case can be made now for the government's reinvolvement, provided such intervention is creative and flexible.

The government has consistently taken the view that the massive growth in U.S. exports since the start of the 1970s has been an unmitigated good. In so doing it has refused to recognize that there are numerous costs attached that are now being paid not by America's foreign customers but by Americans.

First of all, the present system makes little provision for the fact that America's grain resources are not unlimited. Some experts in fact believe that they could even be depleted, the way Middle East oil will eventually be. U.S. farmland can grow crops over and over again, so in that respect grain is a "renewable" resource, whereas oil is not. Yet the resources required to produce grain in modern agriculture are decidedly not renewable. When they run out, grain production will be unimaginably more difficult. Agriculture requires oil and natural gas to run diesel tractors, to power irrigation pumps, to dry grain, and to produce chemical fertilizers, herbicides, and pesticides. These fuels are finite and getting much more expensive. The underground water that irrigates crops in the Western wheat belt in Colorado, Kansas, and Nebraska will not last forever. This underground water table is falling and will take decades to be replenished once it has run dry. The trouble with the present system of pricing grain—based on supply and demand on any given day—is that it does not account for the depletion of land, water, and fossil fuels.

Similarly, food production takes place on agricultural land that is shrinking as cities, highways, airports, and rights-of-way for pipelines and transmission lines claim more and more of it. The House Agriculture Committee has reported that the United States loses 35,000 acres of its agricultural land base each week. An estimated 3,000,000 acres of agricultural land are lost due to soil erosion each year. Some gloomy scenarios envision American food exports ending by the year 2000 as a result of environmental, energy, and economic constraints. This is about the time when Middle East oil supplies will be running low.

Advantageous as huge grain exports may presently be to the United States, they have placed unprecedented and expensive strains on the North American transportation system, and a good deal of the cost of modernizing and improving this system in the United States and Canada will be paid by the taxpayers of those countries rather than by overseas buyers of grain. Federal, state, and provincial governments plan to spend billions of dollars in aid to railroads and in expanding the waterways so that foreign importers will be able to purchase more grain. Both countries plan to invest in improving deteriorated railroad lines and road-beds. The Canadian government has authorized funds for buying new grain hopper cars for the Canadian National Railroad. Congress has approved new waterway projects for the 1980s so that the U.S. Corps of Engineers can continue to expand the barge channels of the Mississippi, Illinois, Ohio, and Arkansas rivers. Some of the costs of building new locks on the Mississippi River will be passed on to barge companies—and ultimately to foreign customers—but the federal government will continue to pay for maintaining a river system that principally benefits the foreign purchasers of U.S. grain.

Belatedly, the Department of Agriculture has become concerned with the effect of the overheated export trade on the farming business itself. The value of farmland rose sharply in the 1970s. Inflation was a factor, but so was the emergence of strong commercial markets overseas. An acre of farmland in Illinois that sold for $500 at the start of the 1970s went for $2,000 at the decade's end. This is fine for farmers who already own their land but devastating to young families who want to get into farming. It is a trend that has accelerated the consolidation of farming in the hands of fewer and fewer businessmen farmers—and some analysts say that the next step will be a takeover of the agricultural sector by corporations and big entrepreneurs. If that happens, the Jeffersonian ideal of an America in which farming is the province of the common man rather than of a small landed class will truly have been lost forever.

The United States has been subsidizing the rest of the world with its grain. In 1979 and 1980 the net income of U.S. farmers was expected to decline—and this at a time when farm exports were at record levels, and on any given week sixty or more freighters were taking on grain at the big elevators along the southern Mississippi River. Our food exports, it is true, have helped to offset the costs of imported oil—and imported food. (The United States is the world's largest food importer, with meat, sugar, coffee, and cocoa among the main items bought overseas.) Foreign countries, however, are buying American food with devalued dollars and with gold that can buy four times as much wheat as it did in 1972. They are getting a bargain.

It seems only fair that foreign customers pay a share of the hidden costs that go along with the exports. Yet many experts argue against this and insist that any attempt by the United States and other grain producers to establish a price for grain outside the "free market," a price based on all the indirect costs to the nation, is doomed to failure and to universal condemnation. They contend that the hungry of the world would suffer and that, in time, America would lose its agricultural markets.

Their moral argument is a compelling and serious one. The United States has a responsibility to countries that need food imports, just as oil-producing countries have a responsibility to oil users not to abuse their economic power. As this book has attempted to show, however, U.S. food exports are not destined primarily for the world's hungry people. The main customers for U.S. grain are rich industrial nations such as Japan and the Soviet Union. Next come some of the wealthier developing countries. Many of these have a miserable record of dealing with malnutrition among their own people and with a lagging agricultural growth on their land. U.S. food imports enable the governments of these countries to carry out other priorities. The food does not reach many of the neediest and most disadvantaged people in those societies.

In any case, the United States has food-aid and credit programs that can be used to directly benefit countries that are genuinely trying to feed their poor, improve their own agriculture, and eliminate malnutrition. If the United States raises grain prices, it could and should expand these programs.

The Carter administration has accepted the conventional wisdom that more government involvement in the pricing of U.S. grain would not work—that other nations would produce more food of their own or switch to other suppliers—but the logic is hard to follow. A global food system has grown up around a grain trade whose volume is unprecedented in history. This system cannot be easily dismantled. In the next twenty years it will be possible for countries to conserve energy. It will be more difficult for them to conserve food, given the population increases that are a certainty. Meanwhile, industrial countries' food economics are built around diets of poultry, meat, milk, and eggs—all of which require soybeans and feed grains that are available in sufficient quantity only in North America. That is why U.S. grain exports now exceed 100 million tons a year.

It is hardly as if other countries have not tried to reduce their dependence on these grain imports. The Soviet Union has spent billions of rubles to overcome its agricultural shortcomings, yet in 1979 President Carter had authorized the Russians to buy up to 25 million tons of U.S. grain in the following year—a record.

The period of easy gains in agricultural production clearly is over. To expand food production will be increasingly costly and difficult in the last decades of this century. Predictions of great new agricultural "breadbaskets" in the Sudan, in the Amazon basin, and in eastern Siberia have not been borne out—these areas have not produced the hoped-for gains. The rising prices of oil-based "inputs" such as chemical fertilizers make it doubtful if they ever will. Japan already has much too little land on which to feed its people. Western Europe has achieved self-sufficiency only in wheat—and that at enormous costs to European taxpayers, who have paid for lavish subsidies to farmers.

The OPEC countries are no exception to the trend toward dependence on foreign sources of food. OPEC's wheat imports grew faster than those of any other bloc of countries in the late 1970s and now stand at 10 million tons, or 14 per cent of the entire world wheat trade. OPEC countries are not underpopulated deserts, for OPEC includes the world's fifth most populous nation (Indonesia), Africa's largest country (Nigeria), Iran, and a densely populated South American nation whose tropical climate is not suited to growing wheat (Venezuela). The United States has been supplying half of OPEC's grain imports, and most of the rest comes from Canada and Australia.

The Iran debacle showed that a food cutoff today can be more painful to the customer than the supplier. True, the five thousand farmers in Washington, Oregon, and Idaho who grow the white wheat favored by Iranian millers did suffer as a result of the curtailment of grain shipments. After the market was cut off, prices for that kind of wheat dropped by some forty cents a bushel. The effect on Iran of a prolonged food cutoff was potentially far more devastating, however.

Before the revolution that deposed the Shah, Iran had obtained a monthly average of 100,000 tons of wheat, 100,000 tons of corn, 40,000 tons of rice, and large quantities of soybean meal and vegetable oil from the United States. Almost one-third of the country's entire food supply was imported. Of that, the United States was the main supplier of staple grains for bread and for feeding the poultry that made up a larger and larger share of the Iranian diet. During the summer, while Ayatollah Khomeini's anti-American rhetoric grew sharper, the grain continued to move from American ports to Iran, but in early November, when the shipments stopped, Khomeini's government began drawing on wheat reserves and hauling wheat from Turkey by truck. Wheat was essential, and Iran was in a bind. During the summer Australia had contracted to provide 100,000 tons of wheat through January 1980, but as Australian longshoremen began to show solidarity with the American trade unionists, these shipments also were delayed. Secretary of Agriculture Bob Bergland acknowledged that Iran faced a "difficult time" buying grain abroad. U.S. officials predicted severe food shortages in major Iranian cities by mid-winter.

It is true that U.S. exports account for only about 8 percent of world grain consumption, but OPEC's oil exports account for less than 10 per cent of the world's supply of energy when non-OPEC sources of oil, gas, and nuclear, hydroelectric, and solar energy are added together. The first and second largest producers of oil in the world are not OPEC countries but the Soviet Union and the United States, in that order. Yet nobody doubts OPEC's power or influence. The reason is that its oil exports, like America's grain exports, are the crucial increment that bridges the gap between adequate supply and scarcity.

For the United States to gain control of its grain resources would require two conditions that do not exist now. The first would be a governmental role in the pricing of grain exports. This could be achieved through the creation of a public authority. Other mechanisms, such as an export tax or an export licensing system, might also serve the same purpose. Second, the major grain exporters would have to establish a system for co-operating and for coordinating the pricing and marketing of their grain. A cartel would be one way of achieving this cooperation; however, a preferable system would bring in consuming countries and give them a say in decisions about price. Countries that cooperated in such an arrangement would be assured of long-term access to grain supplies at stable prices. Above all, Canada and the United States would have to abandon the guerrilla warfare they have used against each other in the world grain markets during much of the postwar era. Mexico, where the Green Revolution in wheat began, would be a logical country to invite into a resource consortium for North America.

Neither of the conditions necessary for adequate public control existed when Henry Kissinger futilely tried to withhold food from the Russians in 1975 in return for cheap Soviet oil. Kissinger failed because he did not have the cooperation of the major exporting countries, who keep on selling, because his initiative did not have a strong political rationale that could be understood by Americans, and because the initiative lacked careful preparation and was, for Kissinger, characteristically ad hoc, secretive and personal in the manner of its execution.

The situation was considerably different when President Carter acted in January 1980 to curtail grain exports in response to the Soviet invasion of Afghanistan. This was a far better executed initiative, and one that could be understood and supported by Americans, even by farmers, as the President's success in the Iowa primary caucus quickly showed. The President also made clear to the Russians that he was not abrogating the 1975 Soviet-American grain agreement that authorized the Russians to purchase a minimum of 8 million tons a year. What he was saying was: 8 million tons and not a bushel more. Put another way, he was telling the Russians that food was an element in national security, and that the United States would not be party to a process that strengthened Soviet national security at a time when Kremlin leadership was ignoring accepted international standards of nonaggression.

When the President acted, he faced the same problem that Kissinger had confronted in 1975: how to control the grain companies. If the grain firms were left in charge, with no government authority to act in the markets, it was certain that the embargo would fail. In this case the President took two vital steps. He sought cooperation from Canada, Australia, the European Common Market, Brazil, and Argentina in limiting the amount of grain that the Russians could obtain elsewhere. Canada and Australia—key countries in Carter's strategy—agreed not to make up the deficit caused by the withholding of U.S. grain.

Second, the President ordered that the U.S. government buy out the contracts the grain firms had with the Russians. It was, in one respect, a bailout—another governmental bailout for a big industry. The grain companies, backed by some international banks, had pleaded for help, arguing that if they could not sell the grain they had acquired for their Soviet customers, they would lose billions of dollars. In another respect, however, it was an essential step for the Carter administration, for it gave the government control, through actual ownership of the Soviet-bound grain. Henceforth, the government would be calling the shots in the grain markets—at least for the grain previously committed to Russia—and this provided some safeguard against leakage in the embargo.

The purpose of establishing a permanent system for controlling America's grain resources would not be to provide administrations in Washington with a new weapon to use against foreign adversaries. In fact, any new public board that made decisions about grain export prices and the volume of these exports would have to be shielded from political pressures, much as the Federal Reserve Board is insulated from such pressures in the monetary and fiscal spheres. Rather, such a system would be aimed at providing an orderly system for cooperation between countries on the pricing and allocation of resources. A public authority that had responsibility for pricing grain exports would protect American consumers and livestock producers against the impact of large disruptive purchases of grain here by foreigners and would equip the United States with stronger leverage in negotiating long-term access to oil and other foreign resources.

The grain companies and business-oriented farm organizations are sure to oppose such steps, just as the oil companies sought to delay the measures taken by OPEC. But American creativity is equal to the task of designing a system that retains the best of the private U.S. grain industry while adding an ingredient of public control.

The Federal Reserve Board and the International Monetary Fund regulate the money supply and international money movements without destroying the banking system. A grain reserve board that performs some similar functions is not difficult to envision. The real obstacles are political and ideological, not technical. The American government's relationship to business and the economy is still modeled on an era when there seemed some hope that the ideology of free trade and free markets would triumph. That, unfortunately, has not come to pass. So the question is whether agricultural policymakers will deal with the world as it really is or continue to deal with it as they wish it could have been.

Acknowledgments

This book, three years in the making, is really the work of many people: friends, scholars, librarians, government officials, diplomats, colleagues, grain merchants, and various other witnesses to history, all of whom generously contributed their information, their advice, and their wisdom. Those in business and government for the most part provided material and information on condition that their names not be used. But even omitting them from the long list of those to whom I am indebted, I would need many pages to express my thanks adequately to all those who have helped me in my work. To them I am grateful.

Several deserve special mention. Without the inspiration, example, and encouragement of Joseph Gauld, Michael Maccoby, and Laurence Stern, this book never would have been finished. Robert G. Kaiser, George Crile III, and J. W. Anderson, who patiently read and commented upon large parts of the manuscript, all helped to improve greatly the final version. As a journalist venturing into the deep waters of historical research, I would have been lost without the help of Wayne D. Rasmussen, historian of the United States Department of Agriculture, and of Professor Morton Rothstein of the University of Wisconsin. Ronald Müller helped me to expand and extend my understanding of multinational corporations.

My editors at *The Washington Post*, Benjamin Bradlee,

Howard Simons, and Richard Harwood, were responsive to the importance of grain as a news story. Later they were generous and patient in giving me the time to see this book to its completion.

I am particularly grateful to Howard Bray and the Fund for Investigative Journalism for a grant that permitted me to travel to European grain centers at a crucial point in the research. I also thank Phyllis Lutyens for her support at another critical moment.

It is traditional to thank book editors, but my acknowledgment of the guidance provided by my editors at The Viking Press is more than *pro forma.* I am grateful to William Decker for his early support, and I am forever thankful to Elisabeth Sifton, who devoted far more time and care to this book than any "first-time" author could expect, and whose many suggestions improved the manuscript.

To others who labored for hours on the research, typing, reading of the manuscript, and dozens of other tasks I am also grateful. I wish to thank especially Victoria Stein, Rebecca Hirsch, Gail Lynch, Mary Washington, Jane Freundel, and Valarie Thomas.

It goes without saying that I alone am responsible for any errors or misinterpretations that may have slipped through despite the best efforts to prevent them.

Notes on Sources

Journalists have an irresistible desire to begin or end every sentence with an "according to." They feel better doing this even if the "according to" is followed by "sources who asked not to be identified"—thereby satisfying editors but not assisting the reader at all. In writing this book I finally overcame this tendency. Early attempts at footnoting and textual sourcing of every statement hindered the flow, seemed stilted, looked silly, and often as not accomplished nothing. So, at the possible risk of seeming to make unsubstantiated assertions, I have left the citation of sources for the back of the book. If my list of sources seems shorter than might be expected for such a vast subject, there are several reasons. One is that this is a book mainly about contemporary times, and living people, rather than documents, are the primary sources for all but a few chapters. And while the amount of material published about grain is indeed voluminous, much of it is exceedingly dry, having to do with agricultural and scientific problems rather than social, political, and economic ones. I am sparing the reader a list of such material. What follows here are references that I believe most nonspecialists would find interesting and instructive.

Chapter 1: One of the best accounts of the Russians' 1975 sneak attack on the American granary is Daniel J. Balz, "Soviet

Grain Purchases Prompt Informal Export Controls," *The National Journal*, September 6, 1975. Congress, sensitized to grain issues by this time, scheduled many hearings: *Russian Grain Sale*, Senate Agriculture Committee, September 4, 1975; and *Who's Making Foreign Agricultural Policy?* the same committee, January 22 and 23, 1976. The sales were also examined in *Sale of Grain to Russia*, Senate Permanent Subcommittee on Investigations, July 31 and August 1, 1975. Other documents touching on the 1975 grain sales include *Issues Surrounding the Management of Agricultural Exports*, Comptroller General, Washington, D.C., May 2, 1977; and *U.S.S.R. and Grain*, Senate Subcommittee on Multinational Corporations, staff report, April 1976. The latter report details Soviet trading techniques and policies. *Potential Implications of Trends in World Population, Food Production and Climate*, CIA, August 1974, reveals as much about CIA fantasies as it does about weather realities. The politics of weather continued to fascinate the agency's analysts, who in May 1976 published *Climatological Research As It Pertains to Intelligence Problems*. A readable and less apocalyptic book on the subject of weather is Fitzhugh Green, *A Change in the Weather*, W. W. Norton, New York, 1977. (Green writes about people who are trying to do something about it!) I also drew from interviews and from diplomatic cables obtained under the Freedom of Information Act.

Chapter 2: A "definitive" history of the growth of the grain trade still waits to be written. The most complete overview that I could find of the trade in the nineteenth century is Graham L. Rees, *Britain's Commodity Markets*, Paul Elek Books, London, 1972, a picturesque, fact-packed, and economically instructive survey. Morton Rothstein, "A British Firm on the American West Coast," *Business History Review*, Vol. XXXVII, No. 4, provides an American connection. George M. Calhoun, *The Business Life of Ancient Athens*, Cooper Square

Publishers, New York, 1968 (reprint of 1926 ed.), reminds us that the chicanery in the food trade is as old as Socrates. Reading Fernand Braudel, *Capitalism and Material Life, 1400–1800,* I wished he had extended his history of commodities in Europe another two centuries. Fortunately, other scholars and historians have also provided fascinating threads and designs of the larger historical tapestry. For the development of Odessa as a wheat port: Patricia Herlihy, "Russian Wheat and the Port of Livorno, 1794–1865," *Journal of Economic History,* Vol. 5, No. 1 (1976), and Herlihy, "Odessa: Staple Trade and Urbanization in New Russia," *Jahrbuecher fuer Geschichte Osteuropas,* No. 21 (1973). For the Argentine wheat segment; James Scobie, *Revolution on the Pampas,* University of Texas Press, Austin, 1964. This book not only provides useful information but also is written with deep compassion for the Italian migrants who made the Argentine wheat trade possible. Also, Harriet Friedmann, *The Transformation of Wheat Production in the Era of the World Market, 1873–1935: A Global Analysis of Production and Exchange,* unpublished Ph.D. dissertation, Harvard University, 1976. For the Irish potato famine: Cecil Woodham-Smith, *The Great Hunger,* Harper & Row, New York, 1962, a classic of social, economic, and political storytelling. Karl Marx, *The Eastern Question,* is the source of his observation about swarthy Greeks in British commodity exchanges. I became absorbed in several books about bread and flour in our past: John Storck and Walter Dorwin Teague, *Flour for Man's Bread,* University of Minnesota Press, Minneapolis, 1952; R. A. Mance and E. M. Widdowson, *Breads White and Brown,* J. B. Lippincott, Philadelphia; and Sir William James Ashley, *The Bread of our Forefathers,* Clarendon Press, Oxford, 1928. A more obscure source on the south Russian wheat trade is Max Winters, *Zur Organization des Suedrussischen Getreide Exporthandels,* Leipzig, 1925. Lighter, faster-paced, but no less revealing is the grain trade section of Edward L. Bernays, *Biography of an Idea*, Simon & Schuster, New York, 1965, the account of someone who actually *met* Leopold Louis-Dreyfus! General reading about the spread of wheat cultivation in the nineteenth century includes D. B. Grigg, *Agricultural Systems of the World*, Cambridge University Press, Cambridge, 1974; Wilfred Malenbaum, *The World Wheat Economy, 1885–1939*, Harvard University Press, Cambridge, 1953. The twenty-volume opus, *Wheat Studies of the Food Research Institute*, Stanford University, Stanford, compiled between 1924 and 1944, contains essential information.

Chapter 3: Frank Norris's *The Pit* and *The Octopus* are part of the American literary pantheon. My favorites among lesser-known books about nineteenth-century American grain are Henrietta M. Larson, *The Wheat Market and the Farmer in Minnesota, 1858–1900*, Ph.D. dissertation, Columbia University, 1926 (hardcover), an unvarnished, compassionate account of how the West was won by courageous farmers; and Gary Paulsen, *Farm: A History and Celebration of the American Farmer*, Prentice-Hall, Englewood Cliffs, N.J., 1977, a book that conveys the pain and hardships and the pleasures and rewards of pioneer farmers. The accounts of the California wheat trade are based on Rodman Paul, "The Great California Grain War," *Pacific Historical Review*, November 1958, and Paul, "The Wheat Trade Between California and the United Kingdom, 1954–c. 1900," *Mississippi Valley Historical Review*, December 1958. Morton Rothstein, "Antebellum Wheat and Cotton Exports: A Contrast in Marketing Organization and Economic Development," *Agricultural History*, Vol. 40 (April 1966), helps explain why wheat, not cotton, finally became king. Some company histories were more helpful than others. James Gray's *Business Without Boundaries: The Story of General Mills*, University of Minnesota Press, Minneapolis, is informative and readable. So is John L. Work, *Cargill Beginnings, An Account of the Early Years*, Cargill, Inc., Minneapolis,

1965, which has an excellent collection of pictures of the early Midwest. Kenneth Douglas Ruble, *The Peavey Story*, Peavey Co., Minneapolis, 1963, is the authorized biography of Frank the Founder. Fortunately, Larson (op cit. above) provides further insights. Harry Fornari, *Bread Upon the Waters*, Aurora Publishers, Nashville, 1973, is a flat account of the growth of exports since Independence, redeemed by excellent illustrations and pages of useful statistics. Two basic references are Murray R. Benedict, *Farm Policies of the United States, 1790–1950*, Twentieth Century Fund, New York, 1953, and Wayne D. Rasmussen and Gladys L. Baker, *The Department of Agriculture*, Praeger, New York, 1972. (The line from Anthony Trollope—"wheat running in rivers"—is from *North America*, London, 1862.)

Chapter 4: World War I: Herbert Hoover, *An American Epic*, Vol. II, Henry Regnery, Chicago, 1960; and *Methods and Operations of Grain Exporters, 1920–1926*, Report of the Federal Trade Commission, Washington, 1926, a four-volume study. For more on U.S. farm policy developments in the 1920s and 1930s, Don F. Hadwiger, *Federal Wheat Commodity Programs*, Iowa State University Press, Ames, 1970; and Murray R. Benedict, *Farm Policies of the United States, 1790–1950*, Twentieth Century Fund, New York, 1953. Books which give an overview of grain markets between the wars include Wilfred Malenbaum, *The World Wheat Economy, 1885–1939*, Harvard University Press, Cambridge, 1953, and Paul de Hevesy, *World Wheat Planning and Economic Planning in General*, Oxford, 1940. (After years of painstaking effort, de Hevesy completed this grand design for a stable world agricultural order and received the page proofs—several days after World War II began!) John Houseman's *Run-Through*, Simon & Schuster, New York, 1972, contains colorful anecdotes of his youthful days as a would-be "merchant prince" in New York and London. Other works include Edward Jerome Dies, *The Wheat Pit*,

Argyle Press, 1925, and David M. Mitrany, *The Land and the Peasant in Romania,* Greenwood Press, New York, 1969 (reprint of 1930 ed.). Alan Palmer, *The Lands Between,* MacMillan, London, 1970, describes the awful impact of the Depression on grain farmers and rural communities in the Danube River basin.

Chapter 5: Lauren Soth, *Farm Trouble,* Princeton University Press, Princeton, N.J., 1957. Willard W. Cochrane and Mary E. Ryan, *American Farm Policy, 1948–1973,* University of Minnesota Press, Minneapolis, 1976. *Khrushchev Remembers: The Last Testament,* translated by Strobe Talbott, Little, Brown, Boston, 1974. Don F. Hadwiger, *Federal Wheat Commodity Programs,* Iowa State University Press, Ames, 1970. *Time Magazine,* "A Hard Row to Hoe," cover story, April 5, 1963. *Northwestern Miller,* accounts of the 1963–64 grain sale to Russia, September 1963 to January 1964. The source of the description of the Novocherkassk food riots is Aleksandr I. Solzhenitsyn, *The Gulag Archipelago, 3,* Harper & Row, New York, 1978.

Chapter 6: Sources that put American agriculture in the 1960s into a global framework—particularly in respect to the policies of the European Common Market—are *U.S. Agriculture in a World Context,* edited by D. Gale Johnson and John A. Schnittker, Praeger, New York, 1974; D. Gale Johnson, *World Agriculture in Disarray,* MacMillan, London, 1973; and Philip M. Raup's "Constraints and Potentials in Agriculture" chapter in *The Changing Structure of Europe,* University of Minnesota Press, Minneapolis, 1970. The "Flanigan Report," the U.S. government's internal blueprint for undermining European tariffs, can be obtained as *Agricultural Trade and the Proposed Round of Multilateral Negotiations,* Senate Agriculture Committee, April 30, 1973. *United States International Economic Policy in an Interdependent World,* Report to the President by the Commission on International Trade and Investment Policy, Washington, D.C., July 1971, is the white paper in which Cargill had a hand. A factual assessment of the "green revolution" is *Measuring the Green Revolution: The Impact of Research on Wheat and Rice Production*, Foreign Agriculture Economic Report No. 106 (USDA), July 1975. Also Dana G. Dalrymple, *Development and Spread of High-Yielding Varieties of Wheat and Rice in the Less Developed Nations*, Foreign Agriculture Economic Report No. 95, August 1976. The CIA's Intelligence Memorandum, *India's Foodgrain Situation, Progress and Problems*, August 1972, summarizes developments in the subcontinent. For China, I consulted Stanley Karnow, *Mao and China*, Viking, New York, 1972.

The best accounts of the 1972 U.S.-Soviet grain transactions are James Trager, *The Great Grain Robbery*, Ballantine Books, New York, 1975 (an updated version of *Amber Waves of Grain*, Arthur Field Books, Inc., 1973), and Joseph Albright, "Some Deal," *The New York Times Magazine*, November 26, 1972. Trager meticulously and engagingly relates the 1972 Soviet buying spree to food prices, history, and politics. His book is an invaluable primer on the U.S. food economy. A critical assessment of the companies and their role is Martha M. Hamilton, *The Great American Grain Robbery and Other Stories*, Agribusiness Accountability Project, Washington, D.C., 1972. Government investigations include *Russian Grain Transactions*, hearings before the Senate Permanent Subcommittee on Investigations, July 20, 23, and 24, 1973; and *Sale of Wheat to Russia*, hearings before the House Agriculture Committee, September 14, 18, and 19, 1972. Also, *Russian Wheat Sales and Weaknesses in Agriculture's Management of the Wheat Export Subsidy Program*, Comptroller General, Washington, D.C., July 9, 1973. The cost of the grain deal was calculated by Albert J. Eckstein and Dale M. Heien, in their *Memo to the National Commission on Supplies and Shortages*, Washington,

D.C., January 1976. The best account of the 1971 grain transactions with the Russians is by Murrey Marder and Marilyn
Berger, "U.S.-Soviet Grain Deal: Case History of Economic
Policy Shift," *The Washington Post*, December 7, 1971; this
was the first article that reported the political and diplomatic
significance of the Nixon administration's shift in grain policy.
CIA reports to the Department of Agriculture on commercial
sales of U.S. grain to the Russians in July and August 1972 were
obtained under the Freedom of Information Act.

Chapter 7: Information on the Born kidnapping was obtained
mostly from private sources knowledgeable about the Montoneros. Some general information about the companies is
found in the series I wrote for *The Washington Post*, "Merchants of Grain," January 1–4, 1976, which inspired further interest and eventually this book. James Trager, *The Great Grain
Robbery*, Ballantine Books, New York, 1975, is useful. An unbiased account of Fribourg's business domain was in the March
11, 1972, cover story of *Business Week*, "The Incredible Empire of Michel Fribourg." Fribourg didn't like it. Cargill is the
best chronicled of the giants: *The Minneapolis Star*, "Cargill—
92 Years as 'Servants to Agriculture,' " August 18, 1957; *Fortune*, "The Two-Billion-Dollar Company That Lives by the
Cent," December 1965; *The Wall Street Journal*, "Cargill Inc.,
a Giant in Troubled Industry Keeps Reaping Riches," November 7, 1975, p. 1; and *NACLA's Latin American & Empire Report*, "U.S. Grain Arsenal," October 1975.

Chapter 8: The brevity of source materials and references for
the chapter on the personalities and families of the merchants
speaks for itself. They are not people who seek the limelight.
Perhaps life histories, personal memoirs, and autobiographies
lie gathering dust in family vaults. If so, I am not privy to
them. Most of the references for the previous chapter also con-
tain some material on the families. But it tends to be sketchy.

All the material I gathered about the late Marc Najar came from interviews. (A relative even played me a tape recording of Najar addressing a business meeting in French.) The same is true of the Borns and Hirsches. Somewhat more is available on Ned Cook. His father was the subject of a biography, *Everett R. Cook—A Memoir*, Memphis Public Library, Memphis, 1971. Ned figured predominantly in James Trager, *The Great Grain Robbery*, Ballantine Books, New York, 1975. Articles about Ned Cook on the rise include *Business Week*, "Cook: An Upstart in the Grain Trade," August 19, 1972; *Grain Age*, "Industry Youngster, Aged 12, Grows Fast in World Market," Bruce W. Smith, February 1975; *Business Week*, "The Grain Trading Maverick," March 10, 1975.

Chapter 9: To learn something about the nuts and bolts of the grain trade, I interviewed many traders in the United States and Europe. It is such an insiders' business that there are few, if any, books for outsiders. The future markets are a different matter. Commodity men exult in them, populists and muckrakers revile them—and both have written about them at length, from Frank Norris on. In the post-1972 commodity boom, the commodity markets were the subject of many articles. Of special interest: *The New York Times Magazine*, "Prince of the Pit," Douglas Bauer, April 25, 1976; *Business Week*, "Commodity Trading—More, More, More . . .," cover story, March 15, 1976; and *The New Republic*, "Reconsideration: *The Pit* by Frank Norris," book review by Joel Solkoff, November 19, 1977. Also see my articles in *The Washington Post*, "Bedlam in the Pits," August 22, 1976, and "Commodity Futures: Rags or Riches Await," August 23, 1976. All of these indicate the continuing wisdom of what one unidentified source said: "The Chicago market is the ninth wonder of the world—if you took it apart, you'd never put it back together again." The information about the international operations of Tradax was brought out in *Multinational Corporations and*

United States Foreign Policy—International Grain Companies, hearings before the Senate Subcommittee on Multinational Corporations, June 18, 23, and 24, 1976. The same hearings also disclosed the Department of Agriculture cables about possible misreporting of grain prices in Europe.

Chapter 10: The material on Continental's problems in getting paid by Mobutu, as well as the documentation on the Canadian Wheat Board's 1976 caper, was obtained from the Department of Agriculture under the Freedom of Information Act. The United Nations Sanctions Committee supplied material concerning the difficulties of enforcing the trade embargo on Rhodesian white maize. Susan George, *How the Other Half Dies—The Real Reasons for World Hunger,* Allanheld, Osmun & Co., Montclair, N.J., 1977, sheds light on the power of the multinationals, especially where soybeans are concerned. Also, *Multinational Corporations and United States Foreign Policy—International Grain Companies,* hearings before the Senate Subcommittee on Multinational Corporations, June 18, 23, and 24, 1976. Three excellent sources on the pros and cons of government grain boards are Don Mitchell, *The Politics of Food; Grain Marketing Systems in Argentina, Australia, Canada and the European Community; Soybean Marketing System in Brazil,* Comptroller General, Washington, D.C., May 28, 1976; and Andrew Schmitz and Alex McCalla, *Comparison of Canadian and U.S. Grain Marketing Systems,* study prepared for National Grain and Feed Association, March 1976. *Improving the Export Capability of Grain Cooperatives,* Farmer Cooperative Service Research Report 34, U.S. Department of Agriculture, June 1976, describes the major multinationals' dominant share of American grain exports.

Chapter 11: Personal interviews with all but one of the participants in the events of the summer and fall of 1975 were the main source for this chapter. (Requests for an interview with

Henry Kissinger were made through his staff, but were not granted.) An excellent, balanced analysis of the realities and myths of American "food power" is *Use of U.S. Food for Diplomatic Purposes—An Examination of the Issues,* prepared for the House Committee on International Relations by Congressional Research Service, Washington, D.C., January 1977; Material on Chile and P.L. 480 was obtained from the Department of Agriculture under the Freedom of Information Act. The International Food Policy Research Institute in Washington provided statistics on foreign countries' dependence on the United States for food. See also "U.S. Food Power Ultimate Weapon in World Politics?" *Business Week,* December 15, 1975; Butz interview in *U.S. News & World Report,* February 16, 1976; Peter Wallenstein, "Scarce Goods as Political Weapons: The Case of Food," *Journal of Peace Research* Vol. XIII, No. 4 (1976); and Lester Brown, *The Politics and Responsibility of the North American Breadbasket,* World Watch Paper 2, Worldwatch Institute, Washington, D.C., October 1975. Also useful was Daniel J. Balz, "Soviet Grain Purchases Prompt Informal Export Controls," *The National Journal,* September 6, 1975. An excellent analysis of the politicization of the U.S. food aid program (P.L. 480) is to be found in Susan DeMarco and Susan Sechler, *The Fields Have Turned Brown,* Agribusiness Accountability Project, Washington, D.C., 1975. Also, Stephen Rosenfeld, "The Politics of Food," *Foreign Policy Magazine,* Spring 1974.

Chapter 12: This chapter relied heavily on documents in the public record: a voluminous, footlocker-size dossier of government reports and correspondence obtained under the Freedom of Information Act; and grand jury indictments and pleadings. For contemporary Korea, I consulted, among other sources, Paul W. Kuznets, *Economic Growth and Structure in the Republic of Korea,* Yale University Press, New Haven, 1977. For contemporary adventures in the commercial rice trade, see

Griffin Smith Jr., "What Your Mother Never Told You About Rice," *Texas Monthly*, March 1975, and my "The Rice Connection," *The Washington Post*, August 7, 1977, B1. Both *The Washington Post* and *The New York Times* gave extensive coverage to the Korean investigation between September 1976 and May 1978.

Chapter 13: The fall of Ned Cook was well reported in the business and trade press. The best account is Lewis Beman, "Ned Cook in the Agonies of Corporate Confession," *Fortune*, May 1977. From this I took Ned's remark, "Agatha Christie could have written the damnedest mystery about this business." Also, H. J. Maidenberg, "U.S. Fights Effort by the Hunts to Corner the Soybean Market," *The New York Times*, April 29, 1977, D1; Shirley A. Jackewicz, "Hunt Brothers' Feud with Agency Grows over Futures Holdings," *The Wall Street Journal*, May 19, 1977; John Huey and Jonathan R. Laing, "How Cook Industries Speculated and Lost Millions on Soybeans," *The Wall Street Journal*, July 14, 1977. Voluminous testimony on grain inspection frauds in New Orleans was given to the Senate Agriculture Committee on June 19, July 8, August 14 and 15, and September 25 and 26, 1975. The Committee published its *Report on Irregularities in the Marketing of Grain* on February 17, 1976. This was a story that might have faded away entirely without two journalists' reporting between June 1975 and June 1976. It was a toss-up whether the Pulitzer Prize would go to James Risser of *The Des Moines Register* or William Robbins of *The New York Times* for their relentless pursuit of the dockside scandal. (The prize was awarded to Risser.) The story of Continental's difficulties with the hectic 1975 trading I put together from my own reporting in the United States and Europe. I also interviewed Ned Cook at length on other aspects of his own troubles.

Chapter 14: There are many books and articles about the persistent problem of hunger, few that address its political and cultural roots. Herewith are several that do: Emma Rothschild, "The Politics of Food," *Foreign Affairs Quarterly*, January 1976; Solon Barraclough, "Agricultural Production Prospects in Latin America," paper, Cornell University, Ithaca, 1977; Susan George, *How the Other Half Dies—The Real Reasons for World Hunger*, Allanheld, Osmun & Co., Montclair, N.J., 1977, and *World Food and Nutrition Study*, The National Research Council, National Academy of Sciences, 1977. Several other documents take what I believe to be an adequately hard-boiled look at this issue, which is so often distorted by emotionalism. For example: *The World Food Situation*, Economic Research Service of the U.S. Department of Agriculture, working paper circulated in October 1974 (an edited version was published later); Harry E. Walters, *International Food Security: The Issues and Alternatives*, paper and speech prepared for 1977 meeting of World Food Council, Rome; and, though it is now outdated, *The World Food Problem, Proposals for National and International Action*, item 9 of the provisional agenda, United Nations World Food Conference, Rome, 1974. Several studies exist on ways governments sabotage food production within their own countries: *Disincentives to Agricultural Production in Developing Countries*, Comptroller General, Washington, D.C., November 26, 1975; Leonard Dudley, Roger J. Sandilands, "The Side Effects of Foreign Aid: The Case of Public Law 480 Wheat in Colombia," *Journal of Economic Development and Cultural Change*, Vol. 23, January 1975, University of Chicago Press.

Beyond these, there are an almost inexhaustible number of documents on hunger and the world grain economy. Of note: Montague Yudelman, *Background Paper on the World Food Situation*, World Bank, Washington, D.C., June 6, 1978; Philip H. Tresize, *Rebuilding Grain Reserves*, Brookings Institution,

Washington, D.C., 1976; *Agricultural Policy Review,* Economic Research Service, U.S. Department of Agriculture, A-FPR-1, Washington, D.C., January 1977; *Recent and Prospective Developments in Food Consumption: Some Policy Issues,* International Food Policy Research Institute, Washington, D.C., July 1977; *Food Needs of Developing Countries,* International Food Policy Research Institute, Washington, D.C., December 1977; and *Grain Reserves: a Potential U.S. Food Policy Tool,* Comptroller General, Washington, D.C., March 26, 1977. And no notes for a chapter on the problems of food production in the developing countries would be complete without a reference to the work of Wolf Ladejinsky, who recognized that political reform and social justice were as necessary for progress in the countryside as technology: Wolf Ladejinsky, *Agrarian Reform as Unfinished Business,* edited by Louis J. Walinsky, Oxford University Press, New York, Oxford, London, Glasgow, 1977.

Index

Aca company, 310
Acheampong, President (Ghana), 457
Achilles (vessel), 411
Adair, Ross, 397
AFL-CIO, 197, 351
Agency for International Development (AID), 380–81, 393
Agricultural Marketing Service, 292
Agriculture, U.S. Department of, 41–44, 49, 50, 51, 101, 135, 143, 144, 148, 150–51, 152, 160, 166, 167, 172–73, 174, 176–83, 185–86, 192, 196, 200, 201, 204, 205, 206, 209, 210–11, 215, 215n., 266, 281, 288, 292–94, 296, 311, 331, 348, 349–50, 382, 385, 395, 396, 411, 429, 444, 494, 495, 496
Agro company, 310
Aiken, George, 161
Albania, 194
Albany Port Authority, 126
Albert, Carl, 392

Albright, Joseph, 491
Alderson, Leonard, 270, 271, 318
Alexandros (vessel), 321
Algeria, 166
Alioto, Joseph, 388, 402
Allende, Salvador, 339, 340, 341, 344, 460
Allied Mills, 167n., 228
Alsop, Joseph and Stewart, 374
Amran, Salvador, 256n.
Anderson-Clayton company, 326
Anderson Co., 310
André, Eric, 249n.
André, Georges, 20, 61–62, 73, 107, 130, 138, 240, 249–50, 268, 321–22
André, Henri, 249n.
André, Pierre, 249n.
André company: Argentine wheat and, 111; banking interests, 240; founder, 20, 62; Garnac and, 128, 138, 210; growth and expansion, 228; maize and, 321–22; operations in Spain, 215n.; secrecy and, 29;

499

RISE TO GLOBALISM
American Foreign Policy, 1938–1980
Second Revised Edition

Stephen E. Ambrose

This completely revised and updated edition of *Rise to Globalism* reviews American foreign policy between 1938 and 1980. World War II, the Cold War, the Korean conflict, the Berlin crisis, the invasion of Cuba, the debacle in Vietnam, America's recent entanglements in the Middle East and Africa, and President Jimmy Carter's actions are among the events that Professor Stephen E. Ambrose relates to the larger themes of America's rise to, and maintenance of, her enormous global power. In his exploration of these themes Ambrose looks at American character traits—economic aggressiveness, racism, fear of Communism—and shows how they have helped shape the nation's foreign policy. It is this probing beneath the surface that makes this a uniquely valuable work.

IRAN: DICTATORSHIP AND DEVELOPMENT

Fred Halliday

Despite the dramatic overthrow of the Shah, Iran is often regarded as one of the rising industrial capitalist nations whose prospects seem bright. But is her future assured and stable? For instance, by the year 2000 Iran may no longer have oil to export—or to bargain with. Fred Halliday provides for the layman a rigorous, readable, and timely analysis of this harsh and divided country. One thing *is* certain, says the author: "If Iran remains in political and cultural terms anything like what it was in the 1970s, then it will remain a brutal, philistine society, marked by extreme inequalities. Such a society will have nothing great and little civilized about it."